THE IMPACT OF MACROECONOMIC POLICIES ON POVERTY AND INCOME DISTRIBUTION

Macro-Micro Evaluation Techniques and Tools

THE IMPACT OF MACROECONOMIC POLICIES ON POVERTY AND INCOME DISTRIBUTION

Macro-Micro Evaluation Techniques and Tools

François Bourguignon

Maurizio Bussolo

Luiz A. Pereira da Silva

Editors

A copublication of Palgrave Macmillan and the World Bank

A copublication of The World Bank and Palgrave Macmillan.

Palgrave Macmillan
Houndmills, Basingstoke, Hampshire RG21 6XS and 175 Fifth Avenue, New York,
NY 10010
Companies and representatives throughout the world

Palgrave Macmillan is the global academic imprint of the Palgrave Macmillan division of
St. Martin's Press, LLC and of Palgrave Macmillan Ltd.

Macmillan® is a registered trademark in the United States, United Kingdom, and other
countries. Palgrave® is a registered trademark in the European Union and other countries.

ISBN: 978-0-8213-5778-1 (soft cover) and 978-0-8213-7268-5 (hard cover)
eISBN: 978-0-8213-5779-8
DOI: 10.1596/978-0-8213-5778-1 (soft cover) and 10.1596/978-0-8213-7268-5 (hard cover)

Library of Congress Cataloging-in-Publication Data
The impact of macroeconomic policies on poverty and income distribution : macro-micro
evaluation techniques and tools / edited by François Bourguignon, Maurizio Bussolo, and
Luiz Pereira da Silva.
    p. cm.
Includes bibliographical references and index.
ISBN 978-0-8213-5778-1 — ISBN 978-0-8213-5779-8 (electronic)
  1. Economic assistance—Evaluation. 2. Poverty. 3. Income distribution. 4. Economic
assistance—Developing countries—Evaluation. 5. Developing countries—Economic
policy—Case studies. I. Bourguignon, François. II. Silva, Luiz A. Pereira da. III. Bussolo,
Maurizio, 1964-
  HC60.I4147 2008
  339.2'2—dc22
                                                                    2007040478

Contents

Part III. Macro-Micro Integrated Techniques

**Part IV. Macro Approach with Disaggregated
Public Spending**

Box

Figures

Tables

Preface

This book assembles methodologies and techniques to evaluate the poverty impact of macroeconomic policies. It takes as a departure point a companion volume, *The Impact of Economic Policies on Poverty and Income Distribution: Evaluation Techniques and Tools* edited by François Bourguignon and Luiz A. Pereira da Silva, published in 2003. That volume was primarily a review of microeconomic techniques aimed at assessing policies that are directly concerned with the welfare of poor households or individuals—such as changing the level of cash transfers to the poorest households, increasing price subsidies for basic consumer goods, and the like. In addition, the second part of that earlier publication introduced basic techniques to deal with the poverty impact of macroeconomic policies that by definition are not targeted and affect the whole population. However, as Nicholas Stern stated in the foreword to the 2003 volume: "[M]ore research is needed to improve the integration of macroeconomic models and the models of household behavior as captured in household surveys. Such an integration is obviously crucial when the distributional incidence and macroeconomic effects of key policies are being studied." Five years later, this book presents the research to which he alluded. It deals with evaluating the impact of macroeconomic policies on poverty and income distribution using cutting-edge approaches.

Policy makers are increasingly becoming aware that despite a positive effect on the average income of their citizens, many macro policies can sometimes produce such a deterioration in the welfare of specific groups that the policies can become socially undesirable and politically unsustainable in terms of the long-run growth objectives for a given economy and society. Similarly, poverty reduction policies designed to target specific individuals and/or households may end up producing macroeconomic (mostly fiscal) consequences. Thus, the selection and implementation of economic policies require a careful assessment of their effects both on aggregate economywide variables—such as employment, inflation, or real GDP growth— and on income distribution and poverty. Modern micro simulation techniques, which use microeconomic data sets to *simulate* the policy impact on all individuals in a sample that is statistically representative of an entire population, are the most promising tool for providing that careful assessment.

This volume presents a comprehensive array of macro-micro modeling frameworks. It begins by highlighting the limitation of macroeconomic models that use representative household groups to link macroeconomic policies and microeconomic data. It then moves to more complex, top-down modeling frameworks, which combine (top) macro models and (down) micro simulation models that, in turn, can be simple micro accounting models or behavioral micro models. The book also explores integrated models, in which the macro and micro parts are either linked by iterative feedback loops or solved simultaneously as a single model. By providing clear access to these techniques, by documenting their analytical underpinnings, their data requirements, and their range of applicability, and even by highlighting some of their limitations, this book provides a unique compendium for practitioners, policy makers, and anyone interested in economic development.

Acknowledgments

This book continued down the path opened by the 2003 companion volume, *The Impact of Economic Policies on Poverty and Income Distribution: Evaluation Techniques and Tools*. Thus, we owe a debt of gratitude to Nicholas Stern and Stanley Fischer, who at the time of its publication, were, respectively, the chief economist of the World Bank and first deputy managing director of the International Monetary Fund. Their initiative inspired the process of reviewing techniques for evaluating the poverty and distributional impact of various policies available for development.

During its four-year lifespan, this project has benefited from the support and advice of many people, including those who contributed comments during the various seminars and conferences at which the authors presented their papers. For their remarks, suggestions, and peer review, we thank in particular Flavio Cunha, Shantayanan Devarajan, Alan Gelb, Coralie Gevers, James Heckman, Thomas Hertel, Jeffrey Lewis, Catherine Pattillo, Guido Porto, and Hans Timmer.

Our greatest debt, obviously, is to the authors of the eight contributed chapters. This book is really the outcome of their original work. Their names and current affiliations are listed in the contributors section, and we truly thank them for their own relevant pieces, for the comments they provided on their colleagues' work, and for their endurance during the long process of producing this volume.

Special thanks go to Nadia Fernanda Piffaretti, Jean Gray Ponchamni, Aban Daruwala, and Roula I. Yazigi, who provided superb administrative support and assistance during various critical phases of this project.

We are very grateful to Kim Kelley for her excellent editorial assistance; to Janet Sasser for managing the editing, typesetting, proofreading, cover design, and indexing of the project and for her dedication and professionalism in assisting the editors at the crucial final stages of the production of this book; and to Santiago Pombo-Bejarano for his enduring support during the long life of this project and for his enthusiastic commitment to converting the manuscript into a finished volume.

Contributors

Editors

François Bourguignon

Professor of economics and director of the Paris School of Economics; former chief economist and senior vice president at the World Bank, Washington, DC

Maurizio Bussolo

Senior economist in the Development Prospects Group at the World Bank, Washington, DC

Luiz A. Pereira da Silva

Chief economist for Brazil's Ministry of Planning and Budget; Deputy Finance Minister for International Affairs, Brazil

Other Contributing Authors

Denis Cogneau

Senior research fellow at the Institut de Recherche pour le Développement (IRD) and the Développement, Institutions et Analyses de Long terme (DIAL), Paris

Carolina Diaz-Bonilla

Economist in the Latin America and Caribbean Region Poverty Sector at the World Bank, Washington, DC

Francisco H. G. Ferreira

Lead economist in the Development Research Group at the World Bank, Washington, DC

Xavier Giné

Economist in the Development Research Group at the World Bank, Washington, DC

Jann Lay

Senior economist and head of the Poverty Reduction, Equity, and Development Research Area at the Kiel Institute for the World Economy, Germany

Phillippe G. Leite	Consultant, Development Economics *World Development Report* team at the World Bank, Washington, DC
Hans Lofgren	Senior economist in the Development Prospects Group at the World Bank, Washington, DC
Michael Lokshin	Senior economist in the Development Research Group at the World Bank, Washington, DC
Denis Medvedev	Economist in the Development Prospects Group at the World Bank, Washington, DC
Paulo Picchetti	Associate professor in the Department of Economics at the Fundação Getulio Vargas, São Paolo, Brazil
Martin Ravallion	Director of the Development Research Group at the World Bank, Washington, DC
Anne-Sophie Robilliard	Research fellow at the IRD and DIAL, Paris
Sherman Robinson	Professor of economics, University of Sussex, Brighton, UK
Luc Savard	Associate professor in the Department of Economics at the Université de Sherbrooke, Quebec, Canada
Robert M. Townsend	Charles E. Merriam Distinguished Service Professor in the Department of Economics at the University of Chicago
Dominique van der Mensbrugghe	Lead economist in the Development Prospects Group at the World Bank, Washington, DC

Abbreviations

BoP	balance of payments
BU	bottom-up (part)
CES	constant elasticity of substitution
CET	constant elasticity of transformation
CGE	computable general equilibrium
CPI	consumer price index
DIAL	Développement, Institutions et Analyses de Long terme
ERR	exchange rate regime
FIES	Family Income and Expenditure Survey
FP	fixed-point (algorithm)
FTAA	Free Trade Area of the Americas
FULLIB	full trade liberalization
GDP	gross domestic product
GNP	gross national product
GTAP	General Trade Analysis Project
HD	human development
IBGE	Instituto Brasileiro de Geografia e Estatística
IFLS	Indonesian Family Life Survey
IFPRI	International Food Policy Research Institute
ILO	International Labour Organization
IMF	International Monetary Fund
IMH	integrated multihousehold (approach, model)
IS-LM	investment savings and liquidity preferences
LAC	Latin America and the Caribbean Region
LAV	linking aggregated variable
LEB	Lloyd-Ellis and Bernhard (2000) model
LES	linear expenditure system
MAMS	Maquette for MDG Simulations
MDG	Millennium Development Goal

MLD	mean log deviation
MSS	micro simulation sequential (approach, method)
NAFTA	North American Free Trade Agreement
PNAD	Pesquisa Nacional por Amostra de Domicílios [National Household Survey]
PV	present value
RH	representative household
RHG	representative household group
RNF	rural nontradable formal
RNI	rural nontradable informal
RTF	rural tradable formal
SAM	social accounting matrix
SES	Socio-Economic Survey
SUSENAS	Survei Sosial Ekonomi Nasional [National Socio-Economic Household Survey]
TD	top-down (part)
UNDP	United Nations Development Programme
UNF	urban nontradable formal
UNI	urban nontradable informal
UTF	urban tradable formal
WPI	wholesale price index

1

Introduction: Evaluating the Impact of Macroeconomic Policies on Poverty and Income Distribution

François Bourguignon, Maurizio Bussolo, and Luiz A. Pereira da Silva

Economists have long been interested in measuring the effects of economic policies on poverty and on the distribution of welfare among individuals and households. Devising satisfactory methods for accurate evaluations has proven to be a difficult task. Progress in economic analysis and the growing availability of microeconomic household data have improved the situation. At the same time, however, calls for rigorous assessment have intensified. Partly because of the fierce debate on the social effects of globalization, economic policy objectives and social demands increasingly have focused on poverty reduction and distribution outcomes.

In this context, development strategies as well as recurrent economic policy choices are being scrutinized ex ante—that is, before they are actually implemented—or assessed ex post—that is, after their execution. The range of policy issues subject to these evaluations is broad and includes the following:

- *Public expenditures.* What is the poverty impact of specific shifts in public spending? How are the poor affected by changes in the delivery of public services, especially in the cases of health and education services?

• *Tax policy.* Do poor people bear a disproportionate burden of taxation or do they really benefit from subsidies designed to assist them?

• *Structural reforms.* How can trade liberalization, domestic markets liberalization, privatization, labor market reforms, and decentralization, among other reforms, help the poor?

• *Macroeconomic policies.* More specifically, what is the poverty impact of changes in the fiscal stance, or in monetary and exchange rate policies? What is the most effective macroeconomic policy setting to foster investment and productivity and to achieve long-term growth that is beneficial to all?

To answer these questions, different methodologies have been devised that can be roughly classified in two groups: (1) microeconomic techniques, based mostly on incidence analyses and econometric evaluation approaches in partial equilibrium settings; and (2) macro-micro techniques, which, with different degrees of integration, combine macro and micro modeling frameworks, usually in a general equilibrium context.

The first set of techniques has been extensively reviewed in the companion volume to this book, *The Impact of Economic Policies on Poverty and Income Distribution: Evaluation Techniques and Tools* (Bourguignon and Pereira da Silva 2003). This group of techniques, well rooted in the public finance literature, has been applied primarily to analyze issues of incidence of tax and public spending (see the questions above related to public expenditures and tax policy). Most of that earlier volume was devoted to case studies that illustrated microeconomic incidence methodologies. Various chapters showed numerous policy applications—changes of indirect taxes, health and education public services, redistributive community programs—and exemplified different methodological perspectives, namely, simpler *accounting* incidence analyses were juxtaposed against more complex *behavioral* approaches. Accounting approaches compute only first-round effects and disregard second-round effects attributable to behavioral reactions. Behavioral incidence analyses explicitly include those reactions. For example,

An individual may decide to work less than otherwise to avoid losing her eligibility for a means-tested transfer, parents may decide to send their children to school to take advantage of free school lunches, or they may pay more attention to their children's health if a public dispensary is built in the neighborhood (Bourguignon and Pereira da Silva 2003: 9).

Other methodological challenges covered by case studies in the first volume included the following: comparing ex ante and ex post approaches; assessing the *average* versus *marginal* effects of a policy; combining *quantitative* with *qualitative* approaches; and evaluating policies with some important geographic dimension (location of infrastructure projects such as roads, irrigation projects, etc.) using *poverty maps*.

The second set of techniques—the integrated macro-micro techniques—was also introduced in the companion volume (Bourguignon and Pereira da Silva 2003). The methodologies and case studies included in the second half of that volume were rather simple and did not include the cutting-edge approaches developed in the literature. This more recent and more sophisticated group of techniques is the focus of the present volume. In fact, the application of the *variants* of a single modeling framework—a macro model linked with a household-level micro model—is the unifying methodological theme of this volume. It is important to emphasize that a macro-micro approach enables different questions to be asked about the poverty and distribution consequences related to policy changes, and answering these questions is a main motivation for this book. First, a macro-micro approach allows assessing the *micro* effects of *macro*economic policy changes and investigating the *second round* effects of policy changes. The pure microeconomic techniques described above cannot consider the poverty impacts of choosing, implementing, or altering macroeconomic policies such as the trade regime, tariffs and non-tariff barriers (NTBs), the exchange rate, interest rates, the policy mix of fiscal and monetary policies, the composition of public spending, and the labor market regulation, among other policies (see the questions on page 2 about structural reforms and macroeconomic policy). Second, even micro policies—that is, policies targeted to specific population groups—when scaled up are likely to have macro consequences. Micro techniques of the type described above may measure the overall financial cost of a specific intervention, such as increasing education coverage through a conditional cash transfer program; however, they stop short of "feeding" this cost to a macro model and thus they cannot gauge what kind of macro (fiscal or growth, for instance) repercussions such a program may have.

A final common thread connects and motivates the various contributions of this volume. This thread is represented by an attempt to measure the complete set of micro, macro, first and second round effects of economic policies by using more than one data set. The studies in this volume show that great gains can be made by using many data sets. Considering standard macro data sets, such as those from a central bank or the national income accounts, together with micro data sets, such as those from household surveys, labor force surveys, population censuses, and community-level surveys, provides analysts better opportunities to "look beyond the averages" in the analysis of the growth-inequality-poverty nexus (Ravallion 2001, 2006). In policy-relevant terms, this basically means a better chance to identify specific interventions that can complement growth-oriented development policies. As shown by the contributions in this volume, looking simultaneously at macro and micro data offers advantages but also presents great challenges. It is well known, for example, that mean consumption from the national accounts and mean consumption from the survey data are different in levels and tend to diverge in growth rates. More specifically, the debate over India's fast growth rate (measured from the national accounts) and slow poverty reduction (measured from the surveys) is not just an academic debate but also a policy debate: sorting it out may have important repercussions on economic policy decisions. In Deaton's words:

> [T]he reformers argue that the survey data are wrong, and the anti-reformers argue that the national accounts data are wrong. [. . . whereas] both of them are in bad shape [and] an enormous amount of work needs to be done on reconciling national accounts and on reconciling them with survey data (2001).[1]

The current volume, in the same way as the 2003 Bourguignon and Pereira da Silva edited volume, is organized along methodological lines. A common macro-micro modeling framework is used across all chapters, but its variants highlight methodological choices dictated by the specific question analyzed and data quality and availability. These choices include the following: (1) the types of macro and micro models; (2) the extent of integration between the macro and micro models; (3) the degree of behavioral response, especially at the micro (household) level; and (4) the time frame of the analysis (ex ante or ex post).

Before presenting a brief survey of these methodological choices and to place the subsequent chapters in a common broad perspective, the next section of this chapter summarizes the role of poverty and distribution in the literature on development. This chapter concludes with a brief summary of lessons learned.

The Relationship between Macroeconomic Policy and Distribution in the Development Literature

The central theme of this volume—the impact of macroeconomic policies on household welfare—has now been generally recognized as a key development question and has received extensive attention

in the theoretical and empirical literature. However, this fc
the distributional consequences of macro policies is very r
recent phenomenon, having entered the development literature trom
fiscal policy incidence analysis in high-income countries. Starting in
the 1940s, four distinct phases emerged in the evolution of economic thinking about the importance of distributional outcomes,
with only the last phase devoting significant attention to impact
analysis at the household level.

During the dawn of development theory and practice, growth
and industrialization were the main objectives. Achieving these
goals—largely through a mechanical, trickle-down effect—would
then bring about development and poverty eradication (Rosenstein-
Rodan 1943). This literature did not ignore the distributional consequences of growth: the well-known inverted U curve (Kuznets
1955) and surplus labor model (Lewis 1954) both acknowledged
that inequality may initially increase as per capita income rises and
labor migrates into a modern, industrial, high-income sector. These
negative distributional consequences were considered transitory and
were an intrinsic part of the growth process, however, and thus not
to be actively managed by policy interventions. Instead, because
higher growth would eventually result in less poverty and inequality, the policy advice of this strand of literature was to focus squarely
on growth.

In the second phase of the evolution of the development
paradigm—during the 1960s and 1970s—concerns over income distribution and poverty intensified. In 1968, World Bank President
Robert McNamara announced poverty reduction as an explicit institutional goal during his first Bank annual meeting speech. This goal
marked an important shift in development thinking: growth alone,
without improvements in the lives of millions of poor people in the
developing world, was no longer sufficient (McNamara, as cited in
Birsdall and Londono 1997). On the research front, economists
showed that a nation's welfare depends on both the *size* of national
income and its *distribution* (Sen 1973). An influential 1974 World
Bank report, *Redistribution with Growth,* concluded that growth
and distributional goals "cannot be viewed independently . . . [but]
should be expressed dynamically in terms of desired rates of growth
of income of different groups" (Chenery and others 1974). In particular, the report sought to explicitly incorporate distributional
outcomes into measures of social welfare by suggesting the use of
the weighted sum of income growth of population subgroups (for
example, income deciles) instead of aggregate GNP or GNP per
capita metrics.

During the third phase—lasting from the mid-1970s to the early
1990s—the development literature reached a broad consensus that

with adequate policies (not necessarily of the redistributive kind) there should be no conflict between accelerated growth and equitable distribution. During this time, models of incidence analysis of public expenditure began to enter the development literature (Meerman 1979; Selowsky 1979; Ahmad and Stern 1991). The scope of policy advice, however, was largely determined by the elements of the Washington Consensus, which did not incorporate explicit distributional objectives. According to Kanbur (2000), this outcome was prompted by several distinct developments. First, a large body of empirical work failed to confirm the U-shaped relationship between levels of per capita income and inequality proposed by Kuznets (1955). The lack of data prevents testing the hypothesis as a time-series phenomenon, while a cross-sectional relationship is difficult to identify once controls for countries with high historical inequality (for example, countries in Latin America) are added. Second, many studies documented the antigrowth and antidistributional consequences of the strongly distortionary policies—including exchange rate overvaluation, high trade barriers, and large state-owned enterprises—adopted by many African and Latin American countries. Most of these studies showed that these distortions were both inefficient and inequitable and argued that policy reform in these areas would have resulted not only in more growth but also in less inequality and less poverty. The third development is represented by the observations of the East Asian "miracle" of strong growth with equity, which showed that growth could benefit everybody equally, although equitable initial distribution of assets was acknowledged as a key determinant of favorable outcomes.

In many ways, the final phase represents a return to the themes of the second phase, albeit with much more sophisticated analytical tools. The recognition of a multifaceted relationship between growth and distribution came about because of the skepticism toward the results of the Washington Consensus policies, and from the discovery that inequality was trending upward in East Asia. A number of countries in Latin America and Sub-Saharan Africa discovered that their performance in terms of growth and income distribution remained disappointing, even after implementing most of the market-friendly reforms. At the same time, living standards of people at the bottom of the distribution became a central issue in the international policy arena, particularly with the adoption of the 2000 United Nations Millennium Declaration. These developments, combined with a realization that little was known about the distributional dynamics of growth, served to draw distributional concerns "back from the cold" (Atkinson 1997).

The renewed focus on the relationship between macro (growth) and micro (distribution) issues has led economists to realize that "growth is quite a blunt instrument against poverty unless that growth comes with falling inequality" (Ravallion 2004). The availability of detailed household surveys and new analytical tools (many of which are described in this volume) has enabled researchers to move beyond concepts of aggregate inequality and focus on the effects of macro policies on specific household groups. Insights generated by this analysis can help in understanding the outcomes of past reforms, design of compensatory mechanisms, and anticipation of challenges inherent in future policy decisions.

Macro-Micro Modeling as a Tool for Poverty and Inequality Analysis

To highlight the differences and the specificity of the methods aimed at assessing the poverty and income distribution effects of *macroeconomic* policies, it is useful to first consider the parallel literature on the evaluation of *microeconomic* policies.

The choice of the evaluation technique in microeconomic policy analyses depends, to use Blundell and Costa Dias' (2007: 1) wording, on three broad concerns: (1) the nature of the question to be answered; (2) the type and quality of data available; and (3) the mechanism by which individuals are allocated to the program or receive the policy (this mechanism is usually called the "assignment rule").

In an ex post evaluation, the policy action has occurred, and researchers and policy makers want to identify whether the implemented policy is working the way they thought it should be, and the nature of the question being asked is thus clearly identified. The evaluation procedure has to properly work out a comparison that clearly separates individuals and households that have been subject to the policy (or "treated") and those that have not but are otherwise similar to the treated. The most convincing method of evaluation is the *social experiment method,* because it builds directly the comparison (or control) group by randomly assigning eligible people to receive (or not receive) the treatment. A series of other methods— for example, natural experiments methods, discontinuity design methods, matching methods, instrumental variables methods, control function methods, and structural econometric methods (for a survey of these methods, see chapter 5 in Bourguignon and Pereira da Silva 2003 or Blundell and Costa Dias 2007)—attempt to mimic the random assignment of the social experiment or use economic theory to model the assignment rule (and thus control for the selection bias). The quality of the data (for example, having long panel data sets) and the complexity of the assignment rule normally dictate the choice of the evaluation method.

In a typical ex ante situation, building the counterfactual is much trickier because the comparison between the situation "before" and "after" the treatment is purely virtual or notional (given that the policy has not been implemented yet). The "theory-free" social experiment method and its close substitutes are not applicable. The dominant approach in ex ante policy evaluations is represented by structural econometric models or, when estimating fully specified structural models is not feasible, simpler reduced-form or nonbehavioral models are used. In this latter case, the main issue is to generate counterfactuals by *simulating* hypothetical situations with the implemented policy and without the policy. The simulation is done using information at the individual or household level, and it is thus labeled *micro simulation.*

Contrasted with the evaluation of microeconomic policy, the assessment of the poverty and income distribution effects of *macroeconomic policies* (ex ante or ex post) presents two distinct problems that require devising novel methods. First, the comparison between groups of individuals and households that are treated (or subject to the experiment) and a control group is much harder. In fact, it is almost impossible to isolate a control group for a macroeconomic policy because, by definition, all individuals and households are affected by the same policy. For example, a devaluation of the real exchange rate affects the whole economy with multiple consequences for households, firms, banks, government, and so on. Therefore—and this is the second problem—one has to figure out not only a micro but also a *macro* counterfactual, and the latter usually has to be done in a general equilibrium setting. These two distinct difficulties justify the use of a macro-micro modeling framework—one that takes into account the macro nature of the policy (or the macro consequences of scaled-up micro interventions) and integrates a microeconomic (that is, individual and household) dimension.

Macro Models with Representative Household Groups: A First Step in Assessing Macroeconomic Policy Effects on Poverty and Distribution

Traditional aggregate macroeconomic models use the simplest and most restrictive assumption that economic policies do not affect the *distribution* of welfare. This is tantamount to assuming that the economy is composed of only one economic agent or that all individuals in a society are identical. This assumption can be relaxed by using the less-stringent hypothesis that economic policies do not affect the distribution of welfare within groups of homogeneous households. This is the idea behind the construction of macroeconomic models in which the single consumer or household is disaggregated into groups of households that share some common characteristics, usually in terms of the structure of their sources of income and their consumption preferences. Identifying—for a given economy—a comprehensive set for such groups would result in building a macro model with a set of representative household groups (RHGs).

The ending point of the 2003 Bourguignon and Pereira da Silva volume was precisely the description of this type of technique. In particular, Lofgren, Robinson, and El-Said (2003, chapter 15) showed how to construct macroeconomic models with RHGs to carry out poverty and inequality analyses in a general equilibrium framework. This class of models has been labeled in the modeling literature as the disaggregated SAM-CGE/RHG model (social accounting matrix [SAM]–computable general equilibrium [CGE]). The best examples start with Adelman and Robinson (1978) and Dervis, de Melo, and Robinson (1982), and continue with Bourguignon, de Melo, and Morrisson (1991) and Agenor, Izquierdo, and Jensen (2006), among others. In this tradition, the typical CGE is a macroeconomic model that separates the household population of an economy into RHGs. Disaggregation aims to capture the various ways through which economic policies would affect the factor allocation and remuneration across RHGs. The SAM-CGE/RHG approach models the functioning of factor markets at the level of aggregation that is compatible with the factor remuneration for each RHG. Under this approach, only the aggregate behavior of these groups—in terms of supply of labor and consumption demand—matters for the general equilibrium of the economy.

Strong assumptions must be made: the distribution of *relative* income within each RHG is policy-neutral, that is, it is not affected by any change in macroeconomic policy; and the demographic weight of households in each RHG is constant. Hence, this approach essentially focuses on changes in the distribution *between* RHGs. Empirically, however, analyses of micro data show that changes of within-RHG inequality can be as important as changes of between-RHG inequality in explaining the evolution of overall inequality. Think, for example, of a case in which the RHGs are formed according to the employment status of the head of household (for example, "small farmers," "unskilled urban workers in the formal sector," and so on) and in which the shock to be simulated results in a strong reduction of unskilled urban workers employed in the formal sector. After the shock, the RHG labeled "unskilled urban workers in the formal sector" is much smaller, but the standard CGE/RHG does not include any mechanisms of adjustment: that is, it does not model which particular household should leave its original group (should it be a poor or a rich household?) nor in which new group it should go. In addition to the criteria used to form RHGs, household-level criteria normally are appropriate only for the head of household, but other members may belong or move to other groups and this cannot be accounted for. These two phenomena are likely and can strongly affect within-RHG inequality, but they are completely ignored by the standard approach.

A direct way to deal with these issues is to introduce as many representative households into the initial CGE/RHG framework as there are in standard household surveys. Indeed, such models do already exist. See, for instance, Cockburn (2006) for an application to a case study of Nepal and see Rutherford, Tarr, and Shepotylo (2007) for a study of Russia. The household sector in these models includes (a few thousand) heterogeneous individual households reflecting those observed in available household surveys; however, as explained below, a restrictive set of conditions need to be assumed to model the behavior of these households.

Is this extension of RHGs to "real" households the way forward? Does it mean that the full integration of household surveys with macro modeling is practically achieved and increasingly will be used as computers and model-solving software become more powerful? The answer to the first question is most certainly yes. Integrating household surveys into macro modeling, whether relying on CGE or other types of models, is undoubtedly the direction to follow to assess the impact of macro policies at the micro level. Most of the chapters in the present volume are about this integration. The answer to the second question must be formed more cautiously. The mere extension of the CGE/RHG approach to individual households taken from household surveys raises methodological issues that cannot be ignored.

The most important difficulty in answering this question relates to estimating heterogeneous economic behavior at the household level. Consider, for instance, the issue of modeling the consumption behavior of households. Within the standard CGE/RHG framework, it is necessary to specify the way each household in the model uses its income, or how the budget coefficients of a particular household depend on the income of that household and on the vector of prices. Starting from the data of a household survey, the behavior of a specific RHG is generally estimated on the basis of observed differences among "real" households belonging to that same RHG. In other words, variability across household incomes and budget shares is used to estimate the way in which the budget share of the representative household of a group changes with income. This variability requires postulating some functional form, which in turn permits inferring price elasticities derived from income effect.

Is such an approach possible with "individual households," namely, in the case when the number of RHGs in the CGE is the same as that for the households in a survey? Yes, but with tighter assumptions. Of course, there is no way to "estimate" a consumption model for a household on a single observation except under two alternative stringent assumptions: (1) observed household budget shares are assumed to be constant—implying a "linear" model with unit income and own-price elasticities of consumption; and (2) observed household budget shares correspond to a common behavioral model where shares depend on income (and prices) with fixed differences between individual shares and what the model implies. As with the RHG approach, the common consumption behavior can be estimated through standard econometric techniques applied to the whole sample of household variations after some assumption has been made on the functional form to use. Residuals in that procedure stand from some unexplained divergence of individual households from the common model. It turns out that these assumptions are far from being innocuous and may influence both the macroeconomic properties of the whole framework and the simulated microeconomic consequences of a macro policy or shock. Assumption 1 would imply that a proportional increase of income of the whole population of households does not modify the aggregate propensity to consume, not a very satisfactory property particularly when aggregated at the macro level. Assumption 2 would imply that the simplicity and homogeneity of such a "common behavioral model" for individual behavior regarding important characteristics of individual decisions would yield very limited responses to policy changes at the macro level. We would be back to the aggregate properties of the macro model itself losing the effort of disaggregation that meant to model hetereogeneity at the start.

A Top-Down Modeling Approach for Integrating Household-Level Data into Macro Models

The CGE/RHG approach is an important first step, but it has inherent limits in terms of modeling the heterogeneity of individuals and households. So how is the impact of macroeconomic policies on heterogeneous individuals measured?

A solution to avoid the problems mentioned in the previous section is to separate the macro and micro parts of the modeling framework. The degree of separation—and the potential alternative ways of linking or integrating (in a different way from the RHG approach)—of these two parts, which are briefly described in the remainder of this introductory chapter, is the distinguishing feature of the various contributions to this volume.

The top-down modeling approach works in a sequential two-step fashion: (1) a macro (top) model is solved and (2) its solution in terms of a vector of aggregate prices, wages, and employment variables—the linking aggregate variables (LAVs)—is used to (a) shock a micro-household-level data set or (b) target the aggregate solution values of a micro (bottom) model (see figure 1.1). In case a, the micro simulation is quite simple and broadly corresponds to the micro *accounting* incidence analysis mentioned above: households (and individuals) do not respond to the price shocks (coming from the top model) by changing the quantities of factor services they supply or the quantities of goods they demand or sell. In case b, the microeconometric model includes *behavioral* responses used to simulate changes in individual wages, self-employment incomes, employment status, and so on. These individual changes are simulated in a way that is consistent with the aggregation of the set of LAVs generated by the macro model. When the micro accounting simulation or the micro behavioral simulation is completed, a full

Figure 1.1 Schematic Representation of the Top-Down Modeling Approach

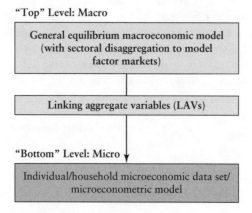

Source: Authors' depiction.

counterfactual distribution of household income is produced and the (macro) policy change can be evaluated. The details of these two top-down approaches are described in the next two subsections.

TOP-DOWN MICRO ACCOUNTING MODELS

This volume features two examples of top-down macro-micro accounting modeling: Ravallion and Lokshin (chapter 2); and Bussolo, Lay, Medvedev, and van der Mensbrugghe (chapter 3). In chapter 2, Ravallion and Lokshin use Morocco's national survey of living standards to measure the short-term welfare impacts of deprotecting cereals (the country's main food staple). The authors find small impacts on mean consumption and inequality in the aggregate and contrary to past claims, find that the rural poor are worse off on average after deprotection. In chapter 3, Bussolo, Lay, Medvedev, and van der Mensbrugghe link a global CGE model with household surveys of Brazil, Chile, Colombia, and Mexico to estimate the first-round impacts on the poor of regional and multilateral trade liberalization scenarios. Their results show that because of different initial positions in terms of economic structure, poverty levels, and trade protection, the poverty effects are quite dissimilar across the four countries studied. Furthermore, for the countries analyzed, the distributional effects of trade are more important than the growth effects (that is, the increase in average incomes following trade reform). Together, the two chapters illustrate the advantages of micro accounting techniques (among others, their ability to capture the largest impacts of reform and their ease of implementation) and highlight an important limitation of this kind of analysis (that is, the fact that the results are likely to be valid only in the short and medium terms). In these micro accounting models, micro data sets are linked to disaggregated macro models by directly applying changes in prices and wages that result from the solution values of the macroeconomic model. For example, sector-specific vectors of macro simulated prices and wages are used to construct a counterfactual income for each individual or household, using simple multiplication or replacement techniques: the actual price and wage rate that explain the components of income for each individual are replaced by the simulated values.

The assumption of no behavior responses has been a major criticism of these micro accounting models, but under certain not overly restrictive conditions, it can be demonstrated that these models are fully consistent with microeconomic behavior. In fact, they estimate first-round effects, which are a good approximation of total welfare effects in situations in which the price (and wage) changes are small and markets are competitive. In other words, behavior responses can be safely ignored when evaluating individual welfare change when the macro policy shock causes only marginal changes in the budget constraints faced by agents and when no agents are rationed or do not operate in a perfect market. Using the well-known utility theory of consumer behavior and relying on the envelope theorem (or Sheppard's lemma or Roy's theorem), a formal demonstration that micro accounting is consistent with behavior is provided in chapter 2. The main conclusion is that the change in the welfare income metric caused by a change in the price of a specific good is equal to the change in the cost of consuming that good because of the variation in its price (with a constant quantity consumed). This conclusion can be generalized to cases in which the agent produces and sells certain goods, including factor services.

Apart from cases in which changes are not marginal and markets are not perfectly competitive and therefore behavioral responses cannot be ignored, an important drawback of this approach is given by the unidirectional link between the macro and micro parts of the modeling framework. This means that distributional changes at the micro level do not provide any feedback to the aggregate variables at the macro level: these are determined exclusively by the macro model.

Additional examples of this approach are found in Chen and Ravallion (2004), who analyze the distributional effects of China's accession to the World Trade Organization; Friedman and Levinsohn (2002), who consider the impact of the Indonesian crisis on poverty; and other examples listed in the survey on poverty and trade by Hertel and Reimer (2005).

TOP-DOWN MICRO SIMULATION MODELS

The second way to conduct top-down macro-micro modeling is to link the macro model to a micro simulation module. This volume features two examples of this modeling framework: Robilliard, Bourguignon, and Robinson in chapter 4; and Ferreira, Leite, Pereira da Silva, and Picchetti in chapter 5. In chapter 4, Robilliard, Bourguignon, and Robinson link a CGE model with a micro simulation model to quantify the effects of the 1997 Indonesian financial crisis on poverty and inequality. Their framework allows for decomposition of the effects of the financial crisis, and their results show that while rural and urban incomes converged in the aftermath of the crisis, overall inequality increased because of the divergence of incomes within these sectors. Thus, the negative income effects of the crisis were augmented by a worsening in the distribution of income. In chapter 5, Ferreira, Leite, Pereira da Silva, and Picchetti use a top-down macro-micro model of the Brazilian economy to examine the impacts of the 1998–99 currency crisis in Brazil on the occupational structure of the labor force and on the distribution of incomes. The authors test the ex ante predictive performance of the model by comparing its simulated results using the 1998 household survey with the actual ex post household survey data observed in 1999. They find that the top-down macro-micro econometric model, while still inaccurate on many dimensions, can actually predict the broad pattern of the incidence of changes in household incomes reasonably well, and much better than the alternative approaches. This chapter thus offers some validation for this macro-micro approach.

The key difference between the simpler accounting approach and micro simulation is that this approach can be used when the envelope theorem is not applicable—for example, when the policy simulated modifies the labor participation decision and/or when there are market imperfections such as rationing. In these circumstances, considering behavioral responses at the micro level becomes essential. These responses are normally simulated by using a structural or reduced-form econometric model, which is initially estimated (or calibrated) from the cross-section data of the household survey. As mentioned, this type of micro model can handle market imperfections. For example, imperfections can be introduced for the labor markets in the macro (CGE) model: wages can be assumed to be rigid in the formal sector in connection with some form of rationing, whereby individuals are not allowed free entry into the formal market segment. This rationing mechanism needs to be replicated or simulated at the micro level, and this can be done using the estimated micro model. Basically, this micro model identifies which individuals switch from jobs in the formal sector to self-employment or to inactivity, or vice versa. In other words, these macro-micro models reconcile the disequilibrium captured by the macro model variables—where prices, wages, and employment will incorporate the effect of market imperfections—and the heterogeneity of individual behavior. Some individuals are more likely to be responsible for the changes observed at the macro sectoral level.

Econometric models of occupational choice by household members allow this allocation to be performed, accounting for individual heterogeneity while using the relevant variables from the macroeconomic general equilibrium model to build the counterfactual distribution. These econometric models essentially consist of multilogit models of occupational choices that are conditional on individual and household characteristics. The micro simulation includes modifying a subset of parameters of the multilogit model to generate aggregate levels of employment by occupational type, skill, gender, and so on, which exactly match the results coming from the CGE macroeconomic model. Practically, the procedure uses the intercepts in multilogit models to match micro simulated employment and the results of the macro model. The intercept is adjusted for each individual in a given group so that the average of the group matches (actually, it converges through all the resulting changes in occupational choices in the group) the average of the same group in the macroeconomic model. This is analogous with "grossing up" a small sample of individuals or households. The procedure remains, however, top down in the sense that there is no feedback between the micro and the macro levels, that is, no explicit link or interaction exists between the micro level results and the actual prices in the macro model. For additional examples of how this technique is used, see chapters 4 and 5, as well as Bussolo, Lay, and van der Mensbrugghe (2006) and Hertel and Winters (2006).

What does this procedure add to the understanding of the impact of macroeconomic policies? Taking into account individual heterogeneity in modeling occupational choices certainly adds accuracy and nuance. The evaluation of the impact of economic policies shows some counterintuitive results when this procedure is used. This is shown when the counterfactual produced by the micro simulation approach is compared with that of the CGE/RHG approach (as in chapter 4) and with the actual distribution (as in chapter 5). The counterfactual distributions obtained under the assumption that distribution of income within RHG (defined by the occupation of household head) is constant provide different results than the distributions obtained with the top-down micro simulation framework shown earlier. The latter is closer to actual distributions and thus allows a better grasp of the impact of macroeconomic policies on specific groups and segments of the distribution: it appears that it constitutes a more accurate and better tool. In particular, the counterfactuals are radically different in an important dimension, namely, the percentiles of the distribution most affected by the experiment. This is a crucial piece of information to design well-targeted compensatory or supportive responses to a given macroeconomic reform.

Toward an Integrated Macro-Micro Model: Feedback Loops from Bottom to Top

Under both the micro accounting and micro simulation top-down models, the results from the LAVs are "injected" into the micro data set that either takes them as givens or adjusts to them. After the changes are computed, however, the aggregated result of, say, the sum of consumption for all households in the micro data set can be different from the result of the aggregate private consumption calculated by the macro model. In other words, there is no feedback from the micro to the macro parts of the modeling framework. Bourguignon and Savard (chapter 6) address this issue by devising feedback loops between the two layers of the framework. In chapter 6, Bourguignon and Savard assess the distributional effects of trade reform in the Philippines, and their results illustrate the bias inherent to methods that ignore feedback effects from the micro to the macro and the assumptions that markets—particularly labor— are fully competitive at the micro level.

The main difference in their model is that the one-step sequential process from the top macro model to the bottom micro model is repeated iteratively and in a bidirectional way; that is, after the first shock, a subset of the LAVs is recalculated by aggregation from the micro data and transmitted to the macro model. This then adjusts again to these new values and once more transmits the new solution to the micro model. The process continues iteratively until convergence is reached. Rutherford, Tarr, and Shepotylo (2007) devised such an iterative algorithm in a CGE/RHG model with thousands of households (see above) and found that, in their case study for Russia and with perfectly competitive markets, most of the micro and macro impacts of an across-the-board trade liberalization were adequately accounted for by the first sequential step. In chapter 6, Bourguignon and Savard propose a different and simpler approach that is applicable to imperfectly competitive environments.

This iterative approach has several advantages over a method that would solve simultaneously for all individual and aggregate equilibrium conditions, as in the CGE/RHG model category with fully disaggregated household groups. First, the macro and the micro parts of the model do not have to be fully consistent in terms of consumption or income aggregates. In many cases, the underestimated aggregate consumption from a household survey does not need to be adjusted to the national accounts generally used in CGE modeling. As Bourguignon and Savard put it, "No correction is necessary for consistency with national account data if it is assumed that the proportion of underestimation is independent from the price of other goods and unit wages" (p. 185 of this volume). A second advantage is that no limit needs to be imposed on the level of disaggregation in terms of production sectors and number of households to be included in the model. A third advantage is that, with respect to other approaches, fewer restrictions apply to the choice of functional forms for the consumption and labor supply behavior of households. In particular, there is no need to choose functional forms with good aggregation properties.

The Fully Integrated Micro-Based CGE Approach

Quite naturally, one wonders whether or not the convergence process described above truly puts microeconomic consistency into the behavior of the macro aggregates. If the ultimate objective is to get a fully consistent macro-micro framework or, in other words, if the goal is to build the poverty impact of macro policies from the strongest basis of micro observations, then a fully integrated micro-based CGE should be the preferred method (Heckman, Lochner, and Taber 1998; Browning, Hansen, and Heckman 1999; Townsend 2002; Townsend and Ueda 2006).

Why not aim to build macroeconomic behavior from all individuals and households in a sample survey? This route is taken in this volume by Cogneau and Robilliard (chapter 7) and Giné and Townsend (chapter 8). In chapter 7, Cogneau and Robilliard develop a macro-micro simulation framework to study the effects of targeted transfer schemes on income distribution and monetary poverty in Madagascar. Their results show that the general equilibrium effects of transfer mechanisms may change the distribution of the benefits between rural and urban households, an effect not accounted for by micro accounting or top-down modeling approaches. In chapter 8, Giné and Townsend apply a general equilibrium occupational choice model to two sectors in Thailand between 1976 and 1996. The authors show that without an expansion of the financial intermediation sector, Thailand would have evolved differently, namely, with a much lower growth rate, a higher residual subsistence sector, and nonincreasing wages but lower inequality. The financial liberalization resulted in welfare gains and losses to different subsets of the population with a limited impact of foreign capital on growth or the distribution of observed income.

Intuitively, it seems logical to circumvent the problems of standard CGE/RHG models using a modeling strategy focusing on each household, but some problems remain. One is the difficulty of calibrating structural behavioral models for individual households with the type of micro data set that is available. The rudimentary way through which some key structural behavior—such as consumption and investment—is modeled at the household level poses a problem for the properties of the overall model when the whole sample (thousands) of households is aggregated. Would the aggregate behavior of all individuals and households for private consumption or investment "react" to macroeconomic policies with the same "known macroeconomic textbook properties" as the observed aggregate variables in national accounts? For example, the macroeconomic literature suggests that aggregate private consumption is sensitive to income, inflation, and interest rates; however, if it is not possible—because of the lack of data at the individual level—to estimate one or all of these elasticities, what would be the overall properties of the macroeconomic model constructed with the aggregation of these insufficiently modeled household behaviors? In addition, econometric problems result from the difference between estimations done in cross-section with the last available household survey and those done with time-series for larger groups, or with panels. The other question—when the modeling of key structural behavioral is limited—is where does the heterogeneity come from? One interpretation is that heterogeneity can be a standard residual in the regression equation across households, which is written to explain the behavior at hand, for example, private consumption. Another interpretation is to accept heterogeneity as a "heterogeneous behavioral coefficient" that can be added to the coefficients used to explain private consumption. But then the identification problem remains for this coefficient, because, as an example and thinking of the consumption function of a given household, the two interpretations of heterogeneity given above are observationally equivalent—up to heteroskedasticity. Yet they have different implications in terms of aggregate behavior.

Macro-Micro Modeling: A Summary of Lessons Learned

An alternative seems to be emerging from the overview of the models and approaches included in this volume and briefly described above. On the one hand, the micro accounting approach uses too restrictive an assumption of constant distribution of income within RHGs, irrespective of the type of macroeconomic policy being examined and of the specific characteristics of the markets being affected. The top-down approach that models household behavior and uses LAVs improves the accuracy of the counterfactual but restricts the instruments of micro simulation to a limited number of LAVs. A complex CGE at the top can be designed, but the transmission of the heterogeneity will be limited to a few dimensions given by the LAVs (for example, occupational choices). On the other hand, the extension of the CGE/RHG approach to the thousands of households in a given survey seems promising as a way to bypass the problems listed above, but this approach has difficulties, too: only *simple* behavior can be properly modeled at the household level—given available data sets—and then properly "aggregated" at a macroeconomic level in the sense that results are consistent with macroeconomic theory.

The alternative can be summarized as follows. The evaluation of the poverty and distributional impact of macroeconomic policies theoretically needs to be conducted with a fully disaggregated general equilibrium model—including as RHGs a sufficiently large and representative sample of the population (possibly tens of thousands); a variety of goods and services produced and consumed in the economy (also thousands); an adequate representation of equilibrium in all major markets; and in particular, consistent modeling of the consumption, investment, production, and savings decisions made by the tens of thousands of RHGs. Although it is theoretically possible to solve such a large model, this volume points to the two major directions found so far to simplify this original—and first best—approach. These two routes should work with a reduced number of RHGs or should solve the full model by successive iterations, working with a top-bottom or a bottom-up approach.

Even by solving the problems noted above, more complex issues remain. In particular, the models described above have nothing to say about the nonincome dimensions of poverty: health, education, and access to infrastructure, among others. Which is the proper macro-micro model that can assess public policies aimed at improving these dimensions? This may seem to be a simple question, but so far, spending on education, health, or cash transfers to households has no direct productive effect in standard CGE or macroeconometric modeling. These tools treat expenditures on physical or human capital identically, even if they have different long-term effects on an economy's growth potential. It is possible to analyze the distributional effect of these expenditures using a micro simulation framework if some behavior is introduced—for example, the demand for schooling or health services. But two difficulties arise: (1) the actual effects on distribution will appear only in the long run (when the young become adults and enter into productive activities); and (2) while these education and health policies are supposed to generate future general equilibrium effects at the macro level (by changing the earnings structure and the growth rate of output), these effects also depend on how the demand side of the economy will evolve (for example, an "excessive" amount of spending on higher education might depress the returns to this kind of "investment"). In this volume, Bourguignon, Diaz-Bonilla, and Lofgren (chapter 9) attempt to construct sectoral (Millennium Development Goal [MDG]-related) demand functions for these services working in a dynamic general equilibrium framework. Although micro data are not directly used to estimate these demand functions, this work could be done and could support the functional form chosen. The attempt provides two messages for policy makers: (1) that dynamic general equilibrium effects of social spending are critical to analyze the allocation of resources to reach the MDGs and (2) that social expenditures are a composite good that produces cross-sectoral or cross-MDG externalities that need to be taken into account (that is, spending on basic infrastructure such as water and sanitation, education, and health in an appropriate proportion are important to achieve better overall development outcomes).

Other methodological issues remain: (1) the importance of modeling heterogeneity of production and investment decisions by firms and (2) micro simulation techniques largely remain comparisons of two cross-sections of households and dynamic modeling and the proper treatment of growth is needed for a better understanding of the links between micro and macro phenomena. These and other issues for further research are briefly discussed in the concluding remarks of this volume.

Note

1. Deaton, Angus (2001). Intervention in a panel discussion on the International Monetary Fund–sponsored conference on "Macroeconomic Policies and Poverty Reduction," April 13, 2001, Washington, D.C.; transcript available at http://www.imf.org/external/np/tr/2001/tr010413.htm.

References

Adelman, Irma, and Sherman Robinson. 1978. *Income Distribution Policy in Developing Countries: A Case Study of Korea*. New York: Oxford University Press.

Agenor, Pierre-Richard, Alejandro Izquierdo, and Henning Tarp Jensen, eds. 2006. *Adjustment Policies, Poverty and Unemployment: The IMMPA Framework*. Malden, MA: Blackwell Publishing.

Ahmad, Ehtisham, and Nicholas Stern. 1991. *The Theory and Practice of Tax Reform in Developing Countries*. New York: Cambridge University Press.

Atkinson, Alexander B. 1997. "On the Measurement of Poverty." *Econometrica* 55 (4): 749–64.

Birsdall, Nancy, and Juan Luis Londono. 1997. "Asset Inequality Matters: An Assessment of the World Bank's Approach to Poverty Reduction." *American Economic Review* 87 (2): 32–37.

Blundell, Richard, and Monica Costa Dias. 2007. "Alternative Approaches to Evaluation in Empirical Microeconomics." Institute for Fiscal Studies. Available at www.ifs.org.uk. An earlier version appeared in *Portuguese Economic Journal* 1 (2002): 91–115.

Bourguignon, François, Jaime de Melo, and Christian Morrisson. 1991. "Poverty and Income Distribution during Adjustment: Issues and Evidence from the OECD Project." *World Development* 19 (1): 1485–508.

Bourguignon, François, and Luiz A. Pereira da Silva, eds. 2003. *The Impact of Economic Policies on Poverty and Income Distribution: Evaluation Techniques and Tools.* Washington, DC: World Bank; Oxford and New York: Oxford University Press.

Browning, M., L. P. Hansen, and J. Heckman. 1999. "Micro Data and General Equilibrium Models." In *Handbook of Macroeconomics*, eds. Taylor and Woodford, vol. 1. Amsterdam: North-Holland.

Bussolo, Maurizio, Jann Lay, and Dominique van der Mensbrugghe. 2006. "Structural Change and Poverty Reduction in Brazil: The Impact of the Doha Round." Policy Research Working Paper No. 3833, World Bank, Washington, DC.

Chen, S., and M. Ravallion. 2004. "Household Welfare Impacts of China's Accession to the WTO." In *China and the World Economy: Policy and Poverty after China's Accession to the WTO*, eds. D. Bhattasali, S. Li, and W. Martin. London and New York: Oxford University Press.

Chenery, Hollis, M. Ahluwalia, C. Bell, J. Duloy, and R. Jolly. 1974. *Redistribution with Growth: Policies to Improve Income Distribution in Developing Countries in the Context of Economic Growth.* London: Oxford University Press.

Cockburn, John. 2006. "Trade Liberalisation and Poverty in Nepal: Computable General Equilibrium Micro Simulation Analysis." In *Globalisation and Poverty: Channels and Policy Responses,* eds. M. Bussolo and J. I. Round, 172–95. London and New York: Routledge/Warwick Studies in Globalisation, Routledge.

Dervis, K., J. de Melo, and S. Robinson. 1982. *General Equilibrium Models for Development Policy.* New York: Cambridge University Press.

Friedman, Jed, and James Levinsohn. 2002. "The Distributional Impacts of Indonesia's Financial Crisis on Household Welfare: A 'Rapid Response' Methodology." *World Bank Economic Review* 16 (3): 397–423.

Heckman, J., L. Lochner, and C. Taber. 1998. "Explaining Rising Wage Inequality: Explorations with a Dynamic General Equilibrium Model of Labor Earnings with Heterogeneous Agents." *Review of Economics Dynamics* 1 (1): 1–58.

Hertel, T. W., and J. J. Reimer. 2005. "Predicting the Poverty Impacts of Trade Reform." *Journal of International Trade and Economic Development* 14 (4): 377–405.

Hertel, Thomas W., and L. Alan Winters, eds. 2006. *Poverty and the WTO: Impacts of the Doha Development Agenda.* New York: Palgrave MacMillan.

Kanbur, Ravi. 2000. "Income Distribution and Development." In *Handbook of Income Distribution*, eds. Alexander B. Atkinson and Francois Bourguignon. Amsterdam: North-Holland.

Kuznets, Simon. 1955. "Economic Growth and Income Inequality." *American Economic Review* 45 (1): 1–28.

Lewis, W. A. 1954. "Economic Development with Unlimited Supplies of Labor." *Manchester School of Economics and Social Studies* 22: 139–81.

Lofgren, Hans, Sherman Robinson, and Moataz El-Said. 2003."Poverty and Inequality Analysis in a General Equilibrium Framework: The Representative Household Approach." In *The Impact of Economic Policies on Poverty and Income Distribution: Evaluation Techniques and Tools,* ed. François Bourguignon and Luiz A. Pereira da Silva, 325–37. Washington, DC: World Bank and Oxford University Press.

Meerman, Jacob. 1979. *Public Expenditure in Malaysia: Who Benefits and Why?* New York: Oxford University Press.

Ravallion, Martin. 2001. "Growth, Inequality and Poverty: Looking Beyond Averages" *World Development* 29 (11): 1803–15.

———. 2004. "Pro-Poor Growth: A Primer." World Bank Policy Research Working Paper No. 3242. World Bank, Washington, DC.

———. 2006. "Looking beyond Averages in the Trade and Poverty Debate." *World Development* 34 (8): 1374–92.

Rosenstein-Rodan, Paul. 1943. "Problems of Industrialization in Southern and Eastern Europe." *Economic Journal* 53: 202–11.

Rutherford Thomas, David Tarr, and Oleksandr Shepotylo. 2007. "The Impact on Russia of WTO Accession and the Doha Agenda: The Importance of Liberalization of Barriers against Foreign Direct Investment in Services for Growth and Poverty Reduction." In *The WTO and Poverty and Inequality,* ed. L. Alan Winters. Cheltenham, UK: Edgar Elgar Publishing.

Selowsky, Marcelo. 1979. *Who Benefits from Government Expenditures? A Case Study of Colombia.* New York: Oxford University Press.

Sen, Amartya. 1973. *On Economic Inequality.* Oxford: Clarendon Press.

Townsend, Robert. 2002. "Safety Nets and Financial Institutions in the Asian Crisis: The Allocation of Within-Country Risk." International Monetary Fund. Prepared for the IMF Conference on Macroeconomic Policies and Poverty Reduction, March 14–15, Washington, DC. Available at http://cier.uchicago.edu/papers/papers.htm.

Townsend, Robert, and Kenichi Ueda. 2006. "Financial Deepening, Inequality, and Growth: A Model-Based Quantitative Evaluation." *Review of Economic Studies* 73 (1): 251–93.

PART I

Top-Down Approach
with Micro Accounting

2

Winners and Losers from Trade Reform in Morocco

Martin Ravallion and Michael Lokshin

As a water-scarce country, Morocco does not have a natural advantage in its production of water-intensive crops such as most cereals—including wheat, which is used to produce the country's main food staples. In the past, the desire for aggregate self-sufficiency in the production of food staples has led to government efforts to foster domestic cereal production—even though cereals can be imported more cheaply. Since the 1980s, cereal producers have been protected by import tariffs as high as 100 percent.

There have been concerns that the consequent reallocation of resources has hurt consumers and constrained the growth of production and trade. Reform to the current incentive system for cereals has emerged as an important issue on the policy agenda for Morocco (World Bank 2003). The major obstacles to reform stem from concerns about the impacts on household welfare, particularly for the poor. Little careful research has been conducted to identify who will gain and who will lose from such reforms.

Nonetheless, much debate about the equity implications has ensued. It is widely agreed that urban consumers will gain from lower cereal prices. More contentious are the impacts in (generally poorer) rural areas. Defenders of the existing protection system have argued that the rural economy will suffer from large welfare losses thanks to trade reform. Critics have argued against this view, claiming that the bulk of the rural poor tend to be net consumers and thus lose out from the higher prices because of trade protection.

These critics argue that the rural poor are likely to gain from the reform, while it will be the well-off in rural areas, who tend to be net producers, who will lose (see, for example, Abdelkhalek 2002 and World Bank 2003).

This chapter studies the household welfare impacts of the relative price changes induced by specific trade policy reform scenarios for cereals in Morocco. Past analyses of the welfare impacts have been highly aggregated, focusing on just one or a few categories of households. The estimates presented here consider the impacts across 5,000 sampled households in the Morocco Living Standards Survey for 1998–99. This allows a detailed picture of the welfare impacts to emerge, thus enabling a more informed discussion of the social protection policy response to trade liberalization.

Past approaches to studying the welfare impacts of specific trade reforms have tended to be either *partial equilibrium analyses,* in which the welfare impacts of the direct price changes caused by tariff changes are measured at the household level, or *general equilibrium analyses,* in which second-round responses are captured in a theoretically consistent way but with considerable aggregation across household types. In general terms, the economics involved in both approaches is well known. And both approaches have found numerous applications.[1]

These two approaches are combined. In particular, the price changes induced by the trade policy change are simulated from a general equilibrium analysis done for a joint government of Morocco and World Bank study. The present study takes the methods and results of that analysis as given and carries them to the Moroccan Living Standards Survey. This approach respects the richness of detail available from a modern integrated household survey, making it possible to go well beyond the highly aggregative types of analysis often found. Not only are the expected impacts measured across the distribution of initial levels of living but how they vary by other characteristics, such as location, are also considered. This chapter is thus able to provide a reasonably detailed map of the predicted welfare impacts by location and socioeconomic characteristics.

In studying the distributional impacts of trade reform, the chapter makes a distinction between the "vertical impact" and the "horizontal impact." The former concerns the way the mean impacts vary with the level of preform income. How does the reform affect people at different preform income levels? The horizontal impact relates to the disparities in impact between people at the same preform level of income. As argued in Ravallion (2004), many past discussions of the distributional impacts of trade and other economywide reforms tended to focus more on the vertical impacts, analogous to standard practices in studying the "benefit incidence" of tax and spending policies. As demonstrated in this chapter, however, that focus may well miss an important component of a policy's distributional impact arising from the horizontal dispersion of impacts at given prereform income levels. The study shows how the impact of a policy on a standard inequality measure can be straightforwardly decomposed into its vertical and horizontal components. The former tells how much of the change in total inequality can be accounted for by the way in which mean impacts that are conditional on prereform income vary with the latter. If there is no difference in the proportionate impact by level of income, then the vertical component is zero. The horizontal component tells the contribution of the deviations in impacts from their conditional means. Only when the impact of the reform is predicted perfectly by prereform income will the horizontal component be zero. The chapter studies the relative importance of these two components of the predicted distributional impact of trade reform in Morocco.

The following section discusses the approach in general terms; the annex to the chapter provides more detail. The detailed results are presented under the heading on the measured impacts of reform, followed by a review of the main findings.

Using Micro Data to Measure and Explain the Welfare Impacts of Reform

This study uses preexisting estimates of the household-level welfare impacts of the price changes generated by a computable general equilibrium (CGE) model. The CGE analysis generates a set of price changes that embody both the direct price effects of the trade policy change and the indirect effects on the prices of both traded and nontraded goods, once all markets respond to the reform. Standard methods of first-order welfare analysis are used to measure the gains and losses at the household level. This approach is sequential rather than integrated. In other words, there is no feedback from the empirical analysis of welfare impacts to the CGE analysis. The alternative approach is to fully integrate the CGE analysis with the household-level data (see, for example, Cockburn 2006).

The study's focus is very much on the short-term welfare impacts of trade policy changes. In keeping with the limitations of the general equilibrium analysis on which it draws, the approach does not capture the dynamic effects of trade reform through labor market adjustment and technological innovation. Nor does it capture potential gains to the environment.[2]

The specifics of the approach to estimating welfare impacts at the household level are outlined in the annex; only the salient features are summarized here.[3] Each household has preferences over consumption and work effort represented by a standard utility function. The household is assumed to be free to choose its preferred combinations of consumptions and labor supplies, subject to its budget constraint. The household also owns a production activity generating a profit that depends on a vector of supply prices and wages. The indirect utility function of the household (giving the maximum utility attainable given the constraints) also depends on prices and wages.

The predicted price impacts from the CGE model are taken as given for the analysis of household-level impacts. In measuring these impacts, the authors are constrained by the data, which do not include prices and wages. This limitation does not pertain to calculating a first-order approximation to the welfare impact in a neighborhood of the household's optimum consumption and labor supply decisions (as outlined in the annex). This calculation provides a measure of the monetary value of the gain for household i, denoted g_i. This value is obtained by adding the proportionate changes in all prices weighted by their corresponding expenditure or revenue shares. The weight for the proportionate change in the jth selling price is the revenue (selling value) from household production activities in sector j; similarly, the consumption expenditure shares are the (negative) weights for demand price changes, and earnings provide the weights for changes in the wage rates. The difference between revenue and expenditure gives (to a first-order approximation) the welfare impact of an equi-proportionate increase in the price of a given commodity. In the specific model used, real wage rates are fixed. The likely implications of relaxing this assumption are discussed in the final section.

By using the calculus in deriving the welfare gains, g_i, for $I = 1, \ldots, n$, the authors implicitly assume small changes in prices. Relaxing this requires more information on the structure of the demand and supply system (see, for example, Ravallion and van de Walle 1991). This relaxation would entail considerable further effort, and given the aforementioned problem of incomplete price and wage data, the reliability of the results would be questionable. For the same reason, the authors have little choice but to largely ignore geographic differences in the prices faced or in the extent to which border price changes are passed on locally.

Having estimated the impacts at the household level, the authors can study how they vary with preform welfare and what impact the reform has on poverty and inequality. Let y_i denote the prereform welfare per person in household i while $y_i^* = y_i + g_i$ is its postreform value, where g_i is the gain to household i. (Ideally, y_i will be an exact money metric of utility, although in practice, it is expected to be an approximation given omitted prices or characteristics.) The distribution of postreform welfare levels is $y_1^*, y_2^*, \ldots y_n^*$. By comparing standard summary measures of poverty or inequality for this distribution with those for the prereform distribution, $y_1, y_2, \ldots y_n$, overall impacts can be assessed.

It is interesting to see how the gains vary with prereform welfare. Is it the poor who tend to gain from these reforms, is it middle-income groups, or is it the rich? Importantly, however, the assignment of impacts to the prereform distribution is unlikely to be a degenerate distribution, with no distribution of its own. There will almost certainly be a dispersion in impact at the given prereform welfare levels. This dispersion will arise from (observable and unobservable) heterogeneity in characteristics and prices. It can also arise from errors in the welfare measure. Averaging across the distribution of impacts at given prereform welfare, one can calculate the conditional mean impact given by the following:

$$(2.1) \qquad\qquad g_i^c = E_i\,(g_i | y = y_i),$$

where the expectation is formed over the conditional distributions of impacts. By including a subscript i in the expectations operator in equation (2.1), one can allow the possibility that the horizontal dispersion in impacts is not identically distributed. In the empirical implementation, equation (2.1) is estimated using a nonparametric regression.

Taking these observations a step further, one can think of the overall impact on inequality as having both vertical and horizontal components.[4] This is straightforward for the mean log deviation (MLD)—an inequality measure known to have a number of desirable features.[5] The MLD defined on the distribution of postreform welfares $y_1^*, y_2^*, \ldots y_n^*$ is given by the following:

$$(2.2) \qquad\qquad I^* = \frac{1}{n} \sum_{i=1}^{n} \ln(\bar{y}^* / y_i^*),$$

where $\bar{y}^* = \sum_{i=1}^{n} y_i^*/n$ is mean postreform welfare. Similarly,

$$(2.3) \qquad\qquad I = \frac{1}{n} \sum_{i=1}^{n} \ln(\bar{y}/y_i)$$

is the prereform MLD. In equations (2.2) and (2.3), it is assumed that $y_i > 0$ and $y_i^* > 0$ for all i. Thus, $I^* - I$ is the change in inequality attributable to the reform. The proposed decomposition of the overall change in inequality can then be written as follows:

$$(2.4) \quad I^* - I = \frac{1}{n}\sum_{i=1}^{n} \ln\left(\frac{1 + \overline{g}/\overline{y}}{1 + g_i/y_i}\right)$$

$$= \frac{1}{n}\sum_{i=1}^{n} \ln\left(\frac{1 + \overline{g}/\overline{y}}{1 + g_i^c/y_i}\right) + \frac{1}{n}\sum_{i=1}^{n} \ln\left(\frac{1 + g_i^c/y_i}{1 + g_i/y_i}\right).$$

vertical component + horizontal component

The vertical component is the contribution to the change in total inequality $(I^* - I)$ of the way in which mean impacts vary with prereform welfare levels. If there is no difference in the proportionate impact by level of welfare ($g_i^c/y_i = \overline{g}/\overline{y}$ for all i), then the vertical component is zero. The horizontal component is the contribution of the deviations in impacts from their conditional means. If the impact of the reform is predicted perfectly by prereform welfare ($g_i = g_i^c$ for all i), then the horizontal component is zero. This decomposition is largely of descriptive interest. There are no immediate policy implications; however, finding that the horizontal component is large could well motivate greater effort by policy makers to understand what characteristics of households are associated with the differences in impacts found empirically.

To help in that task, one can go a step further and try to explain the differences in impacts in terms of observable characteristics of potential relevance to social protection policies. The way the problem of measuring welfare impacts has been formulated allows utility and profit functions to vary between households at given prices. To explain the heterogeneity in measured welfare impacts, one can suppose instead that these functions vary with observed household characteristics. The characteristics that influence preferences over consumption (x_{1i}) are allowed to differ from those that influence the profits from personal production activities (x_{2i}). The gain from the price changes induced by trade reform depends on the consumption, labor supply, and household production choices, which depend in turn on prices and characteristics, x_{1i} and x_{2i}. For example, households with a higher number of children will naturally spend more on food, so if the relative price of food changes, then the welfare impacts will be correlated with this aspect of household demographics.

Similarly, differences in tastes may be associated with various life-cycle stages and education levels. Also, systematic covariates of the composition of welfare are likely.

Generically, the gain can now be written as follows:

$$(2.5) \quad g_i = g(p_i^s, p_i^d, w_i, x_{1i}, x_{2i}).$$

Given that the household-specific wages and prices are not directly observable, further assumptions must be made. In explaining the variation across households in the predicted gains from trade reform, assume that (1) the wage rates are a function of prices and characteristics as $w_i = w(p_i^d, p_i^s, x_{1i}, x_{2i})$, and (2) differences in prices faced can be adequately captured by a complete set of regional dummy variables. Under these assumptions, and linearizing equation (2.5) with an additive innovation error term, the following regression model can be used to represent the gains:

$$(2.6) \qquad g_i = \beta_1 x_{1i} + \beta_2 x_{2i} + \sum_k \gamma_k D_{ki} + \varepsilon_i,$$

where $D_{ki} = 1$ if household i lives in county k, and $D_{ki} = 0$ otherwise, and ε_i is the error term.

Measured Welfare Impacts of Trade Reform in Morocco

Predicted Price Changes and the Survey Data

The price changes (implied by trade reform) used in this analysis were generated by a CGE model that was commissioned by a joint working group of the Ministry of Agriculture of the government of Morocco and the World Bank, as documented in Doukkali (2003). The model was constructed to realistically represent the functioning of the Moroccan economy in 1997–98. The model was explicitly designed to assess the aggregate impacts of deprotecting cereals in Morocco. In addition to allowing for interactions between agriculture and the rest of the economy (represented by six sectors), the model is quite detailed in its representation of the agricultural sector. It allows for 16 different crops or groups of crops, 3 different livestock activities, 13 major agro-industrial activities, and 6 agro-ecological regions. Within each region, the model distinguishes between rain-fed agriculture and four types of irrigated agriculture. The model includes two types of labor, both with fixed real wage rates.

Four policy simulations are undertaken. The simulations then differ in the extent of the tariff reductions for cereals—namely, 10 percent (Policy 1), 30 percent (Policy 2), 50 percent (Policy 3), and 100 percent (Policy 4). In all cases, the government's existing open-market operations, which attempt to keep down consumer prices by selling subsidized cereals, are removed.[6] The loss of revenue from a 50 percent tariff cut approximately equals the savings on subsidies.

Table 2.1 gives the predicted price changes for various trade liberalization scenarios, based on Doukkali (2003).[7] As expected,

Table 2.1 Predicted Price Changes Due to Agricultural Trade Reform in Morocco (percentage change in prices)

Sector	Consumers				Producers			
	Policy 1	Policy 2	Policy 3	Policy 4	Policy 1	Policy 2	Policy 3	Policy 4
Cereals and cereals products	−3.062	−7.786	−12.811	−26.691	−2.858	−7.193	−11.744	−24.107
Fresh vegetables	−0.714	−0.884	−1.051	−1.128	−0.580	−0.767	−0.871	−0.756
Fruits	−0.637	−0.681	−0.683	−0.139	−0.429	−0.301	−0.104	0.843
Dairy products and eggs	−0.472	−0.414	−0.257	0.751	−0.505	−0.487	−0.333	0.637
Meat (red and poultry)	−0.320	−0.109	0.332	1.896	−0.306	−0.078	0.357	1.936
Sugar	−0.200	0.100	0.400	1.300	−0.368	−0.378	−0.354	−0.094
Edible oils	−0.671	−1.064	−1.405	−2.225	−0.632	−0.998	−1.336	−2.061
Fresh and processed fish	0.000	0.696	1.300	2.996	0.000	0.600	1.300	2.881
Other agriculture and processed foods	−0.369	−0.402	−0.421	−0.635	0.268	1.294	2.475	5.388
Services	0.142	0.500	0.758	1.460	0.056	0.500	0.844	1.708
Energy, electricity, and water	−0.060	0.540	1.140	2.580	−0.051	0.549	1.149	2.597
Other industries	0.000	0.600	1.200	2.800	0.000	0.600	1.200	2.793

Source: Authors' calculations based on Doukkali's CGE analysis (2003).
Note: The tariff cuts on imported cereals are 10, 30, 50, and 100 percent for Policies 1, 2, 3, and 4, respectively.

the largest price impact is for cereals, although there are some non-negligible spillovers into other markets, reflecting substitutions in consumption and production and welfare effects on demand. Some of these spillover effects are compensatory—for example, some producer prices rise with the deprotection of cereals.

The survey data set used here is the *Enquête National sur le Niveau de Vie Ménages* (ENNVM) for 1998, produced by the government of Morocco's Department of Statistics, which kindly provided the data set for this study. This is a comprehensive, multipurpose survey that follows the practices of the World Bank's Living Standards Measurement Study.[8] The ENNVM includes a sample of 5,117 households (of which 2,154 are rural) spanning 14 of Morocco's 16 regions; the low-density southernmost region—the former Spanish Sahara—is excluded. The sample is clustered and stratified by region and urban/rural areas. The survey does not include households without a fixed residence (*sans abris*). The survey allows calculation of a comprehensive consumption aggregate (including imputed values for consumption from own production). The consumption numbers calculated by the Department of Statistics were used as the money metric of welfare. Ideally, this would be deflated by a geographic cost-of-living index, but no such index was available given the aforementioned lack of geographic price data.

Implied Welfare Impacts at the Household Level

Tables 2.2 and 2.3 give the budget and income shares at mean points and the mean welfare impacts, broken down by commodity based on the ENNVM; table 2.2 is for consumption, while table 2.3 is for production. (All consumption numbers include imputed values for consumption in kind.) Notice how different the consumption patterns are between urban and rural areas; for example, rural households have twice the budget share for cereals as urban households. Strikingly, the 1.7 percent gain to urban consumers as a whole is largely offset by the general equilibrium effects achieved through other price changes (table 2.2). The income obtained directly from production accounts for about one-quarter of consumption; the rest is labor earnings, transfers, and savings. In rural areas the share is considerably higher, at 87 percent, and about one-third of this is from cereals.[9]

Table 2.4 summarizes the results on the implied welfare impacts. These results indicate that the partial trade reforms have only a small positive impact on the national poverty rate, as given by the percentage of the population living below the official poverty lines for urban and rural areas used by the government of Morocco's

Table 2.2 Consumption Shares and Welfare Impacts through Consumption

Indicator	Consumption shares	Policy 1	Policy 2	Policy 3	Policy 4
National					
Cereals	0.084	0.257	0.654	1.076	2.242
Fresh vegetables	0.042	0.030	0.037	0.044	0.047
Fruits	0.022	0.014	0.015	0.015	0.003
Dairy products and eggs	0.032	0.015	0.013	0.008	−0.024
Meat (red and poultry)	0.112	0.036	0.012	−0.037	−0.213
Sugar	0.015	0.003	−0.002	−0.006	−0.019
Edible oils	0.032	0.021	0.034	0.044	0.070
Fresh and processed fish	0.013	0.000	−0.009	−0.017	−0.038
Agriculture and processed foods	0.101	0.037	0.040	0.042	0.064
Services	0.066	−0.009	−0.033	−0.050	−0.097
Energy, electricity, water	0.148	0.009	−0.080	−0.169	−0.382
Other industries	0.333	0.000	−0.200	−0.400	−0.933
Total	1.000	0.413	0.482	0.551	0.719
Urban					
Cereals	0.066	0.203	0.517	0.851	1.773
Fresh vegetables	0.037	0.026	0.033	0.039	0.042
Fruits	0.022	0.014	0.015	0.015	0.003
Dairy products and eggs	0.034	0.016	0.014	0.009	−0.026
Meat (red and poultry)	0.107	0.034	0.012	−0.035	−0.203
Sugar	0.011	0.002	−0.001	−0.004	−0.014
Edible oils	0.024	0.016	0.026	0.034	0.054
Fresh and processed fish	0.014	0.000	−0.010	−0.018	−0.041
Agriculture and processed foods	0.096	0.035	0.039	0.040	0.061
Services	0.067	−0.010	−0.033	−0.051	−0.097
Energy, electricity, water	0.155	0.009	−0.084	−0.176	−0.399
Other industries	0.368	0.000	−0.221	−0.441	−1.030
Total	1.000	0.348	0.307	0.262	0.123
Rural					
Cereals	0.136	0.415	1.056	1.738	3.622
Fresh vegetables	0.055	0.039	0.049	0.058	0.062
Fruits	0.021	0.014	0.015	0.015	0.003
Dairy products and eggs	0.028	0.013	0.011	0.007	−0.021
Meat (red and poultry)	0.128	0.041	0.014	−0.043	−0.243
Sugar	0.028	0.006	−0.003	−0.011	−0.036
Edible oils	0.053	0.036	0.056	0.075	0.118
Fresh and processed fish	0.010	0.000	−0.007	−0.013	−0.029
Agriculture and processed foods	0.115	0.042	0.046	0.048	0.073
Services	0.066	−0.009	−0.033	−0.050	−0.097
Energy, electricity, water	0.129	0.008	−0.070	−0.147	−0.332
Other industries	0.232	0.000	−0.139	−0.278	−0.650
Total	1.000	0.604	0.996	1.399	2.471

Source: Authors' estimations.

Table 2.3 Percentage Gains from Each Policy: Production
Component

Indicator	Production as a share of total consumption	Policy 1	Policy 2	Policy 3	Policy 4
National					
Cereals	0.089	−0.271	−0.690	−1.135	−2.365
Fresh vegetables	0.053	−0.038	−0.047	−0.056	−0.060
Fruits	0.041	−0.026	−0.028	−0.028	−0.006
Dairy products and eggs	0.051	−0.024	−0.021	−0.013	0.039
Meat (red and poultry)	0.000	0.000	0.000	0.000	0.000
Sugar	0.000	0.000	0.000	0.000	0.000
Edible oils	0.025	−0.017	−0.027	−0.035	−0.056
Fresh and processed fish	0.000	0.000	0.000	0.000	0.000
Agriculture and processed foods	0.002	−0.001	−0.001	−0.001	−0.001
Services	0.000	0.000	0.000	0.000	0.000
Energy, electricity, water	0.000	0.000	0.000	0.000	0.000
Other industries	0.000	0.000	0.000	0.000	0.000
Total	0.262	−0.377	−0.814	−1.269	−2.450
Urban					
Cereals	0.010	−0.031	−0.079	−0.130	−0.272
Fresh vegetables	0.008	−0.006	−0.007	−0.009	−0.009
Fruits	0.016	−0.011	−0.011	−0.011	−0.002
Dairy products and eggs	0.007	−0.003	−0.003	−0.002	0.005
Meat (red and poultry)	0.000	0.000	0.000	0.000	0.000
Sugar	0.000	0.000	0.000	0.000	0.000
Edible oils	0.013	−0.009	−0.014	−0.018	−0.029
Fresh and processed fish	0.000	0.000	0.000	0.000	0.000
Agriculture and processed foods	0.000	0.000	0.000	0.000	0.000
Services	0.000	0.000	0.000	0.000	0.000
Energy, electricity, water	0.000	0.000	0.000	0.000	0.000
Other industries	0.000	0.000	0.000	0.000	0.000
Total	0.054	−0.059	−0.114	−0.170	−0.307
Rural					
Cereals	0.319	−0.978	−2.487	−4.091	−8.524
Fresh vegetables	0.186	−0.133	−0.165	−0.195	−0.210
Fruits	0.113	−0.072	−0.077	−0.077	−0.016
Dairy products and eggs	0.183	−0.086	−0.076	−0.047	0.138
Meat (red and poultry)	0.000	0.000	0.000	0.000	0.000
Sugar	0.000	0.000	0.000	0.000	0.000
Edible oils	0.061	−0.041	−0.065	−0.086	−0.136
Fresh and processed fish	0.000	0.000	0.000	0.000	0.000
Agriculture and processed foods	0.008	−0.003	−0.003	−0.004	−0.005
Services	0.000	0.000	0.000	0.000	0.000
Energy, electricity, water	0.000	0.000	0.000	0.000	0.000
Other industries	0.000	0.000	0.000	0.000	0.000
Total	0.870	−1.313	−2.872	−4.500	−8.753

Source: Authors' estimations.

Table 2.4 Household Impacts of Four Trade Reforms

Indicator	Baseline	Policy 1	Policy 2	Policy 3	Policy 4
National					
Poverty rate (%)	19.61	20.01	20.33	21.04	22.13
Mean log deviation (×100)	28.50	28.92	29.00	29.14	29.17
Gini index (×100)	38.50	38.70	38.90	39.10	39.50
Per capita gain	0	6.52	−23.97	−54.82	−133.81
Mean percentage gain: price changes weighted by mean shares	0	−0.06	−0.51	−0.97	−2.14
Mean percentage gain: weighted by ratios of means (tables 2.2 and 2.3)	0	0.04	−0.33	−0.72	−1.73
Production gain	0	−32.08	−69.01	−106.31	−201.02
Consumption gain	0	38.60	45.05	51.49	67.21
Consumption per capita	9,350.91	9,357.43	9,326.95	9,296.10	9,217.10
Urban					
Poverty rate (percent)	12.19	12.05	11.96	12.05	11.76
MLD (×100)	25.49	25.41	25.32	25.23	24.93
Gini index (×100)	36.60	36.50	36.50	36.40	36.20
Per capita gain	0	35.52	24.80	13.75	−16.49
Mean percentage gain: price changes weighted by mean shares	0	0.36	0.37	0.39	0.44
Mean percentage gain: weighted by ratios of means (tables 2.2 and 2.3)	0	0.29	0.19	0.09	−0.18
Production gain	0	−6.31	−12.10	−17.79	−31.30
Consumption gain	0	41.83	36.90	31.54	14.81
Consumption per capita	12,031.20	12,066.72	12,056.00	12,044.95	12,014.71
Rural					
Poverty rate (percent)	28.28	29.31	30.10	31.54	34.25
MLD (×100)	17.47	17.82	17.82	17.93	17.76
Gini index (×100)	31.20	31.30	31.50	31.80	32.80
Per capita gain	0	−33.53	−91.32	−149.51	−295.85
Mean percentage gain: price changes weighted by mean shares	0	−0.63	−1.74	−2.85	−5.71
Mean percentage gain: weighted by ratios of means (tables 2.2 and 2.3)	0	−0.71	−1.88	−3.10	−6.28
Production gain	0	−67.67	−147.61	−228.56	−435.42
Consumption gain	0	34.14	56.29	79.05	139.57
Consumption per capita	5,649.03	5,615.50	5,557.71	5,499.52	5,353.19

Source: Authors' estimations.

Note: All monetary units are Moroccan dirhams per year. Mean log deviation (MLD) is calculated only over the set of households for which consumption is positive. The mean percentage gains weighted by mean shares are simply the means across the sample of the percentage gains at household level. The second mean percentage gain is weighted by shares at the means points based on tables 2.2 and 2.3.

statistics office.[10] However, a larger impact emerges when complete deprotection is simulated (Policy 4). The national poverty rate then rises from 20 percent to 22 percent. All four reforms entail a decrease in urban poverty (though less than 0.4 percentage point) and an increase in rural poverty. The impacts over the whole distribution are examined later.

Turning to the impacts on inequality, in table 2.4 one finds that the trade reforms yield a small increase in inequality, with the Gini index rising from 0.385 in the base case to 0.395 with a complete deprotection of cereals (Policy 4). Impacts are smaller for the partial reforms (Policies 1–3). The overall per capita gain is positive for the smaller tariff reduction (Policy 1) but becomes negative for Policies 2, 3, and 4. As expected, there is a net gain to consumers and a net loss to producers, though the amounts involved are small overall. There are small net gains in the urban sector for Policies 1–3. Larger impacts are found in rural areas, as expected. The mean percentage loss from complete deprotection is a (nonnegligible) 5.7 percent in rural areas.

Table 2.4 presents the results derived for the impact on poverty as estimated using the government's official poverty lines. It is important to test robustness to alternative poverty lines. For this purpose, the poverty incidence curve, which is the cumulative distribution function up to a reasonable maximum poverty line, is used. The results are given in figure 2.1; for readability, the figure focuses on Policies 1 and 4. The curves for Policies 2 and 3 fall between these two policies.

From this figure, it is clear that there is an increase in overall poverty from complete deprotection; this is robust to the poverty line and poverty measure used (within a broad class of measures; see Atkinson 1987). The impact on poverty is found almost entirely in rural areas; indeed, there is virtually no impact on urban poverty. In rural areas, however, the results in figure 2.1 suggest a sizable impact on poverty from complete deprotection. The mean loss as a proportion of consumption for the poorest 15 percent in rural areas is about 10 percent. There is an increase in the proportion of the rural population living below 2,000 dirhams per person per year, from 6.2 percent to 9.9 percent; the proportion living below 3,000 dirhams rises from 22.2 percent to 26.3 percent. For the country as a whole, the poverty rate for the former poverty line (2,000 dirhams) rises from 2.8 percent to 4.4 percent under Policy 4, while it rises from 11.4 percent to 13.1 percent for the 3,000 dirhams line. The finding of adverse impacts on the rural poor contradicts claims made by some observers who argue that the rural poor tend to be net consumers of cereals, the commodity that incurs the largest price

Figure 2.1 Impacts of Trade Reform Policies on Poverty in Morocco

(Moroccan dirhams)

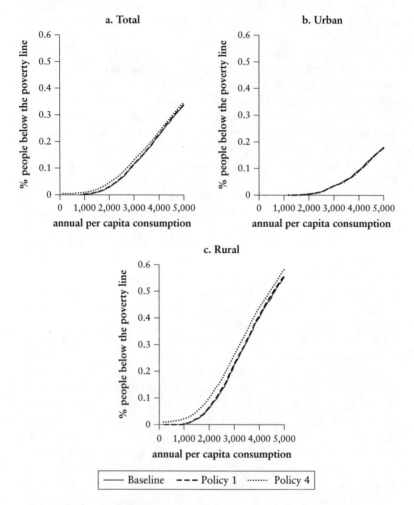

Source: Authors' calculations.
Note: Total population of sites surveyed, urban and rural.

decrease with this trade reform (table 2.1). This point is discussed in more detail in the section on the welfare impacts of these policy reforms.

Table 2.5 presents the mean impacts of Policy 4 by region, split between urban and rural areas. Impacts in urban areas are small in all regions, with the highest net gain as a percentage of consumption being 1.3 percent in Tanger-Tetouan, closely followed by Tensift Al Haouz and Fes-Boulemane. The rural areas with largest mean losses

Table 2.5 Mean Gains from Policy 4, by Region

Region	Total	Urban	Rural	Poorest 15% of rural households
Oued Ed-Dahab-Lagouira	−0.20	−0.20	n.a.	n.a.
Laayoune-Boujdour-Sakia El Hamra	−0.34	−0.34	n.a.	n.a.
Guelmime Es-Semara	−0.96	0.72	−3.47	−0.58
Souss-Massa-Daraa	−1.31	0.42	−2.4	−3.09
Gharb-Chrarda-Beni Hssen	−2.16	0.02	−3.86	0.10
Chaouia-Ouardigha	−4.18	0.32	−8.31	−10.11
Tensift Al Haouz	−0.87	1.12	−2.17	0.31
Oriental	−0.87	0.38	−2.78	0.25
G.Casablanca	0.48	0.41	2.41	n.a.
Rabat-Salé-Zemmour-Zaer	−0.59	0.33	−4.98	0.23
Doukala Abda	−3.13	0.76	−5.92	−3.93
Tadla Azilal	−6.93	−0.71	−11.04	−0.95
Meknes Tafil	−4.89	−0.19	−11.35	−8.48
Fes-Boulemane	−2.4	1.05	−11.52	−13.43
Taza-Al Hoceima-Taounate	−4.47	−0.32	−5.78	−8.39
Tanger-Tetouan	−2.94	1.31	−9.4	−22.03
Total	−2.14	0.45	−5.71	−10.39

Source: Authors' estimations.

Note: Means formed over the household-level percentage gains (equivalent to weighting proportionate price changes by mean shares); n.a. = not applicable.

from deprotection of cereals are Tasla Azilal, Meknes Tafil, Fes-Boulemane, and Tanger-Tetouan. Table 2.5 gives mean impacts for the poorest 15 percent in rural areas (in terms of consumption per person). When the focus is on the rural poor defined in this way, the region incurring the largest mean loss for rural households is Tanger-Tetouan, followed by Fes-Boulemane and Chaouia-Ouardigha. The contrast between the small net gains to the urban sector and net losses to the rural poor is most marked in Tanger-Tetouan.

To begin exploring the heterogeneity in welfare impacts, figure 2.2 illustrates the cumulative frequency distributions of the gains and losses. The figure is simplified by again focusing on Policies 1 and 4. With complete deprotection (Policy 4), about 9 percent of the households incur losses greater than 500 dirhams per year (about 5 percent of overall mean consumption), while about 5 percent lose more than 1,000 dirhams per year. As expected, rural areas have a "thicker tail" of negative gains. About 16 percent of rural households lose more than 500 dirhams and 10 percent lose more than 1,000.

In figure 2.3, the mean gains are plotted against percentiles of consumption per capita for Policies 1 and 4. Both absolute gains/losses and gains/losses as a percentage of the household's consumption are

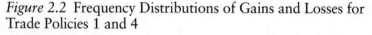

Figure 2.2 Frequency Distributions of Gains and Losses for
Trade Policies 1 and 4

(Moroccan dirhams)

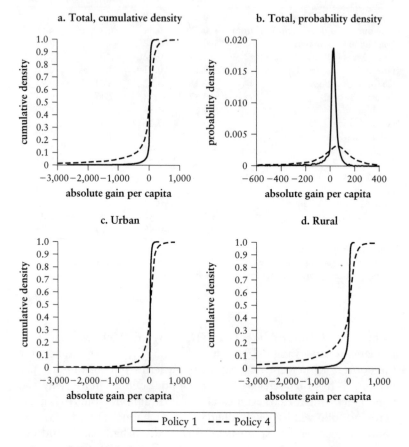

shown. For Policy 1, the mean absolute gain has a tendency to rise as
one moves from the poorest percentile to the richest, though the gradient is small. The mean proportionate gain is quite flat. For Policy 4,
mean absolute impacts also rise up to the richest decile or so, but then
fall. Proportionate gains follow the same pattern, though (again) the
gradient seems small.

What is most striking from figure 2.3 is the wide spread of impacts,
particularly downward (indicating losers from the reform). The variance in absolute impacts is especially large at the upper end of the
consumption distribution, though the dispersion in proportionate

Figure 2.3 Absolute and Proportionate Gains for Policies 1 and 4

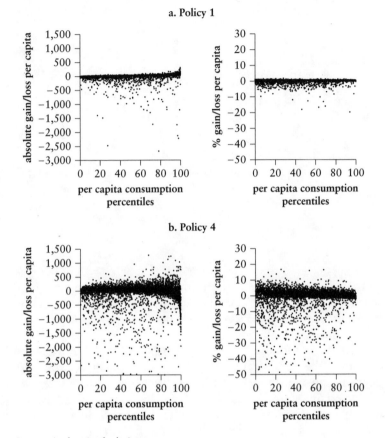

Source: Authors' calculations.

impacts tends to be greater at the other end of the distribution, among the poorest.

Figure 2.4 provides a split between producers and consumers for Policy 4. As expected, to the extent that there is much impact on producers, they tend to lose, although not more so for poor producers than rich ones. For consumption, there tends to be more gainers and a higher variance in impact as one moves up the consumption distribution. However, the downward dispersion in total welfare impacts shown in figure 2.3 is due more to the conditional variance in impacts through production than through consumption.

There are two especially striking findings in figures 2.3 and 2.4. First, notice the sizable losses on the production side among the poor.

Figure 2.4 Production and Consumption Decomposition of the Welfare Impacts for Policy 4

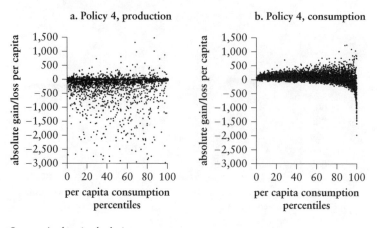

Source: Authors' calculations.

Granted, some large losses are evident for the high-income groups. But the claims that the poor do not lose as producers are clearly false. Furthermore, the poor are often not seeing compensatory gains as consumers.

Second, it is notable that the results in figures 2.3 and 2.4 indicate that the mean gains vary little with mean consumption. Focusing on the "poor" versus the "rich" is of little interest in characterizing gainers and losers from this reform. The diversity in impacts tends to be "horizontal" in the distribution of income—meaning that larger differences in impacts are found at given consumption levels rather than between different levels of consumption.

These two findings are now examined in greater detail.

Who Are the Net Producers of Cereals in Morocco?

In the population as a whole, 16 percent of households are net producers (value of cereals production exceeds consumption). These households are worse off from the fall in cereal prices because of deprotection. In rural areas, this proportion is 36 percent.

However, the survey data do not support the claim that the rural poor in Morocco are (on average) net consumers of cereals. Figure 2.5 illustrates how producers and net producers are spread across

Figure 2.5 Net Producers of Cereals in the Distribution of Total Consumption per Person in Rural Areas of Morocco

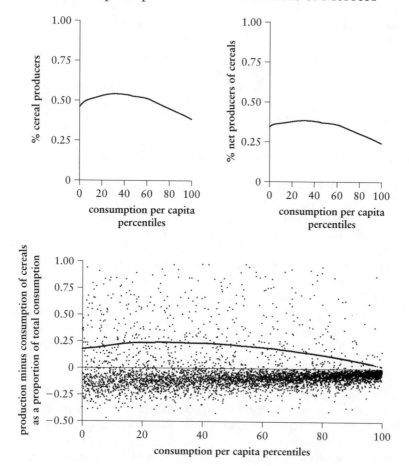

Source: Authors' calculations.

the distribution of total household consumption per person in rural Morocco. Both the scatter of points and the conditional means estimated using the local regression method are given.[11] The first (top left) panel in figure 2.5 shows the proportion of producers, followed by the proportion of net producers (for whom production exceeds consumption of cereals in value terms). Finally, the net production is presented in value terms. In each case, the horizontal axis gives the percentile of the distribution of consumption from poorest to richest.

As shown in this figure, a majority of the rural poor produce cereals. Naturally, much of this is for home consumption. However, even if the focus is solely on net producers, one finds that more than one-third of those in the poorest quintile tend to produce more than they consume. Furthermore, the mean net production in value terms tends to be positive for the poor; in rural areas, the losses to poor producers from falling cereal prices outweigh the gains to poor consumers. More than any single feature of the survey data, it is this fact that lies at the heart of the finding that the rural poor lose from the deprotection reform.

Vertical versus Horizontal Impacts on Inequality

To measure the relative importance of the vertical versus horizontal differences in impact, one can use the decomposition method outlined in the section on micro data near the beginning of this chapter. This decomposition requires an estimate of the conditional mean $E(g \mid y)$, that is, the regression function of g on y. In the study, this was estimated using the nonparametric local regression method of Cleveland (1979).

Table 2.6 gives the results of this decomposition for each of the four policy reforms examined. For the small partial reform under Policy 1, the vertical component dominates, accounting for 73 percent of the impact on inequality. As one moves to the bigger reforms, however, the horizontal component becomes relatively large. Indeed, one finds that 119.8 percent of the impact of Policy 4 on inequality is attributable to the horizontal component, while –19.8 percent is due to the vertical component. So the vertical component was inequality reducing for Policy 4, even though overall inequality rose (table 2.6).

A high degree of horizontal inequality is clear in measured impacts at given mean consumption. Some of this is undoubtedly measurement error, which may well become more important for larger reforms. But some is attributable to observable covariates of consumption and production behavior, as discussed earlier. In trying

Table 2.6 Decomposition of the Impact on Inequality

Indicator	Policy 1	Policy 2	Policy 3	Policy 4
Vertical component	72.69	57.57	38.77	−19.77
Horizontal component	27.31	42.43	61.23	119.77
Total	100.00	100.00	100.00	100.00

Source: Authors' estimations.
Note: The decomposition is implemented only on the sample of households for which both the baseline consumption and the postreform consumption are positive.

to explain this variance in welfare impacts, the characteristics considered include region of residence, whether the household lives in an urban area, the household's size and demographic composition, the age and age-squared of the household head, and education and dummy variables describing key aspects of the occupation and principal sector of employment. Table 2.7 gives summary statistics on the variables to be used in the regressions. Although there are endogeneity concerns about these variables, those concerns are thought to be minor in this context, especially when weighed against the concerns about omitted variable bias in estimates that exclude these characteristics. Under the usual assumption that the error term is orthogonal to these regressors, one can estimate equation (2.6) by ordinary least squares (OLS).

The results are given in table 2.8. These results are averages across the impacts of these characteristics on the consumption and production choices that determine the welfare impact of given price and wage changes. This makes interpretation difficult. These regressions are viewed for their descriptive interest and their ability to isolate covariates of potential relevance in thinking about compensatory policy responses.

Focusing first on the results for Policy 4, larger *losses* from full deprotection of cereals are associated with families that (1) live in rural areas; (2) are relatively smaller (the turning point in the U-shaped relationship is at a household size of about one); (3) have more wage earners, higher education, work in commerce and transport, for example; and (4) live in Chaouia-Ouardigha, Rabat, Tadla Azilal, and Meknes Tafil. Recall that these effects stem from the way household characteristics influence net trading positions in terms of the commodities for which prices change. It appears that larger families tend to consume more cereals and thus gain more from the lower cereal prices. Results are similar for partial deprotection, though education becomes insignificant for Policy 1.

Table 2.9 presents an urban-rural breakdown of the regressions for Policies 1 and 4. There are a couple of notable differences. (Again, the focus is on Policy 4 in the interest of brevity.) There are significant positive effects of having more children and teenagers on the gains from trade reform in rural areas, presumably because such families are more likely to be cereal consumers. The education effect at higher levels of schooling is much more pronounced in urban areas. The effect of working in the transport and commerce sector is more statistically significant in urban areas, though this effect is still sizable in rural areas. The regional effects are more statistically significant in urban areas than in rural areas. There are

Table 2.7 Summary Statistics on Explanatory Variables in the Regression Analysis

Variable	Mean	Standard deviation
Household characteristics		
Urban	0.580	binary
Log household size	1.645	0.550
Log squared household size	3.009	1.621
Female head of household	0.170	binary
Currently unemployed	0.248	binary
Number of wage earners	5.912	2.878
Share of children 0–6 years of age	0.140	0.162
Share of children 7–17 years of age	0.221	0.204
Share of elderly 60+	0.120	binary
Characteristics of household head		
Age of household head	0.505	0.143
Age of household head squared	0.275	0.155
Illiterate head of household	0.582	binary
Primary school not completed	0.100	binary
Primary school completed	0.164	binary
Lower secondary school completed	0.058	binary
Upper secondary school completed	0.059	binary
University completed	0.036	binary
Industry		
Not employed	0.240	binary
Manufacturing/construction	0.004	binary
Commerce/transportation/communication/administration	0.273	binary
Social services	0.085	binary
Other services	0.064	binary
Public servants	0.125	binary
Unemployed or laid-off worker	0.012	binary
Housewife or student	0.037	binary
Young child	0.009	binary
Old or retired	0.074	binary
Sick	0.068	binary
Other inactives	0.010	binary
Region		
Oued Ed-Dahab-Lagouira	0.012	binary
Laayoune-Boujdour-Sakia El Hamra	0.014	binary
Guelmime Es-Semara	0.023	binary
Souss-Massa-Daraa	0.094	binary
Gharb-Chrarda-Beni Hssen	0.058	binary
Chaouia-Ouardigha	0.054	binary
Tensift Al Haouz	0.100	binary
Oriental	0.065	binary
G.Casablanca	0.124	binary
Rabat-Salé-Zemmour-Zaer	0.081	binary
Doukala Abda	0.067	binary
Tadla Azilal	0.047	binary
Meknes Tafil	0.072	binary
Fes-Boulemane	0.051	binary
Taza-Al Hoceima-Taounate	0.058	binary

Source: Authors' estimations.

Table 2.8 Regression of per Capita Gain/Loss on Selected Household Characteristics

	Policy 1		Policy 2		Policy 3		Policy 4	
Variable	Coefficient	Standard error	Coefficient	Standard error	Coefficient	Standard error	Coefficient	Standard error
Household characteristics								
Urban	26.139***	6.275	44.850***	12.948	64.218**	20.068	113.714**	39.213
Log household size	−57.242**	19.583	−78.454*	40.407	−100.548	62.626	−157.373	122.376
Log squared household size	77.337***	16.806	167.523***	34.678	260.865***	53.746	508.026***	105.023
Female-headed household	2.502	7.431	4.072	15.333	5.605	23.765	9.161	46.438
Currently unemployed	10.018*	5.909	23.344*	12.192	36.428*	18.896	67.997*	36.924
Number of wage earners in household	−44.722***	7.019	−101.428***	14.484	−159.842***	22.448	−313.541***	43.865
Share of children ages 0–6	32.783*	17.72	89.774*	36.564	145.705*	56.67	277.637*	110.736
Share of children ages 7–17	25.070*	14.155	69.367*	29.206	113.738*	45.266	221.518*	88.453
Share of elderly 60+	−21.3	15.584	−23.551	32.155	−24.389	49.837	−24.334	97.385
Characteristics of household head								
Age of the head	−38.511	108.759	−151.473	224.41	−272.681	347.809	−624.596	679.642
Age of the head squared	44.097	102.579	142.598	211.658	246.231	328.045	543.07	641.022
Household head is literate only	−8.871	7.983	−23.441	16.472	−38.257	25.53	−76.735	49.888
Incomplete primary education[a]								
Primary school completed	−14.013*	6.757	−40.623**	13.942	−68.220**	21.608	−141.296***	42.224
Lower secondary school	−12.98	10.4	−61.634**	21.458	−112.583***	33.258	−250.335***	64.989
Upper secondary school	−12.462	10.775	−70.619**	22.233	−130.320***	34.458	−286.333***	67.333
University	2.575	13.527	−95.376***	27.912	−197.887***	43.26	−476.077***	84.533
Industry								
Not working or agriculture[a]								
Manufacturing/construction	−3.71	36.465	−0.277	75.242	4.541	116.616	21.281	227.874
Commerce/transportation/ communication/administration	−59.926***	8.198	−122.454***	16.915	−185.113***	26.216	−341.751***	51.228
Social services	4.424	10.036	17.18	20.707	30.536	32.094	66.804	62.714
Other services	−0.2	11.251	9.572	23.214	19.812	35.98	47.874	70.306
Public servants	2.385	8.936	6.785	18.439	10.912	28.579	20.23	55.844
Unemployed or laid-off worker	6.627	21.518	27.715	44.399	49.65	68.813	107.951	134.465

(Continued on the following page)

Table 2.8 (Continued)

Variable	Policy 1		Policy 2		Policy 3		Policy 4	
	Coefficient	Standard error	Coefficient	Standard error	Coefficient	Standard error	Coefficient	Standard error
Housewife or student	2.26	13.49	13.788	27.835	25.401	43.141	55.785	84.301
Young child	7.629	24.5	-3.891	50.553	-16.336	78.352	-51.207	153.104
Old or retired	6.913	11.039	23.527	22.778	40.651	35.303	86.8	68.984
Sick	3.143	10.96	22.092	22.614	42.489	35.049	100.065	68.488
Other inactives	-9.955	22.723	1.817	46.885	15.364	72.667	56.497	141.995
Region								
Oued Ed-Dahab-Lagouira	19.216	22.51	-6.738	46.446	-34.818	71.986	-111.388	140.665
Laayoune-Boujdour-Sakia El Hamra	-1.502	21.067	-20.145	43.47	-40.764	67.374	-98.323	131.652
Guelmime Es-Semara	9.666	16.639	11.901	34.333	12.774	53.212	12.391	103.979
Souss-Massa-Daraa	-7.645	10.868	5.611	22.425	22.766	34.756	85.2	67.916
Gharb-Chrarda-Beni Hssen	-10.087	12.229	-7.485	25.232	-3.592	39.107	10.494	76.418
Chaouia-Ouardigha	-19.542	12.507	-49.255*	25.807	-81.319*	39.998	-169.114*	78.159
Tensift Al Haouz	2.964	10.696	14.527	22.071	27.258	34.207	65.274	66.842
Oriental	-14.038	11.928	-19.198	24.612	-23.918	38.145	-31.056	74.539
G.Casablanca	-3.322	10.429	-15.762	21.518	-28.418	33.35	-60.086	65.169
Rabat-Salé-Zemmour-Zaer	-15.439	11.326	-33.817	23.371	-52.199	36.222	-97.061	70.78
Doukala Abda	-13.169	11.76	-23.668	24.265	-34.315	37.607	-59.462	73.487
Tadla Azilal	-55.774***	13.093	-114.700***	27.016	-174.099***	41.872	-320.810***	81.821
Meknes Tafil	-37.594**	11.54	-74.192**	23.812	-111.929**	36.906	-209.391**	72.117
Fes-Boulemane	-10.249	12.726	-15.356	26.259	-20.651	40.699	-33.326	79.528
Taza-Al Hoceima-Taounate	5.613	12.367	2.43	25.517	-2.415	39.549	-21.329	77.281
Tanger-Tetouan[a]								
Constant	144.096***	34.638	247.104***	71.472	354.469**	110.773	642.381**	216.458
R^2	0.175		0.080		0.062		0.057	

Source: Authors' estimations.

Note: *** and ** denote significance at the 5 percent and 10 percent levels, respectively.

a. Reference category.

Table 2.9 Urban-Rural Split of Regressions for per Capita Gains

| | Urban | | | | Rural | | | |
| | Policy 1 | | Policy 4 | | Policy 1 | | Policy 4 | |
Variable	Coefficient	Standard error	Coefficient	Standard error	Coefficient	Standard error	Coefficient	Standard error
Household characteristics								
Log household size	−32.840*	16.071	45.705	83.159	−89.255*	45.084	−527.017*	294.353
Log squared household size	40.492*	17.841	217.663*	92.32	79.415*	32.524	555.880**	212.348
Female-headed household	−2.696	6.018	−15.603	31.139	11.984	16.902	27.785	110.356
If unemployed present	2.138	4.668	25.238	24.154	11.086	14.482	35.299	94.551
Number of wage earners	−23.972**	8.39	−143.745***	43.414	−45.101***	12.237	−321.182***	79.894
Share of children 0–6	−15.648	15.206	25.903	78.686	95.815**	36.544	609.370*	238.601
Share of children 7–17	−10.44	11.986	−34.073	62.023	81.378**	29.771	622.563**	194.376
Share of elderly 60+	−17.696	13.328	4.67	68.967	−35.448	32.512	−167.42	212.274
Characteristics of household head								
Age of the head	−26.02	96.18	−513.051	497.696	−82.081	216.7	−1.00E+03	1414.846
Age of the head squared	33.769	91.377	263.429	472.842	103.772	202.766	1129.226	1323.868
Household head is literate only	−10.567	6.965	−90.700*	36.042	−8.718	16.11	−75.293	105.182
Incomplete primary education[a]								
Primary school completed	0.157	5.566	−44.272	28.804	−31.613*	14.794	−270.881**	96.589
Low secondary school	6.416	7.632	−119.177**	39.494	−73.971*	31.399	−655.218**	205.005
Upper secondary school	−5.731	7.551	−249.358***	39.074	10.925	49.861	−46.655	325.547
University	9.241	9.282	−433.456***	48.03	20.185	83.244	18.883	543.507
Industry								
Not working or agriculture[a]								
Manufacturing/construction	−4.779	25.641	7.254	132.684	56.769	124.939	366.598	815.737
Commerce/transportation/ communication/administration	−96.116***	10.172	−444.047***	52.634	−43.789**	15.445	−257.349*	100.843
Social services	−1.428	7.574	6.102	39.191	27.61	28.965	247.156	189.116
Other services	−4.7	9.133	6.023	47.259	21.228	25.434	161.257	166.061
Public servants	−2.611	6.884	−19.401	35.621	8.742	23.042	57.723	150.44
Unemployed or laid-off worker	−1.702	15.213	36.377	78.72	60.148	73.543	457.084	480.167

(Continued on the following page)

Table 2.9 (Continued)

| | Urban | | | | Rural | | | |
| | Policy 1 | | Policy 4 | | Policy 1 | | Policy 4 | |
Variable	Coefficient	Standard error	Coefficient	Standard error	Coefficient	Standard error	Coefficient	Standard error
Housewife or student	-4.019	10.145	12.554	52.498	20.295	36.207	110.127	236.4
Young child	-2.268	16.343	-129.322	84.567	107.247	152.23	720.704	993.92
Old or retired	1.108	8.138	48.765	42.112	25.588	34.261	154.32	223.691
Sick	1.847	8.176	63.019	42.308	5.864	30.489	148.543	199.063
Other inactives	-12.094	16.532	23.685	85.547	22.652	67.323	250.306	439.559
Region								
Oued Ed-Dahab-Lagouira	21.2	15.068	-135.288*	77.973	n.a.	n.a.	n.a.	n.a.
Laayoune-Boujdour-Sakia El Hamra	-2.496	14.153	-129.348*	73.236	n.a.	n.a.	n.a.	n.a.
Guelmime Es-Semara	7.558	13.813	-50.41	71.475	23.284	35.563	165.753	232.195
Souss-Massa-Daraa	-1.425	10.023	-54.723	51.863	-8.417	21.371	211.302	139.535
Gharb-Chrarda-Beni Hssen	-44.733***	11.143	-204.020***	57.663	17.31	23.762	208.808	155.141
Chaouia-Ouardigha	-15.625	11.08	-89.734	57.333	-19.527	25.012	-201.804	163.304
Tensift Al Haouz	-8.763	9.759	-37.2	50.5	8.732	21.097	147.015	137.74
Oriental	-18.776*	9.806	-96.129*	50.74	-0.357	25.851	99.206	168.782
G.Casablanca	-9.23	7.849	-112.350*	40.617	5.551	49.268	79.412	321.673
Rabat-Salé-Zemmour-Zaer	-13.825	8.683	-118.444*	44.931	-36.873	30.677	-142.714	200.295
Doukala Abda	-14.916	10.867	-80.126	56.232	-8.244	22.773	-3.679	148.687
Tadla Azilal	-50.624***	12.423	-213.855***	64.285	-51.570*	24.832	-324.785*	162.13
Meknes Tafl	-22.753*	9.622	-126.779*	49.79	-56.111*	24.782	-311.079*	161.8
Fes-Boulemane	-11.946	9.954	-38.193	51.509	-2.002	30.661	-5.31	200.186
Taza-Al Hoceima-Taounate	-20.264	13.982	-161.597*	72.352	16.747	22.229	80.917	145.137
Tanger-Tetouan[a]								
Constant	135.395***	30.386	463.951**	157.234	162.613*	72.909	959.343*	476.029
R^2	0.46		0.08		0.062		0.067	

Source: Authors' estimations.

Note: *** and ** denote significance at the 5 percent and 10 percent levels, respectively.

a. Reference category.

still sizable regional differences in mean impacts in table 2.9, but they are statistically less significant than those found in table 2.8. In fact, the quantitative magnitudes of the regional differences are just as large for the rural areas in table 2.9 as for urban plus rural areas in table 2.8.

The results in tables 2.8 and 2.9 are *conditional* geographic effects (conditional on the values taken by other covariates in the regressions). As in table 2.5, there are pronounced (unconditional) geographic differences in mean impacts in rural areas across different regions. Whether one draws policy lessons more from the conditional or unconditional effects depends on the type of policy being used. If the policy is simply one of regional targeting, then the unconditional geographic effects in table 2.5 will be more relevant. However, finer targeting by household characteristics, in combination with regional targeting, will call for the type of results presented in tables 2.8 and 2.9.

The share of the variance in gains that is accountable to these covariates is generally less than 10 percent. Values of R^2 of this size are common in regressions run on large cross-sectional data sets, although it remains true that a large share of the variance in impacts is not accountable to these covariates. (The exception to the low R^2 is for Policy 1, for which almost half of the variance in gains across urban households is explained.) A sizable degree of measurement error in the gains must be expected—stemming from measurement error in the underlying consumption and production data. No doubt, there are also important idiosyncratic factors in household-specific tastes or production choices.

These regressions try to explain the variance in the gains from the reform. It is interesting to see how one might better explain the incidence of losses from reform among the poor. This is arguably of greater relevance to compensatory policies, which presumably would focus on those among the poor who lose from such reforms. To test how well the same set of regressors could explain who was a "poor" loser from the reforms, a dummy variable was constructed that takes the value unity if a rural household incurred a negative loss and was "poor." To ensure a sufficient number of observations taking the value unity, the poverty line was set higher than the official line—that is, at a per person consumption of 5,000 dirhams per year (rather than at the official line of about 3,000). This was confined to rural areas because that is where the losses are concentrated. In the case of full deprotection (Policy 4), about 14 percent of the variance in this measure can be explained by the set of regressors in table 2.9; for Policy 1, the share is 20 percent.[12] A number of covariates can identify likely losers among the poor, but a large share of the variance is left unexplained.

Another way to assess how effectively this set of covariates can explain the incidence of a net loss from reform among the poor is by comparing the actual value of the dummy variable described earlier with its predicted values from the model, using a cutoff probability of 0.5. For Policy 4,472 households out of 2,100 both were poor and incurred a loss because of the reform. Of these households, the model could correctly predict that this was the case only for 18 percent (86 households). For Policy 1, the model prediction was correct for 27 percent of the 463 households that were both poor and made worse off by the reform.

Most forms of indicator targeting—whereby transfers are contingent on readily observed variables like location—would be based on variables similar to those used in these regressions; indeed, targeted policies use fewer dimensions. This suggests that indicator targeting is of only limited effectiveness in reaching those in greatest need. Self-targeting mechanisms that create incentives for people to correctly reveal their status (such as using work requirements) may be better able to reach these people.

Two Caveats

Although the results presented here are suggestive, two limitations of this analysis should be noted. The first concern stems from the fact that the Doukkali (2003) model assumed fixed wage rates. Sensitivity to alternative labor market assumptions should be checked, but one can speculate on the likely impacts of allowing real wages to adjust to the reforms. Here it can be argued that the export-oriented cash crops that will replace cereals will tend to be more labor intensive than cereals. Thus, higher aggregate demand for the relatively unskilled labor used in agriculture would be expected, and hence higher real wages for relatively poorer groups would be realized. This wage increase will undoubtedly go some way toward compensating the rural poor—and may even tilt the vertical distributional impacts in favor of the poor.

The second concern is that dynamic gains from greater trade openness may not be captured by the model used to generate the relative price impacts; for example, trade may facilitate learning about new agricultural technologies and innovation that brings longer-term gains in farm productivity. These effects may be better revealed by studying time-series evidence combined with cross-country comparisons.

Conclusion

The welfare impacts of deprotection in developing countries have been much debated. Some people have argued that external trade liberalizations are beneficial to the poor, whereas others argue that the benefits will be captured more by the nonpoor. Expected impacts on domestic prices have figured prominently in these debates.

This chapter has studied the welfare impacts at the household level of the changes in commodity prices attributed to a proposed trade reform, namely, Morocco's deprotection of its cereals sector. This deprotection would entail a sharp reduction in tariffs, with implications for the domestic structure of prices and hence household welfare. The analysis presented here draws out the implications for household welfare of the previous estimates of the price impacts of reform undertaken for a joint government of Morocco and World Bank study. The estimates of price impacts are entirely external to (and predate) this analysis. Here some standard methods of first-order welfare analysis are used to measure the gains and losses at the household level using a large sample survey. In future work using this methodology, there may well be more scope for feedback from the household-level analysis to the CGE modeling used to derive price impacts.

In a number of respects, this detailed household-level analysis throws into question past claims about the likely welfare impacts of this trade reform. In the aggregate, one finds a small negative impact on mean household consumption and a small increase in inequality. There is a sizable, and at least partly explicable, variance in impacts across households. Rural families tend to lose; urban households tend to gain. Some provinces experience larger impacts than others, with the highest negative impacts found in rural households in Tasla Azilal, Meknes Tafil, Fes-Boulemane, and Tanger-Tetouan. Mean impacts for rural households in these regions are 10 percent or more of consumption, indicating that there are sizable welfare losses among the poor in these specific regions.

The adverse impact on rural poverty stems, in large part, from the fact that the losses to the net producers of cereals outweigh the gains to the net consumers among the poor. Thus, on balance, rural poverty rises. This contradicts the generalizations that have been made in the past—that the rural poor in Morocco tend to be net consumers of grain and hence gainers from trade reform. Yes, a majority of them are net consumers, but on balance, the welfare impacts on the rural poor are negative.

These results lead to questions about the high level of aggregation common in past claims about welfare impacts of trade reform. Diverse impacts are found at given prereform consumption levels. This "horizontal" dispersion becomes more marked as the extent of reform (measured by the size of the tariff cut) increases. Indeed, it is estimated that all of the impact of complete deprotection of cereals on inequality is horizontal rather than vertical; in this study, the vertical impact on inequality was actually inequality reducing. For a modest reform of a 10 percent cut in tariffs, the vertical component dominates, although a large horizontal component is evident. It is clear from these results that in understanding the social impacts of this reform, one should not look solely at income poverty and income inequality as conventionally measured; instead, one needs to look at impacts along "horizontal" dimensions, at given income levels.

This chapter has identified specific types of households whose consumption and production behavior makes them particularly vulnerable. These results are suggestive of the targeting priorities for compensatory programs. The fact that this analysis also finds a large share of unexplained variance in impacts points to the limitations of targeting based on readily observable indicators, suggesting that self-targeting mechanisms may be needed.

Annex: Measuring Welfare Impacts at the Household Level

The approach used in this study is relatively standard, but it is still worth explaining the specifics on how the analysis in this chapter is done.

Each household is assumed to have preferences over consumption and work effort represented by the utility function $u_i(q_i^d, L_i)$, where q_i^d is a vector of the quantities of commodities demanded by household i and L_i is a vector of labor supplies by activity, including supply to the household's own production activities.[13] The household is assumed to be free to choose its preferred combinations q_i^d and L_i subject to its budget constraint. The production activity owned by the household generates a profit $\pi_i(p_i^s) = \max[p_i^s q_i^s - c_i(q_i^s)]$, where p_i^s is a vector of supply prices, and $c_i(q_i^s)$ is the household-specific cost function.[14] The indirect utility function of household i is given by:

$$(2A.1) \qquad v_i[p_i^s, p_i^d, w_i] = \max_{(q_i^d, L_i)} [u_i(q_i^d, L_i) \,|\, p_i^d q_i^d = w_i L_i + \pi_i(p_i^s)],$$

where p_i^d is the price vector for consumption and w_i is the vector of wage rates.

Taking the differential of expression (2A.1) and using the envelope property (whereby the welfare impacts in a neighborhood of an optimum can be evaluated by treating the quantity choices as given), the gain to household i (denoted g_i) is given by the money metric of the change in utility:

$$(2A.2) \quad g_i = \frac{du_i}{v_{\pi i}} = \sum_{j=1}^{m} \left[p_{ij}^s q_{ij}^s \frac{dp_{ij}^s}{p_{ij}^s} - p_{ij}^d q_{ij}^d \frac{dp_{ij}^d}{p_{ij}^d} \right] + \sum_{k=1}^{n} \left(w_k L_{ik}^s \frac{dw_k}{w_k} \right),$$

where $v_{\pi i}$ is the marginal utility of income for household i—the multiplier on the budget constraint in equation (2A.2)—and L_{ik}^s is the household's "external" labor supply to activity k. (Notice that gains in earnings from labor used in own production are exactly matched by the higher cost of this input to own production.) The proportionate changes in prices are weighted by their corresponding expenditure shares; the weight for the proportionate change in the jth selling price is $p_{ij}^s q_{ij}^s$, the revenue (selling value) from household production activities in sector j. Similarly, $- p_{ij}^d q_{ij}^d$ is the (negative) weight for demand price changes, and $w_k L_{ik}^s$ is the weight for changes in the wage rate for activity k. The term $p_{ij}^s q_{ij}^s - p_{ij}^d p_{ij}^d$ gives (to a first-order approximation) the welfare impact of an equiproportionate increase in the price of commodity j.

Equation (2A.2) is the key formula used to calculate the welfare impacts at household level, given the predicted price changes.

Having estimated the impacts at household level, one can study how they vary with prereform welfare and determine what impact the reform has on poverty and inequality. One can also try to explain the differences in impacts in terms of observable characteristics of potential relevance to social protection policies. The formulation of the problem of measuring welfare impacts presented earlier allows utility and profit functions to vary between households at given prices. To explain the heterogeneity in measured welfare impacts, suppose instead that these functions vary with observed household characteristics. The indirect utility function becomes as follows:

$$(2A.3) \qquad v_i(p_i^s, p_i^d, w_i) = v(p_i^s, p_i^d, w_i, x_{1i}, x_{2i})$$
$$= \max[u(q_i^d, L_i, x_{1i}) \mid p_i^d q_i^d - w_i L_i = \pi_i],$$

where

$$(2A.4) \qquad \pi_i = \pi(p_i^s, x_{2i}) = \max[p_i^s q_i^s - c(q_i^s, x_{2i})].$$

Note that the characteristics that influence preferences over consumption (x_{1i}) are allowed to differ from those that influence the profits from own production activities (x_{2i}). The gain from the price changes induced by trade reform, as given by equation (2A.3), depends on the consumption, labor supply, and production choices of the household, which depend in turn on prices and characteristics, x_{1i} and x_{2i}. Generically, the gain can now be written as equation (2.5).

Notes

The authors are grateful to Touhami Abdelkhalek, Maurizio Bussolo, Jennie Litvack, Sherman Robinson, Hans Timmer, and seminar participants at the World Bank for comments on an earlier version of this chapter, and to Rachid Doukkali for help in using the results of his computable general equilibrium (CGE) analysis. This chapter was originally written as a background paper to the report "Kingdom of Morocco: Poverty Report: Strengthening Policy by Identifying the Geographic Dimension of Poverty," Report No. 28223-MOR (World Bank 2004).

1. See the surveys by McColloch, Winters, and Cirera (2001) and Hertel and Reimer (2005). A number of chapters in part 2 of Bourguignon and Pereira da Silva (2003) describe alternative approaches using general equilibrium models.

2. Although it is not a subject of the analysis in this chapter, arguments are also made about adverse environmental impacts arising from the expansion of protected cereal production into marginal areas. It is claimed that scarce water resources have also been diverted into soft wheat production. For further discussion, see World Bank (2003).

3. There are many antecedents of this study's approach in the literatures on both tax reform and trade reform, but there are surprisingly few applications to point to in the ex ante assessment of actual reform proposals. For another example, see Chen and Ravallion (2004). Hertel and Reimer (2005) provide a useful overview of the strengths and weaknesses of alternative approaches to assessing the welfare impacts of trade policies, including references to empirical examples for developing countries.

4. Antecedents to this type of decomposition can be found in the literature on horizontal equity in taxation. In the context of assessing a tax system, Auerbach and Hassett (2002) show how changes in an index of social welfare can be decomposed into terms reflecting changes in the level and distribution of income, the burden and progressivity of the tax system, and a measure of the change in horizontal equity.

5. For further discussion of the MLD, see Bourguignon (1979) and Cowell (2000). MLD is a member of the general entropy class of inequality measures.

6. In addition to administering the tariffs on imported soft wheat, the government of Morocco buys, mills, and sells around 1 million tons of soft

wheat in the form of low-grade flour that is sold on the open market to help consumers.

7. Rachid Doukkali kindly provided price predictions from the CGE model mapped into the categories of consumption and production identified in the survey. The production revenues were calculated from the survey data by matching these consumption categories to the variables containing information about household production of the corresponding goods.

8. The survey's design and content are similar in most respects to the 1991 Living Standards Measurement Study (LSMS) for Morocco documented in the World Bank's LSMS Web site at http://www.worldbank.org/lsms/.

9. Notice that income from the sale of meat is not recorded in these data. The most plausible explanation is that Moroccan farmers sell livestock to butchers or slaughterhouses (*abattoirs*) rather than selling meat as such. Following conventional survey processing practices, livestock is treated as an asset, so that the proceeds from the sale of livestock are not treated as income. This is questionable. As a test, the main calculations were reworked using the survey data on the transaction in livestock and adding net sales into income. This made a negligible difference to the results. Further details are available from the authors.

10. These have been updated using the consumer price index. The poverty lines were 3,922 dirhams per year in urban areas and 3,037 in rural areas. See World Bank (2001) for details.

11. See Cleveland (1979). This is often referred to as LOWESS (locally weighted scatterplot smoothing). The authors used the LOWESS program in STATA.

12. The R^2 for OLS regressions are 0.139 and 0.191 for Policy 4 and Policy 1, respectively. Using instead a probit model to correct for the nonlinearity, the pseudo-R^2s are 0.135 and 0.196.

13. The standard assumptions are made: that goods have positive marginal utilities while labor supplies have negative marginal utilities.

14. One can readily include input prices in this cost function; see Chen and Ravallion (2004) for a more general formulation. In the present context, this makes no difference to the subsequent analysis, so factor prices are subsumed in the cost function to simplify notation.

References

Abdelkhalek, Touhami. 2002. "De l'impact de la Libéralization du Marche Céréalier Marocain: Enseignements à Partir d'un Modèle de Comportement des Ménages Rureaux." *Critique Economique* 7: 105–14.

Atkinson, Anthony B. 1987. "On the Measurement of Poverty." *Econometrica* 55: 749–64.

Auerbach, Alan J., and Kevin A. Hassett. 2002. "A New Measure of Horizontal Equity." *American Economic Review* 92 (4): 1116–125.

Bourguignon, François. 1979. "Decomposable Inequality Measures." *Econometrica* 47: 901–20.

Bourguignon, François, and Luiz A. Pereira da Silva, eds. 2003. *The Impact of Economic Policies on Poverty and Income Distribution: Evaluation Techniques and Tools.* Washington, DC: World Bank and Oxford University Press.

Chen, Shaohua, and Martin Ravallion. 2004. "Welfare Impacts of Morocco's Accession to the WTO." *World Bank Economic Review* 18 (1): 29–58.

Cleveland, William S. 1979. "Robust Locally Weighted Regression and Smoothing Scatter Plots." *Journal of the American Statistical Association* 74: 829–36.

Cockburn, John. 2006. "Trade Liberalisation and Poverty in Nepal: A Computable General Equilibrium Micro Simulation Analysis." In *Globalization and Poverty: Channels and Policies,* eds. Maurizio Bussolo and Jeffery Round. London: Routledge.

Cowell, Frank. 2000. "Measurement of Inequality." In *Handbook of Income Distribution,* eds. A. B. Atkinson and F. Bourguignon. Amsterdam: North-Holland.

Doukkali, Rachid. 2003. "Etude de Effets de la Libéralisation des Céréales: Resultats des Simulations à L'Aide d'un Modèle Equilibre Général Calculable." Joint Report of the Ministry of Agriculture of Morocco and the World Bank, Rabat and Washington, DC.

Hertel, Thomas W., and Jeffrey J. Reimer. 2005. "Predicting the Poverty Impacts of Trade Reform." *Journal of International Trade & Economic Development* 14 (December 4): 377–405.

McCulloch, Neil, and L. Alan Winters, with Xavier Cirera. 2001. *Trade Liberalization and Poverty: A Handbook.* London: Centre for Economic Policy Research and Department for International Development (UK).

Ravallion, Martin. 2001. "Growth, Inequality, and Poverty: Looking Beyond Averages." *World Development* 29 (11): 1803–815.

———. 2004. "Competing Concepts of Inequality in the Globalization Debate." Brookings Trade Forum, 2004, Brookings Institution Press, Washington, DC.

Ravallion, Martin, and Dominique van de Walle. 1991. "The Impact of Food Pricing Reforms on Poverty: A Demand Consistent Welfare Analysis for Indonesia." *Journal of Policy Modeling* 13: 281–300.

World Bank. 2001. *Kingdom of Morocco: Poverty Update.* Washington, DC: World Bank.

———. 2003. *Kingdom of Morocco: Findings and Recommendations of the Cereals Working Group: A Critical Review.* Washington, DC: World Bank.

3

Trade Options for Latin America: A Poverty Assessment Using a Top-Down Macro-Micro Modeling Framework

Maurizio Bussolo, Jann Lay, Denis Medvedev, and Dominique van der Mensbrugghe

During the past two decades, policy advice given to developing countries has emphasized greater market openness and better integration into the global economy. This advice is based on two major assumptions: (1) that outward-oriented economies are more efficient, are less prone to resource waste, and hence grow faster; and (2) that faster income growth is beneficial for rich and poor alike, thereby contributing to poverty reduction in the developing world.

Both assumptions have been challenged in the recent empirical literature. In particular, research on the second assumption has illustrated that the effects of globalization in general, and trade liberalization in particular, on poverty are uncertain—at least in the short to medium run. Instead, the emerging consensus seems to be that the distributional and poverty impacts of trade liberalization depend critically on the structure of initial protection, the pattern of liberalization, and a number of country characteristics, in particular the functioning of the labor market and the sectoral and skill composition of the workforce (see, for example, Winters, McCulloch, and McKay 2004; Harrison 2005; Hertel and Winters 2005). This uncertainty has brought the issues of possible poverty impacts and the distribution of gains and losses both between and within countries to the center stage of negotiations on multilateral and regional trade reform. The collapse of the Doha Round of global trade talks can be interpreted as a consequence of the uncertainty regarding these distributional effects.

The empirical literature has given rise to several approaches for assessing the ex ante poverty effects of a trade shock, most often by using some form of numerical simulation model (see, for example, Ianchovichina, Nicita, and Soloaga 2000; Harrison and others 2003; Hertel and Winters 2005). This chapter describes one such approach—a framework that links a global computable general equilibrium (CGE) model with household survey data—and relies on it to estimate the effects of multilateral and regional trade reforms on poverty in four major Latin American economies: Brazil, Chile, Colombia, and Mexico. This effort has two main objectives. First, the chapter demonstrates that a simple macro-micro framework— despite a limited set of linkage variables and no behavioral responses by individuals in the survey—is highly superior to alternative methods based on growth-poverty elasticities and to the earlier CGE-based analyses that used the representative household group (RHG) assumption. Second, the chapter assesses the distributional impact of trade reform for a group of countries in which the links between trade liberalization and poverty have been the subject of a large debate. Because earlier trade reform in the region has failed to bring about sizable poverty reduction, the question of whether future liberalization is likely to generate significant inroads in the fight against poverty remains relevant.[1]

The remainder of the chapter is organized as follows. The next section presents the macro and micro aspects of the chapter's methodological framework. This discussion is followed by an explanation of the general equilibrium results of the policy shocks and links them to the poverty outcomes of trade reform. The final section concludes by focusing on the policy implications of the chapter's findings and directions for future research.

The Macro-Micro Framework: Linking a CGE Model to Household Surveys

This section provides the details of the methodological approach of the chapter by focusing on three main areas (divided into three subsections). First, it discusses the pros and cons of the analytical and empirical framework adopted for this exercise. Second, it summarizes the main features of the macro (CGE) model. Third, it introduces the micro module and the household surveys used in the analysis.

Advantages and Drawbacks

The methodological approach of this chapter can be best described as a two-step process. In the first step, a CGE model is used to create two trade reform scenarios and to evaluate the related factor and commodity price changes. In the second step, the general equilibrium price changes are mapped to adjustments of real incomes of individual households in a micro simulation model. Thus, the procedure accounts for two main transmission channels from trade reform to poverty: (1) movements in real prices of different factors and (2) changes in relative prices of different groups of consumption goods (McCulloch, Winters, and Cirera 2001). Variants of the method described here have been used in other case studies, and it is possible to formalize those variants in commonly used terms of welfare analysis (see Chen and Ravallion 2004; Hertel and others 2004; and chapter 2 in this volume). These formal presentations illustrate the major advantages and shortcomings of the current framework, which are only briefly summarized here.

On the macro side, a CGE model has the advantage of being grounded in established trade and general equilibrium theories, of embedding enough data details so that they can be used to simulate realistic trade policy reforms, and of generating price effects that can be directly and unequivocally linked to these reforms. At the same time, CGE models are often criticized for imposing strong assumptions about the structure of an economy (for example, specific functional forms and closure rules) and for the results being largely determined by base year conditions and the chosen values for various elasticities (which, even when econometrically estimated, are susceptible to Lucas' 1976 critique).

The micro modeling approach of this chapter is often referred to as micro accounting. By generating a new counterfactual income distribution for the simulated trade scenarios, the micro module allows for a detailed analysis of the poverty and inequality changes induced by the aggregate trade policy shocks. Households and individuals in the micro module are not allowed to change their optimal choices (in terms of demand for goods and factor supplies) and therefore the welfare impacts can be seen only as first-order approximations. Hence, the method should not be used for large shocks or for medium- to long-term analysis, that is, when such behavioral changes cannot be ignored.

The advantages of the current method include its simplicity as well as the ability to evaluate the trade-induced poverty effects on specific groups of households. For example, as illustrated in this chapter, impact analyses can be conducted separately for rural and urban areas. Other criteria, such as farm and nonfarm households or ethnic groups, may be chosen as well; the only requirement is that the production and consumption behavior of these groups are somehow correlated to the factors and commodities in the CGE model. Furthermore, the survey data allow for detailed distributional analysis, such as an assessment of the importance of redistribution compared with growth effects. Finally, it is relatively easy to extend a CGE model by linking it to a household survey: it requires only some data handling and some straightforward estimation work.

The LINKAGE General Equilibrium Model

The CGE model used in this chapter is the World Bank's LINKAGE model, a relatively standard CGE model with many neoclassical features (for the full model specification, see van der Mensbrugghe 2005). It is based on the Global Trade Analysis Project (GTAP) Release 6.0 data set with a 2001 base year.[2] All markets, including factor markets, clear through flexible prices, and the model exhibits constant returns to scale and perfect competition. The model is global, with a full accounting of bilateral trade flows, and its comparative static (as opposed to recursive dynamic) version has been implemented for the simulations described in this chapter. In each country, a single representative household earns income from skilled and unskilled labor, capital, and land. International factor mobility is not included, and with the exception of labor, intersectoral factor mobility within countries has been limited, so model results should be interpreted as short-term impacts. Labor markets are perfectly segmented by skill level, and unskilled labor is further segmented into farm and nonfarm activities. Therefore, unskilled workers are perfectly mobile within agriculture and nonagriculture, but these workers cannot switch employment between these segments. Skilled workers are perfectly mobile throughout the national economies.

For this application, the GTAP data have been aggregated to 18 countries/regions with an emphasis on the countries in the Western Hemisphere (table 3.1). Canada and the United States have been aggregated together, and most of the major countries in Latin America are identified separately. The remaining high-income countries are aggregated into Western Europe and Asia and Pacific, and the remaining developing countries fall into one of four broad regions: (1) East and South Asia, (2) Middle East and North Africa, (3) Europe and Central Asia, and (4) Sub-Saharan Africa (aggregated with a small residual). The sectoral concordance focuses on some of the major protected commodities, including agricultural and food products, textiles, clothing and footwear, metals, and motor vehicles and parts.

Table 3.1 LINKAGE Model: Regional and Sectoral Groups

Country or group	Sector
Argentina	Cereals
Brazil	Vegetables and fruits
Chile	Oil seeds
Colombia	Sugar
Mexico	Other crops
Peru	Livestock
Uruguay	Other natural resources
República Bolivariana de Venezuela	Fossil fuels
Central America	Cattle meats
Caribbean	Dairy products
Rest of South America	Other food, beverages,
East Asia and Pacific	and tobacco
Europe and Central Asia	Textiles
Middle East and North Africa	Wearing apparel
South Asia	Leather products
Sub-Saharan Africa and the rest of world	Basic manufactures
Canada and United States	Other manufacturing
Western Europe and the European	Metals
Free Trade Area	Motor vehicles and parts
Rest of high-income countries	Other equipment
	Electric and gas utilities
	Construction
	Services

Source: Authors' compilation.

Although services are highly protected in most markets, the levels of protection are hard to measure, and the GTAP data set has little information in this area—thus, the service sectors are highly aggregated.

The Micro Accounting Framework

The LINKAGE model described in the previous section captures some of the most important transmission channels from trade policy to poverty through changes in relative factor and goods prices. Welfare effects can be assessed only for the single representative household in each country; therefore, they provide little information on the distributional consequences of policy reform. This could be remedied by fitting a parametric distribution of changes in welfare (Adelman and Robinson 1978), using a household survey to increase the number of representative households or even to incorporate all sample households into the CGE model (Rutherford, Tarr, and Shepotylo 2005), or by mapping the CGE changes in factor returns and commodity prices to the endowments and consumption patterns of each household in the survey. The latter approach—a less computationally intensive alternative to the inclusion of the entire survey into the CGE model— is the empirical strategy of this chapter.

The micro data are connected to the LINKAGE results through the following variables: the average real wage in each of the four labor market segments (skilled/unskilled and agriculture/nonagriculture), the average nonagricultural real capital rent, the average agricultural (combined) capital and land rent, and the relative prices of food and nonfood commodities. The changes in real incomes of households are then calculated by applying the changes in factor returns to that household's labor and capital endowments, and deflating these with a cost-of-living index. This index is a weighted average of the new food and nonfood prices, with the weights calculated as each household's share of food consumption in the total consumption bundle.[3] A final household income component—composed of all other sources of income, including pensions, public transfers, remittances (internal as well as international), and when available, autoconsumption—is assumed to be constant in real terms.[4]

The micro simulation module is implemented with the following household surveys: 2001 Pesquisa Nacional por Amostra de Domicílios (Brazil), 2000 Encuesta de Caracterización Socioe-conómica Nacional (Chile), 1997 Encuesta de Calidad de Vida (Colombia), and 2001 Encuesta Nacional Ingresos y Gastos de los Hogares (Mexico). These four countries were chosen to highlight various aspects of poverty, inequality, and trade policy in Latin America.[5] Together, these countries account for more than 60 percent of the population and almost 70 percent of GDP in Latin America, and therefore paint a fairly representative picture of the region.

Some preliminary work on the surveys' raw data is needed to ensure a close match to the LINKAGE results; a *perfect* match is quite difficult to achieve (see box 3.1 for more details). Labor incomes for the actively employed population (those 12 years of age and older) enter the analysis at the individual level. Workers are classified as skilled and unskilled based on level of education; if the information on level of education is not satisfactory, occupational variables are used instead. For wage workers, the entire income from employment is considered either skilled or unskilled (agricultural or nonagricultural) labor income. In contrast, income reported by the self-employed is assumed to have both a labor and a capital (plus land for agriculture) component. To separate these two components, a wage was imputed for each self-employed individual. This imputation is based on a wage equation that is estimated separately for wage workers in agriculture and nonagricultural sectors, further differentiated by skill levels. The equations are simple Mincerian wage equations with log wage earnings explained by education and age, the respective squared terms, as well as regional and sectoral dummies. The estimated coefficients of these wage equations are then used to impute a (hedonic) wage for the self-employed. The difference between reported income from self-employment and imputed wage is assumed to represent the capital component of self-employment income. For agricultural activities, the difference should be interpreted as mixed-factor income (from land and capital).[6] In addition to capital income of self-employed individuals, total household capital income includes all dividends, interest, and property rental income earned by household members.

Box 3.1 Consistency Issues

Combining macro and micro models implies working with different types of data sources, including national accounts and primary surveys, which are notoriously inconsistent. The scope of these inconsistencies is illustrated by Deaton (2004), who reports survey income to be, on average, less than 60 percent of GDP. He discusses the reasons for these discrepancies and points to differences in definitions and differences in meeting those definitions, for example, in measuring production. In general, national accounts, in contrast to surveys, are more likely to capture larger transactions than smaller ones. Because these small transactions reflect the living standards of the poor, Deaton (2004) concludes that poverty can be measured only using household surveys.

One of the challenges of the current exercise is to link macro- and micro-based data sets. In principle, one should think of the macro data as aggregations of the micro data (at least for the variables that concern the household sector). Yet, in light of findings by Deaton and others (for example, Robilliard and Robinson 2003; Round 2003) this typically is not the case. Indeed, for the four countries considered in this chapter, large discrepancies are found between the (mainly) national-accounts-based social accounting matrices (SAM) and the household surveys. The extent of the problem is highlighted by the factor shares from the SAM relative to those calculated from the surveys presented in the box table. Of course, the larger the initial discrepancies between these macro and aggregated micro variables, the larger the deviations between macro and micro results after a simulation. If factor shares between the survey and the SAM differ significantly, passing real factor prices from the CGE model to the household survey will provide real household income growth rates that are different from the CGE results.

So what should be done with these discrepancies? Robilliard and Robinson (2003) propose to reconcile the two data sources by adjusting the weights in the survey data. Alternatively, factor markets and the

(Box continues on the following page.)

household sector in the SAM could be rendered consistent with the household survey with regard to the aggregate link variables. The framework proposed in this chapter does not enforce consistency; however, this does not imply that no adjustments are made to the survey data and the SAM. Yet these adjustments are partial and imply a number of discrete decisions by the analyst to reduce discrepancies to a "tolerable" level. What is tolerable remains subject to expert judgment, but so does the decision to put more trust in either national accounts or household survey data.

In fact, there may be good reasons to prefer the survey data in some instances and national accounts data in others—following the general guideline of surveys being the better source for data on small transactions. Eventually, the analyst's choices depend on the type of economic transactions prevalent in the country under consideration, the design of the survey, and the comparative quality of the two data sources. Finally, the problem is mitigated by the fact that SAMs increasingly incorporate information from household surveys—at least with regard to the combination of CGE models with microeconomic data.

Discrepancies between Household Surveys and CGE Model Data

Item	Brazil	Chile	Colombia	Mexico
Value added (percentage of total) in the base year SAM				
Unskilled labor	36	29	43	23
Skilled labor	21	12	18	10
Capital and land	43	59	38	68
Value added (percentage of total) in the household survey				
Unskilled labor	69	74	74	78
Skilled labor	19	11	11	12
Capital and land	13	14	15	9

Source: Authors' calculations.
Note: SAM = social accounting matrices.

Poverty Effects of the Free Trade Area of the Americas and Multilateral Trade Liberalization

This section investigates the poverty and income distribution effects of two different trade liberalization scenarios for Brazil, Chile, Colombia, and Mexico. The simulations are as follows:

• A Free Trade Area of the Americas (FTAA) scenario, where tariffs and export subsidies among the Western Hemisphere countries are eliminated.

- A full trade liberalization (FULLIB) scenario, where tariffs and export subsidies are eliminated for all countries. Domestic support (factors and indirect subsidies) is also eliminated in all countries. Thus, this scenario is a benchmark that represents the best results (in terms of maximizing efficiency gains) a country might expect to achieve.

Each scenario has been modeled separately in a comparative static framework. Before implementing the liberalization scenarios, a series of presimulation shocks are imposed on the model to provide a better starting point for the solution and reflect the global trading environment more carefully. These shocks include, for example, the phase-out of the Multi-Fiber Arrangement quotas as well as China's accession to the World Trade Organization. Having obtained a solution for this "presimulation," the model uses it as a starting point for each of the liberalization scenarios. At the end of the solution period, all model variables are reinitialized to the presimulation starting point, and a new liberalization scenario is solved.

The analysis is carried out in three parts. First, this section discusses the initial conditions in each of the four countries at both the macro and the micro levels. Second, these initial conditions, together with the nature of policy shocks, are used to explain the macro outcomes of trade reform. Third, the macro outcomes are mapped to the household surveys in accordance with the methodology described in the previous section.

Economic Structure, Composition of Tariffs, and Household Income Sources

In addition to the policy shock, the level and sectoral variability of the initial protection as well as the structural features of each economy are key determinants of results in the LINKAGE model. Thus, this section begins with data in table 3.2 that show the import-weighted average tariffs by sector and by origin and destination markets.

In general, tariffs levied against Western Hemisphere trading partners are somewhat lower than tariffs levied against non–Western Hemisphere exporters, mostly because of preferences granted under the region's many preferential trade agreements. This is particularly evident in the case of Mexico, whose import-weighted tariffs on merchandise trade with Western Hemisphere partners are slightly higher than a tenth of its tariffs on trade with countries outside the region. This also suggests that preferential liberalization in Mexico (mainly the North American Free Trade Agreement [NAFTA]) has been taking place behind relatively high external barriers. Similarly, Brazil's

Table 3.2 Trade Protection by Origin, Destination, and Sector (import-weighted 2001 tariffs)

Sector/importer		Exporter						
	Western Hemisphere	Latin America and the Caribbean	Brazil	Chile	Colombia	Mexico	Canada and the United States	Not in the Western Hemisphere
All sectors (excluding services)								
Western Hemisphere	1.9	2.4	5.0	5.4	2.1	0.6	1.6	3.9
Latin America and the Caribbean	5.2	6.7	7.7	9.4	2.8	10.8	4.6	11.6
Brazil	8.3	6.1	—	8.0	10.3	16.4	9.8	10.7
Chile	6.4	6.3	7.0	—	7.0	0.0	6.7	6.5
Colombia	8.5	7.4	13.4	14.2	—	11.5	9.3	12.1
Mexico	1.8	11.4	16.5	2.6	2.8	—	1.2	14.1
Canada and the United States	0.6	1.1	2.5	1.3	1.5	0.0	0.2	2.5
Not in the Western Hemisphere	7.3	11.4	14.2	3.3	7.7	5.8	6.3	3.9
Agriculture and food								
Western Hemisphere	5.3	3.9	6.5	6.4	2.2	1.4	6.5	6.6
Latin America and the Caribbean	8.4	6.5	6.4	14.1	3.3	14.0	10.0	16.5
Brazil	2.2	1.3	—	13.0	18.6	15.9	10.8	12.1
Chile	6.9	6.9	7.0	—	7.0	0.0	7.0	6.7
Colombia	9.7	6.6	14.8	17.1	0	16.4	13.6	13.9
Mexico	9.3	16.5	19.6	9.7	11.5	—	8.6	24.5
Canada and the United States	3.2	2.2	6.5	1.4	1.6	0.3	4.1	4.4
Not in the Western Hemisphere	27.3	24.9	27.6	10.8	17.4	23.0	29.2	10.2

Agriculture

Western Hemisphere	4.4	3.2	7.7	5.5	1.7	0.5	5.6	4.3
Latin America and the Caribbean	8.3	5.0	7.7	14.4	2.3	10.0	10.3	9.8
Brazil	0.8	0.5	—	10.7	10.5	10.4	6.2	9.5
Chile	7.0	6.9	7.0	—	7.0	0.0	7.0	6.7
Colombia	10.5	5.9	8.9	14.7	0	10.8	12.7	10.0
Mexico	10.7	12.7	17.9	16.8	3.2	—	10.5	11.9
Canada and the United States	1.7	2.4	7.7	1.0	1.5	0.2	0.8	2.9
Not in the Western Hemisphere	32.4	31.6	29.4	11.1	20.6	13.0	33.0	12.5

Processed foods

Western Hemisphere	6.1	4.7	5.5	7.2	3.4	2.4	7.2	7.4
Latin America and the Caribbean	8.6	7.6	5.9	13.9	3.7	15.2	9.6	19.3
Brazil	5.2	3.4	—	15.3	20.5	17.1	14.4	13.8
Chile	6.8	6.8	7.0	—	7.0	0.0	7.0	6.7
Colombia	8.8	6.9	17.4	19.3	—	18.7	16.9	17.9
Mexico	7.7	19.4	25.5	2.9	13.0	—	6.3	29.4
Canada and the United States	4.5	1.9	4.9	1.8	2.4	0.4	5.9	4.9
Not in the Western Hemisphere	21.5	17.8	25.4	10.6	3.4	31.4	24.6	9.0

Mining and natural resources

Western Hemisphere	0.9	1.2	2.0	2.6	0.4	0.1	0.4	0.5
Latin America and the Caribbean	3.3	3.7	3.0	4.7	2.3	1.9	2.4	2.1
Brazil	0.7	0.7	—	3.4	0.4	2.4	0.7	0.3
Chile	7.0	7.0	7.0	—	6.7	0.0	6.7	6.7
Colombia	4.7	3.6	5.2	5.0	—	4.0	6.8	7.2
Mexico	1.1	5.4	12.2	0.0	1.1	—	0.6	9.4
Canada and the United States	0.1	0.2	1.5	0.5	0.2	0.0	0.0	0.2
Not in the Western Hemisphere	3.7	4.9	1.5	0.6	0.1	8.0	1.8	1.6

(Continued on the following page)

Table 3.2 (Continued)

Sector/importer	Exporter							
	Western Hemisphere	Latin America and the Caribbean	Brazil	Chile	Colombia	Mexico	Canada and the United States	Not in the Western Hemisphere
Manufacturing								
Western Hemisphere	1.9	2.6	5.1	5.8	3.2	0.7	1.5	4.1
Latin America and the Caribbean	5.1	7.5	7.9	9.3	2.9	11.7	4.3	12.2
Brazil	9.9	9.2	—	9.4	14.5	16.6	10.1	12.3
Chile	6.3	5.9	7.0	—	7.0	0.0	6.7	6.5
Colombia	8.3	7.6	13.7	14.3	—	11.6	8.9	12.2
Mexico	1.4	11.7	16.5	0.5	3.0	—	0.7	14.2
Canada and the United States	0.6	1.1	2.3	1.5	4.0	0.0	0.2	2.7
Not in the Western Hemisphere	4.9	7.1	11.1	3.3	2.0	4.7	4.6	3.8

Source: Authors' calculations from the GTAP data.
Note: — = not available.

tariffs on imports from other Latin American countries are relatively low, reflecting its participation in MERCOSUR (the Southern Common Market). It is also noteworthy that for Brazil tariffs on agriculture and food commodities are much lower than on manufactured goods, while the opposite is true for Mexico. The tariff structure in Chile and Colombia is largely uniform across different sectors, and the level of duties in the former country is, on average, lower than in other Latin American countries.

The tariff patterns shown in table 3.2 are also reflected in the structural features of the four economies, which are summarized in table 3.3. For example, exports and imports figure most prominently in the GDP of Chile and Mexico, the two countries with the lower average tariffs. Table 3.3 provides important sector detail by summarizing import intensities (measured as the ratio of sectoral imports over sectoral GDP), export intensities (ratios of exports to GDP), and factor intensities (measured as the factor's percentage contribution to total sectoral value added) for each production sector in the LINKAGE model. According to the data in table 3.3, in Brazil the highest dependency on imports is in the capital goods sectors (which have elevated protection rates) and fossil fuels. Therefore, these sectors are likely to be most affected by import competition following trade reform. Conversely, Brazil's export strength is concentrated in export crops, food processing, natural resources, and some manufacturing. As expected, export-oriented sectors (within agriculture) require intensive use of land and unskilled labor, and light manufacturing requires unskilled labor. Apart from the service sectors, the protected import competing sectors are major employers of skilled labor—in conjunction with unskilled workers.

The poverty consequences of trade reform are determined to a large extent by the factor endowments and consumption patterns of households in the neighborhood of the poverty line. This information is summarized in table 3.4, which shows the contributions of labor, capital, and transfers to total household income for rural and urban households above and below the poverty line. Several important patterns are captured in this table. First, although the rural/urban classification is in no way synonymous with the farm/nonfarm distinction, the majority of incomes in rural areas are earned through farm activities, whereas urban dwellers rely mainly on nonfarm earnings. Second, poor households derive a large share of their income from unskilled labor and have almost no skill endowments. Third, no clear pattern in the distribution of transfer income emerges by regions or income levels, most likely because of the differences in definitions across countries. In some cases, transfer income may be mainly auto-consumption, more likely to be observed among the rural poor, while

Table 3.3 Economic Structure for Brazil, Chile, Colombia, and Mexico (percent)

	Brazil						Chile					
Sector	GDP	Imports/ GDP	Exports/ GDP	Un- skilled	Skilled	K+L	GDP	Imports/ GDP	Exports/ GDP	Un- skilled	Skilled	K+L
Cereals	1	53	30	24	1	74	1	26	15	46	1	53
Vegetables and fruits	0	38	42	23	1	76	5	1	55	46	1	53
Oil seeds	1	5	92	23	1	76	0	308	68	47	0	53
Sugar	1	1	63	35	4	61	0	14	0	43˙	2	56
Other crops	1	7	52	23	1	76	0	51	101	46	1	53
Livestock	2	1	3	23	1	76	2	2	3	46	1	53
Other natural resources	1	21	152	43	5	52	5	2	91	24	4	73
Fossil fuels	1	142	42	27	5	68	0	1,427	141	13	3	84
Cattle meat	0	5	72	37	6	56	0	98	14	45	8	47
Dairy products	0	10	2	28	5	68	0	15	23	29	4	67
Other food	2	12	63	38	6	55	6	16	91	32	6	62
Textiles	1	41	36	34	5	61	1	82	18	39	6	55
Wearing apparel	1	9	11	79	13	8	1	133	15	43	7	50
Leather products	0	20	165	53	9	39	0	251	43	45	7	48
Basic manufactures	4	20	42	58	10	32	6	43	87	31	5	64
Other manufacturing	4	72	29	38	6	56	3	148	74	36	9	55
Metals	1	64	179	27	4	68	4	22	227	27	5	68
Motor vehicles and parts	1	119	145	28	5	67	0	455	51	32	7	60
Other equipment	4	131	62	40	7	53	1	980	88	44	12	44
Electric and gas utilities	3	16	0	42	13	45	4	1	0	19	9	73
Construction	9	0	0	19	4	76	6	0	0	44	8	48
Services	63	5	3	38	30	33	52	11	9	24	19	57
Total	100	17	16	36	21	43	100	34	37	29	12	59
Agriculture	5	11	39	25	1	74	9	8	37	46	1	53
Mining	2	97	83	33	5	62	6	71	94	23	4	73
Light manufacturing	5	15	56	42	7	51	9	42	67	34	6	60
Other manufacturing	14	78	58	43	7	50	15	134	123	32	7	61
Services	75	5	3	36	26	38	62	10	8	26	17	58

Source: Authors' calculations from the Global Trade Analysis Project data.
Note: Unskilled and Skilled = labor categories by education level; K+L = payments to capital and land.

	Colombia						Mexico				
GDP	Imports/ GDP	Exports/ GDP	Un-skilled	Skilled	K+L	GDP	Imports/ GDP	Exports/ GDP	Un-skilled	Skilled	K+L
1	53	0	50	2	48	1	48	3	46	1	53
3	6	22	46	1	53	1	8	37	46	1	53
0	40	1	46	1	53	0	438	11	46	1	53
1	4	33	33	4	63	1	2	4	27	2	71
2	8	77	46	1	53	1	14	8	46	1	53
4	1	2	46	1	53	1	13	9	46	1	53
1	7	2	74	6	20	2	7	5	21	2	76
4	2	134	18	3	79	2	26	86	8	2	90
1	5	3	74	12	14	1	24	1	16	3	81
1	15	11	32	5	63	0	50	4	14	2	83
4	23	21	45	7	47	6	11	11	14	3	83
1	126	75	56	8	36	2	58	51	26	4	70
1	12	85	61	9	30	1	32	101	23	4	73
0	53	88	72	11	17	1	26	18	29	5	66
3	47	53	49	8	43	6	42	33	19	4	77
3	124	67	38	8	54	5	82	36	19	5	77
1	111	80	56	9	35	2	53	30	22	4	74
0	472	190	65	13	22	2	129	197	24	6	70
1	636	100	62	15	23	7	149	201	25	7	68
2	0	1	18	8	73	0	3	1	17	8	75
5	0	0	41	7	52	4	0	2	54	10	35
61	6	4	44	27	30	54	5	4	20	14	66
100	19	18	43	18	38	100	28	31	23	10	68
12	10	24	46	1	53	5	20	15	44	1	55
4	2	110	28	4	69	4	19	55	13	2	85
7	29	35	51	8	42	11	23	26	18	3	79
8	158	70	47	9	44	21	96	105	22	5	73
69	5	4	43	25	33	59	5	4	22	14	64

Table 3.4 Household Incomes by Source, Segment, and Poverty Status
(percentage of total)

Country/household	Farm			Nonfarm				Food
	Skilled	Unskilled	Capital	Skilled	Unskilled	Capital	Transfer	
Brazil								
Total	0	9	2	15	46	8	20	30
Poor-urban	0	12	1	4	64	7	12	28
Poor-rural	1	63	8	1	16	4	7	40
Nonpoor-urban	0	2	1	21	49	9	18	28
Nonpoor-rural	3	35	11	5	21	3	23	40
Chile								
Total	0	18	3	8	34	7	31	38
Poor-urban	0	9	0	3	52	2	35	32
Poor-rural	0	41	1	1	22	0	36	46
Nonpoor-urban	0	3	1	18	43	12	23	32
Nonpoor-rural	1	36	7	3	24	4	25	46
Colombia								
Total	0	14	4	8	39	7	27	46
Poor-urban	0	4	1	4	63	8	21	45
Poor-rural	0	36	9	1	18	1	35	57
Nonpoor-urban	0	1	1	20	46	14	18	30
Nonpoor-rural	0	23	12	10	26	6	22	48
Mexico								
Total	0	10	2	8	41	4	35	37
Poor-urban	0	6	0	3	60	2	29	41
Poor-rural	0	32	1	1	20	1	45	48
Nonpoor-urban	0	1	0	18	45	7	29	27
Nonpoor-rural	0	16	5	5	32	5	37	36

Source: Authors' calculations from household surveys.

Note: Transfers include autoconsumption; and the last column, Food, represents the share of food items in the consumption basket.

in other cases, it may be mainly pensions, found primarily among the better-off urban residents.

The last column of table 3.4 shows the share of income that each household group spends on food products. For Brazil and Chile, these shares are the same for poor and nonpoor households because of the lack of detailed expenditure data. Data from Colombia and Mexico, however, show that poor households devote a much larger share of their income to food expenditures. Furthermore, in all four countries, food expenditures are significantly higher among rural households because of lower incomes in these rural areas. This suggests that the poverty outcomes of trade reform, especially in the rural areas, are likely to be particularly sensitive to changes in food prices.

Macroeconomic Results of Trade Reform

Because the model is solved in a comparative static mode and factor mobility is restrained, the adjustment process after the trade liberalization shock is carried out almost entirely through price changes. To trace the links between these price changes and the liberalization scenario, this section begins by examining the pattern of sectoral adjustment in table 3.5.

First, consider the FTAA scenario for Brazil, Chile, and Mexico. For Western Hemisphere partners, Brazil's tariffs are significantly higher against imports of manufactured goods, whereas the converse is true for Mexico, and Chile's tariffs are largely uniform across sectors. Tariff reductions result in increased import inflows and a reallocation of resources away from sectors that face more intense competition from foreign producers. Consequently, in Brazil, manufacturing imports rise the most; in Mexico, the agricultural sector experiences the largest growth in import volumes. In Chile, the effect is largely the same across agriculture and manufacturing. This pattern of increased import inflows is also borne out in the behavior of prices of domestic goods sold locally. In Brazil, the largest price declines are observed in manufacturing sectors; in Mexico, the prices of agricultural commodities register the greatest changes. This behavior testifies to the market share losses experienced by domestic producers as a result of tariff reform.

Turning to the exports side, notice that the sectors with the largest increase in import volumes are often also the sectors with the greatest increase in exports volumes. This reflects greater incentives to export through lower domestic producer prices. The export response varies across sectors and generally is linked to the structure of each country's comparative advantage, revealed partly in the sectoral exports-to-GDP ratio in table 3.3. Thus, for Brazil, which exports more than

Table 3.5 Sectoral Adjustments
(percentage change with respect to initial levels)

Country/sector	Exports volume		Imports volume		Production volume	
	FTAA	FULLIB	FTAA	FULLIB	FTAA	FULLIB
Brazil						
Total	12.4	21.5	11.6	25.5	0.1	−0.2
Agriculture	2.1	17.8	2.7	46.2	0.2	3.1
Mining	2.9	6.0	2.0	7.8	0.1	−1.1
Light manufacturing	9.3	40.9	18.9	69.2	0.5	1.0
Other manufacturing	21.6	26.0	16.0	30.4	0.3	−2.1
Services	−1.6	−5.4	0.8	4.0	−0.1	0.2
Chile						
Total	5.9	7.2	7.9	10.1	0.1	0.0
Agriculture	3.5	3.4	17.8	6.7	0.1	0.8
Mining	4.1	5.3	7.3	9.2	0.3	0.3
Light manufacturing	13.6	17.1	16.4	19.6	0.7	0.5
Other manufacturing	8.0	7.4	7.8	10.6	0.3	−1.0
Services	−1.9	2.2	1.7	2.9	−0.1	0.2
Colombia						
Total	8.5	10.7	7.0	11.6	−0.1	−0.4
Agriculture	9.5	39.6	19.3	36.7	0.1	0.6
Mining	1.8	1.1	13.3	24.9	0.5	0.1
Light manufacturing	25.5	12.2	25.2	35.0	0.7	−1.9
Other manufacturing	7.8	5.6	5.4	8.9	−1.3	−3.8
Services	6.2	8.4	−3.4	−3.3	0.0	0.4
Mexico						
Total	3.3	11.8	3.8	14.8	0.0	0.0
Agriculture	17.0	32.9	18.9	37.1	−0.2	0.2
Mining	0.8	1.7	3.1	9.0	−0.1	−0.9
Light manufacturing	6.2	69.8	10.3	52.0	0.0	1.6
Other manufacturing	3.0	6.6	2.8	10.8	0.3	−0.7
Services	0.2	−3.0	−0.1	2.5	−0.1	0.0

Source: Authors' calculations.
Note: FTAA = Free Trade Area of the Americas; FULLIB = full trade liberalization.

half of its production of other manufactures, the increase in exports volume more than offsets the decrease in domestic prices, leading to an overall expansion in sectoral production. Conversely, Mexico, which exports a relatively low share of its production of agricultural goods, is unable to compensate for the fall in domestic demand with rising export sales and consequently, experiences a contraction in that sector. In general, the sectoral adjustments brought about by FTAA reform are quite modest. This is likely because of the already low tariffs on most imports from Western Hemisphere trading partners.

The pattern of adjustment in the FULLIB scenario differs somewhat from the changes likely to take place with trade reform under the FTAA. Relative to the latter scenario, Brazil, Colombia, and to a lesser extent, Chile orient their production structure much more toward agriculture and away from heavy manufacturing. This pattern reflects the comparative advantage of these countries in producing agricultural goods and the high levels of protection their agricultural exports face among non–Western Hemisphere trading partners. For Mexico, the FTAA scenario further reinforces the regional bias of the country's production structure and therefore global trade reform implies a quite different adjustment pattern for exports, imports, and domestic output. For example, in contrast to the FTAA, full liberalization is likely to result in a much larger increase in exports and production of processed food, but a contraction in the output of textiles and leather products (largely because of competition from East Asian countries).

The adjustments in main factor and consumption prices, as well as real consumption changes, are summarized in table 3.6. In all simulations, Brazil and Chile experience an increase in the payments to unskilled farm workers and a decrease in the skilled/unskilled wage gap for the agricultural sector. In Colombia, unskilled agricultural labor experiences gains only in the case of multilateral liberalization; in Mexico, unskilled agricultural workers lose in all cases. These results are consistent with the structure of individual simulations, and differences across countries reflect their particular patterns of protection and comparative advantage. For example, Brazil's comparative advantage lies in agricultural products and it tends to protect its manufacturing sectors more than the others. Consequently, trade reform leads to an expansion in production of agricultural goods, and because labor is not able to move between agricultural and nonagricultural activities, wages in the farm sectors increase significantly. Conversely, domestic prices decline in the previously protected manufacturing sectors, which reduces production and wages in that sector. The same effect takes place in Mexico, only with the sectoral roles reversed—because Mexico's agriculture is relatively more protected, farm wages suffer relative to nonfarm earnings. The case of Mexico is particularly interesting because, in addition to the aforementioned price effect, another phenomenon takes place—that is, preference erosion. Within each of the liberalization scenarios above, Mexico loses the significant margin of preference it enjoys as a NAFTA member with respect to other Latin American countries. This is one of the reasons why Mexico's nonfarm wages do not experience a significant increase—it already enjoys virtually tariff-free access to

Table 3.6 Price (Factors, Consumption Aggregates) and Real Income Changes (percentage change)

Indicator	Brazil		Chile		Colombia		Mexico	
	FTAA	FULLIB	FTAA	FULLIB	FTAA	FULLIB	FTAA	FULLIB
Nonfarm skilled wage	0.30	0.52	1.32	1.47	-1.53	-2.11	0.04	0.64
Nonfarm unskilled wage	0.45	-0.30	1.82	1.29	-1.41	-2.97	0.20	0.72
Nonfarm capital rent	1.57	4.42	1.98	2.02	-0.46	-0.96	0.32	1.84
Farm skilled wage	0.30	0.52	1.32	1.47	-1.53	-2.11	0.04	0.64
Farm unskilled wage	3.13	51.44	3.34	20.21	-2.34	19.76	-6.40	-3.26
Farm capital and land rent	1.70	21.52	1.62	5.87	-0.61	5.63	-1.16	1.27
Nonfarm skill/unskilled wage gap	-0.15	0.82	-0.49	0.18	-0.12	0.88	-0.15	-0.08
Farm skill/unskilled wage gap	-2.75	-33.63	-1.95	-15.59	0.83	-18.26	6.88	4.03
Food prices	0.55	10.97	1.06	4.84	-2.75	2.10	-1.54	6.51
Nonfood prices	0.09	-0.33	0.23	-0.64	-1.70	-2.91	-0.08	-0.76
Consumer price index (CPI)	0.16	1.28	0.44	0.71	-1.99	-1.76	-0.42	0.76
Real consumption	0.11	1.24	0.39	0.51	-0.30	0.23	0.09	0.23

Source: Authors' calculations.
Note: FTAA = Free Trade Area of the Americas; FULLIB = full trade liberalization.

its biggest market, the United States and Canada, and further regional or global liberalization serves only to open the North American markets for its competitors.

The bottom rows of table 3.6 report the percentage changes in food and nonfood prices, the consumer price index (CPI), and real consumption. With rising farm wages in Brazil and Chile, food prices increase in both FTAA and FULLIB scenarios (despite downward pressure from cheaper imports) and drive the increase in the overall CPI. In Colombia and Mexico, food prices fall in the FTAA simulation as factor returns in agriculture decline. This lowers domestic production costs and combined with increased access to cheaper imports, contributes to the decrease in the overall CPI. Conversely, farm factor prices increase in these countries in the FULLIB scenario, which is sufficient to change the sign of changes in the aggregate CPI for Mexico, but not for Colombia.

With the exception of Colombia under the FTAA scenario, all countries experience positive changes in consumption volumes. Because the FULLIB scenario includes larger tariff cuts and represents the "first-best" world trade scenario, consumption gains in this simulation are larger than under the FTAA and are always positive. The aggregate gains in either scenario are rather small, which can be attributed to several model features, including the following: limited factor mobility, no changes in capital accumulation, and a fixed fiscal closure, where tariff revenue losses are compensated by increases in direct taxes on household income. These aggregate gains, however, are much more indicative of changes at the top of the income distribution than at the bottom, because richer households have a larger weight in the expenditure pattern of the single representative household in the LINKAGE model. To determine the distribution of these gains in the population— and consequently, their repercussions for poverty—the next section translates the changes in macro aggregates into welfare effects at the household level.

Poverty and Income Distribution Results of Trade Reform

The initial poverty conditions of the four countries under analysis, as well as the estimated poverty effects of the two liberalization scenarios, are shown in table 3.7. The initial poverty conditions in Brazil, Chile, Colombia, and Mexico are fairly typical for developing countries. Poverty especially affects rural areas, and the rural poor are more likely to be further away from the poverty lines than the urban poor (as shown by the poverty gap and squared poverty gap statistics, which account for inequality among the poor, with squared poverty gap being more sensitive to changes in inequality).[7]

Table 3.7 Initial Poverty Levels and Percentage Changes Resulting from Trade Reforms

Indicator	Brazil			Chile			Colombia			Mexico		
	H	PG	P2	H	PG	P2	H	PG	P2	H	PG	P2
Initial poverty level (percent)												
All	23.5	9.6	5.3	21.0	7.3	3.8	60.7	32.6	21.8	50.2	20.7	11.2
Urban	19.5	7.6	4.0	20.4	7.1	3.7	53.7	27.1	17.6	43.7	16.6	8.5
Rural	44.7	20.3	11.8	24.6	8.5	4.4	79.1	46.7	32.7	69.3	32.7	19.2
FTAA (percentage change from initial levels)												
All	−0.64	−1.32	−1.70	−1.82	−2.04	−1.85	−0.21	−0.51	−0.54	−0.32	0.47	1.04
Urban	−0.21	−0.85	−1.07	−1.56	−1.92	−1.73	−0.16	−0.66	−0.72	−0.61	−0.48	−0.25
Rural	−1.64	−2.24	−2.82	−3.14	−2.68	−2.45	−0.29	−0.28	−0.30	0.24	1.88	2.71
FULLIB (percentage change from initial levels)												
All	−5.97	−10.77	−13.77	−4.42	−4.53	−4.01	−0.12	−1.18	−1.78	1.17	2.05	2.72
Urban	−0.69	−2.74	−4.08	−2.64	−3.06	−2.70	1.12	0.95	0.93	1.14	1.66	2.15
Rural	−18.05	−26.46	−30.99	−13.40	−11.92	−10.59	−2.31	−4.38	−5.55	1.23	2.62	3.46

Source: Authors' calculations.

Note: FTAA = Free Trade Area of the Americas; FULLIB = full trade liberalization; H = the poverty headcount; PG = the poverty gap; P2 = the squared poverty gap: FGT(0), FGT(1), and FGT(2), respectively. All are estimated at the national poverty line for each country.

In Brazil and Chile, aggregate poverty declines across all scenarios. The reduction in rural and urban headcounts is in line with the factor price changes in table 3.6 and the structure of household earnings shown in table 3.4. Therefore, the rural poor benefit much more from trade reform than the urban poor. The strong decrease in the squared poverty gap shows that the poorest of the poor gain the most under both scenarios—and much more under FULLIB than under the FTAA. In Colombia, the aggregate poverty effects of all simulations are quite small, but again, the results are consistent with factor and consumption price changes given by the macro model (in all cases, however, the decline in rural poverty is significant).[8] In Mexico, poverty decreases under the FTAA, but the reduction is entirely accounted for by a nationwide distributional shift caused by a widening rural-urban gap. The same pattern takes place under the FULLIB scenario, with the urban poor losing less than the rural poor.

The most interesting dynamics are observed when comparing the impact of multilateral and regional liberalization across countries. For Brazil and Chile, multilateral liberalization is unequivocally superior to regional scenarios, and the order of magnitude of poverty reductions is proportional to the scale of tariff reductions. In Colombia, the difference between scenarios can be explained by the virtually unchanging rural-urban gap under FTAA and a major closing of this gap under the full trade liberalization scenario. As before, this is consistent with the factor price changes in table 3.6 and the endowments of poor households shown in table 3.4. For Mexico, only the regional liberalization scenarios are poverty reducing, but multilateral liberalization actually increases poverty. The reason for this result is the previously mentioned preference erosion—with regional liberalization, Mexico only loses its preference margin relative to other Latin American and Caribbean countries. With multilateral liberalization, however, it is now forced to compete on equal grounds with all U.S. and Canadian trading partners.

Perhaps the most persuasive way to highlight the poverty and distributional effects of trade liberalization is to compare the poverty results obtained by a distribution-neutral growth with those generated by the micro-accounting methodology of this chapter. This comparison is summarized in table 3.8 in terms of poverty elasticities. The growth elasticity in table 3.8 is calculated by applying the same (distribution-neutral) growth rate to the incomes of every household in the survey. Thus, this elasticity represents the percentage change in the poverty headcount that corresponds to a 1 percentage point increase in the growth rate in the *average* per capita income in a given country. The trade elasticity, on the other hand, considers changes in

Table 3.8 Income Elasticity of Poverty Headcount

Country	Growth elasticity	Trade elasticity scenario	
		FTAA	FULLIB
Brazil	−1.0	−1.5	−12.7
Chile	−1.6	−1.8	−4.1
Colombia	−0.5	−0.3	−0.7
Mexico	−1.0	0.3	

Source: Authors' calculations.

Note: FTAA = Free Trade Area of the Americas; FULLIB = full trade liberalization. Mexico's full liberalization trade elasticity is not reported because average growth rates are negative.

the shape of the income distribution and is calculated using actual heterogeneous income growth rates for each household.[9] Comparing the two sets of elasticity illustrates three major points: (1) both trade and growth elasticities vary across countries because of differences in initial conditions, such as income inequality; (2) trade elasticities are almost always larger than growth elasticities; (3) trade elasticities are higher when reform is more extensive.

The initial level of inequality, that is, the shape of the initial income distribution, and the level of the poverty line determine how many individuals escape poverty with a 1 percent increase in average incomes. A common but important feature of the elasticities is that they are all rather small, mainly because of the fact that Latin America is a region with high levels of inequality. Cross-country empirical evidence convincingly shows that, all other things being equal, inequality reduces the growth elasticity of poverty reduction (see Ravallion 2001; Bourguignon 2002). Colombia, which shows the smallest growth elasticity in table 3.8, is the country with the highest initial level of inequality. This means that many of its poor people are still quite distant from the poverty line, and a lot of growth is needed to lift them out of poverty.[10] In fact, summary statistics of the income distribution around the poverty line such as the poverty gap and the squared poverty gap are much more relevant for determining the extent of poverty reduction than aggregate inequality measures. The Gini coefficient of Chile is six points below that of Colombia; but even more important, the former's poverty gap and squared poverty gap are much lower than the latter's gaps (table 3.7). This means that the growth of average incomes can be fairly effective in reducing poverty in Chile. Intermediate situations are observed for Mexico and Brazil.

If trade liberalization raises the prices of factors owned by the poor or reduces the prices of the goods consumed by them more than the average, the growth elasticity will underestimate the pro-poor potential of reform. The results of this chapter show that this is the case for Latin America: trade liberalization induces pro-poor growth in most of the scenarios examined here, as evidenced by the fact that trade elasticities are generally higher than growth elasticities. Trade reform generates large poverty reductions for the initially poorer households, namely, those earning large shares of their incomes from agricultural sectors. Much lower trade-induced reductions are observed for households that depend on nonagricultural incomes. These poverty reductions show that trade reform, if implemented successfully, can have a significant pro-poor distributional effect in addition to the positive effect that it has on average incomes. The difference between the growth elasticity in the first column of table 3.8 and the trade elasticities in the right-hand columns represents the equalizing effect of trade reform—that is, the fact that trade liberalization benefits the poor more than the rich (although the growth and the inequality effects are not strictly additive). Table 3.8 also shows that the degree of poverty reduction is positively correlated with the scope of trade liberalization, with deeper reforms generally bringing about larger reductions in poverty. This larger reduction occurs because the poor gain not only when their own countries liberalize, but also when other nations reduce their trade barriers. Thus, the scope and design of trade reforms determine their distributional outcomes.

Conclusion

This chapter has illustrated an application of a relatively simple macro-micro model to the analysis of trade reforms and poverty in Latin America. Several important lessons can be learned from this exercise. First, the chapter provides empirical evidence that trade liberalization, at both the regional and multilateral levels, can be poverty reducing in Latin America. The strength and even sign of the impact depends critically on the design of reforms and the initial situation of a country. Second, the chapter clearly shows that a policy approach that considers only the effects of growth on poverty is misleading when analyzing trade reform shocks. In most cases, the aggregate poverty changes that are calculated based on such an approach are substantially different from the results obtained under a full survey approach that accounts for changes in the distribution. Third, the chapter has illustrated the advantages and flexibility of macro-micro models, including their ability to focus on specific groups of households by income level, location, or any other characteristic.

The empirical analysis in this chapter has shown that the poverty impact of trade reform can vary greatly depending on the type of liberalization and the initial conditions of a country. The results point to large declines in the poverty headcount in Brazil and Chile following both the FTAA and a full global trade reform. In both cases, rural poverty declines the most, and some of the largest income gains are observed among the poorest of the poor. In Colombia, the poverty reduction potential of trade reform is much more modest, partially because of conflicting poverty trends in rural and urban areas. Although both urban poverty and rural poverty are likely to decline marginally following the implementation of the FTAA, rural poverty falls but urban poverty rises as a result of full trade reform. Finally, in the case of Mexico, rural poverty could rise under both reform scenarios, although the increase in rural poverty would be offset by the decline in urban poverty under the FTAA.

The results of this chapter convincingly show that the differences in rural and urban real income growth induce important distributional shifts that must be considered when judging the poverty impact of trade reform. As shown in the calculations of growth and trade elasticities, the distributional consequences of reform can either reinforce or counteract changes in average incomes brought about by trade liberalization. Alternatively, even if the overall impact on poverty is not too large, its dispersion across households (because of their heterogeneity in terms of factor endowments and consumption patterns) is significant, and recognizing this distribution may help when designing compensatory policies. Thus, macro-micro approaches should be a preferred vehicle for comprehensive analysis of the poverty effects of policy because of their ability to take into account both the endowments of the poor and the relative factor price changes induced by trade liberalization.

The particular macro-micro methodology used in this chapter offers a number of important advantages. First, the current approach represents a reasonable approximation to changes in household welfare in the short term. Second, the method is not too computationally intensive and does not require extensive efforts to reconcile the inconsistencies between the macro and micro data. Third, the methodology allows the researcher to exploit the full heterogeneity of the household survey and focus on groups that are not explicitly represented in the macro model, such as rural and urban households.

Conversely, the empirical strategy of this chapter has some potential drawbacks. For example, the limited detail of the macro model allows prices to be determined only at the national level, rather than regional or even local levels. In other words, the pass-through effects of trade shocks to prices are the same in border areas and remote regions. In addition, trade liberalization usually triggers more than just factor price changes, especially in the longer run. In particular, liberalization is likely to induce different types of labor market switching. People migrate from rural to urban areas, and they move between sectors or different occupational categories (from self-employment into wage-employment or vice versa). The simple household survey-based approach used in this chapter does not allow for labor market switching. And this drawback becomes more serious as longer time periods are considered—and as individuals become more mobile across geographic areas, sectors, and occupations. Other long-run implications of trade reform—for example, potential effects on capital accumulation, productivity, and stability of the macro environment—are not considered in this analysis.

Notes

The authors thank Hans Timmer for his comments on this chapter and Abhijeet Dwivedi for his excellent research assistance. An earlier version of this chapter was presented as a paper at the Second CEPII-IDB Conference: Economic Implications of the Doha Development Agenda for Latin America and the Caribbean, October 6–7, 2003, Washington, DC.

1. Although contrary to policy makers' expectations, postreform growth and poverty reduction have been disappointing, a number of studies caution that without reforms the situation would have been even worse. See, for example, ECLAC (1996), Burki and Perry (1997), Easterly, Loayza, and Montiel (1997), IADB (1997), and Lora and Barrera (1997).

2. The Global Trade Analysis Project (GTAP) database and model are disseminated by Center for Global Trade Analysis of Purdue University. See http://www.gtap.org and Hertel (1999).

3. An important assumption in the micro simulations is that price changes are equal across the whole country. This is not always the case and pass-through effects can be different according to the distance from the border, the types of traded goods, and other factors that can be household specific. For an example of an analysis that takes into account geographic price differentials in Mexico, see Nicita (2005).

4. For some of the surveys analyzed in this chapter, these transfers can be finely disaggregated up to the point at which it is possible to identify specific government transfer policies (such as food stamps, health care reimbursements, and other social transfer expenditures).

5. For instance, although in Chile the poverty incidence is almost the same in both rural and urban areas, rural poverty in Brazil is twice the urban rate, and the same ratio is 1.5 in Mexico and Colombia. The distribution of income is much more equal in Chile and Mexico than it is in Colombia. Brazil tends to protect its manufacturing sector, but Mexico's tariffs are heavily biased toward agriculture, and Chile has a uniform tariff structure.

6. For some individuals, this procedure yields negative differences that are set to zero. The proportion of self-employed with an imputed wage

higher than their reported self-employment earnings is significant for Brazil and Colombia but quite low for Chile and Mexico.

7. The rural and urban poverty measurement obtained in this way may be misleading. Price levels and the corresponding purchasing powers in rural and urban sectors of the economy can be quite different; so instead of a single international level applied to the whole population, zone-specific poverty lines could be used to guarantee more accurate estimates.

8. Because the initial level of poverty in Colombia is much higher than in the other countries under consideration, a smaller percentage decrease in the poverty headcount represents a larger reduction in terms of number of people.

9. As for the case of the growth elasticity, to calculate the trade elasticity, the growth rate of the *average* per capita income is normalized to 1 percentage point, although different households experience different growth rates of their incomes.

10. The initial inequality, measured by the Gini coefficient, for each country is as follows: Brazil 59, Chile 57, Colombia 63, and Mexico 53.

References

Adelman, I., and S. Robinson, 1978. *Income Distribution Policy in Developing Countries: A Case Study of Korea.* New York: Oxford University Press.

Bourguignon, François. 2002. "The Growth Elasticity of Poverty Reduction: Explaining Heterogeneity across Countries and Time Periods." In *Growth and Inequality*, eds. T. Eicher and S. Turnovski. Cambridge, MA: MIT Press.

Burki, J., and G. Perry. 1997. *The Long March: A Reform Agenda for Latin America and the Caribbean in the Next Decade.* Washington, DC: World Bank.

Chen, Shaohua, and Martin Ravallion. 2004. "Welfare Impacts of China's Accession to the World Trade Organization." *World Bank Economic Review* 18: 29–57.

Deaton, A. 2004. "Measuring Poverty in a Growing World (or Measuring Growth in a Poor World)." *Review of Economics and Statistics* 87 (1): 1–19.

Easterly, W., N. Loayza, and P. Montiel. 1997. "Has Latin America's Post-Reform Growth Been Disappointing?" *Journal of International Economics* 43: 287–311.

ECLAC (Economic Commission for Latin America and the Caribbean). 1996. "Economic Panorama of Latin America, 1996." United Nations, Santiago, Chile.

Encuesta de Calidad de Vida. 1997. Departamento Administrativo Nacional de Estadística. Bogotá, Colombia.

Encuesta de Caracterización Socioeconómica Nacional. 2000. Ministerio de Hacienda, Gobierno de Chile. Santiago, Chile.

Encuesta Nacional Ingresos y Gastos de los Hogares. 2001. Instituto Nacional de Estadística, Geografía e Informática. Aquascalientes, Mexico.

Harrison, A. 2005. "Globalization and Poverty: An NBER Study." University of California at Berkeley and NBER (Draft). National Bureau of Economic Research.

Harrison, G. W., T. F. Rutherford, D. Tarr, and A. Gurgel. 2003. "Regional, Multilateral, and Unilateral Trade Policies of MERCOSUR for Growth and Poverty Reduction in Brazil." Working Paper No. 3051. World Bank, Washington, DC.

Hertel, T. W. 1999. *Global Trade Analysis: Modeling and Applications.* New York: Cambridge University Press.

Hertel, Thomas W., Maros Ivanic, Paul Preckel, and John Cranfield. 2004. "The Earnings Effects of Multilateral Trade Liberalization: Implications for Poverty in Developing Countries." GTAP Working Paper No. 16 Revised. Center for Global Trade Analysis, Global Trade Analysis Project, Purdue University.

Hertel, T., and L. A. Winters. 2005. *Poverty and the WTO. Impacts of the Doha Development Agenda.* Washington, DC: Palgrave and World Bank.

IADB (Inter-American Development Bank). 1997. "Latin America after a Decade of Reforms: Economic and Social Progress in Latin America, 1997 Report." IADB, Washington, DC.

Ianchovichina, Elena, Alessandro Nicita, and Isidro Soloaga. 2000. "Trade Reform and Poverty: The Case of Mexico." *The World Economy* 25 (7): 945–73.

Löfgren, H., R. Lee Harris, and S. Robinson. 2002. "A Standard Computable General Equilibrium (CGE) Model in GAMS." Microcomputers in Policy Research No. 5. International Food Policy Research Institute, Washington, DC.

Lora, E., and F. Barrera. 1997. "A Decade of Structural Reforms in Latin America: Growth, Productivity and Investment Are Not What They Used to Be." Working Paper No. 350. Inter-American Development Bank, Office of the Chief Economist, Washington, DC.

Lucas, Robert E., Jr. 1976. "Econometric Policy Evaluation: A Critique." *Carnegie-Rochester Conference Series on Public Policy* 1: 19–46.

McCulloch, N., L. A. Winters, and X. Cirera. 2001. "Trade Liberalization and Poverty: A Handbook." U.K. Department for International Development and the Centre for Economic Policy Research, London.

Nicita, A. 2005. "Multilateral Trade Liberalization and Mexican Households: The Effect of the Doha Development Agenda." Policy Research Working Paper No. 3707. World Bank, Washington, DC.

Pesquisa Nacional por Amostra de Domicílios. 2001. Instituto Brasileiro de Geografia e Estatística. Rio de Janeiro, Brazil.

Ravallion, M. 2001. "Growth, Inequality, and Poverty: Looking beyond the Averages." *World Development* 29 (11): 1803–815.

Robilliard, A. S., and S. Robinson. 2003. "Reconciling Household Surveys and National Accounts Data Using a Cross-Entropy Estimation Method." *Review of Income and Wealth* 49 (3): 395–406.

Round, J. I. 2003. "Constructing SAMs for Development Policy Analysis: Lessons Learned and Challenges Ahead." *Economic Systems Research* 15 (2): 161–83.

Rutherford, Thomas, David Tarr, and Oleksandr Shepotylo. 2005. "Poverty Effects of Russia's WTO Accession: Modeling 'Real' Households and Endogenous Productivity Effects." Policy Research Working Paper Series No. 3473. World Bank, Washington, DC.

van der Mensbrugghe, D. 2005. "Prototype Model for Real Computable General Equilibrium Model for the State Development Planning Commission, P. R. China." http://siteresources.worldbank.org/INTPROSPECTS/Resources/334934-1100792545130/LinkageTech Note.pdf.

Winters, L. A., N. McCulloch, and A. McKay. 2004. "Trade Liberalization and Poverty: The Evidence So Far." *Journal of Economic Literature* 42 (1): 72–115.

PART II

Top-Down Approach with Behavioral Micro Simulations

4

Examining the Social Impact of the Indonesian Financial Crisis Using a Macro-Micro Model

Anne-Sophie Robilliard, François Bourguignon, and Sherman Robinson

Determining the social cost of a macroeconomic crisis like the one that struck Indonesia in 1997 is not an easy task. One year after the crisis, the World Bank (1998) argued that if real gross domestic product (GDP) declined by 12 percent in 1998, then the incidence of poverty in Indonesia could affect up to 14.1 percent of the population in 1999—compared with a level of 10.1 percent in mid-1997. Other estimates released at about the same time were more pessimistic. Indonesia's Central Board of Statistics (CBS 1998) predicted a fourfold increase of the poverty headcount (rising from 11.3 percent in 1996 to 39.9 percent by mid-1999), whereas the International Labour Organization (ILO 1998) predicted a sixfold increase (of up to 66.3 percent) by the end of 1999.[1] Ex post estimates were much lower than these dramatic predictions. In a study based on data collected in Indonesia's National Labor Force Surveys (*Survei Angkatan Kerja Nasional,* or SAKERNAS) from August 1997 through 1998, Manning (2000) found that the "traditional" features of the Indonesian labor markets helped cushion the economic shock of the crisis. Finally, more recent estimates published by the World Bank (Suryahadi and others 2000), based on a comparison of the poverty level between two National Social Economics Surveys (*Survei Sosial Ekonomi Nasional,* or SUSENAS), show that the poverty headcount rose from 9.7 percent to 16.3 percent between 1996 and 1999.

These various estimates illustrate the basic methodological ambiguity in predicting either what will happen to the poor just after an economic crisis strikes or in deciphering what did happen ex post (after the fact, based on actual data). In both cases, an explicit counterfactual scenario is needed. In the first case, the scenario must show departures from the precrisis evolution of the economy. In the second case, it must permit assessing what would have happened without the crisis and help disentangle the effects of the crisis from other exogenous shocks that are present in the data—such as the climatic effects of the El Niño drought in the case of Indonesia. This counterfactual scenario may be simple. For instance, it is natural to assume that decreases in household income or consumption depend on the economic activity of the social groups being considered. A scenario would thus consist of a set of predictions about the rate of growth of either the various sectors of the economy or the aggregate income of the various factors of production. The early rough estimates of the effect of the Indonesian crisis on poverty were based on this type of approach. But the divergence between those estimates suggests that establishing even a simple counterfactual scenario of this type is not easy—and requires more than a rough model of the economy.

The use of more rigorous multisector models would probably yield more consensual predictions for the economy as a whole and for its various sectors and factors of production. It is not clear, however, that this would also result in satisfactory predictions for the distribution of income and poverty. Associating household incomes with sector activity or factor remuneration rates is, in effect, equivalent to defining representative household groups (RHGs) that derive income from a predetermined combination of factors. Models that incorporate several sectors and several RHGs with some exogenous distribution *within* those groups have been used for some time now—see, for example, Derviş, de Melo, and Robinson (1982) and the survey by Adelman and Robinson (1989). Whether these models are used to analyze either structural reforms like trade regimes or short-run macroeconomic issues—as in Bourguignon, Branson, and de Melo (1992)—this approach is problematic, as well. In particular, by ignoring changes in the distribution of income *within* RHGs, these models may ignore major sources of change in the distribution of economic welfare and poverty. In most studies of changes in inequality over time,[2] it is indeed shown that changes in the relative income and weight of a few groups of households with identical selected characteristics leave a sizable unexplained residual. Focusing on the inequality *between* representative groups (as multisector, multihousehold models presently do) may thus lead to a biased view of the impact of macro or structural policies on the distribution of income.

A simple example may explain the nature of the problem. A majority of households in Indonesia generate income from various sources: (1) salaried employment of some members in the formal sector, (2) wage work in the informal sector of others, and (3) self-employment of yet another group. If RHGs are defined, as is typically done, by the sector of activity and employment status of the household heads (small farmers, urban unskilled workers in the formal sector, and so forth), it may not be too much of a problem to account for this multiplicity of income sources. Thus, the change in the inequality *between* the groups of small farmers and urban unskilled workers in the formal sector may account for the fact that both groups have different secondary sources of income—because of differences in household composition, labor supply behavior, and the occupation of secondary members. Two difficulties arise, however. First, say that a macroeconomic crisis or a trade reform modifies the number of unskilled urban workers employed in the formal sector. What should be done with the number of households with households heads in that occupation? Should it be modified? If so, from which groups must new households in that RHG be taken, or to which groups should they be allocated? First, could this operation be completed based on the assumption that the distribution of income within all RHGs remains the same? Second, assuming that changes in occupation affect only secondary members and not household heads (so that RHGs are unchanged), is it reasonable to assume that all households in a group are affected in the same way by this change in the activity of some of their group members? A secondary member may move out of the formal sector and back into family self-employment, but this may happen only in a subgroup of households within a given representative group, which may seriously affect the distribution within this group. It is phenomena of this kind that may help explain changes in the "within" component of inequality decomposition exercises. But these changes are ignored in multisector, multihousehold group models.

This chapter presents a new approach that can be used to quantify the effects of macroeconomic shocks on poverty and inequality by overcoming difficulties such as these.[3] This new approach combines a micro simulation model with a standard multisector computable general equilibrium (CGE) model. The two models are used in a sequential fashion to simulate the full distributional impact of a financial crisis and generate meaningful counterfactual scenarios.[4] The CGE model is based on a standard social accounting matrix (SAM) and is intended to capture both the structural features of an economy and the general equilibrium effects of the macroeconomic constraints that arise from macro shocks. The micro simulation model is based on a subsample of the 1996 SUSENAS survey and simulates income generation mechanisms for approximately 10,000 Indonesian households. The two models are treated separately. The macro (or CGE) model communicates with the micro model by generating a vector of prices, wages, and aggregate employment variables that correspond to a given shock or policy. The micro model is then used to generate changes in individual wages, self-employment incomes, and employment status in a way that is consistent with the set of macro variables fed by the macro model. When this is done, the full distribution of real household income corresponding to the simulated shock or policy may be evaluated. This framework is designed to capture important channels through which a financial crisis of the type that struck Indonesia in 1997 may affect household incomes. Its main focus is the structure and functioning of labor markets, but this approach also captures part of the expenditure-side story by taking into account any increases in the relative price of food.

The following section shows the structure of the micro simulation module and explains how it is linked to the CGE part of the model. The general features of the CGE model are then discussed, followed by scenarios, simulation results, and conclusions.

The Micro Simulation Model

This section briefly describes the specification of the household income generation model used for micro simulation and then focuses on how consistency is achieved between micro simulation and the predictions of the CGE model. A more detailed discussion of the specification and econometric estimates of the various equations of the household income generation model and simulation methodology can be found in Alatas and Bourguignon (2005).[5]

In the notations used in the remainder of chapter 4, the household income generation model for household m with working-age members k_m consists of the following set of equations:

(4.1) $\text{Log } w_{mi} = \alpha_{g(mi)} + x_{mi}\beta_{g(mi)} + v_{mi}$ $i = 1, \ldots k_m$

(4.2) $\text{Log } y_m = \gamma_{f(m)} + Z_m\delta_{f(m)} + \lambda_{f(m)}N_m + \eta_m$

$$(4.3) \qquad Y_m = \frac{1}{P_m} \left(\sum_{i=1}^{k_m} w_{mi} IW_{mi} + y_m \, \mathrm{Ind}(N_m > 0) + y_{0m} \right)$$

$$(4.4) \qquad\qquad\qquad P_m = \sum_{k=1}^{K} s_{mk} p_k$$

$$(4.5) \quad IW_{mi} = \mathrm{Ind}\left[a^w_{h(mi)} + z_{mi} b^w_{h(mi)} + u^w_{mi} \right.$$
$$\left. > \mathrm{Sup}\left(0, \, a^s_{h(mi)} + z_{mi} b^s_{h\,(mi)} + u^s_{mi}\right) \right]$$

$$(4.6) \qquad N_m = \sum_{i=1}^{k_m} \mathrm{Ind}\left[a^s_{h(mi)} + z_{mi} b^s_{h(mi)} + u^s_{mi} \right.$$
$$\left. > \mathrm{Sup}\left(0, \, a^w_{h(mi)} + z_{mi} b^w_{h(mi)} + u^w_{mi}\right) \right].$$

Equation (4.1) expresses the (log) earnings of member i of household m as a function of that member's personal characteristics, x. The latter include age, education level, and geographic region. The residual term, v_{mi}, describes the effects of unobserved earning determinants. This earning function is defined separately on various "segments" of the labor market defined by gender, skill level (less than secondary or more than primary education), and area (urban/rural). Thus, $g(mi)$ is an index function that indicates the labor market segment to which member i in household m belongs.

Equation (4.2) is the (net) income function associated with self-employment, or small entrepreneurial activity, which includes the opportunity cost of household labor and profit. This function is defined at the household level and depends both on the number of household members actually involved in that activity, N_m, and on some household characteristics, Z_m. These characteristics include area of residence, the age and schooling of the household head, and land size for farmers. The residual term, η_m, summarizes the effects of unobserved determinants of self-employment income. A different function is used depending on whether the household is involved in farm or nonfarm activity. This is exogenous and is defined by whether or not the household has access to land, as represented by the index function $f(m)$.

Equation (4.3) is an accounting identity that defines total household real income, Y_m, as the sum of wage income of its members, profit from self-employment, and (exogenous) nonlabor income, y_{0m}. In this equation, the notation IW_{mi} stands for a dummy variable that is equal to unity if member i is a wage worker and zero otherwise. Thus wages are summed over only those household members actually engaged in wage work. Likewise, income from self-employment has to be taken into account only if at least one member of the household is engaged in self-employment activity ($N_m > 0$). Total income is then deflated by a household-specific consumer price index (CPI), P_m, which is derived from the observed budget shares, s_{mk}, of household m and the price, p_k, of the various consumption goods, k, in the model—equation (4.4).

Equations (4.5) and (4.6) represent the occupational choices made by household members. This choice is discrete. Each individual must choose from three alternatives: being inactive, a wage worker, or self-employed. This choice is represented within a discrete utility-maximizing framework. The utility associated with the first alternative (inactivity) is arbitrarily set to zero, whereas the utility of being a wage worker or self-employed is a linear function of a set of individual and household characteristics, z_{mi}. The intercept of these functions has a component, a^w or a^s, that is common to all individuals, and an idiosyncratic term, u_{mi}, which represents unobserved determinants of occupational choices. The coefficients of individual characteristics, z_{mi}, b^w, or b^s, are common to all individuals. However, they may differ across demographic groups indexed by $h(mi)$. For instance, occupational choice behavior, as described by coefficients a^w, a^s, b^w, and b^s, may be different for household heads, spouses, and male or female children. The constants may also be demography-specific.

Given this specification, an individual will prefer wage work if the utility associated with that activity is higher than that associated with the two other activities. This is the meaning of equation (4.5). Likewise, the number of self-employed workers in a household is the number of individuals for whom the utility of self-employment is higher than that of the two alternatives, as represented in equation (4.6).[6]

The model is now complete. Overall, it defines the total real income of a household as a nonlinear function of the observed characteristics of household members (x_{mi} and z_{mi}), some characteristics of the household (Z_m), its budget shares (s_m), and unobserved characteristics (v_{mi}, η_m, u_{mi}^w, and u_{mi}^s). This function depends on five sets of parameters: (1) for the earning functions (α^g and β^g), for each labor market segment, g; (2) for the self-employment income functions (γ^f, δ^f, and λ^f); (3) for the farm or nonfarm sector, f; (4) for the utility of the alternative occupational choices (a_h^w, b_h^w, a_h^s, and b_h^s), for the various demographic groups, h; and (5) for the vector of prices, p. As is shown later, it is through several of these parameters that the results of the CGE part of the model may be transmitted to the micro module.

The micro simulation model gives a rather complete description of household income generation mechanisms by focusing on both earning and occupational choice determinants. However, a number of assumptions about the functioning of the labor market are incorporated in this specification. The fact that labor supply is considered to be a discrete choice between either inactivity or full-time work for wages (or for self-employment income) within the household calls for two sets of remarks. First, the assumption that individuals are inactive or work full time is essentially justified by the fact that no information on the number of hours worked is available in the micro data source used to estimate the benchmark set of the model's coefficients. As a practical matter, this implies that estimated individual earning functions—equation (4.1)—and profit functions—equation (4.2)—may incorporate some labor supply dimension. Second, distinguishing between wage work and self-employment is implicitly equivalent to assuming that the Indonesian labor market is imperfectly competitive. If this were not the case, then returns to labor would be the same in both types of occupation; and self-employment income would be different from wage income only because it would incorporate the returns to nonlabor assets being used. The specification that has been selected is justified, in part, by the fact that assets used in self-employment are not observed, so one cannot distinguish between self-employment income derived from labor and that derived from other assets. But it is also justified by the fact that the labor market may be segmented (in the sense that labor returns are not equalized across wage work and self-employment). There may be various reasons for this. On the one hand, there may be rationing in the wage labor market. People unable to find jobs as wage workers move into self-employment, which is a kind of shelter. On the other hand, there may be externalities that make working within and outside the household imperfect substitutes. These two interpretations are consistent with the way in which the labor market is represented in the CGE part of the model.[7]

It is now time to consider how the link is made between the CGE part and the micro part of the model—and how the effects of macroeconomic shocks and policies are simulated on each household represented in the database. The principle behind these simulations is quite simple. It associates macroeconomic shocks and policies simulated in the CGE part of the model with changes in the set of coefficients of the household income generation model—equations (4.1)–(4.6). With a new set of coefficients (α^g, β^g, γ^f, δ^f, λ^f, a_h^w, b_h^w, a_h^s, b_h^s) and the observed and unobserved individual and household characteristics (x_{mi}, z_{mi}, Z_m, s_m, v_{mi}, η_m, u_{mi}^w, u_{mi}^s), these equations allow one to compute the occupational status of all household members, their earnings, their self-employment income, and finally, the total real income of their household. But this association must be done in a consistent way. Consistency with the equilibrium of aggregate markets in the CGE model requires that (1) changes in average earnings (with respect to the benchmark in the micro simulation) must be equal to changes in wage rates in the CGE model for each segment of the market for wage labor; (2) changes in self-employment income in the micro simulation must be equal to changes in informal sector income per worker in the CGE model; (3) changes in the number of wage workers and those self-employed by labor market segment in the micro simulation model must match those same changes in the CGE model; and (4) changes in the consumption price vector, p, must be consistent with the CGE model.

The link between the CGE part of the model and the micro part is obtained through the resolution of the following system of equations:

$$\sum_m \sum_{i,g(mi)=G} \text{Ind}\left[a^{w^*}_{h(mi)} + z_{mi}\hat{b}^w_{h(mi)} + \hat{u}^w_{mi} \right.$$
$$\left. > \text{Sup}(0, a^{s^*}_{h(mi)} + z_{mi}\hat{b}^s_{h(mi)} + \hat{u}^s_{mi})\right] = E^*_G$$

$$\sum_m \sum_{i,g(mi)=G} \text{Ind}\left[a^{s^*}_{h(mi)} + z_{mi}\hat{b}^s_{h(mi)} + \hat{u}^s_{mi} \right.$$
$$\left. > \text{Sup}(0, a^{w^*}_{h(mi)} + z_{mi}\hat{b}^w_{h(mi)} + \hat{u}^w_{mi})\right] = S^*_G$$

$$\sum_m \sum_{i,g(mi)=G} \text{Exp}\left(\alpha^*_G + x_{mi}\hat{\beta}_G + \hat{v}_{mi}\right) \text{Ind}\left[a^{w^*}_{h(mi)} + z_{mi}\hat{b}^w_{h(mi)} + \hat{u}^w_{mi} \right.$$
$$\left. > \text{Sup}(0, a^{s^*}_{h(mi)} + z_{mi}\hat{b}^s_{h(mi)} + \hat{u}^s_{mi})\right] = w^*_G$$

$$\sum_m \sum_{i,f(m)=F} \text{Exp}\left(\gamma^*_F + Z_m\hat{\delta}_F + \hat{\lambda}_F\hat{N}_m + \hat{\eta}_m\right) \text{Ind}\left[N_m > 0\right] = I^*_F,$$

with $\quad \hat{N}_m = \sum_i \text{Ind}\left[a^{s^*}_{h(mi)} + z_{mi}\hat{b}^s_{h(mi)} + \hat{u}^s_{mi} \right.$
$$\left. > \text{Sup}(0, a^{w^*}_{h(mi)} + z_{mi}\hat{b}^w_{h(mi)} + \hat{u}^w_{mi})\right],$$

where the unknowns are α^{g^*}, γ^{f^*}, $a^{w^*}_h$, and $a^{s^*}_h$. This system of equations has as many equations as unknowns and has a unique solution that can be obtained through standard Gauss-Newton techniques.[8] Once the solution is obtained, it is a simple matter to compute the new income of each household in the sample, according to the model in equations (4.1)–(4.6), with the new set of coefficients α^{g^*}, γ^{f^*}, $a^{w^*}_h$ and $a^{s^*}_h$, and then to analyze the modification that this implies for the overall distribution of income.

The justification for using the intercepts is that it implies a "neutrality" of the changes being made with respect to individual or household characteristics. For example, changing the intercepts of the log earning equations generates a proportional change of all earnings in a labor market segment, regardless of individual characteristics outside those that define the segments (skill, gender, and geographic area). The same is true of the change in the intercept of the log self-employment income functions. A similar argument applies to the criteria associated with the various occupational choices. Indeed, it is easily shown that changing the intercepts of the multilogit model implies the following neutrality property: the relative change in the ex ante probability that an individual has some occupation depends only on the initial ex ante probabilities of the various occupational choices, rather than on individual characteristics.

In the Indonesian case, the number of variables that allow the micro and the macro parts of the overall model to communicate, that is, the vector $(E_G^*, S_G^*, w_G^*, I_F^*, q^*)$, is equal to 26 plus the number of consumption goods used in defining the household-specific CPI deflator. The labor market has eight segments. The employment requirements for each segment in the formal (wage work) and informal (self-employment) sectors (E_G^* and S_G^*) lead to 16 restrictions. In addition, there are eight wage rates in the formal sector (w_G^*) and two levels of self-employment income (I_F^*) in the formal and the informal sectors. Thus, simulated changes in the distribution of income implied by the CGE part of the model are obtained through a procedure that allows numerous degrees of freedom.

Two elements must be added to describe the full scope of the model. First, the household-specific price index, P_m, is based on the disaggregation of expenditure into only two goods, food and nonfood. This disaggregation is the most relevant one for the analysis of the consequences of the Indonesian financial crisis. Second, other incomes, y_{0m}, are considered as exogenous (in real terms) in all simulations. They include housing and land rents, dividends, royalties, imputed rents from self-occupied housing, and transfers from other households and institutions. It would have been possible to endogenize some of these items in the CGE model, but this was not done.

The CGE Model

The CGE model presented in this chapter is based on a 1995 SAM. The SAM has been disaggregated using cross-entropy estimation methods (Robinson, Cattaneo, and El-Said 2001) to include

38 sectors, 14 goods, 14 factors of production (8 labor categories and 6 types of capital), and 10 household types, as well as the usual accounts for aggregate agents (firms, government, rest of the world, savings-investment). The CGE model starts from the standard neoclassical specification in Derviş, de Melo, and Robinson (1982) but also incorporates the disaggregation of production sectors into formal and informal activities and associated labor market imperfections.

Markets for goods, factors, and foreign exchange are assumed to respond to changing demand and supply conditions, which are, in turn, affected by government policies, the external environment, and other exogenous influences. The model is Walrasian in that it determines only relative prices and other endogenous real variables in the economy. Financial mechanisms are modeled implicitly, and only their real effect is accounted for in a simplified way. Sectoral product prices, factor prices, and the real exchange rate are defined relative to the producer price index of goods for domestic use, which serves as the *numeraire*. The exchange rate represents the relative price of tradable goods with regard to nontraded goods (in units of domestic currency per unit of foreign currency).

Activities and Commodities

Indonesia's economy is dualistic, and the model captures this by distinguishing between formal and informal "activities" in each sector. Both subsectors differ in the type of factors they use—a distinction that allows for treating formal and informal factor markets differently. Informal and formal sectors are further differentiated by the fact that formal sectors are assumed to rely on foreign credit to operate, whereas informal sectors do not.

For all activities, the production technology is represented by a set of nested constant elasticity of substitution (CES) value added functions and fixed (Leontief) intermediate input coefficients. On the demand side, imperfect substitutability is assumed between formal and informal products. Thus, consumers demand an aggregate of the formal and informal products. Domestic prices of commodities are flexible, varying to clear markets in a competitive setting where individual suppliers and demanders are price-takers.

Following Armington (1969), the model assumes imperfect substitutability, for each good, between the domestic commodity (which itself results from a combination of formal and informal activities) and imports. What is demanded is a composite good, which is a CES aggregation of imports and domestically produced goods. For export commodities, the allocation of domestic output between exports and domestic sales is determined on the assumption that domestic producers maximize profits subject to imperfect transformability between these two alternatives. The composite production good is a constant elasticity of transformation (CET) aggregation of sectoral exports and domestically consumed products.

These assumptions of imperfect substitutability and transformability grant the domestic price system some degree of autonomy from international prices and serve to dampen export and import responses to changes in the producer environment. Such treatment of exports and imports provides a continuum of tradability and allows two-way trade at the sector level—which reflects what is observed empirically at the level of aggregation of the model.

Factors of Production

Eight labor categories are included in the Indonesia CGE model: urban male unskilled, urban male skilled, urban female unskilled, urban female skilled, rural male unskilled, rural male skilled, rural female unskilled, and rural female skilled. The designations male and female, as well as skilled and unskilled labor, are assumed to be imperfect substitutes in the production activity of urban or rural sectors.

In addition, labor markets are assumed to be segmented between formal and informal sectors. In the formal sector labor markets, imperfect competition mechanisms are assumed to result in some increasing wage-employment curve; and real wages are defined by the intersection of that curve and competitive labor demand. Informal sector labor is equivalent to self-employment, and wages in that sector are set to absorb any labor not employed in the formal sectors. Wages adjust to clear all labor markets in the informal sectors, whereas employment adjusts in the formal sectors.

Land appears as a factor of production in the agricultural sectors. Only one type of land is considered in the model. It is competitively allocated among the different crop sectors so that marginal value added is equalized across activities.

Capital markets are segmented into six categories: owner-occupied housing, other unincorporated rural capital, other unincorporated urban capital, domestic private incorporated capital, public capital, and foreign capital. Given the short-term perspective of the model, it is assumed that capital is fixed in each activity.

The model also incorporates working capital requirements by all sectors. Sectors demand domestic working capital in proportion to their demands for domestically produced intermediate inputs. They also demand working capital denominated in foreign exchange in proportion to their demands for imported intermediate inputs. Informal sectors are assumed not to require any imported intermediate inputs.

Working capital is treated as a factor input that is strictly complementary to physical capital. The model incorporates a nested production function in all sectors, with aggregate "capital" consisting of an aggregation of physical capital, domestic working capital, and foreign working capital (foreign exchange). Both types (domestic and foreign) of working capital are assumed to be required in fixed proportions to physical capital. When the supplies of aggregate domestic and foreign working capital are reduced (as an effect of the financial crisis), they are assumed to be competitively allocated across sectors, so that their marginal revenue product is the same. Because physical capital is fixed, this causes capacity underutilization in some sectors.

The effect of this treatment is to make aggregate output sensitive to any reduction in the supply of working capital. With cuts in working capital, the utilization of physical capital will also decline.[9] The sector impact depends on a sector's dependence on intermediate inputs, both domestic and imported.

Households

The disaggregation of households in the CGE model is not central to this discussion, because changes in factor prices are passed on directly to the micro simulation model without use of the RHGs used in the original SAM. Consumption demand by households at the CGE level is determined by the linear expenditure system (LES), in which the marginal budget share is fixed and each commodity has a minimum consumption (subsistence) level.

Macro Closure Rules

Equilibrium in a CGE model is defined by a set of constraints that need to be satisfied by the economic system but are not directly considered in the decisions of micro agents (Robinson 1989). Aside from the supply-demand balances in product and factor markets, three macroeconomic balances are specified in the Indonesia CGE model: (1) the fiscal balance, with government savings equal to the difference between government revenue and spending; (2) the external trade balance (in goods and nonfactor services), which implicitly equates the supply and demand for foreign exchange (flows, not stocks, because the model has no assets or asset markets); and (3) savings-investment balance. Practically, a balanced macro closure is used, in which aggregate investment and government spending are assumed to be in a fixed proportion to total absorption. Any shock affecting total absorption is thus assumed to be shared proportionately among government spending, aggregate investment, and aggregate private consumption. While simple, this closure effectively assumes a successful structural adjustment program in which a macro shock is assumed not to cause particular actors (government, consumers, and industry) to bear a disproportionate share of the adjustment burden.

Scenarios and Simulations

As mentioned earlier, both parts of the model are handled separately, with the macro level communicating with the micro part through a vector of "linking variables" (for prices, wages, and aggregate employment). The overall structure is top-down in that there is no feedback from the micro model back to the macro CGE model. This top-down sequential structure allows running various kinds of experiments. In the first set of experiments (labeled "historical simulation"), historical changes in the linking variables are derived from price statistics and labor market surveys taken during and after the crisis and fed directly into the micro model, without any use of the macro CGE model. Thus, this historical simulation is essentially meant to test the capacity of the micro model to generate income distribution predictions on the basis of a few observed macro indicators. In the second set of simulations (labeled "policy simulations"), the value of linking variables is taken from the results of the CGE model. These simulations are used to decompose the historical shock into various elementary components.

Time Horizon

The question of time horizon requires comment. The financial crisis that struck Indonesia during the summer of 1997, and the resulting turmoil, spanned approximately 20 months—extending until March 1999, when the first signs of output recovery were recorded.[10] Given the equilibrium nature of the macro framework and of the linking variables between the macro and micro models discussed in this chapter, the crisis is not tracked month by month. Instead, the impact of the shock is analyzed using comparative statics. The deviations from base values used as historical references are thus computed for a period extending from July–August 1997 to September–October 1998. The latest date corresponds to the peak of the crisis with respect to both macroeconomic indicators (Azis, Azis, and Thorbecke 2001) and poverty indicators (Suryahadi and others 2000).

The analysis of this short-term shock in a CGE framework is made possible by imposing a number of rigidities in the specification of factor markets, as shown earlier. The base year for the macro model is the 1995 SAM, with both the consumption structure and the factor disaggregation based on the 1996 SUSENAS. The sample used for the micro simulation is a subsample of the 1996 SUSENAS. Some inconsistency could arise between the macro and the micro parts of the model because they do not refer to the same year. In fact, due to the sequential nature of the framework used in this chapter, full consistency is not required between the macro and the micro sides of the model. Indeed, all of the analysis using this model may be performed in terms of deviations from benchmarks that may not fit perfectly together.[11]

Historical Changes in Poverty

As mentioned earlier, diverse estimates have been published on the before-and-after impact of the Indonesian financial crisis on poverty and income distribution. The results reported by Suryahadi and others (2000) are used as a reference to analyze the historical change in poverty and income distribution. These authors used various household surveys to compute changes in real income over the period from 1996 to 1999. Although poverty rates derived from SUSENAS data would be consistent with the household sample used in the model presented in this chapter, changes derived from the Indonesian Family Life Survey (IFLS), adjusted to achieve consistency with other estimates (Suryahadi and others 2000), were used as a general benchmark. This choice is justified, on the one hand, by the fact that the SUSENAS (conducted every three years) does not allow isolation of the crisis period and, on the other hand, by the fact that the second wave of the IFLS was specifically designed to help determine how the crisis affected welfare (Frankenberg, Thomas, and Beegle 1999). Based on IFLS estimates adjusted by Suryahadi and others (2000), poverty incidence is shown to have increased by 164 percent between September 1997 and October 1998.[12]

Because the IFLS results reported by Suryahadi and others (2000) do not distinguish between the urban and the rural sectors, the present authors report estimates based on both the 1996 and 1999 SUSENASs—to compare how urban and rural households

Table 4.1 Evolution of Poverty in Indonesia, 1996–99

Households/indicator	1996	1999	Percentage change
All			
Headcount index (P0)	9.75	16.27	66.8
Poverty gap index (P1)	1.55	2.79	80.2
Poverty severity index (P2)	0.39	0.75	91.9
Urban			
Headcount index (P0)	3.82	9.63	152.3
Poverty gap index (P1)	0.53	1.51	183.0
Poverty severity index (P2)	0.12	0.37	201.6
Rural			
Headcount index (P0)	13.10	20.56	56.9
Poverty gap index (P1)	2.12	3.61	70.5
Poverty severity index (P2)	0.54	0.99	83.6

Sources: SUSENAS 1996 and 1999, cited by Suryahadi and others (2000).

fared over the period (table 4.1). The overall increase in poverty appears to be much smaller than the one that Suryahadi and others (2000) obtained using IFLS data. This result is consistent with the difference in the time coverage of both sources, because poverty decreased with the recovery after October 1998. The data in table 4.1 show that poverty increased more in the urban sector than in the rural sector. Nevertheless, poverty remains higher in the rural sector because of the initial disadvantage of that sector. The strong increases in the poverty gap indicator (P1) and the poverty severity index (P2) also show that from 1996 to 1999, the situation deteriorated more for the poorest of the poor.

Historical Experiment

The first experiment, called "historical," uses historical vectors of the linking variables (prices, wages, and aggregate employment changes) to feed into the micro model. Changes in the last two sets of variables, shown in table 4.2, are derived from the comparison of two SAKERNASs (for 1997 and 1998). Consumer price changes (not reported) are taken from reports by Badan Pusat Statistik (BPS). SAKERNASs do not indicate changes in self-employment incomes. The authors assume that these are equal to changes in wages; but because of the effect of increases in relative output prices, this assumption is probably unsatisfactory in the case of rural self-employment incomes. A comparison of the 1997 and 1998 employment surveys shows a dramatic drop in real wages

Table 4.2 Evolution of Occupational Choices and Wages by Segment, 1997–98

Segment	Inactive	Wage worker	Self-employed	Nominal wage	Real Wage
Urban male unskilled	−0.9	−6.5	5.7	8.2	−40.8
Urban male skilled	11.9	−12.7	9.9	5.3	−42.3
Urban female unskilled	−2.6	5.1	5.9	21.8	−33.4
Urban female skilled	5.9	−15.5	2.3	10.3	−39.6
Rural male unskilled	−1.8	−13.6	5.1	27.9	−30.0
Rural male skilled	2.5	−13.3	9.3	16.8	−36.1
Rural female unskilled	−5.5	0.0	7.5	47.3	−19.4
Rural female skilled	2.7	−14.3	3.4	12.2	−38.6
All segments	−0.3	−10.2	5.8	11.7	−38.9

Sources: SAKERNAS 1997 and 1998; authors' calculations.

Note: Numbers in the first three columns are percentage changes in proportions. Real wage is equal to nominal wage deflated by consumer price index base year 1996 = 100.

and an important shift out of wage work and into self-employment over the period. It also suggests that overall inactivity did not increase significantly. The picture differs slightly, however, across labor types. The movement out of wage work and into self-employment activities is observed for all but two categories, urban and rural unskilled females. Concerning the employment rate, although stable overall, it decreases for all skilled categories but increases for all unskilled categories.[13]

Table 4.3 shows the results on poverty and inequality derived from the micro model (under the preceding assumptions). They show a 238.6 percent increase in poverty, higher than the historical change of 164 percent reported by Suryahadi and others (2000) based on the comparison of the 1997 and 1998 IFLS. This overestimation can be explained by the simulation, which ignores the fact that self-employment incomes decreased less than real wages. The poverty increase appears to be fueled by the dramatic income shock—a 40.4 percent drop in mean per capita income. Results also show an increase in inequality driven by the increase of *within-sector* inequality: although rural and urban mean per capita incomes converge (that is, the fall in per capita income in the urban sector is bigger than in the rural sector, −44.8 percent and −26.5 percent, respectively), the decrease in *between-sector* inequality does not compensate for the increases within the urban and rural sectors. In terms of the rural-urban divide, the results appear consistent with the historical record shown in table 4.1, although those data refer to a distinct time period.

Table 4.3 Historical Simulation Results

Income and relative price changes	All households		Urban households		Rural households	
	Base	Percentage change	Base	Percentage change	Base	Percentage change
Per capita income[a] (Rp, thousands[b])	121.1	−40.4	171.0	−44.3	90.6	−35.9
Entropy index 0 (×100)	35.5	2.7	38.7	10.2	25.6	9.0
Entropy index 1 (×100)	49.3	0.9	53.9	8.7	33.1	4.9
Gini index (%)	45.6	0.2	47.5	3.9	38.7	2.9
Headcount index (P0)	9.2	238.6	4.0	432.9	12.4	200.4
Poverty gap index (P1)	2.2	340.5	1.0	528.8	2.9	299.0
Poverty severity index (P2)	0.9	408.8	0.4	648.5	1.2	355.9

Source: Results from the authors' micro simulation module, using historical changes in prices, wages, and occupational choices by segment (see table 4.2). Self-employment income is assumed to drop by the same magnitude as male unskilled wage, that is, −40 percent in the urban sector and −30 percent in the rural sector.

Note: Base values are used for the Base column and percentage change for other simulations.

a. Per capita income is total monthly income.

b. Rp = rupiah, Indonesia's official currency.

The poverty increase in the urban sector is much higher than in the rural sector, but poverty remains higher in the rural sector.

These different results show the capacity of the micro simulation framework to generate plausible income distribution predictions on the basis of a few observed macro indicators.

CGE Experiments

In the following experiments, the vector of linking variables fed into the micro simulation is derived from the results of the CGE model. The set of experiments presented attempts to reproduce and decompose the effect of the crisis within the framework of the CGE model.

The base CGE scenario seeks to reproduce the evolution of the Indonesian economy between 1997 and 1998 in terms of changes in employment, wages, and macroeconomic aggregates. The most important external shocks during that period are the financial crisis and the extended drought caused by El Niño. The drought is simulated through a negative 5 percent shock on the total productivity factor in agricultural sectors. A 25 percent increase in the marketing cost of food is assumed. This increase reflects the fact that traders, more than producers, are expected to benefit from the food price increase. The financial crisis is simulated through a combination of different shocks. It is assumed that the need to adjust the current account led to a real devaluation that is simulated through a 30 percent decrease in the exogenous foreign saving flows to the economy (SIMDEV scenario). As a result of the devaluation, all sectors experienced a "credit crunch," simulated through a cut in the supply of working capital. As shown earlier, two types of working capital are considered. In a first stage, the impact of a 25 percent cut in the availability of foreign working capital is examined in combination with the real devaluation described above (the DEVCCF scenario). In a second stage, the impact of a 20 percent cut in the availability of domestic credit is considered (the FINCRI scenario). Because the domestic credit crunch shock is viewed as stemming from the foreign credit crunch, it is simulated in combination with the two previous components of the financial crisis. The resulting simulation can then be analyzed as mimicking a "pure" financial crisis shock, without any other historical shock. The effect of the El Niño drought is first simulated alone (SIMELN scenario) and then in combination with the financial crisis, thus yielding something that should be close to what actually happened in Indonesia between 1997 and 1998 (the SIMALL scenario).

Table 4.4 shows how different elements of the crisis contributed to the total negative real GDP shock. The historical simulation captures the main changes observed over the period: a 14.4 percent drop in GDP, a fall in imports and a surge of exports, an increase in the relative price of food commodities, and a drop in real wages. Combining the different shocks shows that the credit crunch is the major force explaining the collapse of GDP, while the drought combined with increases in the marketing cost of food appears to be the main driving force behind increases in the relative price of food commodities.

In terms of the impact of the macro shocks on poverty and income distribution, the results in table 4.5 show that the modeling exercise yields a 143.4 percent increase in the poverty headcount ratio when all components of the crisis are taken into account (SIMALL). This surge in poverty appears to be fueled by the drop in the average income per capita and by an important increase in inequality indicators. Both the financial crisis and the El Niño drought contribute to the negative income impact and the increase in inequality.

In terms of the rural-urban divide, the CGE experiments presented in this chapter capture (to some extent) the differences in per capita income changes shown in the historical simulation. This

Table 4.4 Simulation Results: Macro Aggregates

Indicator	BASE	SIMELN	SIMDEV	DEVCCF	FINCRI	SIMALL
GDP at factor costs (Rp, thousands of billions)[a]	535.6	−0.5	−0.9	−10.7	−14.1	−14.4
Exports (Rp, thousands of billions)	122.7	−0.4	28.8	19.4	15.4	13.1
Imports (Rp, thousands of billions)	126.8	−0.3	−19.2	−28.4	−32.2	−34.4
Exchange rate	1.0	−5.1	31.8	27.3	27.2	24.3
Food/nonfood terms of trade	1.0	27.3	15.4	−4.2	−3.3	21.0
Incorporated capital income[b]	1.0	−13.2	7.8	43.0	32.2	19.7
Agricultural self-employment income[c]	1.6	−5.9	8.2	−8.0	−18.5	−23.4
Nonagricultural self-employment income	4.5	−19.9	−4.1	−16.1	−16.1	−30.7
Skilled labor wage[c]	4.9	−17.5	−12.8	−37.5	−42.2	−50.9
Unskilled labor wage[b]	2.7	−14.5	−12.6	−32.3	−35.5	−43.0

Source: Results from the authors' CGE module.

Note: Base values for BASE column and percentage change for other simulations; SIMELN = El Niño drought; SIMDEV = real devaluation; DEVCCF = real devaluation + foreign credit crunch; FINCRI = real devaluation + foreign credit crunch + domestic credit crunch; SIMALL = real devaluation + foreign credit crunch + domestic credit crunch + El Niño drought; GDP = gross domestic product.

a. Rp = rupiah, Indonesia's official currency.

b. Incorporated capital income includes private, public, and foreign capital income.

c. Self-employment and wage incomes are equal to value added divided by quantity of labor units in the social accounting matrix.

Table 4.5 Simulation Results: Per Capita Income, Inequality, and Poverty Indicators

Indicator	BASE	SIMELN	SIMDEV	DEVCCF	FINCRI	SIMALL
All areas						
Per capita income[a]						
(Rp, thousands[b])	121.1	−12.4	−5.1	−16.3	−19.5	−27.9
Entropy index 0 (×100)	35.5	2.9	1.4	−3.0	1.3	5.2
Entropy index 1 (×100)	49.2	4.5	1.7	−2.9	1.0	6.7
Gini index (%)	45.5	1.3	0.3	−1.8	0.2	2.2
Headcount index (P0)	9.2	49.7	17.1	51.6	80.2	143.4
Poverty gap index (P1)	2.2	54.6	25.2	61.9	101.0	182.0
Poverty severity index (P2)	0.9	54.1	31.3	68.2	111.6	197.5
Urban						
Per capita income[a]						
(Rp, thousands[b])	170.9	−14.0	−7.7	−23.8	−25.3	−33.5
Entropy index 0 (×100)	38.7	6.8	5.4	4.5	8.0	15.0
Entropy index 1 (×100)	53.9	7.9	5.3	4.5	6.8	15.1
Gini index (%)	47.5	3.3	2.4	2.1	3.5	6.9
Headcount index (P0)	4.0	70.4	44.1	130.8	167.1	301.4
Poverty gap index (P1)	1.1	70.6	55.4	135.1	186.6	324.8
Poverty severity index (P2)	0.4	72.0	67.3	146.9	216.6	353.4

Rural

Per capita income[a]						
(Rp, thousands[b])	90.6	-10.5	-2.0	-7.7	-12.8	-21.5
Entropy index 0 (×100)	25.6	4.1	3.7	5.1	8.8	12.0
Entropy index 1 (×100)	33.1	5.2	3.6	5.5	9.8	14.6
Gini index (%)	38.7	1.8	1.3	1.9	3.7	5.1
Headcount index (P0)	12.4	45.6	11.8	36.0	63.1	112.2
Poverty gap index (P1)	2.9	51.0	18.6	45.7	82.1	150.5
Poverty severity index (P2)	1.2	50.1	23.4	50.8	88.5	163.1

Source: Results from the authors' micro simulation module using changes in prices, wages, and occupational choices by segment generated by the computable general equilibrium module.

Note: Base values for BASE column and percentage change for other simulations; SIMELN = El Niño drought; SIMDEV = real devaluation; DEVCCF = real devaluation + foreign credit crunch; FINCRI = real devaluation + foreign credit crunch + domestic credit crunch; SIMALL = real devaluation + foreign credit crunch + domestic credit crunch + El Niño drought.

a. Per capita income is total monthly income.

b. Rp = rupiah, Indonesia's official currency.

divide is apparent in terms of poverty changes, because urban poverty increases by 301.4 percent and rural poverty increases by only 112.2 percent. This can be explained by differential income shocks in the urban and rural sectors. Results also show that the inequality indicators increase in both sectors.

Conclusion

The income changes generated by the new macro-micro framework introduced in this chapter (drawn from a sample of households in an Indonesian household survey) are consistent, once they have been aggregated, with the predictions of a multisector CGE-like macro model. Chapter 4 shows that this framework captures important channels through which the 1997 financial crisis affected household incomes in Indonesia. This result is obtained through an explicit representation of the actual combination of different income sources within households and how this combination may change—through desired or undesired modifications in the occupational status of household members.

Compared with standard CGE, or before-and-after analysis, the framework developed in this chapter allows for an original analysis of the distributional effects of a financial crisis like the one that struck Indonesia in 1997. At the macro level, the analysis shows that the credit crunch was an important force behind the collapse of GDP in Indonesia, while the devaluation (combined with increases in the marketing cost of food) appears to be the primary driving force behind increases in the relative prices of food with respect to nonfood commodities. At the micro level, heterogeneity of households (with respect to factor endowments), consumption behavior, and occupational choices, whether free or forced, prove to be important in explaining the poverty and distribution effect of the crisis.

These are pure simulations intended to be consistent with what was observed in aggregate terms in Indonesia—and cannot be compared with actual data at the microeconomic level. Under these conditions, it is difficult to say that one simulation or methodology is better than another. The appeal of the framework developed in this chapter is that it accounts for realistic shocks on household economic conditions, especially with regard to the occupational status of household members. That it does so in a way that is selective, across household types, is also appealing—as suggested by the casual observation of household conditions during crisis periods. The main problem, however, is that this selectivity is essentially introduced by translating observed cross-sectional differences in household income generation behavior into the time dimension. In other words, the simulation methodology presented in chapter 4 relies on the standard assumption in economics that a household that faces specific conditions of crisis in a future labor market will behave like a household that is observed under those same current conditions. Determining whether this is justified could be accomplished only with panel data—and so is left for future work.

Notes

The authors are grateful to Indonesia's Badan Pusat Statistik (BPS). They also thank Vivi Alatas for valuable help with the data and programming; and thank Benu Bidani, Dave Coady, Gaurav Datt, Tamar Manuelyan Atinc, Emmanuel Skoufias, and Jaime de Melo for comments and helpful discussions on the text. Other useful comments were made by seminar participants at the International Food Policy Research Institute (IFPRI), the World Bank, The Institute for Economic and Social Research (LPEM) at the University of Indonesia, the University of Nottingham in the United Kingdom, the Annual World Bank Conference on Development Economics in Europe (ABCDE-Europe 2002), and Développement Institutions et Analyses de Long terme (DIAL) in Paris.

1. Results from these International Labour Organization and Central Bureau of Statistics reports are taken from Booth (1998).

2. Starting with Mookherjee and Shorroks's (1982) study of the United Kingdom.

3. A detailed comparison of the approach used in this chapter with the representative household group approach is presented in a companion paper (see Bourguignon, Robilliard, and Robinson 2005).

4. A tighter integration of the micro and macro models has been attempted within a simpler framework by Cogneau (2001) and Cogneau and Robilliard (2001) and applied to Madagascar (as discussed in chapter 7 of this volume). For a general discussion of the link between CGE modeling and micro-unit household data, see Plumb (2001).

5. A more general discussion of the model can be found in Bourguignon, Ferreira, and Lustig (1998) and Bourguignon, Fournier, and Gurgand (2001).

6. The model also considers the possibility that a person may have concurrent income from both wage work and self-employment. This is taken as an additional alternative in the discrete choice model—equation (4.5). A dummy variable controls for this in the earning equation (4.1), and this person is assumed to count for half of a worker in the definition of N_m. To simplify presentation, the authors do not insist on this aspect of the data (or the model). See Alatas and Bourguignon (2005).

7. This rationing interpretation of the functioning of the labor market leads to reinterpreting the "utility" function—defined in equations (4.5) and (4.6)—as a combination of both utility aspects and the way in which the rationing scheme depends on individual characteristics.

8. For the Jacobian used in the Gauss-Newton method to make sense in the present framework, the number of households and the dispersion of their characteristics must be sufficiently high. If this were not the case, then the discontinuity implicit in the Ind( ) functions would create problems.

9. This representation of the output effect of the crisis fits the analysis made by Stiglitz. See, for example, Furman and Stiglitz (1998).

10. Azis, Iwan J., Erina E. Azis, and Erik Thorbecke. 2001. "Modeling the Socio-Economic Impact of the Financial Crisis: The Case of Indonesia." Ithaca, NY: Cornell University Press. (photocopy)

11. In particular, no attempt was made to reconcile the household survey data with the national accounts data.

12. To be consistent with the latest available estimates of the poverty headcount for 1996, the percentage changes reported by Suryahadi and others (2000) between 1996 and 1997 are applied to the base value computed by Pradhan and others (2000). This generates an estimate of the poverty headcount of 9.7 percent in 1997. The present authors then chose an income poverty line that would generate the same headcount for the sample and used that poverty line as the reference value.

13. Because the SAKERNAS does not permit deriving the evolution of self-employment income for agricultural and nonagricultural activities, in this historical simulation, self-employment incomes were assumed to decrease in real terms by the same magnitude as unskilled male wages in the urban and rural sectors.

References

Adelman, Irma, and Sherman Robinson. 1989. "Income Distribution and Development." In *Handbook of Development Economics,* eds. Hollis Chenery and T. N. Srinivasan, Vol. II, 949–1003. Amsterdam: Elsevier Science Publishers.

Alatas, V., and François Bourguignon. 2005. "The Evolution of Income Distribution during Indonesia's Fast Growth, 1980–96." In *The Microeconomics of Income Distribution Dynamics in East Asia and Latin America,* eds. François Bourguignon, Francisco H. G. Ferreira, and Nora Lustig. Washington, DC: Oxford University Press and World Bank.

Armington, Paul S. 1969. "The Geographic Pattern of Trade and the Effects of Price Changes." *International Monetary Fund Staff Papers* 16 (2): 179–201.

Booth, Anne E. 1998. "The Impact of the Crisis on Poverty and Equity." *ASEAN Economic Bulletin* 15 (3): 353–62.

Bourguignon, François, W. Branson, and Jaime de Melo. 1992. "Adjustment and Income Distribution: A Micro-Macro Model for Simulation Analysis." *Journal of Development Economics* 38 (1): 17–40.

Bourguignon, François, Francisco H. G. Ferreira, and Nora Lustig. 1998. "The Microeconomics of Income Distribution Dynamics." A Research Proposal. The Inter-American Development Bank and the World Bank, Washington, DC.

Bourguignon, François, Martin Fournier, and Marc Gurgand. 2001. "Fast Development with a Stable Income Distribution: Taiwan, 1979–1994." *Review of Income and Wealth* 47 (2): 139–63.

Bourguignon, François, Anne-Sophie Robilliard, and Sherman Robinson. 2005. "Representative versus Real Households in the Macroeconomic Modeling of Inequality." In *Frontiers in Applied General Equilibrium Modeling: In Honor of Herbert Scarf,* eds. Timothy J. Kehoe, T. N. Srinivasan, and John Whalley. Cambridge, UK, and New York: Cambridge University Press.

Central Bureau of Statistics (CBS). 1998. "Perhitungan Jumlah Penduduk Miskin dengan GNP Per Kapita Riil." Jakarta, Indonesia: CBS.

Cogneau, Denis. 2001. "Formation du revenu, segmentation et discrimination sur le marché du travail d'une ville en développement: Antananarivo fin de siècle." DIAL Working Paper 2001-18. Paris: Développement Institutions et Analyses de Long terme.

Cogneau, Denis, and Anne-Sophie Robilliard. 2001. "Growth, Distribution, and Poverty in Madagascar: Learning from a Micro-simulation Model in a General Equilibrium Framework." Working Paper 61. International Food Policy Research Institute (IFPRI), Washington, DC.

Derviş, Kermal, Jaime de Melo, and Sherman Robinson. 1982. *General Equilibrium Models for Development Policy*. New York: Cambridge University Press.

Frankenberg, Elizabeth, Duncan Thomas, and Kathleen Beegle. 1999. "The Real Costs of Indonesia's Economic Crisis: Preliminary Findings from the Indonesian Family Life Surveys." RAND Document DRU-2064-NIA/NICHD. RAND Corporation, Santa Monica, CA.

Furman, Jason, and Joseph E. Stiglitz. 1998. "Economic Crises: Evidence and Insights from East Asia." *Brookings Papers on Economic Activity* 1998 (2): 1–114.

International Labour Organization (ILO). 1998. *Employment Challenges for the Indonesian Economic Crisis*. Jakarta, Indonesia: ILO Regional Office for Asia and the Pacific and the United Nations Development Program.

Manning, Chris. 2000. "Labour Market Adjustment to Indonesia's Economic Crisis: Context, Trends, and Implications." *Bulletin of Indonesian Economic Studies* 36 (1): 105–36.

Mookherjee, Dilip, and Anthony F. Shorrocks. 1982. "A Decomposition Analysis of the Trend in U.K. Income Inequality." *Economic Journal* 92 (368): 886–902.

Plumb, Michael. 2001. "Empirical Tax Modeling: An Applied General Equilibrium Model for the U.K. Incorporating Micro-unit Household Data and Imperfect Competition." PhD Thesis, Nuffield College, University of Oxford.

Pradhan, M., A. Suryahadi, S. Sumarto, and L. Pritchett. 2000. "Measurements of Poverty in Indonesia: 1996, 1999, and Beyond." SMERU Working Paper. Social Monitoring & Early Response Unit Research Institute, Jakarta, Indonesia.

Robinson, Sherman. 1989. "Multisectoral Models." In *Handbook of Development Economics,* eds. Hollis Chenery and T. N. Srinivasan, Vol. II, 885–947. Amsterdam: Elsevier Science Publishers.

Robinson, Sherman, A. Cattaneo, and M. El-Said. 2001. "Updating and Estimating a Social Accounting Matrix Using Cross Entropy Methods." *Economic Systems Research* 13 (1): 47–64.

Suryahadi, A., S. Sumarto, Y. Suharso, and L. Pritchett. 2000. "The Evolution of Poverty during the Crisis in Indonesia, 1996–99." SMERU Working Paper. Social Monitoring & Early Response Unit Research Institute, Jakarta, Indonesia.

World Bank. 1998. *Indonesia in Crisis: A Macroeconomic Update.* Washington, DC: World Bank.

5

Can the Distributional Impacts of Macroeconomic Shocks Be Predicted? A Comparison of Top-Down Macro-Micro Models with Historical Data for Brazil

Francisco H. G. Ferreira, Phillippe G. Leite, Luiz A. Pereira da Silva, and Paulo Picchetti

This chapter analyzes the predictive performance of a top-down macro-micro simulation model in reproducing the impact on individual and household income of a large macroeconomic shock, such as an exchange rate and currency crisis. It compares model simulation results with actual distributions. Currency and financial crises such as those experienced in Mexico during 1996, in various countries in East Asia between 1997 and 1999, in Russia during 1998, and in Brazil during 1999 can have devastating effects on both government budgets and private sector balance sheets. But such macroeconomic shocks do not affect all households alike. Occupational structures across the labor market respond to changes in relative prices and to new expenditure aggregates. The distributions of earnings generated in those labor markets also respond to these changes, and thus the distributions of household income per capita—even when aggregated measures of poverty and inequality appear to be minimal or not affected.

There is now an established typology of the common elements that precede and cause financial crises in emerging markets,[1] and there is a growing body of literature documenting the impact of different types of crises and shocks on poverty and inequality.[2] Much less progress has been made on understanding the actual transmission mechanisms through which aggregate shocks affect individual incomes and occupations across the economy in a way that would help policy makers.[3] Given its general equilibrium nature, this problem has traditionally been approached through computable general equilibrium (CGE) models, in which all individuals and households in an economy are lumped together into a much smaller number of representative household groups (RHGs). See, for example, chapter 1 in this volume or Adelman and Robinson (1988). Although the literature applying CGEs to developing countries has generated a number of useful insights, the use of CGEs in addressing distributional questions has been particularly problematic. As discussed in the introduction to this volume, CGE/RHG models are limited because changes in individual occupations and earnings can be very heterogeneous—even within the sectors of economic activity and skill levels traditionally used to construct the RHGs. In chapter 4, Robilliard, Bourguignon, and Robinson show, for the case of Indonesia in 1998–99, that poverty and distributional effects simulated using RHGs can be different from those effects simulated on disaggregated real households.

There are two novelties in this chapter when compared with chapter 4. First, this analysis uses a different type of macro model on "top." The macro model used is based on a set of investment savings and liquidity preference money supply (IS-LM) equations estimated econometrically on time-series data—not a typical CGE model calibrated with ad hoc parameters. As many parameters as possible are obtained, using time-series national accounts and aggregated household survey data from Brazil for 1981–2000. This "top" is then linked to a microeconomic simulation model of household income formation, estimated on cross-section data from a household survey, at the "bottom." Second, and most important, the counterfactual model simulation results for 1999 are compared with the actual changes revealed by the 1999 household survey data, thus providing the first rigorous test (known to the authors) on the performance of a top-down macro-micro model against real data. This is possible for Brazil given the annual frequency and comparability of the household survey data (the Pesquisa Nacional por Amostra de Domicílios or PNAD).

More specifically and going further, this chapter compares three types of model predictions with the observed (ex post) impact of the crisis. This model operates on two levels: the macro general equilibrium model of the economy on top and the reduced-form household income determination model on the bottom. Linking the two are the key linking aggregated variables (LAVs) that represent the price, wage, and employment vectors generated by the macro model. The framework described in figure 5.1 can be used to construct three types of experiments to assess the predictive performance of this top-down model.

The first experiment is designed to define the counterfactual income distribution that would arise from an RHG approach. To distinguish errors from the RHG assumption from those arising from the macro model, this analysis uses on top (as LAVs that should come out of the top macro model) the historically observed—or actual, rather than predicted—LAVs. Average actual values (for each RHG) of the LAVs are imputed to individual households in the 1998 data set, as chapters 1, 2, and 3 in this volume would do in what might be called a micro accounting approach. In the second experiment, the same observed LAVs are used, but the disaggregated micro simulation model is now used to simulate changes to the income of individual households. In the third experiment, the results of simulations using the macro model (LAVs) are combined with the simulations derived from the micro model. The three experiments can be summarized as shown in table 5.1. When compared with the actual 1999 distribution, the results of these three experiments help to identify

Figure 5.1 A Simplified Overview of the Top-Down Macro-Micro Framework

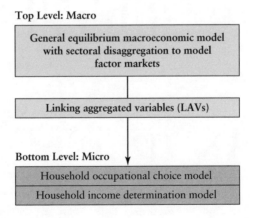

Source: Authors' depiction.

Table 5.1 An Overview of the Three Experiments Conducted

Experiment	Top-level macro model	Linking aggregated variables (LAVs)	Bottom-level micro model
1. Representative household group (RHG)	No macro simulation	LAVs: actually observed changes of average income and employment for each RHG	No micro simulation: each individual receives the average income and employment change of the RHG he/she belongs to
2. Pure micro simulation using the household income micro simulation model	No macro simulation or "perfect disaggregated macro model" using actually observed average income and employment change of the economy's RHGs	No LAVs	Pure micro simulation: micro model runs so that its average results for each RHG converge to the actual observed average income and employment change of the economy's RHGs
3. Full macro-micro linking model	Macro simulation: macro model runs to replicate the 1999 financial crisis	LAVs: simulated changes of average income and employment for each RHG	Micro simulation: micro model runs so that its average results for each RHG converge to the simulated average income and employment change of the model's RHGs

Source: Authors' depiction.

possible sources of discrepancy for each level of the framework (the top macro and the bottom micro).

This exercise admittedly contains an array of perils and pitfalls. Perhaps most important, the parameters in reduced-form macro models usually conflate "deep" taste and technology parameters with policy parameters, and are thus subject to the Lucas critique that estimates obtained under a certain policy regime may no longer be valid under another. But there are other issues: national accounts data used to estimate the macro model may be at odds with the aggregated picture arising from the household survey data used to estimate the micro model; assumptions about labor market closures are inevitably oversimplifications of a much more complex reality and are likely to involve a search-driven equilibrium unemployment rate; and so forth.

This chapter pursues this approach, despite these serious data and methodological limitations, because of the sheer importance of the question. The ability to predict, with some degree of confidence, the direction and magnitude of the impacts of large macroeconomic events (shocks or policy changes) on the incomes and occupations of individuals across the income distribution would be a major asset to policy making in a number of countries, particularly those unfortunate enough to have the combined characteristics of being both volatile—or shock prone—and poor. Although this chapter does not fully achieve that objective, comparisons of the model predictions with the actual data, and the decomposition of the errors into elements attributable to each of the macro and micro components, may be useful to other applied researchers working on this important question.

The chapter is organized as follows. The following section briefly describes the event to be modeled—the 1998–99 currency crisis (with the floating and devaluation of the Brazilian real)—and the structure of the macro model used for Brazil. The procedure to generate LAVs and the precise scenario of the currency crisis that is simulated are then presented, followed by a discussion of the micro model of income determination at the household level and the results of the micro simulation based on them. The chapter concludes with a discussion of micro model accuracy, the simulations, and concluding remarks.

The 1998–99 Currency Crisis and the Macro Model

The macro model outlined in this section was designed to simulate the macro shock corresponding to the macroeconomic policy package implemented in Brazil in 1998–99 responding to an exchange rate and currency crisis. It consisted chiefly of the abandonment of Brazil's crawling-peg exchange rate regime (ERR) and related fiscal adjustment measures.

During most of the first period of the four-year Real Plan (July 1994–January 1999), Brazil maintained a crawling-peg ERR. After the Asian crises in 1997–98, the crisis in Brazil began around the third and fourth quarters of 1998, with pressure on the pegged exchange rate coming from capital outflows. The pressure continued during the first quarter of 1999, after the floating of the Brazilian real. The policy response included—among other less salient policies—changes in the following variables:

• The "float" of the currency on January 15, 1999, whose average annual parity with the U.S. dollar went up from R$1.161 (annual 1998 average) to US$1, to R$1.816 (annual 1999 average, corresponding to a 56.4 percent nominal devaluation).

• A temporary rise in the central bank policy rate (the Banco Central or BACEN's Selic) from October 1998 until May 1999. The monthly rate was raised from 1.47 percent in August 1998 to 3.33 percent in March 1999 (corresponding to annualized rates of almost 50 percent). However, thanks to the rapid resolution of the crisis, the annual average base nominal rate in 1999 actually ended up lower than in 1998. In nominal terms, the Selic was set in 1997, 1998, and 1999 at 24.8 percent, 28.8 percent, and 25.6 percent, respectively, corresponding to real average rates of 16.1 percent, 26.6 percent, and 4.7 percent, respectively.

• A renegotiation of the terms of Brazil's Stand-By Arrangement (SBA) with the International Monetary Fund (IMF) to strengthen the credibility of the policy framework, and hence tighten the fiscal stance corresponding to a reduction of the consolidated public sector borrowing requirements (PSBRs), from R$68 billion to R$56 billion (7.5 percent of gross domestic product [GDP] down to 5.8 percent of GDP, that is, a cut of R$12 billion, or 1.7 percent of GDP).

• The implementation of an inflation target anchor in 1999 to replace the exchange rate anchor for inflation expectations; the provision of hedge-to-market participants (through the issuance of government foreign exchange–indexed domestic bonds); and undisclosed occasional interventions on the spot market, drawing on international reserves, within the limits agreed on under the new SBA arrangement with the IMF.

The goal of this analysis is to model this event at the macro level in the simplest possible way, consistent with the objective of generating LAVs for wage, price, and employment variables that can be applied to the microeconomic simulation model using household data. At the bottom or household level, using the household survey database, the model will transmit those average changes across households, with a view to predicting occupational and distributional impacts.

At the top of the framework, a conventional IS-LM macroeconometric general equilibrium model is used, but with a disaggregated labor market and a financial sector. The model is estimated on time-series data, and some equations are specified with a dynamic specification (lags, for example) that allows for some dynamic in the solution of the model. Data availability issues imposed some constraints on the choice of estimators.[4] In spite of these inevitable constraints, several equations are estimated using two-stage least squares when endogeneity of the regressors was considered to be particularly likely. The parameters of the model are estimated on 1981–2000 annual data, both from the national accounts and from a time-series of averages from the PNAD household surveys, which have been fielded annually by the Brazilian census bureau (Instituto Brasileiro de Geografia e Estatística, IBGE) since 1976.[5]

The basic layout of the macro model is a disaggregated but still standard IS-LM framework (as in the Klein-Goldberger model, MPS[6] in the United States, or DMS and METRIC[7] in France; also see Artus, Deleau, and Malgrange 1986).[8] The functioning of these large models is complex but can be reduced to the interaction of three basic modules. First, a real economy module determines production, components of aggregate demand (such as private consumption and investment), and factor demand (discussed in the following section). Then, a wage-prices module determines the aggregate price level, wage rates, and labor market characteristics. And finally, a financial and monetary module determines the interest rate and equilibria in asset markets. Because of its modular structure, the macro model can function under various configurations (for example, by assuming that some of the modules can be "frozen" and thus actual or exogenous values for its components can be used instead). Or instead of modeling a variety of financial assets equilibria, the financial asset market can be reduced to just one local currency market.

The key transmission mechanism in the macro model—between the real economy and the financial markets—comes from the linking of real private consumption and investment to the endogenous domestic interest rate, which is determined by equilibrium in the financial sector. In particular, (1) real private consumption is a standard function of disposable income, the general price index, and the real deposit interest rate (to account for a "wealth" or portfolio effect); and (2) real private investment is decomposed into its building and construction versus machinery components. Both components follow a standard specification, including aggregate demand (an accelerator) and the price of capital, decomposed into the real exchange rate (given the importance of imported equipments) and the domestic working capital interest rate. In a nutshell, a higher base policy (central bank) interest rate would achieve the following: increase real domestic interest rates, lower private consumption and investment, lower the current account deficit, increase demand for domestic financial assets, and thus put pressure for an appreciation of the nominal exchange rate after an adjustment of the current account of the balance of payments (BoP). The workings of the model respond to the standard stabilization package implemented during most, if not all, of the exchange rate and currency crises of the 1990s.

In addition, the BoP is modeled in a fairly detailed way, with real services, real imports, and exports of goods disaggregated into major types of commodities and services. The general specification for all these items makes each of them dependent (respectively for debit and credit components) on domestic and external demand and relative prices, that is, the real exchange rate. The current account balance is constructed by accounting identities. Capital movements follow uncovered interest parity conditions and are assumed to depend on only the interest rate differential, the expected depreciation of the exchange rate, and country risk. Historical simulations in the current version of the macro model are based on an exogenous nominal exchange rate that is compatible with the two regimes that recently prevailed in Brazil.[9] Details of the macro model, including the exact specification of each equation in each module and the estimation results, are not presented here, but they can be found in Pereira da Silva, Picchetti, and Samy de Castro (2004).

Factor Markets in the Real Economy Model

AGGREGATE SUPPLY AND DEMAND MODELING STRATEGIES

The main motivation behind the breakup of supply into different sectors is the ability of the macro model to differentiate the effects of macro and external shocks on different types of products—and on the workers producing them. Accordingly, the supply side in the model is divided into six sectors:

- urban tradable formal (UTF)
- urban nontradable formal (UNF)
- urban nontradable informal (UNI)
- rural tradable formal (RTF)
- rural nontradable formal (RNF)
- rural nontradable informal (RNI)

For each of these sectors, production is modeled as value added, and factor demand functions are derived from factor price equals marginal product conditions.

FACTOR MARKETS

Factor demand functions determine the demand for capital and for labor by skill level. To relate the employment and earnings predictions of this level of the model to the household survey data used in the micro simulation stage, the classification of workers by skill level had to be made in terms of observed characteristics for the individuals. Skill level was defined according to years of formal education as reported in the PNAD. Low-skill workers have between 0 and 4 years of formal education, whereas intermediate-skill workers have between 5 and 11 years and high-skill workers have more than 11 years.

The demands for these different types of labor and for capital are derived by equating factor prices to the marginal products from the production functions for each of the six sectors, which are represented by a three-level nested constant elasticity of substitution (CES) model. The motivation for this approach is to provide for flexibility in the rates of substitution between capital and labor, and between the different types of labor. The first level of the CES allows for substitution between capital and a composite measure of labor. In the second level, this composite labor can be decomposed between skilled and unskilled jobs. The third level accounts for the fact that unskilled jobs can be performed by either low-skill or intermediate-skill workers, whereas skilled jobs can be performed by either intermediate-skill or high-skill workers. Therefore, as in Fernandes and Meneses-Filho (2001), it is assumed that there is substitution between all types of labor, except between high-skill and low-skill labor. The production function for each one of the six sectors can then be represented as follows:

$$(5.1) \qquad y = \beta\left[\lambda K^{-\rho} + (1 - \lambda)L_a^{-\rho}\right]^{-1/\rho},$$

where

$$(5.2) \qquad L_a = \left[\delta L_Q^{-\Psi} + (1 - \delta)L_U^{-\Psi}\right]^{-1/\Psi}$$

$$(5.3) \qquad L_Q = \left[\phi L_{iQ}^{-\varepsilon} + (1 - \phi)L_h^{-\varepsilon}\right]^{-1/\varepsilon}$$

$$(5.4) \qquad L_U = \left[\xi L_l^{-\gamma} + (1 - \xi)L_{iU}^{-\gamma}\right]^{-1/\gamma};$$

K = capital; L_a = composite labor; L_Q = composite labor for skilled jobs, can be performed either by L_i (intermediate-skill workers) or by L_h (high-skill workers); L_U = composite labor for unskilled jobs, can be performed either by L_i (intermediate-skill workers) or by L_l (low-skill workers).

(5.5)   Elasticities of substitution:
$$\begin{cases} \sigma_{ka} = \dfrac{1}{1 + \rho} \\[2mm] \sigma_{QU} = \dfrac{1}{1 + \psi} \\[2mm] \sigma_{ih} = \dfrac{1}{1 + \varepsilon} \\[2mm] \sigma_{li} = \dfrac{1}{1 + \gamma} . \end{cases}$$

Having defined factor demand functions based on these sectoral production functions, the authors turn to factor supply functions. These functions are separately specified by skill level (in the case of labor) and by economic sector (for both labor and capital). Labor supply is assumed to be perfectly inelastic for each skill group and to correspond to the economically active population (EAP) in those groups.

Factor market equilibrium conditions are obtained by simultaneously solving equation pairs $\begin{matrix} L_{ij}^d(w) + U_i = L_{ij}^s \\ w_{ij} = f(U_i, \ldots) \end{matrix}$ for each labor type i and sector j. In each of these pairs, the second equation is a wage curve, which relates equilibrium wage levels to skill-specific unemployment levels. This setup generates 48 equations for 30 unknowns: 24 endogenous factor prices and 6 endogenous skill-specific unemployment rates.[10] A detailed degree of disaggregation is a requirement for a model that purports to focus on occupational and distributional consequences of shocks.

The solution to the system generates most of the LAVs required for transmission to the micro model. Specifically, it generates 18 wage rates (three labor types in six sectors) and 21 occupation rates (six employment levels, and one unemployment level for each of three types of workers). The only missing LAVs now are consumption price aggregates. To obtain those, however, it is necessary to move from the factor markets to the product markets, and then incorporate the financial markets to derive an endogenous set of interest rates from the IS-LM equilibrium. The first step, while moving to the product markets, is to recognize that this modeling strategy implies that the number and definition of final demand sectors are different from those of production sectors. This assumption creates the issue of reconciling the output and price variables on both sides of the model, which is done through a conversion matrix.

CONVERSION MATRIX

The approach discussed in this chapter follows Fisher, Klein, and Shinkai (1965). On the one hand, the output demanded by the final demand sectors must be distributed over the production sectors; on the other hand, the prices generated by the price-formation equations in the production sectors must be aggregated to obtain prices for the final demand sectors. In this model, data are available on total output by formal production sector, derived from national accounts. But in the case of the informal sector, there is no readily available statistic on production. Therefore, value added for these sectors was estimated based on reported incomes from informal workers in the household surveys. The output conversion matrix was estimated with the natural restrictions (that nontradable sectors do not export, for example), and the resulting weights were used to convert sector prices into gross national product deflators.

Figure 5.2 illustrates this macro model. The key elements are the transmissions from the standard IS-LM macro aggregates (depicted on the right-hand side of the figure) into the disaggregated labor market (on the left-hand side). The demand for each labor factor—broken down by the three skills of the six sectors defined earlier (UTF, UNF, UNI, RTF, RNF, and RNI)—modeled in the framework comes from the appropriate disaggregation of output from the standard IS-LM macro model, taking into account the role of private disposable (after tax) incomes, government financing needs (tax revenue versus debt and other payments), demand elsewhere in the world (the BoP), and central bank policies (setting the base BACEN Selic rate) that affects both the government's financing needs and private aggregates (consumption and investment). These demands (sectoral outputs) are depicted in figure 5.2 by arrows that extend from the aggregation matrix to the sectoral boxes depicted above them.

The LAVs of the macro model are then produced as explained and depicted by the arrows that link the sectoral boxes and the "Labor market" box.

The LM Curve and the Financial Sector

Like employment levels and factor prices, product prices and interest rates are also endogenous in the macro model and related to the IS-LM framework. A financial sector was modeled with several agents and markets, roughly following Bourguignon, Branson, and de Melo (1989). Specifically modeling a financial sector was necessary to refine the transmission of financial crises—external and domestic—to the rest of the model and, in particular, to the disaggregated sectoral demand for labor and to the real macro variables (real private consumption and investment). Indeed, during financial crises, many

Figure 5.2 An Overview of the Main Blocks of the Macro Model

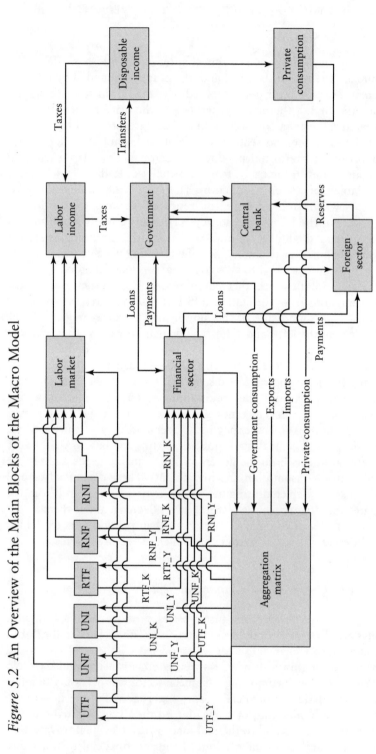

Source: Authors' depiction.

Note: RNF = rural nontradable formal; RNI = rural nontradable informal; RTF = rural tradable formal; UNF = urban nontradable formal; UNI = urban nontradable informal; UTF = urban tradable formal.

traditional policy instruments lose their ability to affect the behavior of households, firms, investors, and banks, both domestic and foreign. This exercise attempts to capture some of these episodes and their characteristics—despite the fact that the model's simulation has an annual periodicity, while most of the manifestations of these crises are infra-annual. Finally, this modeling strategy is modular, allowing the financial sector's part of the framework to be activated fully or in part.

In particular, two domestic interest rates in local currency are endogenous in the model: the domestic deposit rate for household deposits, and the domestic borrowing rate for firms (working capital interest rate). Two other interest rates are exogenous: one national (the Selic, Brazil's Central Bank policy rate) and one foreign (a short-term London interbank-offered interest rate in U.S. dollars). Brazil experienced an abrupt change in its ERR during 1999, moving from an exchange rate anchor to a floating exchange rate with inflation targeting and a corresponding change in emphasis for the Selic. This regime change was integrated for simulations in which the inflation-targeting objective prevails. Once the base policy rate is set, the structure of interest rates (domestic borrowing and deposit rates) is determined by modeling the spreads (see Cardoso 2003; Favero and Giavazzi 2002). Spreads over the base real policy rate will determine the real deposit rate given the supply of bank deposits by households and their first-layer choice between local and foreign currency. Spreads over the deposit rate will determine the real working capital rate given the supply of new credit by commercial banks after their first-layer choice for government domestic bonds and the demand for new credit by firms. This part of the model is important to capture the short-term effect of hikes in the country's base policy rate that can result from either (1) the need under a pegged exchange rate to defend the regime by matching the rise in the country-risk premium and the expected devaluation, or (2) the need under a floating ERR with inflation targeting to establish the credibility of the anti-inflation stance of the central bank.

Estimation and Standard Results of the Macro Model

As mentioned earlier, the macro model comprises equations estimated by ordinary least squares on time-series data.[11] The performance of the macro model (for example, multipliers and deviations from a base in the case of standard simulation exercises of fiscal and monetary shocks) is comparable to that of the macro models of industrial economies (France and the United States), but its investment multiplier is much weaker. These results are summarized in table 5.2.

Table 5.2 Standard Multipliers of the Macro Model
Compared with Other Macro Models

Model	$\Delta Y / \Delta G$	$\Delta C / \Delta G$	$\Delta I / \Delta G$	$-(\Delta IM / \Delta G)$ $+(\Delta X / \Delta G)$
PPSC model				
(Brazil)	1.31	0.27	0.29	−0.25
French models				
DMS	1.10	0.31	0.35	−0.55
Metric	1.38	0.31	0.66	−0.60
PITI	1.54	0.22	0.82	−0.48
DECA	1.26	0.37	0.58	−0.69
U.S. models				
Brookings	2.79	1.11	0.82	−0.14
HC	1.74	0.31	0.53	−0.10

Sources: Artus and Muet 1980; Pereira da Silva, Picchetti, and Samy de Castro 2004.

With regard to the counterfactual simulation of the 1999 currency crisis, the macro model fares reasonably well in a historical simulation mode. Tables 5.3 and 5.4 present partial results (1995–99), extracted from a dynamic historical simulation for 1986–99. The run captures the major consequences of the crisis, such as the slowdown in real private consumption and the fall in real disposable income and private investment, which explain the modest real GDP growth rate (0.8 percent) in 1999. The major components of the external sector balances are reasonably well captured by the simulation. The Brazilian currency crisis is milder than the large output contraction that characterized other financial crises experienced elsewhere during the late 1990s.

The historical simulation also captures the stabilization period under the Real Plan (mid-1994 to 1998) in its real and price/monetary manifestations. The major feature of the period—consumer price index (CPI) inflation brought down from more than 2,200 percent per year in 1994 to 8.5 percent in 1997—is portrayed by the consistent fall in inflation measured by several price indexes (general price index, INFL_GPIF; wholesale price index, INFL_WPI; and GDP deflator, INFL_DEF_AGG_Y). Deflation, however, did not ignite sustainable aggregate growth that remained erratic as captured by real GDP growth, total gross fixed capital formation (FBK_TOTAL_REAL_GROWTH), and private consumption real growth (HHS_CONS_REAL_GROWTH). In fact, deflation and the real appreciation of the Brazilian real (seen in the upward trend of the real exchange rate, RER_DEV) until late 1998 produced an increasing deterioration in both the trade (BOP_TB) and the current account (BOP_CA) balances. Despite a growing ratio of tax revenues

Table 5.3 Some Results of the Macro Model, Historical Simulation for 1999

Indicator	1995	1996	1997	1998	1999
Real GDP growth (percent)					
Actuals	4.2	2.7	3.3	0.1	0.8
Baseline	4.7	1.9	0.3	0.7	0.5
FBK_TOTAL_REAL_GROWTH (percent)					
Actuals	7.3	1.2	9.3	−0.3	−7.2
Baseline	5.2	−3.6	0.2	2.5	−6.1
HHS_CONS_REAL_GROWTH (percent)					
Actuals	4.8	5.6	3.3	−1.5	0.5
Baseline	5.2	5.0	0.9	−0.2	−0.8
XBSZN (R$ thousands)					
Actuals	49,916,655	54,430,127	65,356,311	67,862,415	100,135,527
Baseline	47,834,680	57,002,630	65,265,190	70,423,570	103,217,900
MBSZN (R$ thousands)					
Actuals	61,314,054	69,310,584	86,000,488	87,768,795	115,153,991
Baseline	59,486,390	68,346,620	85,603,290	84,773,800	123,693,100
BOP_CA (US$ millions)					
Actuals	−18,382	−23,442	−30,555	−33,435	−25,335
Baseline	−18,173	−20,762	−29,613	−26,205	−29,205
BOP_TB (US$ millions)					
Actuals	−3,464	−5,539	−6,856	−6,594	−1,199
Baseline	−2,660	−1,045	−7,317	−2,091	−3,608
AGG_NH_L (units of workers)					
Actuals	4,076,944	4,298,040	4,590,574	4,924,643	4,975,319
Baseline	4,073,141	4,279,046	4,544,963	4,918,456	5,080,301
AGG_NI_L (units of workers)					
Actuals	22,762,114	24,027,848	24,756,877	25,971,134	27,121,571
Baseline	22,245,900	24,340,140	25,658,480	25,778,510	26,534,570
AGG_NL_L (units of workers)					
Actuals	27,075,090	24,592,552	24,886,158	24,110,653	23,777,927
Baseline	26,260,380	24,462,200	25,116,370	24,350,920	23,894,390

Source: Authors' estimates based on Pereira da Silva, Picchetti, and Samy de Castro (2004).

Note: FBK_TOTAL_REAL_GROWTH = growth of total gross fixed capital formation; HHS_CONS_REAL_GROWTH = growth of private consumption real growth; XBSZN = exports of goods and nonfactor services; MBSZN = imports of goods and nonfactor services; BOP_CA = current account; BOP_TB = trade account; AGG_NH_L = total skilled labor force; AGG_NI_L = total semi-skilled labor force; AGG_NL_L = total unskilled labor force. Currencies: R$ = Brazilian reais; US$ = United States dollars.

Table 5.4 Major Results of the Public Sector and Financial
Sector Modules, Historical Simulation for 1999

Indicator	1995	1996	1997	1998	1999
AGG_TAX_TRIB_REAL					
(percentage of GDP)					
Actuals	18.65	17.96	18.19	18.48	20.37
Baseline	17.08	18.27	20.18	19.67	19.50
AGG_TAX_INSS_REAL					
(percentage of GDP)					
Actuals	5.92	7.13	6.01	7.37	7.34
Baseline	6.04	7.22	6.19	7.46	7.40
AGG_TAX_OTH_REAL					
(percentage of GDP)					
Actuals	3.92	3.50	4.37	3.46	3.33
Baseline	4.00	3.54	4.50	3.50	3.36
CARGA					
(percentage of GDP)					
Actuals	28.44	28.63	28.58	29.33	31.07
Baseline	27.12	29.03	30.86	30.63	30.26
FIN_CG_INTPAY_Y					
(percentage of GDP)					
Actuals	2.90	2.93	2.36	5.95	9.13
Baseline	4.40	3.13	2.27	5.96	7.33
FIN_PS_PRIM_Y					
(percentage of GDP)					
Actuals	−0.27	0.09	0.95	−0.01	−3.19
Baseline	1.59	−0.31	−0.24	−0.67	−2.31
FIN_PS_INTPAY_REAL					
(percentage of GDP)					
Actuals	96,325	80,037	74,040	115,172	181,344
Baseline	119,859	83,422	69,630	111,567	146,627
FIN_GG_DBT_DOM					
(R$ millions)					
Actuals	136,904	206,068	261,842	317,212	394,441
Baseline	168,963	182,763	238,856	320,860	383,905
FIN_CG_DBT_DOM_Y					
(percentage of GDP)					
Actuals	9.84	14.40	16.79	20.92	22.07
Baseline	13.34	10.75	15.80	22.24	21.93
INFL_WPI (percent)					
Actuals	58.77	6.33	8.13	3.55	16.58
Baseline	66.53	8.32	8.66	5.89	15.25
INFL_DEF_AGG_Y					
(percent)					
Actuals	77.55	17.41	8.25	4.85	5.70
Baseline	76.91	17.68	7.83	5.03	6.36

Table 5.4 (Continued)

Indicator	1995	1996	1997	1998	1999
RER_DEV (percent)					
Actuals	−7.22	5.43	−0.82	1.37	35.27
Baseline	−11.55	3.49	−1.30	0.87	36.82
Real interest rate, certificates of deposit					
Actuals	32.40	15.60	15.60	25.30	4.40
Baseline	29.69	15.39	15.01	23.97	5.33
WC_REAL (average percentage points/month)					
Actuals	75.21	33.46	28.39	32.06	12.21
Baseline	75.21	33.46	28.39	32.06	12.21
SELIC_REAL (average percentage points/month)					
Actuals	33.40	16.50	16.10	26.60	4.70
Baseline	33.37	16.53	16.09	26.63	4.68

Source: Authors' estimates based on Pereira da Silva, Picchetti, and Samy de Castro (2004).

Note: AGG_TAX_TRIB_REAL = total tax burden; AGG_TAX_ INSS_REAL = social security taxes; AGG_TAX_OTH_REAL = other taxes; CARGA = total tax burden; FIN_CG_INTPAY_Y = central government interest payments; FIN_PS_PRIM_Y = public sector primary fiscal result; FIN_PS_INTPAY_REAL = public sector interest payments; FIN_GG_DEBT_DOM = general government domestic debt; FIN_CG_DEBT_DOM_Y = central government domestic debt; INF_WPI = annual inflation, wholesale prices; INF_DEFL_AGG_Y = annual inflation, GDP deflator; RER_DEV = real exchange rate, depreciation; WC_REAL = real interest on working capital; SELIC_REAL = real central bank base rate.

to GDP (CARGA), public sector fiscal primary surplus as a percentage of GDP (FIN_PS_PRIM_Y) was clearly insufficient until a turnaround in policy in 1999, which aimed to stabilize the government's domestic debt-to-GDP ratio (FIN_CG_DBT_DOM_Y). Following the standard models on currency crises, the risk of a change in market perception of the sustainability of the pegged real was clearly growing by the end of 1997 to mid-1998, particularly after the East Asian crises.

The macro model also depicts the 1999 financial crisis reasonably well in historical simulation mode. Stocks, issuance, and holdings of the key financial asset (government domestic bonds, FIN_CG_DBT_DOM) increase, and interest payments (FIN_PS_INTPAY_REAL) jump. The model captures adequately the increases in domestic prices (general price index, the CPI, and the WPI) brought by the pass-through effect of the depreciation of the Brazilian real that follows its floating in January 1999. The change in the ERR resulted in an average 56.4 percent depreciation of the average annual nominal exchange rate that, given the pass-through on domestic prices, translated into a

35 percent real devaluation of the index (RER_DEV). The model captures the fall of the domestic real interest rates that accompanied the surge in domestic prices after the crisis. Finally, the model overshoots slightly its imports projection—although the expected corrections in both the trade and current account balances are picked up.

Generating the LAVs to Link the Macro and Micro Models

As indicated earlier, the factor markets module of the macroeconomic model generates 20 LAVs for occupational status (three employment levels, by sector, and one unemployment level, for five area/skill combinations), and 15 LAVs for incomes (the earnings rates in each sector, in each of the five area/skill combinations).[12] In addition, there are 6 LAVs for changes in the output prices of the six sectors. There are 41 LAVs in total. The LAVs were generated by area (urban and rural); by skills—low (0 to 4 years of schooling), intermediate (5 to 11 years of schooling), and high (12 or more years of schooling); and by occupational sector (tradable, nontradable, and informal). Tables 5.5 and 5.6 show the estimates produced using the macro model runs for 1999, the actual values observed at the PNAD 1998 and 1999 data, and the errors produced by the macro model.

The storyline for the 1998–99 crisis is well known: the financial crisis resulted in an overall decline in urban employment across the country. Unemployment grew in both urban and rural areas and for all skill levels, but more markedly for high-skill workers. Informality also grew, particularly in urban areas. Formal employment fell across all skill groups in urban areas, and more markedly in nontradable sectors, as one would expect. In rural areas, however, the currency depreciation produced a positive output response leading to an increase in employment in the tradable sectors for all skill groups.

Table 5.5 presents the occupational structure of the Brazilian population, aggregated by these three sectors and three skill groups, for both urban and rural areas. Column A shows absolute numbers and proportions for 1998, and column B shows the same information *as actually observed* in 1999, and calculates the actual changes between the two years, which is sometimes referred to as the "true LAVs." Column C presents the corresponding prediction results from the macro module for 1999. The entries in this column are counterfactual occupational numbers and shares, as predicted by the model, when calibrated to simulate the crisis, on the basis of 1998 data. It includes the "model LAVs," that is, the predicted change in employment shares in each category. The last column in the table subtracts the actual LAVs (in column B) from the predicted

Table 5.5 Aggregate Results from the Macro Model, Occupations

Location/skill level/employment	1998 actual from PNAD (A)		1999 actuals from PNAD (B)			1999 simulated by the macro model only (C)			Errors of the macro model (D)
	Units of workers	Percentage of workers by category	Units of workers	Percentage of workers by category	Percentage of actually observed changes (true LAVs)	Units of workers	Percentage of workers by category	Percentage change in each category (model LAVs)	Absolute error (percent)
Urban sector	48,809,911		50,317,141			51,620,283			
Low skill	17,372,833	54.6	17,259,832			18,043,135	56.0		
Unemployed	1,497,575	4.7	1,606,782	5.1	8.49	1,623,210	5.0	6.93	−1.56
Formal tradable sector	2,184,630	6.9	2,071,504	6.6	−4.08	2,112,696	6.6	−4.58	−0.51
Formal nontradable sector	3,338,557	10.5	3,206,221	10.2	−2.76	3,098,839	9.6	−8.34	−5.58
Informal sector	10,352,071	32.5	10,375,325	33.0	1.38	11,208,390	34.8	6.87	5.49
Intermediate skill	26,632,953	66.7	28,153,740			28,290,953	67.4		
Unemployed	3,703,688	9.3	4,245,037	10.2	9.49	4,265,261	10.2	9.62	0.13
Formal tradable sector	4,345,438	10.9	4,475,094	10.7	−1.65	4,556,787	10.9	−0.22	1.44
Formal nontradable sector	7,809,610	19.6	7,923,915	18.9	−3.12	7,872,205	18.8	−4.06	−0.94
Informal sector	10,774,217	27.0	11,509,694	27.5	2.00	11,596,700	27.6	2.44	0.44
High skill	4,804,125	79.2	4,903,569			5,286,195	79.3		
Unemployed	321,052	5.3	380,467	6.1	14.56	381,562	5.7	8.26	−6.29
Formal tradable sector	709,379	11.7	723,085	11.5	−1.54	782,972	11.8	0.53	2.07

(Continued on the following page)

Table 5.5 (Continued)

Location/skill level/employment	1998 actual from PNAD (A) Units of workers	Percentage of workers by category	1999 actual from PNAD (B) Units of workers	Percentage of workers by category	Percentage of actually observed changes (true LAVs)	1999 simulated by the macro model only (C) Units of workers	Percentage of workers by category	Percentage change in each category (model LAVs)	Errors of the macro model (D) Absolute error (percent)
Formal nontradable sector	2,274,160	37.5	2,217,602	35.3	−5.76	2,323,764	34.9	−6.92	−1.15
Informal sector	1,499,534	24.7	1,582,415	25.2	2.02	1,797,897	27.0	9.25	7.23
Rural sector	10,049,477		10,267,135			10,415,081			
Low skill	7,522,219	68.8	7,484,557			7,649,800	71.0		
Unemployed	174,659	1.6	176,238	1.7	3.75	180,065	1.7	3.10	−0.65
Formal tradable sector	958,768	8.8	984,502	9.3	5.94	942,946	8.8	−1.65	−7.59
Formal nontradable sector	365,199	3.3	347,372	3.3	−1.80	340,327	3.2	−6.81	−5.01
Informal sector	6,023,593	55.1	5,976,445	56.4	2.36	6,186,462	57.4	2.70	0.34
Intermediate + high skill	2,527,258	66.5	2,782,578			2,765,281	67.4		
Unemployed	233,247	6.1	276,675	6.7	9.45	279,455	6.8	19.81	10.36
Formal tradable sector	480,512	12.6	538,314	13.1	3.40	533,627	13.0	11.05	7.65
Formal nontradable sector	424,539	11.2	470,756	11.4	2.33	399,930	9.8	−5.80	−8.12
Informal sector	1,388,960	36.6	1,496,833	36.4	−0.55	1,552,270	37.9	11.76	12.30
Total urban and rural	58,859,388		60,584,276			62,035,364			

Source: Authors' estimates based on IBGE (1998; 1999).

Note: LAV = linking aggregated variable; PNAD = Pesquisa Nacional por Amostra de Domicílios (National Household Survey).

LAVs (in column C), and thus measures the absolute errors of the macro model in predicting occupational change.

On the whole, the model gets the directions of change right: there are only four errors of direction, corresponding to 20 percent of the simulations. Three of these errors occurred in rural areas, where overall confidence on the underlying data is lower. In terms of precision, however, the macro module performs rather poorly. Ten predictions (50 percent) are off by 5 percentage points or more, in absolute terms. In relative terms, the errors are large, indeed, and on seven occasions are greater than 100 percent (with respect to the actual changes).

Table 5.6 presents the results in terms of changes in nominal earnings (labor incomes). As expected, output contraction in urban areas translated not only into falls in employment (as seen in table 5.5), but also into falling wages (even in nominal terms). Interestingly, this was the case for all categories, except workers with low or intermediate skills in the formal nontradable sector. In rural areas, a much more mixed picture emerged. Interestingly, there were large actual rises in the wages of all workers in the formal nontradable sector. For low-skill workers, this was a rise of 32 percent in nominal terms, which was well predicted by the model. Conversely, wages in the rural formal tradable sector fell marginally.

As in table 5.5, the performance of the macro model can be judged in table 5.6 by comparing the predicted changes in wages for each worker category (the model LAVs in column E) with the changes actually observed (the "true LAVs" in column D). Absolute errors are again presented in column F. Fortunately, the performance of the macro model is better for earnings than for occupations. None of the 15 counterfactual changes in earnings for household groups reported went in the opposite direction to the changes actually observed for those groups.

There were, however, four significant errors in the magnitude of change (those of more than 5 percentage points) in the urban sector. The nominal monthly wages of workers with low-level skills working in the formal tradable sector were projected to grow by 13.9 percent; instead, they grew by only 5 percent. For intermediate-skill workers in the formal tradable sector, a fall of 14 percent was projected, but these wages fell by only 4 percent. For high-skill workers working in the formal tradable sector, a fall of 7 percent was expected, yet wages fell by only 0.7 percent. Finally, for workers with intermediate- and high-level skills in the formal tradable rural sector, growth of 29.7 percent was projected, but their nominal wages grew by only 12.5 percent. The macro model systematically tends to predict larger declines in wages than the ones actually experienced by workers. In

Table 5.6 Aggregate Results from the Macro Model, Earnings

Location/skill level/employment	Wage (nonzero earnings) in nominal R$ per month			Linking aggregate variables (LAVs) in percentage change for each category for 1998–99		
	1998 actual from PNAD (A)	1999 actual from PNAD (B)	1999 simulated by the macro model only (C)	Percentage of actually observed changes (true LAVs) (D)	LAVs macro model (percent) (E)	Error (percent) (F)
Urban sector						
Low skill						
Formal tradable	454.67	450.81	449.94	−0.85	−1.04	−0.19
Formal nontradable	385.27	404.02	439.01	4.87	13.95	9.08
Informal	264.53	259.82	258.76	−1.78	−2.18	−0.40
Average for the category	316.34	314.77	317.38	−0.49	0.33	0.82
Intermediate skill						
Formal tradable	627.25	605.30	541.31	−3.50	−13.70	−10.20
Formal nontradable	546.28	547.12	548.47	0.15	0.40	0.25
Informal	398.91	388.51	385.44	−2.61	−3.38	−0.77
Average for the category	492.46	481.73	468.42	−2.18	−4.88	−2.70

High skill						
Formal tradable	2,011.96	1,997.40	1,869.99	-0.72	-7.06	-6.33
Formal nontradable	1,759.46	1,682.85	1,678.20	-4.35	-4.62	-0.26
Informal	1,391.10	1,327.12	1,315.27	-4.60	-5.45	-0.85
Average for the category	1,676.54	1,608.90	1,575.78	-4.03	-6.01	-1.98
Rural sector						
Low skill						
Formal tradable	341.14	337.88	322.60	-0.96	-5.44	-4.48
Formal nontradable	252.03	333.78	333.50	32.44	32.33	-0.11
Informal	164.69	172.02	171.47	4.45	4.12	-0.34
Average for the category	192.83	202.52	197.93	5.02	2.64	-2.38
Intermediate + high skill						
Formal tradable	551.13	529.68	507.13	-3.89	-7.98	-4.09
Formal nontradable	527.82	593.85	684.36	12.51	29.66	17.15
Informal	275.19	273.70	266.69	-0.54	-3.09	-2.55
Average for the category	380.28	389.10	385.50	2.32	1.37	-0.95

Source: Authors' estimates based on IBGE (1998; 1999).

Note: LAV = linking aggregated variable; PNAD = Pesquisa Nacional por Amostra de Domicílios (National Household Survey); R$ = Brazilian reais.

rural areas, the underprediction affects only intermediate- and high-skill workers. Nevertheless, in one-third of these cases, prediction errors were quite low in absolute terms, and less than 20 percent in relative terms.

Although the overall performance of the macro model in predicting short-term changes in the occupational structure of Brazil's population between 1998 and 1999 was disappointing, the performance in terms of earnings changes was better. Predictions of changes in earnings that are accurate in direction and less than 20 percent off in magnitude may begin to be of some use for policy makers seeking to assess which groups may be in greater need of social protection during a crisis episode. Nevertheless, aggregate predictions, defined in terms of groups (such as intermediate-skill workers in the formal nontradable sector), may not provide effective policy handles for the design of safety nets. This is the advantage of combining the macro model with the micro module—that is, to allocate the average changes predicted for each representative group of households to actual individuals in the household survey sample. This is an appropriate time to turn to the definition of the micro model.

The Micro Model

The occupational responses to a devaluation such as the one considered in this chapter may differ between men and women within the same area and skill groups, or indeed across women with different numbers of children. It may also differ across workers with the same levels of education but different age and experience profiles. Changes in earnings may be different depending on whether the informal nontradable sector job is in manufacturing in a unionized sector, or in own account service provision in an urban slum. To capture some of the sources of heterogeneity across the diverse population of individuals and households lumped into these groups of agents, a simple reduced-form model of household income determination is estimated, which is based on Bourguignon, Ferreira, and Lustig (2005) and Ferreira and Barros (1999). Once the model has been estimated,[13] it can be used to simulate individual and household responses to the sectoral mean changes (in employment probabilities and in earnings) predicted by the macro module, while respecting the conditional distribution of wages and employment on observed individual characteristics.

The model, similar to the one in chapter 4, consists of three simple blocks. Because the goal is to obtain a measure of welfare, the first block simply defines the household's income per capita, aggregating it across its components. The second block seeks to estimate a descriptive relationship between individual earnings and some of its observed determinants, while the third block estimates a relationship between occupational choice and some of its key correlates.

The first block, which is given by equation (5.6), simply defines household per capita income, by adding all labor incomes across occupations (indexed by s) and household members (indexed by i). The sum of nonlabor incomes of the individuals in the household is represented by y_{0h}. The size of the household is denoted n_h. I_{is} is an indicator variable that takes a value of one if household member i works in sector s and zero otherwise. At the simulation stage, nonlabor incomes and public sector wages are assumed to remain constant in real terms (meaning they are deflated to 1999 using the CPI computed from September 1998 to September 1999,[14] which is equal to 1.0598).

$$(5.6) \qquad y_h = \frac{1}{n_h}\left[\sum_{i=1}^{n_h}\sum_{s=1}^{3} I_{is}\, w_{ih}^s + y_{0h}\right].$$

The second block of equations is represented by a set of standard Mincerian earnings regressions:

$$(5.7) \qquad \log w_{ih} = \alpha_{gs} + x_{ih}\beta_{gs} + \varepsilon_{ih}.$$

This equation relates the earnings (w) of an individual i in household h to his or her observed (x) and unobserved (ε) characteristics in the standard manner. The model is estimated separately across occupations (denoted by s) and across area/skill household groups (g).[15] The population was partitioned into the same groups used in the macro model. There are three occupation sectors s (formal tradable, formal nontradable, informal). Household groups g are defined by urban or rural locations, and along education dimensions: low (0 to 4 years of schooling), intermediate (5 to 11 years of schooling), and high (12 or more years of schooling). As before in the macro model, the individuals who live in rural areas with intermediate or high skills are aggregated. In each of these groups, the vector x includes the following characteristics: intercept, education (and its square), experience (and its square), occupation, race, Brazilian geographic regions, and dummy variables for gender and metropolitan areas.

For purposes of this chapter, these regressions are interpreted merely as descriptions of multivariate correlations. The coefficients are not interpreted causally, as they are likely to be biased because of selectivity and the correlation between unobserved ability and some of the regressors. The key assumption made, and which allowed the earnings equations to be used for the micro simulations, was that any such selection and endogeneity biases are stable between 1998 and 1999.

The occupational choice model is defined in the last block. The constrained choice of occupation by the worker as a function of his or her household and individual characteristics is represented as follows:

$$(5.8) \qquad I_{j=s} = I(z_{ib}\gamma_s + \eta_{ib} > z_{ib}\gamma_j + \eta_{ib} | \forall j \neq s),$$

where I is an indicator function, which takes the value one if the inequality within the bracket holds, and zero otherwise. z is a vector of observed individual and household characteristics, and η captures unobserved individual-level determinants of occupational choice. Elements of z include education; labor market experience; gender; race; occupation, education, experience, and race of the household head; Brazilian geographic regions; a dummy variable if the household is in a metropolitan area; housing status; and a categorical variable for other incomes. This occupational choice model may be estimated empirically by means of a discrete choice model such as a multinomial logit, for which the probability of choosing the category s (inactivity, unemployment, work in the informal sector, work in the formal tradable sector, and work in the formal nontradable sector) is modeled as follows:

$$(5.9) \qquad \Pr(j = s) = \frac{e^{z_{ib}\gamma_s}}{\sum_j e^{z_{ib}\gamma_j}}.$$

Six such models with identical specifications were estimated: one for household heads, another for spouses, and a third for other household members (each of these in both rural and urban areas). Each individual makes a choice according to whether the criterion within the bracket is higher for that sector than for any of the other four. The parameter vector γ is specific to each occupation and can be interpreted in two ways: either as a vector of the marginal utilities of each characteristic in Z, in the occupation s; or as a descriptive parameter of the distribution of observed occupations, conditional on the elements of Z. The occupational choice model is written in the reduced form—that is, it does not include the wage rate of individuals or family members in the vector Z of explanatory variables. Marginal effects calculated from the estimation results for all six models are reported in the annex, at the end of this chapter.

The model, equations (5.7) through (5.9), is estimated on household-level data from the PNAD, which is fielded annually (except in census years) by the Brazilian Census Bureau, IBGE. This chapter uses the unit-record data for the 1998 survey, which had a sample size of 88,356 households (and 333,074 individuals), and for the 1999 survey, which had a sample size of 91,523 households (and 340,986 individuals). The PNAD is the staple household survey for analysis of the Brazilian income distribution. It is representative for both urban and rural areas in all five Brazilian geographic regions, except in the north, where for cost-related reasons, rural areas are fielded only in the state of Tocantins. Income data from the PNAD do, however, suffer from considerable measurement error. The PNAD questionnaires, although much improved during the 1990s, still contain insufficient detail on capital incomes, production for own consumption, and incomes-in-kind. As a result, some evidence suggests that some of the incomes are underreported, particularly in rural areas—and this problem is more severe at both tails of the distribution.[16] In what follows, rural incomes are included for the sake of completeness of coverage. Caution is urged, however, because the income levels reported here are likely to reflect substantial measurement error. In addition, the labor earnings estimations are restricted to the sample for people who are 15 to 80 years old.

After estimating the model, the authors use equations (5.7) through (5.9), with the estimated coefficients reported in the annex and with the individual residual terms from the estimation, and equation (5.6) to simulate the effects of the 1998–99 Brazilian crises on the distribution of household per capita incomes, poverty, and inequality. Then the counterfactual distribution thus constructed is compared with the original distribution taken from 1999 PNAD data.

Formally, the micro simulations consist of finding the solution of the following system of 21 equations based on the 1998 PNAD data:

$$(5.10) \qquad I_s^g(z_{ih}\hat{\gamma}_s + \eta_{ih}^s > z_{ih}\hat{\gamma}_j + \eta_{ih}^j \,|\, \forall j \neq s) = f_s^g \dots \dots \forall s,g$$

$$(5.11) \qquad \sum_{i \in g} \sum_{s \in g} \mathrm{Exp}(\hat{\alpha}_{gs} + x_{ih}\beta_g + \varepsilon_{ih}) = \pi_s^g \omega_s^g \dots \dots \dots \forall g.$$

Equation (5.10) corresponds to the first six equations of the system: one for household heads, one for spouses, and one for other household members, by rural and urban areas. Equation (5.11) corresponds to the remaining 15 equations: the earnings regressions were separately estimated for each group (occupational choice, skills, and area). This system would be overidentified if more than one element in each vector γ were allowed to vary. Therefore, exactly 21 unknowns are solved for: 6 γ_0 and 15 α terms.

The authors' interpretation follows. The first six equations—represented by equation (5.10)—require that the intercept term of the multinomial logit for occupation s (relative to inactivity) be such that the fraction of the population who belong to household group g and choose to work in occupation s is equal to the share of the population (who belong to that household group) that is predicted by the "top" macro model to be employed in occupation s, f_s^g.[17] The remaining equations—represented by (5.11)—require that the intercept term of the earnings equation estimated for household group g be such that the mean of the real wage in the counterfactual distribution be equal to the sector/group wage predicted by the factor markets module of the macro model, ω_s^g.

The system is fully simultaneous, and it is solved numerically by the application of a Newton-Raphson algorithm, which essentially alters values of the 12 "unknown" parameters progressively to minimize the sum of squared differences between the left- and the right-hand sides of equations (5.10) and (5.11). This procedure is analogous to the one used by Bourguignon, Robilliard, and Robinson (2005). As in that analysis, the authors offer no formal existence or uniqueness proofs for the equilibrium of the system, and their algorithm does converge to reach a seemingly plausible equilibrium.

Once the system of equations represented by equations (5.10) and (5.11) converges to a solution, the solution values for the γ_0 and α vectors are substituted into equations (5.7) and (5.9). Equation (5.9) will determine the new distribution of occupations in the population, which is consistent with the macroeconomic changes simulated by the macro model. Taking these counterfactual individual occupations into account, equation (5.7) determines the new predicted earnings for each employed worker. Equation (5.6) aggregates the new earnings distribution, generating the final counterfactual distribution of household incomes.[18] These simulated distributions are therefore consistent (by construction) with both the actual conditional earnings distributions and the conditional occupational distribution observed in 1998, and with the predictions of the macro model for the effects of the devaluation on the Brazilian economy. In what follows, these distributions (referred to as the counterfactual 1999 distributions) are compared with the actual distributions observed in 1999.

Results from the Complete Top-Down Macro-Micro Simulation: Employment and Earnings Rates

The main results for the occupational simulations are presented in table 5.7, for urban and rural areas by skill category and by occupation sector. Employment changes were simulated to target the new distribution of employment across all sectors, but not by the exact number of individuals in each segment. Of the six columns (A to F) in this table, the first four (A to D) contain the observed data and the results of the model's simulations; columns E and F analyze the errors of the procedure and decompose them into macro and micro error components.

Column A, "1998 actual from PNAD," presents actual 1998 employment numbers and the distribution of workers by skill category and occupational sector. Column B, "1999 simulated by the macro model only," provides the counterfactual 1999 (absolute and relative) employment numbers *predicted by the macro model only*, and the proportional changes (the LAVs) implied by these numbers, with respect to the actual 1998 data. These are the same LAVs that were presented earlier, in column C of table 5.6. Column C, "1999 simulated by the macro-micro model," presents the corresponding counterfactual employment numbers and LAVs *predicted by the full top-down macro-micro model*. Column D, "1999 actual from PNAD," presents the real employment numbers from the 1999 PNAD and the proportional changes (the "true" LAVs) with respect to the actual 1998 figures (as in column B of table 5.6).

Column E, "Errors of the macro-micro simulation," analyzes differences between the top-down macro-micro simulations and the actual changes, in absolute terms. Errors of sign in the direction of change and at over- or underpredictions above a threshold of 5 percentage points are reported. Column F, "Total error of the macro-micro simulation," reports the absolute errors in worker shares and then decomposes them into two categories: those attributable to prediction errors from the macro model, and those coming from the micro simulation model.

Somewhat surprisingly, the performance of the top-down macro-micro model is far superior to that of the macro model alone. For occupations in the urban sector, the absolute error is less than 5 percentage points for all but three categories: the formal nontradable sector for workers with low skills, the formal nontradable sector for workers with high skills, and the informal sector with high skills. For occupations in the rural sector, the top-down macro-micro model also performed adequately, except for rural households in the formal nontradable sector and for workers with intermediate and high skills.

Overall, out of the 20 occupational LAVs, the top-down macro-micro model makes six errors with regard to the observed data (the "true LAVs") that are significant (or about 30 percent of the results). Two of these were errors in direction only, one was an error of both magnitude and direction, and three were errors of magnitude only. As column F indicates, the bulk of these errors can be attributed to

Table 5.7 Detailed Results from the Top-Down Macro-Micro Models, Occupations by Skill and Sector

Location/skill level/employment	Units of workers	Percentage of workers by category	Units of workers	Percentage of workers by category	Percentage change in each category (model LAVs)	Units of workers	Percentage of workers by category	Percentage change in each category predicted by macro-micro model
	1998 actual from PNAD (A)		*1999 simulated by the macro model only (B)*			*1999 simulated by the micro-macro model (C)*		
Urban sector	48,809,911		51,620,283			49,119,235		
Low skill	17,372,833	54.6	18,043,135	56.0		17,739,441	55.9	
Unemployed	1,497,575	4.7	1,623,210	5.0	6.93	1,602,373	5.1	7.22
Formal tradable sector	2,184,630	6.9	2,112,696	6.6	−4.58	2,081,482	6.6	−4.51
Formal nontradable sector	3,338,557	10.5	3,098,839	9.6	−8.34	3,046,427	9.6	−8.58
Informal sector	10,352,071	32.5	11,208,390	34.8	6.87	11,009,159	34.7	6.55
Intermediate skill	26,632,953	66.7	28,290,953	67.4		26,746,944	67.3	
Unemployed	3,703,688	9.3	4,265,261	10.2	9.62	4,060,079	10.2	10.14
Formal tradable sector	4,345,438	10.9	4,556,787	10.9	−0.22	4,280,151	10.8	−1.10
Formal nontradable sector	7,809,610	19.6	7,872,205	18.8	−4.06	7,411,419	18.6	−4.65
Informal sector	10,774,217	27.0	11,596,700	27.6	2.44	10,995,295	27.7	2.52
High skill	4,804,125	79.2	5,286,195	79.3		4,632,850	78.8	
Unemployed	321,052	5.3	381,562	5.7	8.26	347,442	5.9	11.72
Formal tradable sector	709,379	11.7	782,972	11.8	0.53	683,461	11.6	−0.60
Formal nontradable sector	2,274,180	37.5	2,323,764	34.9	−6.92	2,015,842	34.3	−8.57
Informal sector	1,499,534	24.7	1,797,897	27.0	9.25	1,586,105	27.0	9.15
Rural sector	10,049,477		10,415,081			10,123,593		
Low skill	7,522,219	68.8	7,649,800	71.0		7,595,335	70.5	
Unemployed	174,659	1.6	180,065	1.7	3.10	182,628	1.7	6.25
Formal tradable sector	958,768	8.8	942,946	8.8	−1.65	957,336	8.9	1.48
Formal nontradable sector	365,199	3.3	340,327	3.2	−6.81	343,156	3.2	−4.49
Informal sector	6,023,593	55.1	6,186,462	57.4	2.70	6,112,215	56.7	1.47
Intermediate + high skill	2,527,258	66.5	2,765,281	67.4		2,528,258	67.1	
Unemployed	233,247	6.1	279,455	6.8	19.81	259,220	6.9	12.05
Formal tradable sector	480,512	12.6	533,627	13.0	11.05	489,727	13.0	2.85
Formal nontradable sector	424,539	11.2	399,930	9.8	−5.80	361,605	9.6	−14.06
Informal sector	1,388,960	36.6	1,552,270	37.9	11.76	1,417,706	37.6	2.98
Total urban and rural	58,859,388		62,035,364			59,242,828		

Source: Authors' esimates based on IBGE (1998; 1999).

Note: LAV = linking aggregated variable; PNAD = Pesquisa Nacional por Amostra de Domicílios. (National Household Survey)

Units of workers	1999 actual from PNAD (D)		Errors of the macro-micro simulation (E)				Total error of the macro-micro simulation (in percentage points) (F)		
	Percentage of workers by category	Actually observed changes (true LAVs)	Sign and absolute error over 5%	Sign error	Absolute error (over 5%)	Total error (in units of workers) difference between units predicted by macro-micro model and actual	Difference between percentage change predicted by macro-micro model and actual	Percentage of the error coming from the macro model	Percentage of the error coming from the micro simulation model
50,317,141									
17,259,832									
1,606,782	5.1	8.49				(4,409)	−1.27	84.35	15.65
2,071,504	6.6	−4.08				9,978	−0.44	87.60	12.40
3,206,221	10.2	−2.76			1	(159,794)	−5.82	95.94	4.06
10,375,325	33.0	1.38			1	633,834	5.16	94.39	5.61
28,153,740									
4,245,037	10.2	9.49				(184,958)	0.65	19.95	80.05
4,475,094	10.7	−1.65				(194,943)	0.55	61.86	38.14
7,923,915	18.9	−3.12				(512,496)	−1.53	61.50	38.50
11,509,694	27.5	2.00				(514,399)	0.52	85.07	14.93
4,903,569									
380,467	6.1	14.56				(33,025)	−2.84	64.54	35.46
723,085	11.5	−1.54				(39,624)	0.94	64.70	35.30
2,217,602	35.3	−5.76				(201,760)	−2.80	41.06	58.94
1,582,415	25.2	2.02			1	3,690	7.13	98.58	1.42
10,267,135									
7,484,557						110,778	2.56	81.72	18.28
176,238	1.7	3.75				6,390	2.50	29.10	70.90
984,502	9.3	5.94				(27,166)	−4.45	79.44	20.56
347,372	3.3	−1.80				(4,216)	−2.69	79.78	20.22
5,976,445	56.4	2.36				135,770	0.69	60.65	39.35
2,782,578									
276,675	6.7	9.45				(17,455)	2.61	59.80	40.20
538,314	13.1	3.40				(48,587)	−0.55	78.97	21.03
470,756	11.4	2.33	1	1	1	(109,151)	−16.38	91.59	8.41
1,496,833	36.4	−0.55		1		(79,127)	3.53	87.34	12.66
60,584,276			1	2	4				

the macro part of the model. This is clearly the major obstacle for these types of procedures, but the link with a macro model of some sort is nevertheless essential for simulating counterfactual economy-wide policies.

The model seems to capture a good deal of the occupational effect of the 1999 crisis on the occupational structure in Brazil. The shock led to the following key changes (change in actually observed data/change predicted by the top-down macro-micro model):

• A significant increase (+13 percent/+13 percent) in unemployment in both rural and urban areas

• A particularly large rise in unemployment for workers with intermediate- and high-skill levels in urban areas (+9.5 percent/+10 percent and +15 percent/+12 percent, respectively)

• An increase in the level of informality in both rural and urban areas (+1 percent/+4 percent and +4 percent/9 percent, respectively)

• A growth of informality in particular in urban areas for workers with intermediate and high levels of skills (+2 percent/+2.5 percent and +2 percent/+9 percent, respectively).

These four general characteristics are picked up fairly well by the top-down macro-micro model, with the exception of an overprediction for the increase in urban high-skill informality. Overall, it seems that the micro simulation stage of the procedure contributes to a considerable reduction in the prediction errors in occupations that plagued the macro stage, as reported in table 5.5. Table 5.7 suggests that the predictions of the combined model do seem to capture the main general effects of the financial crisis on the Brazilian labor market.[19] Naturally, these changes in occupational status were accompanied by changes in earnings. The top-down macro-micro model also runs the counterfactual simulation for earnings.

The Main Results for the Counterfactual Structure of Earnings

The predictive performance of the top-down macro-micro model simulations for earnings (nonzero nominal monthly wages) is presented in table 5.8. Nominal monthly wages (in Brazilian reais, R$) are presented in columns A, B, E, and F. The actual wages for 1998 and 1999 are in columns A and E, respectively. Columns B and F list the nominal monthly wages simulated by the authors' macro component alone, and by the top-down macro-micro model, respectively.

For Brazil as a whole, the model seems to slightly underestimate absolute earnings levels in 1999. The errors reported in table 5.8 are

Table 5.8 Aggregate Results from the Top-Down Macro-Micro Models, Earnings

Location/skill level/employment	Wage (nonzero earnings) in nominal R$ per month — 1998 actual from PNAD (A)	1999 simulated by the macro model only (B)	Linking aggregate variables (LAVs) in percentage change for each category for 1998–99 — Model LAVs (C)	Actually observed (true LAVs) (D)	Wage (nonzero earnings) in nominal R$ per month — 1999 actual from PNAD (E)	1999 simulated by the micro-macro model (F)	Difference between percentage change predicted by macro-micro model and actual — In nominal R$ per month	Difference between percentage change predicted by macro-micro model and actual	Percentage of error coming from macro model	Percentage of error coming from micro-simulation model	Sign and absolute error over 5%	Sign error	Absolute error (over 5%)
Urban sector													
Low skill													
Formal tradable	454.67	449.94	−1.04	−0.85	450.81	450.10	−0.71	−0.16	84.70	15.30	0	0	0
Formal nontradable	385.27	439.01	13.95	4.87	404.02	438.88	34.86	8.63	99.64	0.36	0	0	1
Informal	264.53	258.76	−2.18	−1.78	259.82	259.78	−0.04	−0.02	51.01	48.99	0	0	0
Average for the category	316.34	317.38	0.33	−0.49	314.77	318.42	3.65	1.16	71.32	28.68	0	1	0
Intermediate skill													
Formal tradable	627.25	541.31	−13.70	−3.50	605.30	540.31	−64.99	−10.74	98.47	1.53	0	0	1
Formal nontradable	546.28	548.47	0.40	0.15	547.12	543.40	−3.71	−0.68	21.13	78.87	0	0	0
Informal	398.91	385.44	−3.38	−2.61	388.51	385.87	−2.64	−0.68	87.69	12.31	0	0	0
Average for the category	492.46	468.42	−4.88	−2.18	481.73	466.54	−15.19	−3.15	87.63	12.37	0	0	0

(Continued on the following page)

Table 5.8 (Continued)

Location/skill level/employment	Wage (nonzero earnings) in nominal R$ per month		Linking aggregate variables (LAVs) in percentage change for each category for 1998–99		Wage (nonzero earnings) in nominal R$ per month		Total error of the macro-micro simulation						
	1998 actual from PNAD (A)	1999 simulated by the macro model only (B)	Model LAVs (C)	Actually observed (true LAVs) (D)	1999 actual from PNAD (E)	1999 simulated by the micro-macro model (F)	In nominal R$ per month	Difference between percentage change predicted by macro-micro model and actual	Percentage of error coming from macro model	Percentage of error coming from micro-simulation model	Sign and absolute error over 5%	Sign error	Absolute error (over 5%)
High skill													
Formal tradable	2,011.96	1,869.99	−7.06	−0.72	1,997.40	1,876.85	−120.55	−6.04	94.90	5.10	0	0	1
Formal nontradable	1,759.46	1,678.20	−4.62	−4.35	1,682.85	1,674.90	−7.95	−0.47	58.48	41.52	0	0	0
Informal	1,391.10	1,315.27	−5.45	−4.60	1,327.12	1,321.97	−5.15	−0.39	63.90	36.10	0	0	0
Average for the category	1,676.54	1,575.78	−6.01	−4.03	1,608.90	1,576.74	−32.16	−2.00	97.18	2.32	0	0	0
Rural sector													
Low skill													
Formal tradable	341.14	322.60	−5.44	−0.96	337.88	323.41	−14.48	−4.28	94.96	5.04	0	0	0
Formal nontradable	252.03	333.50	32.33	32.44	333.78	334.18	0.40	0.12	29.46	70.54	0	0	0
Informal	164.69	171.47	4.12	4.45	172.02	173.62	1.60	0.93	20.41	79.59	0	0	0
Average for the category	192.83	197.93	2.64	5.02	202.52	201.16	−1.36	−0.67	58.66	41.34	0	0	0
Intermediate + high skill													
Formal tradable	551.13	507.13	−7.98	−3.89	529.68	502.08	−27.60	−5.21	81.71	18.29	0	0	1
Formal nontradable	527.82	684.36	29.66	12.51	593.85	650.29	56.44	9.50	72.65	27.35	0	0	1
Informal	275.19	266.69	−3.09	−0.54	273.70	267.56	−6.13	−2.24	88.92	11.08	0	0	0
Average for the category	380.28	385.50	1.37	2.32	389.10	379.77	−9.33	−2.40	38.59	61.41	0	0	0

Source: Authors' estimates based on IBGE (1998; 1999).

Note: LAL = linking aggregated variable; PNAD = Pesquisa Nacional por Amostra de Domicílios (National Household Survey); R$ = Brazilian reais.

mostly small and driven by the urban areas, which account for 80 percent of the population. The model tends to systematically predict larger declines in wages than were in fact observed. In the rural areas, the underprediction affects only intermediate- and high-skilled workers. For the six basic groupings that underpin table 5.8 (the three skill levels in urban and rural areas), the model predictions really missed the target in only 5 out of 15 LAVs, for a success record of about 66 percent.

Overall, the top-down macro-micro model can be said to capture a great deal of the actually observed changes in earnings in Brazil from 1998 to 1999. The shock led to the key changes outlined below, including the percentage change in actually observed data and (shown in parentheses) the percentage change predicted by the top-down macro-micro model:

• Mean earnings fell for all three urban categories of workers: by −0.49 percent (+0.33 percent) for workers with low-skill level, by −2.18 percent (−4.88 percent) for workers with intermediate-skill level, and by −4.03 percent (−6.01 percent) for workers with high-skill level.

• The picture is more mixed in rural areas. There, the only winners among low-skill workers were those employed in the formal nontradable and the informal sectors (and this is well predicted by the model). The main losers (−3.89 percent) among intermediate- and high-skill workers were those in the formal tradable sector (and this is overpredicted by the model, −7.98 percent). The main winners (+12.51 percent) among intermediate- and high-skill workers were those in the formal tradable sector—which the model overpredicted by 29.66 percent.

Results from the Top-Down Macro-Micro Model: Household Incomes from Three Experiments

Having thus described the results of the full top-down macro-micro simulation in terms of group means for occupation and earnings rates, the natural next step is to look at the predicted impacts on the disaggregated distribution of household income per capita. After all, had one been interested only in the changes in mean earnings for workers in each of those area/skill/sector groupings, the applied macro model might have sufficed. The whole point of integrating the macro model with a micro simulation module is to better account for heterogeneities within those groups.

This section presents the disaggregated simulation results for household incomes and compare them with the actually observed changes. In fact, to compare the performance of the top-down macro-micro model with alternative modeling strategies, the authors actually conduct three experiments. Experiment 1 mimics a "traditional" RHG approach—that is, the average effects of the 1999 shock are applied uniformly to all individuals belonging to the same representative group of households. However, instead of using the macro model's simulated results, the changes actually observed (the "true LAVs" from tables 5.5 and 5.6) are used, as if the macro model were capable of generating perfect predictions. This first experiment corresponds to the RHGs approach used by most macro CGE models. The LAVs are the actually observed changes of average income and employment for each RHG. There is no micro simulation: each individual receives the average income and employment change of his or her RHG.

Experiment 2 still uses the observed changes in earnings and employment levels (the "true LAVs"), but now, instead of imputing the LAVs uniformly to all members of a household group, the authors allow the microeconomic model to allocate them—by finding the solution to system equations (5.10) and (5.11), which take heterogeneity in personal characteristics (observed and unobserved) into account. This second experiment corresponds to a pure simulation using the micro simulation model. The micro model runs so that its average results for each RHG converge to the actually observed average income and employment change of the economy's RHGs. This experiment tests the predictive capability of the micro simulation model.

Finally, Experiment 3 combines both previous approaches (that is, the simulated results of the macro model with the functioning of the micro simulation model). However, this time the LAVs generated by the macro economic model are used instead of the observed LAVs, so that the third experiment corresponds to the full top-down macro-micro linking model. The macrosimulation consists of running the macro model to replicate the 1999 financial crisis. The run generates LAVs consisting of simulated changes of average earnings and employment levels (as well as prices) for each RHG. Then the micro simulation model runs so that its average results for each RHG converge to the simulated average income and employment change of the model's RHGs. This experiment tests the predictive capability of the full top-down macro-micro linking model.

The results for the distributions of household income per capita are used to construct three incidence curves for changes in nominal incomes. The authors compare the results of each of these three experiments with the actually observed changes in the distribution of household per capita income for Brazil between 1998 and 1999. The comparison is presented graphically in figures 5.3, 5.4, and 5.5.

COMPARING THE MAIN RESULTS FOR THE OVERALL DISTRIBUTION FOR THE THREE EXPERIMENTS

Figures 5.3, 5.4, and 5.5 present the income incidence curves resulting from the 1999 financial crisis on the distributions of household incomes in Brazil. In all cases, the curves plot the difference in logarithms of the mean incomes in each hundredth of the distribution. For instance, the difference in logs between the actual 1999 and the actual 1998 incomes for each percentile of the distribution is represented by the thick black line. That line constitutes the "benchmark" against which the curves of the three experiments will be assessed. Actual data show that the 1999 financial crisis was inequality decreasing. Apart from the first decile (where changes are often affected by the change in the proportion of households reporting zero incomes), the upper deciles of the distribution suffer much larger losses (real falls of 4 to 5 percent) than the first deciles of the distribution, whose real losses are limited to about 1 to 2 percent.

Figure 5.3 presents the comparison between the actual 1998–99 change in incomes for each percentile of the distribution and the incidence curve of the RHG experiment (Experiment 1). The model under this type of experiment correctly predicted the fall in real incomes for the entire distribution, which can be seen by the line that

Figure 5.3 Comparison between Actually Observed Changes and Experiment 1, Using Representative Household Groups

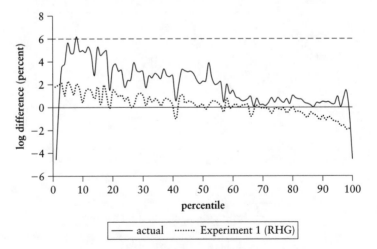

Source: Authors' estimates based on IBGE (1998; 1999).

Note: RHG = representative household group. The x axis represents the percentage change between 1999 and 1998 in nominal income (R$, reais) per month for each percentile of the distribution in Brazil.

represents inflation (at 6 percent) during the period. Beyond that, the model substantially underestimates the rises in nominal earnings in all segments of the distribution. In other words, it consistently overestimates the real wage losses during the crisis.

Figure 5.4 adds to the previous figure the incidence curve of the pure micro simulation experiment (Experiment 2). This experiment performs much better than the first one: the distance between the predicted curve and the real change is much lower now, for the entire distribution and, in particular, between the 50th and 90th deciles. Nevertheless, errors do remain, especially in the bottom half of the distribution and for the richest 5 percent of the population.

Figure 5.5 finally adds to the previous figure the incidence curve of the full top-down macro-micro simulation experiment (Experiment 3). The top-down model performs better than the RHG simulations from Experiment 1, but not as well as Experiment 2. Because Experiment 2 was conducted using "true LAVs," its errors (the differences between its incidence curve and the thick line for the actual

Figure 5.4 Comparison between Actually Observed Changes and Experiment 1, Using Representative Household Groups, and Experiment 2, Using Pure Micro Simulation Model

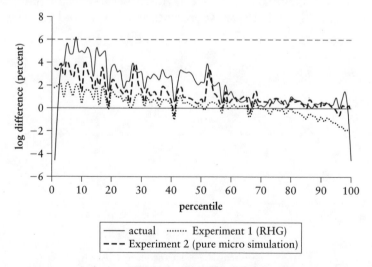

Source: Authors' estimates based on IBGE (1998; 1999).

Note: RHG = representative household group. The x axis represents the percentage change between 1999 and 1998 in nominal income (R$, reais) per month for each percentile of the distribution in Brazil.

Figure 5.5 Comparison between Actually Observed Changes and Experiment 1, Using Representative Household Groups, Experiment 2, Using Pure Micro Simulation Model, and Experiment 3, Using Full Macro-Micro Linking Model

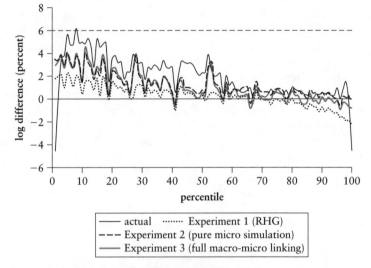

Source: Authors' estimates based on IBGE (1998; 1999).

Note: RHG = representative household group. The x axis represents the percentage change between 1999 and 1998 in nominal income (R$, reais) per month for each percentile of the distribution in Brazil.

changes in figures 5.3 to 5.5) are due entirely to prediction errors from the micro simulation model. The additional distance between the incidence curves from Experiments 3 and 2 corresponds to additional errors arising from the macro module.

The important overall message to take from figure 5.5—which in a sense graphically summarizes the main results of the chapter—is that while top-down macro-micro models such as these are not capable of perfectly predicting the incidence profile of a macroeconomic phenomenon such as the 1999 Brazilian currency crisis, they nevertheless perform reasonably well in predicting both the direction of changes in earnings and the broad pattern of their incidence along the income distribution. In particular, top-down models such as these perform much better than standard RHG approaches, even when macro errors in RHG approaches are eliminated (as was shown here by the use of true LAVs for Experiment 1).

All three incidence curves drawn on figures 5.3, 5.4, and 5.5 are derived, in one way or another, from household survey data. The line for actual changes simply represents a line of differences between centile means across two surveys. The other three lines are predictions obtained by adding different amounts of income to those same means. In any case, these curves are clearly a graphical representation of collections of sample statistics and, therefore, differences across them contain—in addition to modeling (prediction) errors—an element of sampling error. Strictly speaking, therefore, the preceding statements about centile differences should be subject to statistical tests for significance. The simplest suitable test is the paired t test. In this exercise, the same variable (income) is measured in different ways on the same condition. Assuming that the incomes were generated from the same random sample, it is easy to test the means. Treating the difference of the two variables as a random sample from a normal distribution, the test is given by the following:

$$H_0: \mu_{\text{actual}} - \mu_{\text{exp } i} = 0 \qquad \times \qquad H_1: \mu_{\text{actual}} - \mu_{\text{exp } i} \neq 0$$

$$t = \frac{(\bar{x} - \mu_0)\sqrt{n}}{s} \sim t_{n-1}$$

$$s = \sqrt{\left(\sum_{i=1}^{n}(x_i - \bar{x})^2/n - 1\right)}.$$

Table 5.9 presents the results of the paired t test for statistical significance for each of the three experiments. At the 5 percent level of confidence, one can reject the null hypothesis H_0 that the mean of the logarithms of the actual incomes and those simulated under Experiment 1 are equal. One cannot, however, reject the hypotheses that the lines representing Experiments 2 and 3—the micro model based on true LAVs and the fully top-down macromicro model, respectively—are equal to the line for the actually observed changes.

Table 5.9 Paired t Test

Hypothesis test	t	$P > |t|$	Result
$H_0: \mu_{\text{actual}} = \mu_{\text{exp } 1}$	-2.7403	0.0073	H_0 rejected
$H_0: \mu_{\text{actual}} = \mu_{\text{exp } 2}$	0.3919	0.6959	H_0 accepted
$H_0: \mu_{\text{actual}} = \mu_{\text{exp } 3}$	0.3753	0.7082	H_0 accepted

Source: Authors' estimates based on PNAD/IBGE 1998–99.

The interpretation of these test results is that while the differences between the RHG simulations and the actual changes were too large to be attributable to sampling errors alone, the differences between the predictions from the other two experiments and reality were small enough that they *may* be attributed only to sampling error. Broadly similar results were also found using two alternative test formulations: the Welch test for samples from two different population distributions, and the Smirnov-Kolmogorov nonparametric test for distributional differences. In all three cases, the *p*-values for the null hypothesis under Experiments 2 and 3 were higher than under Experiment 1.

Conclusion

This chapter has outlined a top-down macro-micro model of the Brazilian economy that investigates the link between macroeconomic shocks and the distributions of employment, earnings, and household incomes. The approach estimates a macro model based on time-series data and a micro model based on household-level cross-section data. The macro model generates three sets of LAVs: employment and unemployment levels per household group and sector, wage levels per household group and sector, and consumer price levels per sector. These linking variables are then used to recalibrate parameters in the earnings and occupational models at the microeconomic level, and thus to simulate changes in the distribution of earnings and incomes at the household level.

This approach, adapted from Bourguignon, Robilliard, and Robinson (2005) was applied to an investigation of the employment, earnings, and income distribution effects of the 1998–99 devaluation of the Brazilian real. Unlike previous studies, the authors took advantage of the benefit of hindsight and compared the counterfactual distributions generated by their model for 1999 with the distributions actually observed in 1999.

The shock observed—together with the standard policy response of tightening both the monetary and fiscal stances to ensure price stability after the currency floated—was expected to be rather negative. However, the massive devaluation in Brazil (nominal 56 percent) did not result, as it did in East Asia, in a collapse of the financial sector with devastating effects on the credit market and (eventually) on the real economy.[20] Increases in poverty were correspondingly smaller in Brazil than in Indonesia, Thailand, or, for that matter, Argentina. Nevertheless, real incomes in Brazil fell across the entire distribution, and aggregated poverty measures rose accordingly. The headcount index rose from 28.1 percent to 29.2 percent. Because income falls were greatest for the richest households, inequality fell for most commonly used measures. The Gini coefficient fell from 0.593 to 0.587.

The main effect on the distribution of occupations was a substantial increase in unemployment levels across the board, but predominantly in urban areas and for more skilled workers. In urban areas the informal sector registered small increases in employment (+3.5 percent), whereas the formal sector retrenched by 0.5 to 1 percent, regardless of skill level or the tradable nature of the goods. In rural areas, the picture was mixed. There was a pronounced move from employment in the informal and formal nontradable sectors toward the formal tradable sector (the sector that benefited from the real devaluation). The actual effects on the distribution of earnings were reasonably muted, at least in urban areas. Real wages fell for most groups but rose substantially for workers in the rural nontradable sector. Household incomes fell across the distribution—but less so for the poor than for the rich. The changes were thus generally equalizing in the sense that skilled workers had greater declines than those with fewer years of schooling.

The predictive performance of the top-down macro-micro model was uneven. Comparing occupational and earnings predictions from the macro model alone with the observed changes (aggregated from the observed 1999 PNAD for the same household groups) yielded at best a mixed picture. As shown in the section on generating LAVs, the model made a number of mistakes even in the direction of employment changes, and the errors were generally large in magnitude. The performance for the earnings LAVs was better, but not stellar either. In this case, however, at least there were no errors of direction, and only about one-third of the predictions were off by 5 or more percentage points.

When the macro and micro levels were combined, however, so that the LAV predictions were not uniformly attributed to households in the corresponding groups but instead allocated in ways that respected the correlations present in the household data, performance improved substantively. In the section on results, errors in occupational predictions were shown to be smaller for the macro-micro model than they had been for the macro model alone. The same pattern held for earnings. Indeed, looking at the distribution of incomes in a truly disaggregated manner, as was done in the section on results, reveals a somewhat less damning verdict on the top-down macro-micro modeling exercise. While the top-down model failed to replicate the incidence of changes in incomes along the distribution perfectly, it did get both the direction and the basic pattern of incidence right. In fact, prediction errors in the top-down model were statistically indistinguishable from the sampling errors inherent in comparing two separate PNAD samples (1998 and 1999). Importantly, the top-down model performed much better than the simple RHG approach would have, even under the assumption that the latter would get all of the macro changes exactly right.

All in all, the authors definitely do not claim that this approach has delivered the ability to predict the distributional outcomes of macroeconomic shocks or policy packages with anything near perfect accuracy. They also recognize that both the macro and the micro modeling are data- and computation-intensive tools, and that large macroeconometric models are not the most elegant tools in the professional toolkit. Nevertheless, they do find evidence that the top-down approach delivers a capacity to predict the distributional impacts of a macro shock in a manner that is both broadly acceptable and considerably superior to existing alternative approaches, such as the RHG approach, for which the crucial element in this improvement over RHG approaches seems to be the use of the microeconomic simulations.

(*Chapter continues on the following page.*)

Annex: Main Equations of the Micro Simulation Model

Table 5A.1 Log Earnings Regression

Indicator	Urban formal tradable						Rural formal tradable			
	Low		Intermediate		High		Low		Intermediate + high	
	Coefficient	P-value	Coefficient	P-value	Coefficient	P-value	Coefficient	P-value	Coefficient	P-value
R^2	0.27		0.40		0.36		0.22		0.42	
#obs	4,449		9,004		1,378		1,910		967	
Education	0.069	0.01	-0.051	0.06	-0.505	0.09	0.195	0.00	0.033	0.40
Education2	0.008	0.14	0.011	0.00	0.024	0.02	-0.021	0.01	0.006	0.00
Experience	0.037	0.00	0.059	0.00	0.079	0.00	0.021	0.00	0.040	0.00
Experience2	0.000	0.00	-0.001	0.00	-0.001	0.00	0.000	0.07	0.000	0.03
Race: white	0.189	0.00	0.168	0.00	0.380	0.00	0.186	0.00	0.198	0.00
North	-0.064	0.13	-0.124	0.00	-0.038	0.76	0.123	0.25	-0.062	0.67
Northeast	-0.326	0.00	-0.348	0.00	-0.099	0.10	-0.197	0.00	-0.153	0.01
South	-0.073	0.00	-0.075	0.00	-0.060	0.21	0.045	0.26	0.037	0.46
Center-West	0.066	0.05	-0.085	0.00	0.205	0.01	0.199	0.00	0.215	0.00
Metropolitan area	0.134	0.00	0.087	0.00	0.235	0.00	0.093	0.06	0.119	0.01
Gender: male	0.407	0.00	0.389	0.00	0.370	0.00	0.280	0.00	0.392	0.00
Intercept	4.322	0.00	4.534	0.00	7.872	0.00	4.381	0.00	4.142	0.00

Indicator	Urban formal nontradable						Rural formal nontradable			
	Low		Intermediate		High		Low		Intermediate + high	
	Coefficient	P-value	Coefficient	P-value	Coefficient	P-value	Coefficient	P-value	Coefficient	P-value
R^2	0.24		0.35		0.38		0.29		0.47	
#obs	7,557		17,959		4,866		803		897	
Education	0.018	0.31	-0.065	0.00	-0.101	0.50	0.094	0.03	-0.046	0.27
Education2	0.008	0.06	0.012	0.00	0.010	0.05	-0.014	0.17	0.010	0.00
Experience	0.033	0.00	0.054	0.00	0.067	0.00	0.015	0.01	0.045	0.00
Experience2	0.000	0.00	-0.001	0.00	-0.001	0.00	0.000	0.15	-0.001	0.00

Continued regression table (coefficients with p-values):

Variable	Coef	p	Coef	p	Coef	p	Coef	p	Coef	p
Race: white	0.148	0.00	0.195	0.00	0.283	0.00	0.085	0.02	0.301	0.00
Region										
North	-0.098	0.00	-0.082	0.00	0.017	0.76	0.175	0.12	0.087	0.58
Northeast	-0.287	0.00	-0.297	0.00	-0.217	0.00	-0.238	0.00	-0.144	0.01
South	0.014	0.44	0.010	0.42	-0.038	0.18	0.098	0.03	0.003	0.96
Center-West	0.055	0.02	0.040	0.01	0.107	0.00	0.121	0.04	0.209	0.00
Metropolitan area	0.117	0.00	0.102	0.00	0.285	0.00	0.131	0.00	0.255	0.00
Gender: male	0.490	0.00	0.417	0.00	0.469	0.00	0.456	0.00	0.434	0.00
Intercept	4.492	0.00	4.518	0.00	4.936	0.00	4.612	0.00	4.274	0.00

	Urban informal				Rural informal					
Variable	Coef	p	Coef	p	Coef	p	Coef	p	Coef	p
R^2	0.29		0.36		0.35		0.25		0.33	
#obs	22,630		24,459		3,353		11,136		2,740	
Education	0.037	0.00	-0.049	0.02	-0.692	0.00	0.072	0.00	-0.044	0.16
Education2	0.013	0.00	0.010	0.00	0.033	0.00	0.006	0.17	0.010	0.00
Experience	0.054	0.00	0.067	0.00	0.066	0.00	0.032	0.00	0.048	0.00
Experience2	-0.001	0.00	-0.001	0.00	-0.001	0.00	0.000	0.00	-0.001	0.00
Race: white	0.142	0.00	0.179	0.00	0.182	0.00	0.143	0.00	0.140	0.00
Region										
North	-0.169	0.00	-0.142	0.00	-0.137	0.04	-0.158	0.00	0.061	0.46
Northeast	-0.439	0.00	-0.391	0.00	-0.277	0.00	-0.375	0.00	-0.354	0.00
South	-0.122	0.00	-0.030	0.03	-0.078	0.04	-0.024	0.33	-0.089	0.03
Center-West	-0.037	0.04	-0.007	0.66	0.239	0.00	0.153	0.00	0.100	0.02
Metropolitan area	0.223	0.00	0.133	0.00	0.238	0.00	0.290	0.00	0.272	0.00
Gender: male	0.646	0.00	0.608	0.00	0.489	0.00	0.578	0.00	0.503	0.00
Intercept	3.736	0.00	4.090	0.00	8.598	0.00	3.726	0.00	4.050	0.00

Sources: IBGE 1998 and authors' calculation.

Table 5A.2 Occupational Structure Multinomial Logit Model: Marginal Effects, Rural

Indicator	Inactive	Unemployed	Formal tradable	Formal nontradable	Informal
Heads					
Probability	0.05	0.01	0.13	0.04	0.77
Gender: male	-0.12	-0.01	0.11	-0.02	0.04
Education	0.00	0.00	0.01	0.01	-0.02
Education2	0.00	0.00	0.00	0.00	0.00
Experience	0.00	0.00	0.00	0.00	0.00
Experience2	0.00	0.00	0.00	0.00	0.00
Race: white	0.00	0.00	0.01	0.00	-0.01
Status of house occupation (tenant or owner)	0.01	0.00	-0.11	0.00	0.10
Other incomes	0.00	0.00	0.00	0.00	0.00
Age (years)					
0–9	0.00	0.00	0.01	0.00	-0.01
10–18	0.00	0.00	0.02	-0.01	-0.02
19–64	-0.01	0.00	0.00	0.00	0.01
65+	0.00	0.00	0.00	0.00	0.01
Region					
North	-0.03	0.00	-0.07	-0.01	0.11
Northeast	-0.02	-0.01	-0.11	-0.03	0.16
South	-0.02	0.00	-0.04	-0.02	0.08
Center-West	-0.04	-0.01	-0.03	-0.03	0.10
Metropolitan area	0.05	0.01	0.03	0.06	-0.14
Spouse					
Probability	0.67	0.02	0.01	0.04	0.26
Gender: male	-0.42	0.01	0.03	0.08	0.30
Education	-0.01	0.00	0.00	0.01	0.00

Education2	0.00	0.00	0.00	0.00	0.00
Experience	−0.03	0.00	0.00	0.00	0.02
Experience2	0.00	0.00	0.00	0.00	0.00
Head's education	0.00	0.00	0.00	0.00	0.00
Head's experience	0.00	0.00	0.00	0.00	0.00
Dummy if head is formal tradable	0.05	0.00	0.02	0.01	−0.08
Dummy if head is formal nontradable	−0.05	0.00	0.01	0.03	0.01
Head's race	0.00	0.00	0.00	0.00	0.00
Race: white	0.03	−0.01	0.00	0.00	−0.03
Status of house occupation (tenant or owner)	0.01	0.01	0.00	0.00	−0.01
Other incomes	0.00	0.00	0.00	0.00	0.00
Age (years)					
0–9	0.00	0.00	0.00	0.00	0.00
10–18	0.01	−0.01	0.00	0.01	−0.02
19–64	−0.03	0.00	0.00	0.00	0.03
65+	0.02	0.00	0.00	−0.01	0.00
Region					
North	−0.06	−0.01	−0.03	−0.02	0.12
Northeast	−0.06	−0.02	−0.01	0.00	0.09
South	−0.12	0.00	0.01	0.01	0.10
Center-West	−0.05	−0.01	0.00	−0.01	0.06
Metropolitan area	0.03	0.01	0.00	0.02	−0.06
Others					
Probability	0.43	0.06	0.04	0.03	0.45
Gender: male	−0.47	0.00	0.06	0.00	0.41
Education	−0.03	0.01	0.00	0.01	0.01
Education2	0.00	0.00	0.00	0.00	0.00
Experience	−0.04	0.00	0.00	0.01	0.03

(Continued on the following page)

Table 5A.2 (Continued)

Indicator	Inactive	Unemployed	Formal tradable	Formal nontradable	Informal
Others					
Experience2	0.00	0.00	0.00	0.00	0.00
Head's education	0.02	0.00	0.00	0.00	−0.02
Head's experience	0.00	0.00	0.00	0.00	0.00
Dummy if head is formal tradable	0.05	0.01	0.05	0.00	−0.11
Dummy if head is formal nontradable	0.02	0.02	0.00	0.02	−0.06
Head's race	0.00	0.00	0.00	0.00	0.00
Race: white	0.03	−0.01	0.00	0.01	−0.03
Status of house occupation (tenant or owner)	0.04	−0.01	−0.02	−0.01	−0.01
Other incomes	0.00	0.00	0.00	0.00	0.00
Age (years)					
0–9	0.00	0.00	0.00	0.00	−0.01
10–18	0.02	−0.01	0.00	−0.01	0.00
19–64	−0.01	0.00	0.00	0.00	0.02
65+	−0.02	0.00	0.00	0.00	0.02
Region					
North	0.08	−0.04	−0.04	−0.01	0.01
Northeast	0.07	−0.02	−0.04	−0.01	0.00
South	−0.08	−0.02	0.02	0.00	0.08
Center-West	0.00	−0.02	−0.01	−0.01	0.05
Metropolitan area	0.13	0.04	0.01	0.03	−0.21

Sources: IBGE 1998 and authors' calculation.

Table 5A.3 Occupational Structure Multinomial Logit Model: Marginal Effects, Urban

Indicator	Inactive	Unemployed	Formal tradable	Formal nontradable	Informal
Heads					
Probability	0.15	0.04	0.13	0.22	0.47
Gender: male	−0.22	−0.02	0.15	0.02	0.08
Education	0.01	0.00	0.01	0.00	−0.02
Education2	0.00	0.00	0.00	0.00	0.00
Experience	0.01	0.00	0.00	0.00	0.00
Experience2	0.00	0.00	0.00	0.00	0.00
Race: white	0.01	−0.01	0.00	0.00	−0.01
Status of house occupation (tenant or owner)	0.01	−0.01	0.01	0.00	−0.01
Other incomes	0.00	0.00	0.00	0.00	0.00
Age (years)					
0–9	0.01	0.01	0.00	0.01	−0.02
10–18	0.03	0.01	0.00	−0.01	−0.02
19–64	−0.02	0.00	0.01	0.00	0.01
65+	−0.01	0.00	0.00	−0.01	0.02
Region					
North	−0.03	−0.01	−0.09	−0.06	0.18
Northeast	−0.01	−0.01	−0.07	−0.04	0.12
South	−0.04	0.00	0.01	0.01	0.02
Center-West	−0.03	0.00	−0.07	0.02	0.08
Metropolitan area	0.01	0.02	0.00	0.05	−0.07
Spouse					
Probability	0.60	0.05	0.02	0.10	0.23
Gender: male	−0.50	0.04	0.06	0.14	0.26

(Continued on the following page)

167

Table 5A.3 (Continued)

Indicator	Inactive	Unemployed	Formal tradable	Formal nontradable	Informal
Spouse					
Education	0.01	0.00	0.00	0.00	-0.01
Education2	0.00	0.00	0.00	0.00	0.00
Experience	-0.02	0.00	0.00	0.00	0.01
Experience2	0.00	0.00	0.00	0.00	0.00
Head's education	0.01	0.00	0.00	0.00	-0.01
Head's experience	0.00	0.00	0.00	0.00	0.00
Dummy if head is formal tradable	0.05	0.00	0.02	0.00	-0.08
Dummy if head is formal nontradable	0.00	0.00	0.00	0.05	-0.05
Head's race	0.00	0.00	0.00	0.00	0.00
Race: white	0.05	-0.01	0.00	-0.01	-0.03
Status of house occupation (tenant or owner)	0.01	-0.01	0.00	0.00	0.00
Other incomes	0.00	0.00	0.00	0.00	0.00
Age (years)					
0–9	0.00	0.00	0.00	0.01	-0.01
10–18	0.05	0.00	0.00	-0.02	-0.03
19–64	-0.02	0.00	0.00	0.00	0.01
65+	0.05	0.00	-0.01	-0.03	-0.02
Region					
North	0.02	-0.01	-0.01	-0.03	0.04
Northeast	0.02	-0.01	-0.01	-0.02	0.03
South	-0.08	0.01	0.01	0.03	0.03
Center-West	-0.01	0.00	-0.02	0.00	0.03
Metropolitan area	-0.01	0.02	0.01	0.01	-0.02

Others

Probability	0.41	0.13	0.05	0.13	0.28
Gender: male	−0.21	0.01	0.05	0.02	0.14
Education	−0.04	0.01	0.01	0.02	0.00
Education2	0.00	0.00	0.00	0.00	0.00
Experience	−0.05	0.00	0.01	0.02	0.02
Experience2	0.00	0.00	0.00	0.00	0.00
Head's education	0.03	0.00	0.00	−0.01	−0.02
Head's experience	0.00	0.00	0.00	0.00	0.00
Dummy if head is formal tradable	0.01	0.00	0.04	0.00	−0.05
Dummy if head is formal nontradable	−0.01	0.00	0.00	0.04	−0.04
Head's race	0.00	0.00	0.00	0.00	0.00
Race: white	0.02	−0.01	0.00	0.01	−0.01
Status of house occupation (tenant or owner)	−0.01	0.01	0.00	0.01	−0.01
Other incomes	0.00	0.00	0.00	0.00	0.00
Age (years)					
0–9	−0.02	0.00	0.01	0.01	0.00
10–18	0.02	0.00	0.00	−0.01	−0.01
19–64	0.01	0.00	−0.01	−0.01	0.01
65+	0.00	0.00	0.00	−0.01	0.01
Region					
North	0.11	−0.02	−0.06	−0.08	0.04
Northeast	0.12	−0.02	−0.06	−0.07	0.02
South	−0.02	−0.01	0.01	0.01	0.01
Center-West	−0.01	−0.01	−0.04	0.00	0.05
Metropolitan area	0.01	0.04	−0.01	0.02	−0.06

Sources: IBGE 1998 and authors' calculation.

Notes

The authors thank François Bourguignon and Anne-Sophie Robilliard for their guidance and inspiration and Armando Castelar Pinheiro, Aart Kraay, and Alexandre Samy de Castro for useful comments on a previous version of this chapter.

1. Most if not all financial crises in emerging markets (a) occurred after significant financial liberalization under rigid exchange rate regimes; (b) were preceded by massive capital inflows that allowed the accumulation of significant unhedged foreign currency liabilities by domestic agents that became illiquid or insolvent when these capital flows suddenly reversed; and (c) tended to cause contagion and spread to other countries. The literature has proposed interpretations of the origin and spread of the crises ranging from a "fundamentalist" view (that the crises resulted from weak macroeconomic and financial fundamentals) to a "financial panic" view (that the crises were self-fulfilling due to investor behavior unrelated to economic conditions. For a survey, see Pereira da Silva (2001).

2. See, for example, Lokshin and Ravallion (2000) on the case of Russia, and Kakwani (1998) on Thailand. Baldacci, de Mello, and Inchauste (2002) use cross-country analysis to show that financial crises tend to have a negative impact on the income distribution and to increase poverty. There is also comparative work on the impact of financial crises in Asia and Latin America on labor markets and household incomes; see, for example, Fallon and Lucas (2002). These analyses conclude that employment fell by much less than production in crisis-hit countries, but that there were considerable changes in employment status, location, and sectoral composition. They also show that cuts in real wages (resulting from real depreciation of the currency) were accompanied by small rises in unemployment, and that families smoothed their incomes through increased participation and private transfers.

3. Policy makers may want to compare the likely distributional impacts of alternative stabilization strategies, such as a tighter monetary policy with regard to a tighter fiscal policy—or may like to know whether the negative impact of a devaluation on the balance sheets of (predominantly urban) firms indebted in hard currencies might be offset by income gains in the rural tradable sector. In designing safety nets to cope with the crisis, policy makers may wonder which sectors would be most hurt by declines in the demand for labor, and whether those sectors are likely to respond predominantly through lower wages or through higher unemployment.

4. Data on wages and employment for the disaggregated labor market could be obtained only through the household surveys, which start in the late 1970s and are available yearly. Likewise, data for the financial sector are not available with consistent methodologies for a time span that allows a large sample.

5. PNAD data are annual except for census years and a few other exceptions, such as 1994.

6. MPS was named for the initials of the institutions that helped develop it: Massachusetts Institute of Technology, the University of Pennsylvania, and the Social Science Research Council.

7. Both the DMS and METRIC were macroeconometric models developed in France in the late 1970s and 1980s. DMS stands for the French words *Dynamic multisectoriel,* that is, multisectoral dynamic; METRIC stands for *Modèle économétrique trimestriel de la conjuncture,* that is, quarterly econometric model of the economic situation.

8. Macroeconometric models usually have an ad hoc treatment of expectations (naïve, adaptive mechanisms). They are also subject to the Lucas critique; parameters in most equations are not invariant to a change in regime. The critique forced macro models not only to give more emphasis to theory, long-run relationships, and the supply side, but to specify and estimate dynamic adjustments more robustly. Models tried to incorporate rational expectations or model-consistent expectations to address the Lucas critique. The estimation strategy in the authors' "top" macro model addresses only some of these issues. Most of the behavioral equations are estimated by ordinary least squares, some with an error-correction mechanism. Attempts to construct macro models based purely on a bottom-to-top aggregation of microeconomic behavior are under way (see Townsend and Ueda 2001); for an example, see chapter 8 of this volume.

9. In most macro frameworks there are two possible ERRs. Under a fixed regime, the central bank intervenes in the foreign exchange market to maintain a fixed parity or a crawling peg path with respect to a specific foreign currency target (the U.S. dollar, for example). Thus, the change in the demand for money by households is affected by this foreign component (an exogenous element in the supply of money). Under a flexible regime, the central bank does not intervene, and the BoP equation determines the freely floating exchange rate.

10. The 30 unknowns are four factor prices for each of six sectors (24) and six unemployment levels (one for each skill type, and separately for urban and rural areas). Capital is assumed to be fully utilized in all sectors. In practice, however, insufficient numbers of observations for high-skill workers living in rural areas required that skill type be grouped with intermediate-skill workers in rural areas. Since the price of capital is not an LAV either, this reduces the number of LAVs in practice to three factor prices in five sectors (15) and five unemployment levels. To these 20 LAVs obtained from the solution of these systems of equations, 15 employment levels will be added. LAVs are later discussed in this chapter in a section on LAV links.

11. Details in Pereira da Silva, Pichetti, and Samy de Castro (2004). In the present version, the simulations describe essentially movements between long-term solutions in levels. However, one of the main forthcoming

extensions involves enhancement of the dynamics of the solutions by estimating movements of the variables in differences, through an error-correction mechanism. The idea, in line with the basic motivation for the proposed model, is to gain further insight into the paths of adjustment of the endogenous variables in response to shocks, allowing the analysis of trade-offs not only in terms of macro stability versus social indicators, but also in terms of the time periods involved.

12. Recall that there are only five area/skill combinations because the intermediate- and high-skill workers in rural areas are being considered together due to an insufficient number of observations.

13. While the macro model is estimated on aggregated time-series data, the micro model is estimated on a single cross-section of the household survey (PNAD 1998). In both cases, identical definitions of skills and sectors are used, to guarantee a consistent mapping of individuals into groups.

14. September is the reference month of the survey.

15. For simplicity, the corresponding g and s subscripts are dropped from the variables (w, x, and ε) in equation (5.7).

16. See Ferreira, Lanjouw, and Neri (2003) and Elbers and others (2001) for an assessment of these measurement problems that is based on comparisons between the PNAD and an alternative Brazilian household survey, the Pesquisa de Padrões de Vida (PPV).

17. One difficulty is that the macro module allows for changes in the relative skill composition of labor demand when constructing the employment LAVs, but this micro simulation does not allow for changes in the education level of the worker. This may be economically realistic for the short term, but it implies that there are six actual unknowns for potentially 18 exogenous variables (f_s^g targets). In the simulations, the adjustment occurs through the number of people left over for unemployment and inactivity from each skill category, which corresponds to a quantity closure to the labor market.

18. These counterfactual distributions assume that a number of features of the population and economy remained constant at their 1998 levels. These include the spatial, racial, gender, and education composition of the population; the distribution of nonlabor incomes; and the internal composition of the households.

19. Whether or not much consolation should be derived from this improvement will depend on how much of the improvement is attributable to mechanical factors behind the convergence of the Newton-Raphson algorithm.

20. The real GDP growth rates in Brazil for 1997, 1998, and 1999 were, respectively, 3.27 percent, 1.32 percent, and 0.81 percent—still in positive territory—as opposed to the dramatic changes from positive 6 to 8 percent real growth down to −5 percent to −15 percent in the same period in East Asian crisis-hit countries such as Thailand and Indonesia.

References

Adelman, Irma, and Sherman Robinson. 1988. "Macroeconomic Adjustment and Income Distribution: Alternative Models Applied to Two Economies." *Journal of Development Economics* 29 (1): 23–44.

Artus, Patrick, Michel Deleau, and Pierre Malgrange. 1986. *Modélisation Macroéconomique.* Paris: Economica.

Artus, P., and P. A. Muet. 1980. "Une Etude Comparative des Proprietes Dynamiques de Dix Modeles Americains et Cinq Modeles Français." *Revue Economique* 31 (1).

Baldacci, Emanuele, Luiz de Mello, and Maria G. Inchauste. 2002. "Financial Crises, Poverty, and Income Distribution." IMF Working Paper 02/4. International Monetary Fund, Washington, DC.

Bourguignon, Francois, W. Branson, and Jaime de Melo. 1989. "Macroeconomic Adjustment and Income Distribution: A Macro-Micro Simulation Model." OECD Technical Paper 1. Organisation for Economic Co-operation and Development, Paris.

Bourguignon, François, Francisco H. G. Ferreira, and Nora Lustig. 2005. *The Microeconomics of Income Distribution Dynamics in East Asia and Latin America.* Washington, DC: World Bank; New York: Oxford University Press.

Bourguignon, François, Anne-Sophie Robilliard, and Sherman Robinson. 2005. "Representative versus Real Households in the Macroeconomic Modeling of Inequality." In *Frontiers in Applied General Equilibrium Modeling: In Honor of Herbert Scarf,* eds. Timothy J. Kehoe, T. N. Srinivasan, and John Whalley. Cambridge, UK, New York: Cambridge University Press.

Cardoso, Eliana. 2003. "Seigniorage, Reserve Requirements, and Bank Spreads in Brazil." In *Taxation of Financial Intermediation: Theory and Practice for Emerging Economies,* ed. Patrick Honohan, 241–68. Washington, DC: World Bank and Oxford University Press.

Elbers, C., J. O. Lanjouw, Peter Lanjouw, and Philippe G. Leite. 2001. "Poverty and Inequality in Brazil: New Estimates from Combined PPV-PNAD Data." World Bank, Development Economics Research Group, Washington, DC.

Fallon, Peter, and Robert E. B. Lucas. 2002. "The Impact of Financial Crises on Labor Markets, Household Incomes, and Poverty: A Review of Evidence." *World Bank Research Observer* 17 (1): 21–45.

Favero, Carlo A., and Francesco Giavazzi. 2002. "Why Are Brazil's Interest Rates So High?" SSRN Electronic Paper Collection. University of Bocconi Innocenzo Gasparini Institute for Economic Research and IGIER, University of Bocconi, Milan, Italy.

Fernandes, Reynaldo, and Naércio A. Meneses-Filho. 2002. "Escolaridade e Demanda Relativa por Trabalho: Uma Avaliação para o Brasil nas

Décadas de 80 e 90." In Chahad J. P. Zeetano and N. Meneses-Filho (eds.), *Mercado Do Trabalho No Brasil*. Sao Paulo: Ltr Editora.

Ferreira, Francisco H. G., and Ricardo Paes de Barros. 1999. "The Slippery Slope: Explaining the Increase in Extreme Poverty in Urban Brazil, 1976–1996." *Brazilian Review of Econometrics* 19 (2): 211–96.

Ferreira, Francisco H. G., Peter Lanjouw, and Marcelo Neri. 2003. "A Robust Poverty Profile for Brazil Using Multiple Data Sources." *Revista Brasileira de Economia* 57 (1): 59–92.

Fisher, Franklin, L. R. Klein, and Y. Shinkai. 1965. "Price and Output Aggregation in the Brookings Econometric Model." In *The Brookings Quarterly Econometric Model of the U.S.*, ed. J. Duesenberry, 653–79. Washington, DC: Brookings Institution.

IBGE (Instituto Brasileiro de Geografia e Estatística). 1998. *Pesquisa nacional por amostra de domicílios (PNAD)*. Rio de Janeiro.

_____. 1999. *Pesquisa nacional de domicílios (PNAD)*. Rio de Janeiro.

Lokshin, Michael, and Martin Ravallion. 2000. "Welfare Impacts of the 1998 Financial Crisis in Russia and the Response of the Public Safety Net." *The Economics of Transition* 8 (2): 269–95.

Kakwani, Nanak. 1998. "Impact of Economic Crisis on Employment, Unemployment, and Real Income." Bangkok, Thailand: National Economic and Social Development Board.

Pereira da Silva, Luiz A. 2001. "Boom and Bust in East-Asia: How the East-Asia Miracle Produced the Financial Bubbles That Ended in the 1997–98 Crises." World Bank, Development Economics Research Group, Washington, DC.

Pereira da Silva, Luiz A., Paulo Picchetti, and Alexandre Samy de Castro. 2004. "A Macroeconometric Financial Model for Brazil Estimated with the PNAD." World Bank Development Economics Research Group, Washington, DC.

Townsend, Robert M., and Kenichi Ueda. 2001. "Transitional Growth with Increasing Inequality and Financial Deepening." IMF Working Paper WP/01/108, International Monetary Fund, Research Department, Washington, DC.

PART III

Macro-Micro Integrated Techniques

6

Distributional Effects of Trade Reform: An Integrated Macro-Micro Model Applied to the Philippines

François Bourguignon and Luc Savard

Analyzing the micro impact of policy reforms is essential to understand their impact on poverty and more generally on income distribution, and therefore their social acceptability. When reforms are shown to be beneficial for society as a whole but not to particular groups, such an analysis gives policy makers information on the measures to be taken to compensate losers and on the cost of these measures. The Philippines' government is faced with numerous policy choices that are all the more difficult because of concerns voiced by various pressure groups about the impact of these policies on vulnerable groups. An important policy choice has to do with unilateral trade liberalization. This policy likely will have beneficial aggregate effects in the medium run when markets will have fully adjusted. Domestic agents, however, likely will benefit unevenly from this reform, some of them running the risk of being net losers. Moreover, the presence of market imperfections may substantially modify the overall gain of the reform and increase individual losses.

The identification of the distributional effects of a policy reform, and in particular of the losers and the way they could possibly be compensated, is difficult. The reason for this difficulty is the need to jointly evaluate two types of effect: (1) the aggregate effects of the policy reform, something that is generally done through conventional macro modeling—with more or less sectoral disaggregation; and (2) the heterogeneous effects of the reform on individual agents, an analysis that requires an essentially microeconomic perspective. Recent years have witnessed a flourishing body of literature about this macro-micro nexus in modeling the poverty and distributional impact of macro policies, including trade reforms. The integration of the macro and the micro perspectives remains somewhat imperfect or rather cumbersome, however. The present chapter proposes an alternative approach and applies it to the issue of trade liberalization in the Philippines.

The chapter is organized as follows. The first section discusses the various methodological approaches to the macro-micro link in the analysis of policy reforms and presents the original approach applied in the chapter. The second section presents the original features of the application of that methodology to the Philippines and, in particular, the way it accounts for labor market imperfections. The third section shows the results of simulating the distributional effects of across-the-board trade liberalization in the Philippines. It compares the results obtained from the methodology used in this chapter with those derived from alternative approaches.

An Iterative Top-Down Approach to the Macro-Micro Link

This section starts by briefly reviewing the existing methodologies that link the macro and micro parts of a modeling framework, highlighting their advantages and limitations. It then proposes an alternative approach and describes its implementation.

Existing Approaches to the Modeling of the Macro-Micro Link

Three main approaches are being used in the literature to link macro reforms to changes in income distribution and poverty within the framework of economywide computable general equilibrium (CGE) models. The first and most common is the representative household (RH) approach. The population of households is partitioned into groups, and each group is represented by a virtual household assumed to behave as the mean of the group. Income distribution within groups is taken as exogenous, so this approach considers only between-group sources of variations in the distribution of income and poverty. This is a severe drawback given the importance of the within-group components in existing empirical evidence on the sources of change in income distribution.

The second approach may be referred to as the CGE micro simulation sequential (MSS) method. This is essentially a top-down approach. At the top, a conventional CGE model—with or without representative households—is used to simulate policy reforms and estimate changes in prices and factor rewards resulting from the reform. These changes are then fed into a conventional household survey database to yield estimates of the change in the income and expenditures of individual households under the assumption of no behavioral response. It is known that with perfect markets and marginal changes in the price system, the difference between these two amounts yields a money metric measure of the change in the individual welfare of households. Applying these changes to initial incomes derives the change in the distribution of real income within the population and in poverty. This simple approach to the micro consequences of macro policy reforms combines conventional CGE modeling and micro simulation and is being used increasingly—see, for instance, chapters 2 and 3 in this volume by Lokshin and Ravallion and by Bussolo, Lay, Medvedev, and van der Mensbrugghe; Coady and Harris (2001); King and Handa (2003); Vos and De Jong (2003); and Chen and Ravallion (2004). A more complicated approach that considers labor force participation behavior, labor market imperfections, and possibly nonmarginal price changes has been explored by Bourguignon, Robilliard, and Robinson (2005); and Ferreira, Leite, Pereira da Silva, and Picchetti (chapter 5 in this volume).

An obvious critique of the MSS approach is the lack of feedback from the micro side of that methodology (the micro simulation based on household surveys) to the macro side (that is, the CGE model). Household behavioral responses to price changes may well be ignored when computing marginal changes in welfare at the micro level under the assumption of perfect markets. As noted by Hertel and Reimer (2004) or Bourguignon and Spadaro (2006), however, these responses are not necessarily negligible at the macro level, and the approximation may be grossly incorrect in the case of market imperfections or nonmarginal changes in the price system. This top-down approach is also inappropriate when policy changes are specified at the household level, for instance, with cash transfer programs.

A third approach that is being explored in recent work handles the micro and the macro parts of the modeling in a fully integrated way, rather than sequentially as with the MSS approach or through intermediate aggregation as with the RH approach. Practically, this approach is simply an extension of the latter. It includes as many "representative households" as there are actual households in the household survey that would be used with the MSS approach. In the prototype model by Decaluwé, Dumont, and Savard (1999), each household is characterized by its share in total factor endowments in the economy (as computed from the income part of the household survey), its saving rate, and the allocation of its consumption budget among the various goods and services appearing in the CGE model. All these shares and rates are fixed, and the model solves for the complete equilibrium of the economy, including saving and consumption demand for each household in the sample. Cogneau and Robilliard (2001) applied this type of integrated approach of micro-macro modeling to the Malagasian economy, based on a set of 2,000 households observed in a household survey and under the assumption of a dualist labor market.

In comparison with the other approaches, this integrated multihousehold (IMH) approach appears as the only one based on a rigorous theoretical framework that considers all the observed heterogeneity of the population of households. Yet it raises several difficulties at the implementation stage. First, reconciliation between the aggregate data in the macro part of the model and micro data coming from the household survey can be problematic—especially concerning the definition of aggregate goods and services to be used in both the micro (household expenditure) and macro (sectoral production) sides of the model; see Rutherford, Tarr, and Shepotylo (2005) or Cockburn (2006). Second, the numerical resolution can be challenging. Boccanfuso, Cabral, and Savard (2005) were able to handle an integrated model including around 3,500 Senegalese households, but Rutherford, Tarr, and Shepotylo (2005) found it almost impossible when including 50,000 households in their analysis of the effect of Russia's accession to the World Trade Organization. Finally, detailed microeconomic behavior or micro consequences of market imperfections can be difficult to model in this context. For instance, the introduction of involuntary unemployment in the modeling of the labor market requires specifying rationing schemes at the individual level that somehow imply externalities among individuals or households. This feature may be difficult to handle within a standard CGE framework. Cogneau and Robilliard (2001) provide an example of such a model that includes externalities among households. This example, however, seems to have been provided at the cost of an oversimplified macro framework.

It is likely that advances in computing power will soon make it possible to include a much larger number of households in a CGE framework. It is less clear whether that will permit solving the other difficulties. It is thus important to explore other approaches to micromacro modeling that permit the full integration of standard CGE modeling and a detailed representation of a large population of individual households.

The MSS method may be seen as a first iteration in the IMH approach. Introducing some feedback from the micro simulation level into the CGE model and then applying the whole MSS again seems like a natural iterative way of integrating the micro and macro analyses of policy reforms. Rutherford, Tarr, and Shepotylo (2005) devised such an iterative algorithm and found that in the case of Russia and with perfectly competitive markets, most of the micro and macro impacts of an across-the-board trade liberalization were satisfactorily accounted for by the first MSS step. This chapter proposes a different and simpler approach that can be applied to imperfectly competitive environments. It examines whether the same practical conclusion can be obtained in the case of trade liberalization in the Philippines in the presence of strong imperfections of the labor market.

An Iterative MSS Solution to the IMH Model

An elementary Walrasian representation of the economy is used here to present and discuss the iterative method proposed in this chapter to solve an IMH model. The model actually used for the Philippines' application in the second part of the chapter is more elaborated.

Let $C_{h,i}(y_h, \eta_h, p)$ be the consumption function of good i ($=1, \ldots, I$) by household h, where y_h is the income of household h ($=1, \ldots, H$), η_h is a set of demographic characteristics, and p is the vector made of the prices of goods and services. Let $L_{h,n}(\pi_h, \eta_h, w, p, R_h)$ be the supply of labor of type n ($=1, \ldots, N$) by household h, where π_h is the vector of the specific productivities of household h in the various types of labor (say, skilled-unskilled), w is the corresponding vector of unit wages, and R_h is nonlabor income. Finally, let $Y_i(k_i, w, p)$, $P_i(k_i, w, p)$, and $L_i^d(k_i, w, p)$ be, respectively, the supply, the profit, and the vector of labor demands of the sector producing good i, with k_i standing for the fixed factors of production.

The competitive equilibrium of that economy is given by the solution in (p, w) of the following system of equations:

$$\sum_{h=1}^{H} C_{h,i}(y_h, \eta_h, p) = Y_i(k_i, w, p) \quad \forall i = 1, \ldots, I$$

$$\sum_{h=1}^{H} \pi_{hn} L_{hn}(\pi_h, \eta_h, w, p, R_h) = \sum_{i=1}^{I} L_{in}^d(k_i, w, p) \quad \forall n = 1, \ldots, N$$

(6.1)

$$y_h = \sum_{n=1}^{N} \pi_{hn} w_n L_{hn}(\pi_h, \eta_h, w, p, R_h) + R_h;$$

$$R_h = \sum_{i=1}^{I} \alpha_{hi} P_i(k_i, p, w) \quad \forall h = 1, \ldots, H,$$

where α_{hi} is the share of the profits of sector i that goes to household h.

This simple model includes the main features of an IMH model. What makes it somewhat difficult to solve is that the number of H households, and therefore the total number of equations, may be extremely large. Things would be much simpler if it were possible to group the H households into a much smaller number of aggregate households for which the consumption and labor supply would depend only on their aggregate characteristics, including productivity and nonlabor income. Then the solution of the system of equations (6.1) could be cast in terms of these RHs and the income and consumption of each individual household could be assumed to be proportionate to that of the RHs in the group to which it belongs. In effect, such an approach combines the RH and the MSS approach into the solution of the IMH model. Introducing some heterogeneity among households, however, or making the consumption functions and labor supply functions nonlinear with respect to income, is enough to make aggregation and the preceding simplification invalid.[1]

A simple algorithm for solving an equilibrium system like (6.1) is the familiar fixed point. The structure of the algorithm is shown in figure 6.1.

Formally, let w^m, p^m be the vector of unit wages and prices at iteration m, and let Γ^m, Λ^m be the corresponding vectors of aggregate household demand for goods and labor supply at those prices and

Figure 6.1 Iterative Resolution of the Integrated Multihousehold CGE Model

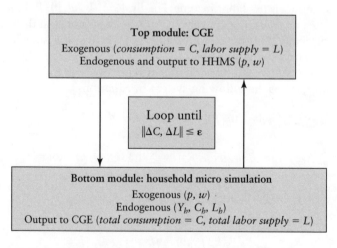

Source: Authors' representation.
Note: CGE = computable general equilibrium.

wages, as given by the left-hand side of the first two sets of equations in (6.1):

$$\Gamma_i^m = \sum_{h=1}^{H} C_{h,i}(y_h^m, \eta_h, p^m) \quad \forall i = 1, \ldots, I$$

$$\Lambda_n^m = \sum_{h=1}^{H} \pi_{hn} L_{hn}(\pi_{h.}, \eta_h, w^m, p^m, R_h^m) \quad \forall n = 1, \ldots, N$$

(6.2)
$$\text{with} \quad y_h^m = \sum_{n=1}^{N} \pi_{hn} w_n^m L_{hn}(\pi_{h.}, \eta_h, w^m, p^m, R_h^m) + R_h^m$$

$$\text{and} \quad R_h^m = \sum_{i=1}^{I} \alpha_{hi} \cdot P_i(k_i, p^m, w^m) \quad \forall h = 1, \ldots, H .$$

Simplifying this set of equations, the preceding definition may be rewritten as a bottom-up (BU) equation:

$$\Gamma^m = \Phi(w^m, p^m)$$

(6.3)
$$\Lambda^m = \Psi(p^m, w^m) .$$

Equation (6.2) corresponds to the MSS approach to the micro impact of macro policies. It simulates the impact of changes in the price system (p, w) on individual incomes. Aggregating the micro responses to those changes provides the BU part of the iterative algorithm proposed in equation (6.3). This step feeds household responses to price changes back to the top of the CGE part of the algorithm, a feedback that is missing in the standard noniterative MSS approach. Aggregate demand and labor supply being considered as exogenous in iteration $m + 1$, aggregate equilibrium conditions in equation (6.1) can now yield new values for the price system. This particular step of the iteration writes now as a top-down (TD) equation:

$$Y_i(k_i, w^{m+1}, p^{m+1}) = \Gamma_i^m \quad \forall i = 1, \ldots, I$$

(6.4)
$$\sum_{i=1}^{I} L_{in}^d(k_i, w^{m+1}, p^{m+1}) = \Lambda_n^m \quad \forall n = 1, \ldots, N ,$$

which yields a new vector of prices and wages (p^{m+1}, w^{m+1}). This new vector is then sent down to micro simulation at the household level for a new iteration. This system of equations thus provides the TD part of the algorithm that solves the integrated household model.

Writing the solution of the preceding system as follows:

$$(w^{m+1}, p^{m+1}) = \Psi(\Gamma^m, \Lambda^m),$$

it is now possible to put the two parts, BU and TD, of the algorithm together, leading to the following fixed-point (FP) algorithm:

$$(6.5) \qquad (w^{m+1}, p^{m+1}) = \Psi[\Phi(w^m, p^m), \Theta(w^m, p^m)].$$

Convergence of the algorithm is obtained when the distance between two successive iterations on the vectors (p^m, w^m) is below some arbitrary small threshold.[2]

With a single market, the preceding algorithm is the familiar cobweb model. Some conditions must hold for this algorithm to converge, namely, the elasticity of the demand side of the market must be smaller than the elasticity of the supply side near the equilibrium. In a multimarket framework, the condition for multimarket equilibrium stability is that the matrix $(J - I)$, where J is the Jacobian of the system of FP equations (6.5) and I is the unit matrix, is definite negative.

An interesting property of this FP algorithm is that its first iteration essentially corresponds to the MSS approach. Starting from some initial equilibrium situation, suppose that a shock hits the economy on the supply side. As a first approximation, the MSS approach is equivalent to supposing that aggregate demand and labor supply are not modified. Then the TD solution of equation (6.4) gives the resulting shocks in the price system. The BU part of the algorithm identifies the effect of this shock on the income and welfare of each household in the sample being used. The MSS approach would stop there, ignoring the possible feedback of the initial shock on aggregate demand and labor supply. An interesting question is whether considering feedback effects of the household sector on the economy, as is done in the iterative procedure proposed here, eventually leads to different estimates from those obtained at the first iteration.

It is possible to get closer to final effects using a single iteration or the MSS approach by introducing some behavioral response on the demand side of the goods markets and on the supply side of the labor markets into the CGE model. This can be done by introducing in that model an RH whose behavior has some similarity with the aggregate behavior of the sample of individual households.[3] The first iteration of the algorithm would thus rely on a CGE model that has a single aggregate household with a demand system. Aggregate income and price elasticities of the demand for goods and services and the supply of labor would have to be close to the elasticity obtained from aggregating individual households' behavior.

The iterative top-down, bottom-up resolution method shown above—which applies to much richer representations of the economy than equation (6.1)—has several advantages over a method that would solve simultaneously for all individual and aggregate equilibrium conditions. First, there is no obligation to make the macro and the micro parts of the model fully consistent in terms of consumption or income aggregates. Some rule would be needed that permits converting the aggregates obtained from the BU part of the algorithm into the aggregates used in the CGE part of the model. For instance, the household survey may be underestimating the aggregate consumption of a particular good as given by the national accounts generally used in CGE modeling. No correction is necessary for consistency with national account data if it is assumed that the proportion of underestimation is independent from the price of other goods and unit wages. In other words, income and expenditure data in household income and expenditure surveys can be used as they are. A second advantage is that there is no limit to the level of disaggregation in terms of production sectors and number of households to be included in the model. This issue is discussed in Chen and Ravallion (2004) and Rutherford, Tarr, and Shepotylo (2005). The third advantage is that the flexibility of the functional forms used to model the consumption and labor supply behavior of households is greater than in other approaches. In particular, there is no need to choose functional forms with good aggregation properties. Finally, as can be seen in the following section, it is possible to introduce labor market imperfections without major difficulty and to explicitly consider the externality among households when rationing occurs on one side of the market.

Labor Market Imperfections

Like many other developing countries, the Philippines is characterized by a dual labor market with a formal sector in which most employees are wage workers, most often under a labor contract, and an informal sector dominated by self-employment and family business (Riveros 1993). Taking this dualism into account is important because workers with the same characteristics are not remunerated at the same rate in the two sectors, and the allocation of workers between the two sectors has a direct impact on poverty and the distribution of income. This feature is introduced in the present micro-macro model using the well-known specification first presented by Roy (1951), revisited by Heckman and Sedlacek (1985), and further enriched by Magnac (1991), in which workers decide which sector, if any, they want to join depending on the wages they are offered or anticipate.

Another feature of the Philippine economy seems to be the wage rigidity in the formal sector of the economy.[4] This implies that some rationing takes place in the formal sector of the economy that forces workers who would have preferred a job in that sector to work in the informal sector or to be inactive. This feature of the labor market is taken into account by following closely the micro framework proposed by Magnac (1991).

Formally, the representation of the labor market in the present model of the Philippine economy is as follows. Assume in a first stage there is only one type of labor but that productivity, π_h, varies across individuals h—who momentarily will be assumed to coincide with household heads. Productivity is assumed to depend on individual characteristics according to a Mincerian model type. Then the wage, ω_h^j, of individual h in the segment j (=1 for formal, 2 for informal) of the labor market is given by the following:

$$(6.6) \qquad \omega_h^j = \pi_h\, w_j \quad \text{with} \quad \log \pi_h = H_h.\gamma^j + u_h^j,$$

where w_j is the general level of earnings in segment j, as given by the solution of the aggregate CGE model; H_h stands for the human capital characteristics of individual h (essentially education, age, and gender); γ^j is a vector of coefficients specific of segment j; and u_h^j is a residual term for the effect of unobserved characteristics on individual productivity in segment j. The key assumption is that the elasticity of individual labor productivity with respect to human capital characteristics is segment specific.

Participation decisions are taken by comparing the potential wages in the various market segments to a reservation wage, ω_h^0, given by the following:

$$(6.7) \qquad \ln \omega_h^0 = H_h\gamma^0 + Z_h\delta + u_h^0,$$

where γ^0 stands for the semi-elasticities of the reservations wage with respect to the observable characteristics of workers, δ is for the semi-elasticities with respect to household characteristics, and Z_h and u_h^0 summarize the effect of unobserved variables. The reservation wage, ω_h^0, is not directly observed and must be inferred from the observed participation behavior of individuals in the sample.

With these three distinct wage variables, it is possible to represent the decision process of an individual who has to choose among three alternatives: being inactive, working in sector 1, or working in sector 2. To take into account the possible imperfection of the labor market and entry restrictions in the formal sector, it is convenient to introduce a cost of entry in that sector. A simple assumption is that this cost is proportional to the formal wage, so that it represents something like the waiting time to get a job in the formal sector. Accordingly, the net (logarithm of the) gain in the formal segment of the labor market can be defined as follows:

$$(6.8) \qquad \ln\omega_h^1 + u_h^c,$$

where u_h^c stands for the logarithm of the proportion of earnings in the formal sector that is actually received by the worker—after taking into account the cost of entry. The labor market may be said to be perfectly competitive when this cost is nil, which implies that u_h^c is nil instead of negative.

Taking into account the cost of entry into the formal sector, the employment decision process can be described by the following set of conditions:

$$\text{formal employment: } \ln\omega^1 - u_h^c > \ln\omega^2,$$
$$\text{and} \quad \ln\omega^1 - u_h^c > \ln\omega_h^0;$$
$$(6.9) \qquad \text{informal employment: } \ln\omega^2 > \ln\omega^1 - u_h^c,$$
$$\text{and} \quad \ln\omega^2 > \ln\omega_h^0;$$
$$\text{inactive: } \ln\omega_h^0 > \ln\omega^1 - u_h^c,$$
$$\text{and} \quad \ln\omega_h^0 > \ln\omega^2.$$

Observing the sector of employment of individuals (and their earnings in that sector) and making some simplifying assumptions on the distribution of the unobserved terms, u_{ji}, it is possible to estimate the parameters of equations (6.6) and (6.7). Under the assumption of a normal distribution of the unobserved terms, Magnac (1991) provides a two-step estimation method of the Heckman type that starts with a bivariate probit on the sectors of employment and participation. It is not possible, however, to estimate precisely the unobserved components, u_{ji}, of the various earning equations. Only one unobserved term may be directly derived from the estimation for employed individuals. It is the residual of the earning equation in the segment of the market where they are employed. For the other equations, these unobserved terms are drawn randomly in the appropriate conditional distributions. For instance, the estimated $\hat{u}_h^1$, $\hat{u}_h^c$, and $\hat{u}_h^0$ terms for an individual employed in the informal sector must be drawn according to the following rule:

$$\hat{u}_h^1 \approx N(0, \sigma_1) \quad \hat{u}_h^0 \approx N(0, \sigma_0) \quad \hat{u}_h^c \approx N(0, \sigma_c)$$

$$(6.10) \qquad \hat{u}_h^1 + \hat{u}_h^c \leq \ln w^2 - \ln w^1 + H_h(\hat{\gamma}^2 - \hat{\gamma}^1) + \hat{u}_h^2$$

$$\hat{u}_h^0 \leq \ln w^2 + H_h(\hat{\gamma}^2 - \hat{\gamma}^0) - Z_h\hat{\delta} + \hat{u}_h^2.$$

For the sake of brevity and given the scope of the present chapter, the detail of the estimation procedure and the results obtained in the case of the Philippines are not provided. A simplified version of Magnac's (1991) method was applied to household heads with the additional assumption that all employed individuals in a household were in the same segment of the labor market as the head.[5]

This micro specification of the labor market implied several departures from the simple Walrasian model discussed in the previous section. At the top level, formal and informal are considered as two different types of labor input in the production process of the various sectors of the aggregate CGE model. A basic labor market imperfection is introduced by postulating a fixed real wage (w^1/P) in the formal segment of the labor market,[6] which results in some rationing, whereas the informal labor market is supposed to clear through a flexible wage w^2. Numerous CGE models actually represented the labor market in that way (see, for instance, Fortin, Marceau, and Savard 1997; Decaluwé, Martens, and Savard 2001; Agénor and El Aynaoui 2005). Labor supply in the two markets is taken as exogenous in the first iteration, but results from the micro simulation are used to endogenize the labor supply in the subsequent iterations. At the micro simulation level, the general level of wages obtained in the top part of the algorithm is used to scale up or down the potential earnings of individuals in the various segments of the labor market with respect to initial estimates of individual earnings. The reservation wage is reasonably assumed to be scaled up or down using a consumer price index (P). These potential earnings can then be used to revise the employment choices of households. Some rationing will possibly take place if employment in the formal sector is below the spontaneous supply of workers. The rationing scheme is analyzed in further detail below.

The consequences of such a functioning of the labor market have already been analyzed in the CGE literature, particularly in the RH context (see, for instance, Thomas and Vallée 1996; Fortin, Marceau, and Savard 1997; Savard and Adjovi 1998; Devarajan, Ghanem, and Thierfelder 1999; Agénor, Izquierdo, and Fofack 2003). Evaluating the aggregate and distributional impact of this imperfection of the labor market requires more care in a fully disaggregated representation of the population of households.

Evaluating the aggregate supply of labor in the two segments of the labor market at iteration $m + 1$ in the micro simulation module can be done by counting the number of people in the various cases defined by equation (6.9) with the prices and wages of iteration m. Thus, the total labor supply $L_{.1}^{m+1}$ to the formal sector is given by the cardinal of the following:

$$\{\ln\omega_h^{1,m} + u_h^c > \ln\omega_h^{2,m}, \quad \text{and} \quad \ln\omega_h^{1,m} + u_h^c > \ln\omega_h^{0,m}\},$$

which also writes as follows:

(6.11)

$$L_{.1}^{m+1} = Card\left\{\begin{array}{l} \ln\dfrac{w^{1m}}{w^{2m}} + H_h(\hat{\gamma}^1 - \hat{\gamma}^2) + \hat{u}_h^1 + \hat{u}_h^c - \hat{u}_h^2 > 0 \text{ and} \\[2ex] \ln\dfrac{w^{1m}}{P^m} + H_h(\hat{\gamma}^1 - \hat{\gamma}^0) - Z_h\delta + \hat{u}_h^1 + \hat{u}_h^c - \hat{u}_h^0 > 0 \end{array}\right\},$$

where $Card\{C\}$ stands for the cardinal of the set of individuals defined by the conditions C. Likewise, the labor supply, $L_{.2}^{m+1}$, to the informal sector is given by the following:

(6.12)

$$L_{.2}^{m+1} = Card\left\{\begin{array}{l} \ln\dfrac{w^{1m}}{w^{2m}} + H_h(\hat{\gamma}^1 - \hat{\gamma}^2) + \hat{u}_h^1 + \hat{u}_h^c - \hat{u}_h^2 \leq 0 \text{ and} \\[2ex] \ln\dfrac{w^{2m}}{P^m} + H_h(\hat{\gamma}^2 - \hat{\gamma}^0) - Z_h\delta + \hat{u}_h^2 - \hat{u}_h^0 > 0 \end{array}\right\}.$$

Other people are inactive.

Now consider the case in which the formal labor supply exceeds the demand at the fixed real wage w^{1m}/P^m. Then some people who want to work in that segment of the market will not find a job there. Likewise, it may be the case that the demand exceeds the supply, in which case the formal sector will have to attract workers who were initially inactive or employed in the informal sector. How is this adjustment implemented in the model?

The entry cost in the formal sector is used to adjust the labor supply in the formal labor market to match the actual demand. If the demand of formal labor initially exceeds the supply of workers, then the cost of entry in the formal sector is reduced in the same proportion for all individuals, so that some individuals will move from the informal to the formal sector and others will switch from inactivity to formal employment. In the opposite case of excess supply in the formal labor market, the adjustment takes place by increasing the cost of entry. Fewer people are then willing to work in the formal sector, some of them preferring the informal sector and others becoming (or remaining) inactive. Modifying the entry cost is like changing $\hat{u}_h^c$ by the same amount for all individuals.

Equilibrating the formal labor market through entry cost thus requires determining the amount ε^{m+1} by which all the $\hat{u}_h^c$ terms must be modified for the constrained labor supply to the formal sector $\overline{L}_{.1}^{m+1}(\varepsilon^{m+1})$ to be equal to the demand, L_1^{dm}. From equation (6.11), it can be seen that ε^{m+2} is given by the solution of the following equation:

$$(6.13) \quad \overline{L}_{.1}^{m+1}(\varepsilon^{m+1}) = L_1^{dm}$$

$$= Card \left\{ \begin{array}{l} \ln\dfrac{w^{1m}}{w^{2m}} + H_h(\hat{\gamma}^1 - \hat{\gamma}^2) + \hat{u}_h^1 + \hat{u}_h^c - \hat{u}_h^2 + \varepsilon^{m+1} > 0 \quad \text{and} \\[2ex] \ln\dfrac{w^{1m}}{P^m} + H_h(\hat{\gamma}^1 - \hat{\gamma}^0) - Z_h\delta + \hat{u}_h^1 + \hat{u}_h^c - \hat{u}_h^0 + \varepsilon^{m+1} > 0 \end{array} \right\}.$$

This modification of the cost of entry in the formal sector also modifies the labor supply to the informal segment of the market, which now writes as follows:

$$(6.14) \quad \overline{L}_{.2}^{m+1}(\varepsilon^{m+1})$$

$$= Card \left\{ \begin{array}{l} \ln\dfrac{w^{1m}}{w^{2m}} + H_h(\hat{\gamma}^1 - \hat{\gamma}^2) + \hat{u}_h^1 + \hat{u}_h^c - \hat{u}_h^2 + \varepsilon^{m+1} \leq 0 \quad \text{and} \\[2ex] \ln\dfrac{w^{2m}}{P^m} + H_h(\hat{\gamma}^2 - \hat{\gamma}^0) - Z_h\delta + \hat{u}_h^1 + \hat{u}_h^c - \hat{u}_h^0 > 0 \end{array} \right\}.$$

Taking into account the imperfection of the labor market is thus equivalent to replacing the labor supplies coming from the BU part in the initial algorithm by the constrained labor supplies, $\overline{L}_j^{m+1}(\varepsilon^{m+1})$. In effect, the equilibrium on the formal labor segment always holds—at the prices of iteration m—so that, practically, the introduction of a fixed real wage in that segment of the market is equivalent to replacing a quantity variable of the initial model by a shadow price, that is, the cost of entry into the formal labor market.

It is also possible to dispense with this shadow price and implement more directly the rationing process. Consider the case of an excess supply in the formal labor market. The preceding mechanism is equivalent to expelling $N = L_{.1}^{m+1} - L_1^{dm}$ individuals from the notional labor supply in the formal labor market. To see which individuals will be expelled, it is sufficient to rank all people in $L_{.1}^{m+1}$ given by equation (6.11) according to the following criterion, G_h:

$$(6.15) \quad \begin{array}{l} G_h = Inf\lfloor H_h(\hat{\gamma}^1 - \hat{\gamma}^2) + \hat{u}_h^1 + \hat{u}_h^c - \hat{u}_h^2, \\ H_h(\hat{\gamma}^1 - \hat{\gamma}^0) - Z_h\hat{\delta} + \hat{u}_h^1 + \hat{u}_h^c - \hat{u}_h^0 \rfloor, \end{array}$$

which happens to be independent of the price system and thus can be established once for all individuals when estimating the labor supply model in equation (6.9). By definition of the notional labor supply, there are $L_{.1}^{m+1}$ individuals such that the criterion G_h is positive. Rationing employment in the formal segment of the labor market to only L_1^{dm} individuals is equivalent to selecting the L_1^{dm} individuals with the highest G_h. Put another way, it is equivalent to expelling from the notional labor supply the N individuals with the lowest score G_h. Whether those individuals will go to the informal sector or to inactivity depends on which one of the two terms on the right-hand side of equation (6.14) is binding. The opposite procedure can be applied to the case in which there is excess demand in the formal segment of the labor market.

The preceding procedure has to be applied independently for the various types (n) of labor, depending on whether there is a potentially binding minimum wage for both skilled and unskilled workers. Practically, however, the minimum wage is assumed to be binding only for skilled workers. In other words, the market for unskilled workers is assumed to clear through the wage scale factor w_2.

The description of the way the segmentation of the labor market and the rigidity of wages are taken into account in the present IMH model of the Philippine economy is now complete, except for a last detail. The framework that has just been presented is based on the heterogeneity of individual productivities, π_h. This heterogeneity implies that, at the aggregate level, there is a relationship between the number of people being employed in one segment, j, of the labor market and their productivity. As can be seen from the ranking given by equation (6.14), people who leave the formal labor market in case of a contraction are not taken randomly in the initial population of employees in the formal sector. The same is true of those who would join if the formal sector were expanding, and consequently, it is true of the informal segment of the labor market. This means that the average productivity of workers in the two segments of the labor market depends on the number of people working there. This endogeneity of the labor productivity must be taken into account in the CGE part of the model. Thus, for each type of labor, the BU part of the algorithm must return at each iteration not only the (constrained) total labor supply in the two segments $j = 1, 2$ of the labor market, $\bar{L}_{.j}^{m+1}(\varepsilon^{m+1})$, but also the mean productivity of the two groups of workers, $\hat{\pi}_{.j}^{m+1}(\varepsilon^{m+1})$, which is a function of the cost of entry into the formal segment.

The original algorithm has now been generalized to noncompetitive mechanisms that affect microeconomic agents in a way that depends on their comparative individual characteristics. These mechanisms are likely to matter in determining the distributional impact of a policy reform. The fact that this can be done in a rather simple way within the present sequential algorithm may be an important advantage in comparison with the simultaneous resolution of a fully integrated micro-macro CGE model.

Application to a Trade Reform in the Philippines

This section discusses the results obtained in applying the above described IMH model to the study of the distributional effects of a trade reform in the Philippines. Important details of the actual specification of the model are discussed before focusing on the results of a few simulations.

The CGE model used in this chapter is based on the EXTER model (externally open model) of a standard small developing economy provided by Decaluwé, Martens, and Savard (2001), with extensions that take into account the dualism of the labor market. The CGE model is disaggregated into 20 sectors and includes 873 equations. The bottom part of the overall micro-macro model is based on a sample of 39,520 households.

The main data sources used in that exercise are the 1997 Family Income and Expenditure Survey (FIES), the Labor Force Survey (LFS) for 1997 to 1998, and the 1990 social accounting matrix (SAM). The FIES and LFS were used first to estimate the structural econometric labor supply model described in equation (6.9) and then were used in the micro simulation module. Both surveys are based on the same master sample, and 98 percent of the households are found in the FIES and LFS. The FIES and SAM were used for the macro CGE module. The main data manipulation required was the conversion of the FIES nomenclature into the national accounts nomenclature found in the SAM. This conversion was relatively easy and straightforward, because the level of aggregation was quite high in the FIES. It is not necessary to have perfect consistency between the income and expenditure accounts at the micro and macro levels, because the effects are transmitted from the aggregate results of the micro module to the macro CGE model through percentage variations. This way of linking the micro module and the CGE model also avoids the adjustment of the structure of households' expenditure observed in the micro data.

The household micro simulation module relies on a representation of the spending and labor supply behavior of the household. Household consumption is modeled with a linear expenditure demand system (LES) based on total consumption expenditures. The calibration method proposed by Dervis, de Melo, and Robinson (1982), with all households having the same income elasticity for all goods, as well as the same Frisch parameter, is used. The resulting demand for consumption goods is made consistent with observed spending in the FIES through household-specific additive shift parameters.[7] Total expenditure is derived from total income after savings and income taxes. Both the savings rate and the income tax rate are taken to be fixed and household specific.[8] All transfers received and given are exogenous.

On the income side, capital endowments are supposed to be proportional to the level of capital income observed in the 1997 FIES. Labor incomes are given by the model discussed in the preceding section. Based on information provided in the FIES and LFS, workers were classified as employed in the formal or informal sector depending on their occupations as specified in the survey.[9]

At the macro level, the main features of the CGE model are as follows.[10] Producers in the various sectors of the economy are assumed to maximize profits in a fully competitive environment subject to a Cobb-Douglas production function for effective labor and capital and to a Leontief function for intermediate inputs. In each sector, it is assumed that formal and informal firms produce the same aggregate good and that they can be aggregated in a single representative firm, employing simultaneously formal and informal labor.[11] The aggregate labor input in the Cobb-Douglas production function is supposed to be the cost-minimizing combination of formal and informal labor under the assumption of a constant elasticity of substitution (CES) between them. In all sectors, the model distinguishes between skilled and unskilled labor. Both types of labor are fully mobile across sectors, but capital is assumed to be fixed, which generates branch-specific returns to capital. This assumption is consistent with a medium-term perspective on the effect of trade liberalization.

In terms of trade, the Philippines is assumed to be a small open economy. The demand of imported goods is derived from Armington's (1969) specification of a CES between domestic and foreign goods. Likewise, domestic production is allocated to the domestic or foreign markets (exports) through a standard constant elasticity of transformation (CET) function.

On the consumer side, the income of the RH is composed of earnings from skilled and unskilled labor, capital payments, dividends, and transfers from other agents (households and remittances from abroad). As consumption is determined by the micro module, the aggregate saving rate of households is implicitly allowed to vary.

The government levies an income tax (on households and firms), taxes on goods and services, and import duties and transfers from the rest of the world. Its expenditures include various subsidies, the production of public services, and public investments.

As for closure rules, total investment is exogenous and current government expenditures are scaled up or down to balance investment and savings. The exchange rate is endogenous and adjusts to meet an exogenous current account constraint. Finally, the gross domestic product (GDP) deflator is used as a *numéraire*. These closure rules are equivalent to assuming that the burden of the adjustment to any reform is born by households, either directly through their income or expenditures or indirectly through current government expenditures.

The policy simulation reported in this chapter consists of an across-the-board reduction in import duties of 30 percent. This is a rather conventional exercise in the analysis of the effects of trade reforms. The Philippines is a rather open economy—the average tariff rate is around 12 percent—and thus no large effect is expected from such a reform. Because initial protection is heterogeneous across sectors, such a reform entails some restructuring of the economy, which should have some effect on the price system and on the distribution of welfare.

The simulation is performed under different specifications of the overall micro-macro model and assumptions about the functioning of the labor market (see table 6.1). In a first specification, the labor market is supposed to be fully competitive with market-clearing wages in both the formal and informal segments. In the second specification, the real wage is assumed to be fixed in the formal sector, and adjustments are supposed to take place in the way described in the preceding section. The objective of the third specification is essentially methodological. Only the first iteration of the algorithm described above was performed, which is equivalent to the MSS approach. The objective of the comparison of the second and third specifications is to get some idea about the consequences of ignoring the feedback effects from the micro simulation to the macro part of model and to get some idea about the overall precision of the MSS approach. To maximize the precision of the MSS approach, the first iteration at the CGE level was performed with a single RH that

Table 6.1 Definition of Model Specification Used

Definition of specification	Acronym
Integrated multihousehold model with flexible wages	IMH_FL_w
Integrated multihousehold model with fixed formal wage	IMH_FX_w^1
Micro simulation sequential approach with flexible wages	MSS_FL_w
Micro simulation sequential approach with fixed formal wage	MSS_FX_w^1

Source: Authors' classification.

approximated the aggregate consumption and labor supply behavior implied by the micro part of the algorithm.

Aggregate Effects

The direct effect of liberalizing trade is to reduce the price of imports and, therefore, to increase the domestic demand for the most protected goods. Given the fixed current account balance, the real exchange rate has to go up, thus reducing imports and increasing exports to balance out the current account. More important, the government income is negatively affected by the drop in tariffs. As total investment is exogenous, government consumption must be cut down to balance savings and fixed investments. It is this direct revenue effect of the trade reform that produces the most important general equilibrium effects in the model. Other effects are due to the shifting of part of consumption from nontradable to tradable goods caused by change in relative prices (numerical results are shown in the first column of table 6.2).

The strong reduction in government expenditure puts downward pressure on the labor market as civil servants are laid off. In the first and third specifications, real formal wages are flexible and they are

Table 6.2 Macro Results

Variable	Base	IMH_FL_w (percentage change)	IMH_FX_w[1] (percentage change)	MSS_FL_w (percentage change)	MSS_FX_w[1] (percentage change)
Gross domestic product	104,510.0	−0.04	−0.69	−0.05	−1.27
Real household income	86,476.0	1.45	1.13	1.37	0.64
Household real consumption	72,607.0	1.00	1.40	1.35	1.03
Formal wage (index)	1.0	−3.18	0	−3.86	0
Informal wage (vs. formal)	0.5	0.61	−1.25	0.67	−0.46
Government income	20,367.0	−8.39	−8.43	−8.32	−8.84
Real public spending	16,818.0	−6.63	−11.34	−9.48	−13.02
Real investment	23,684.0	2.25	2.26	2.02	2.17
Firm income	26,172.0	0.60	0.55	0.74	0.14
Firm savings	7,810.0	1.04	0.95	1.29	0.24
Employment rate	0.8316.0	≈0	−0.66	≈0	−2.03
Exchange rate (index)	1.0	0.23	0.30	0.17	0.27

Source: Authors' calculations.
Note: The Base column units are billion pesos, except as otherwise specified.

driven down by this drop in labor demand. This reduces the overall cost of labor and pushes employment up in other sectors, including informal employment. As the public sector is more intensive in formal labor, the end result is a drop in real formal wages and a slight increase in informal wages. This result is partly due to the fact that nontradable sectors, which gain relative to the tradable sectors from the change in relative prices, are on average more intensive in informal labor.

On the supply side, these changes in relative wages induce some workers to move from the formal to the informal segments of the labor market and induce other workers to become inactive, in accordance with the labor supply model discussed above. The change in relative wages is not big enough to produce substantial changes in output. Thus, GDP decreases only slightly. On the demand side, the drop in government expenditures is compensated by an increase in real investment, which is caused by the drop in the relative prices of imports and, to a lesser extent, by the drop in household consumption.

Things are somewhat different when wages are assumed to be rigid in the formal sector (see table 6.2, second column). As before, formal workers are laid off by the government sector, but as formal wages do not fall, these workers do not find jobs in the other sectors and move to inactivity or to informal work at a lower productivity. This excess supply of formal labor in turn leads to a slight drop in informal wages—unlike in the preceding specification. Interestingly enough, this movement of labor comes with some changes in the average productivity of labor in the two sectors. Average productivity, of both skilled and unskilled workers, increases by 1.03 percent in the formal sector and decreases by 0.61 percent in the informal sector. Overall, GDP falls by 0.69 percent in the IMH model, while 0.7 percent of the labor force goes to inactivity. On the demand side, the price rigidity induced by wage rigidity reduces the substitution of public spending by investment or household consumption. In effect, households are more severely affected by the trade reform, and their real income falls by substantially more than with flexible wages. Because of the lack of response of domestic prices in sectors employing predominantly formal workers, the devaluation is more pronounced, amounting to 50 percent more than in the full-employment simulation.

Sectoral Effects

Changes in the structure of production shown in table 6.3 are easily interpreted in light of the preceding arguments. These changes result from the combination of four types of effects: (1) the contraction of public spending; (2) changes in labor costs as analyzed above; (3) changes caused by the drop in tariffs—lower input prices but

Table 6.3 Structural Effects of the Trade Reform, Output (Value Added) Change by Sector

Sector	Base (pesos, billion)	IMH_FL_w (percentage change)	IMH_FX_w[1] (percentage change)	MSS_FL_w (percentage change)	MSS_FX_w[1] (percentage change)
Palay[a] and corn	5,198	0.29	0.41	0.42	0.13
Fruit and vegetable	4,211	0.19	0.51	0.28	0.26
Coconut	1,790	0.38	0.63	0.47	0.21
Livestock	4,474	0.42	0.68	0.57	0.37
Fishing	3,997	0.27	0.81	0.37	0.28
Other agriculture	1,846	−0.26	0.92	−0.20	−0.08
Logging and timber	857	0.54	0.76	0.65	0.40
Mining	1,604	1.50	1.59	1.62	1.16
Manufacturing	13,112	0.83	0.72	0.96	0.30
Rice manufacturing	2,023	0.46	0.56	0.61	0.27
Meat industry	2,081	0.57	0.78	0.77	0.41
Food manufacturing	3,696	−0.03	0.39	0.03	0.06
Electricity, gas, and water	2,341	0.04	−0.52	0.04	−1.05
Construction	6,848	1.15	1.49	1.26	1.24
Commerce	15,150	0.64	0.68	0.77	0.28
Transport and commerce	5,206	0.44	0.46	0.55	0
Finance	3,580	−0.02	−0.81	−0.05	−1.33
Real estate	7,314	0.87	0.49	1.16	0.24
Services	6,960	0.91	0.31	0.98	−0.39
Public services	12,223	−6.06	−10.40	−7.32	−12.24

Source: Authors' calculations.

a. *Palay* is the term used in the Philippines to designate the rice grain in its husk that cannot be consumed directly.

also enhanced competition of imports; and (4) changes caused by the devaluation, which dampens the effect of the tariff cut and favors export sectors. The contraction of the public sector is more pronounced with rigid wages because the effect of lower revenues caused by the fall in tariffs is not compensated for by a drop in labor cost. It can be seen that the difference is quite substantial—the drop is 60 percent more pronounced with rigid formal wages. Through backward links, the drop in public spending has a negative effect on various sectors. This effect is uncompensated by other effects in the finance and utility sectors when wages are rigid. Output thus falls in both sectors, but when wages are flexible, it is compensated by the drop in labor cost.

The flexibility of labor costs tends to compensate for the reduction of protection in sectors exposed to foreign competition, except when those sectors are relatively more intensive in informal labor, the cost of which was seen to increase in the flexible wage specification. This is the case in the other agriculture and food manufacturing sectors, the output of which tends to decline. This fall is not observed in the case of rigid formal wages, because the cost of informal labor tends to fall, thus compensating for the enhanced exposition of these sectors to foreign competition.

Favorable consequences of the trade reform and the accompanying devaluation of the domestic currency can be seen on export-oriented sectors like mining, logging, and some agricultural subsectors. The drop in tariffs is favorable in sectors with import-intensive inputs like construction. In all these cases, the direction and intensity of output changes are comparable across the flexible and rigid formal wage specifications, with the slight differences in output changes being mostly attributable to the differences in labor costs.

Overall, it is interesting to see that assumptions made about the flexibility or rigidity of formal wages do make a difference in both the aggregate and the structural effects of trade reform. The contraction of the public sector is more pronounced in the case of rigid wages, which entails a contraction of GDP and a contraction in sectors that depend on public demand. More than this rather mechanical effect occurs, however. Differences in the changes in labor costs and the asymmetry in the changes in the cost of informal labor are responsible for additional structural effects.

All of these effects would be magnified if the trade reform had been more ambitious, for example, with the total elimination of tariffs. In that case, however, the assumption that most of the adjustment would be borne by recurrent public expenditures would have been untenable. Part of this assumption should have been applied to investment, with the effects being difficult to analyze in an essentially static framework.

Poverty Effects

The main objective of the methodology used in this chapter is to derive the impact of policy reforms defined at the macro level on the distribution of income and, in particular, on poverty. Table 6.4 shows the impact of the trade reform analyzed in this section on poverty according to the three specifications that have been used. Poverty is summarized by the three usual Foster-Greer-Thorbecke (1984) indicators. FGT_0 stands for the poverty headcount, which is the proportion of people below the poverty line. FGT_1 is the depth of poverty, which measures the amount of money that should be transferred to the poor

Table 6.4 Effects on Poverty (FGT Poverty Indexes) for the Whole Population and by Education Groups

Poverty index	Groups	Base	IMH_FL_w (percent)	IMH_FX_w[1] (percent)	MSS_FL_w (percent)	MSS_FX_w[1] (percent)
FGT$_0$	All	0.311	−2.19	−1.46	−2.21	−1.79
FGT$_1$	All	0.096	−2.82	−1.67	−2.90	−2.25
FGT$_2$	All	0.040	−3.63	−1.75	−3.54	−2.68
	0	0.564	−1.33	−1.48	−1.47	−1.55
	1	0.501	−1.91	−1.38	−2.15	−1.58
	2	0.384	−2.02	−0.81	−1.79	−1.25
FGT$_0$	3	0.317	−2.78	−2.11	−1.84	−2.45
	4	0.184	−3.93	−3.08	−3.97	−3.28
	5	0.092	−2.78	−0.34	−3.38	−2.06
	6	0.021	−3.91	−1.96	−4.63	−3.42
	0	0.185	−2.47	−2.47	−2.13	−2.46
	1	0.168	−2.47	−1.75	−2.59	−2.15
	2	0.116	−2.97	−1.56	−3.09	−2.17
FGT$_1$	3	0.090	−3.23	−1.79	−3.26	−2.57
	4	0.048	−3.31	−1.68	−3.64	−2.29
	5	0.022	−3.48	1.56	−3.85	−2.51
	6	0.005	−3.78	0.03	−4.76	−3.42
	0	0.080	−3.36	−3.07	−2.87	−3.06
	1	0.075	−3.26	−2.12	−3.28	−2.68
	2	0.048	−3.86	−1.60	−3.74	−2.54
FGT$_2$	3	0.035	−3.94	−2.07	−3.87	−3.30
	4	0.018	−4.04	−0.62	−4.24	−2.11
	5	0.007	−4.52	6.37	−4.62	−2.19
	6	0.002	−4.04	3.35	−4.44	−3.73

Source: Authors' calculations.

Note: FGT = Foster-Greer-Thorbecke (1984) indicators; FGT$_0$ = poverty headcount; FGT$_1$ = depth of poverty; FGT$_2$ = severity of poverty. Education groups are defined in annex 6B.

to eliminate poverty under perfect targeting. It may be expressed as the product of the headcount and the poverty gap, or the relative distance at which poor people are from the poverty line. Severity of poverty, FGT$_2$, corresponds to the same concept but uses the square of the distance from the poverty line, and thus gives more weight to extreme poverty. Because micro-macro modeling allows for taking into account the whole distribution, it would be possible to use any other poverty indicator available in the literature. A more comprehensive representation of the change in the distribution caused by the trade reform is shown below. At this stage, the analysis concentrates only on these three poverty measures in the whole population or in groups defined by the education of household heads.

Before getting into the detail of table 6.4, it is worth insisting on the various forces behind changes in the three poverty indexes. There are two sources of changes. The first is purely distributional. It arises because the income of different households changes in different ways and proportions caused by the trade reform and its general equilibrium effects on household incomes. The second is found in the changes that take place in the structure of prices and that modify the real income of households, possibly in different ways depending on their consumption basket. Two possibilities can be used to take this into account. The first one corrects all changes in (nominal) household incomes by a price index that is based on their consumption, maintaining the poverty line (nominally) fixed. The second approach modifies the poverty line only, using a price index meant to fit the average consumption basket of the poor. This second approach is pursued in the calculations summarized in table 6.4, with the price index being based on the minimum basket of consumption goods used in the LES representation of household consumption behavior in the micro part of the micro-macro algorithm.[12]

This effect of the changes in the final price of goods on the poverty line—that is, the price effect—is undoubtedly negative. The trade liberalization directly reduces the price of imported goods and of those domestic goods that compete with them, and indirectly reduces the price of goods that use imported inputs. Other things equal, poverty would thus fall, this being true for all poverty indexes. But one has to consider the income effect or, in other words, the way the nominal income of households is modified through the general equilibrium effects. With flexible wages, it may be expected that the income effect will reduce poverty further. It is true that formal labor incomes are lower because of the trade reform, but the opposite is true of informal labor incomes. Moreover, it was seen that changes in the volume and the structure of employment were minimal. As informal labor incomes are likely to be of greater importance among the poor, it may thus be expected that the income effect also contributes to reducing poverty when wages are flexible.

This pattern is precisely what can be seen in the fourth column of table 6.4. For the whole population, poverty is falling because of the trade reform, and the higher the severity of the poverty index, the higher it falls. This shows that the price effect and the income effect are at work. It can be proven that, by itself, the price effect should reduce FGT_1 and FGT_2 more or less in the same proportion.[13] The fact that FGT_2 falls by proportionally more than FGT_1 means that the relative income of the poorest households is increasing. The same pattern may be observed for the various education groups, except for the most educated ones—for which changes in table 6.4 may not be relevant because of low initial poverty. But the income effect is likely not to be important in those groups for which most labor income is likely to come from the formal segment of the labor market.

The examination of the changes in poverty indexes by education group with the flexible wage specification seems to suggest that the higher the education level of household heads, the stronger the impact of the trade reform on poverty. This correlation must be taken with much care. If, indeed, most of the drop in poverty with flexible wages comes from the lowering of the poverty line, then there may be something purely mechanical, evident in the fact that the change in poverty indexes increases with the education level. For instance, the elasticity of the poverty headcount (FGT_0) with respect to the poverty line, z, is given by the ratio $zf(z)/F(z)$, where $f(\ )$ is the density of the distribution of income and $F(\ )$ is the cumulative function. It is conceivable that this ratio changes in a systematic way with the level of poverty across education groups. Checking this would require a rather detailed estimate of the density of the distribution of income in the various groups.

More interesting is the fact that different patterns in poverty changes are obtained under the assumption of rigid wages in the formal sector and the rationing scheme that is supposed to apply to the labor market in that case. At the aggregate level, first, it can be seen that the drop in poverty is much less important than with flexible wages. Moreover, the difference tends to be bigger when moving from headcount to depth of poverty and then to severity of poverty. Not only are fewer people lifted out of poverty, but welfare improvements are also lower for the poorest.

As the initial effect of the drop in tariffs on the poverty line is comparable in the two specifications, the explanation of that difference must be found in different income effects. Indeed, the fact that informal labor incomes decrease with rigid formal wages and that some workers withdraw from the labor force has an impact on poverty that goes in the direction opposite of the decline in the poverty line and that is opposite to the income effect seen with flexible formal wages. The same phenomenon is behind the disappearance of the pattern that was present in the drop in poverty by education groups with flexible wages. Opposite income effects affect all groups—not only the low-education groups that are more affected by the drop in informal labor incomes, but also the higher-income groups in which some people are forced into informal work or into inactivity.

At this stage, the interest of modeling explicitly the effect of the trade reform on the distribution of income at the individual level appears quite clearly. The phenomena just described could not be considered properly using a traditional RH approach. The impact of such a reform on poverty depends on individual household circumstances: how much of the initial income comes from informal labor, how many people are forced out of their jobs in the formal sector, and so on. An aggregate analysis would, at best, be able to give information on the effect of lower prices on the poverty line, and possibly make a tiny change in the mean income of some household groups.

Changes in the Overall Distribution

Rather than focusing on poverty, the macro-micro framework used in this chapter allows for an analysis of the change in the whole distribution of income within the population. In what follows, this change is described by the growth incidence curve that shows the changes in real income by percentile of households before and after trade reform. Figure 6.2 illustrates the results of the specification with a flexible (IMH_FL_w^1) and a fixed real wage in the formal sector.

Figure 6.2 indeed shows substantial differences in the distributional impact of the reform with these two specifications. The top of the distribution, between percentiles 88 and 97, are the relative losers

Figure 6.2 Comparative Growth Incidence Curves for Total Population: IMH_FX_w^1 versus IMH_FL_w

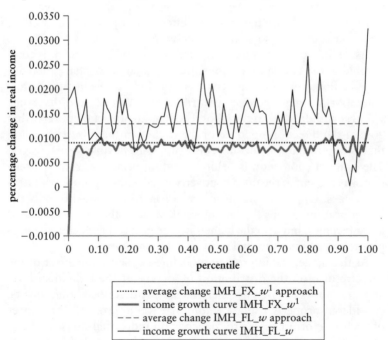

Source: Authors' calculations.

(although net gainers) in the specification; flexible wage rates and the top two percentiles are relative winners. Conversely, the growth incidence curve is rather flat with the fixed wage rate specification except for the very bottom percentiles, which are both relative and absolute losers.

The explanation of that difference is both simple and interesting. With the flexible wage rates, it was seen in table 6.2 that the trade reform had a negative effect on the wage rates in the formal sector of the economy. Households that derive income almost exclusively from labor in the formal sector belong mostly to the 87 to 97 percentiles of the distribution, whereas other households with members in the formal sector derive income from other sources as well, such as land or capital. Likewise, households in the top three percentiles include business owners in the export and informal sectors.

These effects largely disappear with the fixed wage specification, because costs and profits are essentially rigid. In that case, what drives the negative part of the growth incidence curve in the first percentiles is the fact that, because of the rigidity in the labor market, some households lose their job and end up inactive. In effect, households in the bottom percentiles are being replaced by households that were initially at a higher rank in the distribution but that are affected by job losses. In other words, the relative drop in formal wages with the flexible wage specification is replaced by formal employment contraction, with some workers being absorbed by the informal sector—moving down in the income ranking but with limited impact on average income—and other workers losing jobs.

Comparison of Micro Simulation Sequential and the Complete Algorithm

It is now time to examine the third and fourth specifications appearing in tables 6.2–6.4, which are simply the first TD iterations of the micro-macro model rather than its complete resolution. The issue is to determine whether this simpler micro simulation approach used by several authors is a satisfactory approximation of the overall effects of the simulated reform.

The answer to that question depends on the type of result and the specification that is being examined. With the flexible wage specification, gaps between the first iteration and the complete resolution are quite limited. The first iteration only exaggerates the contraction of public spending, because it misses the household consumption feedback in the complete algorithm, even though the macro model tries to mimic the aggregate consumption behavior of the whole population of households. The same is true with the rigid wage specification except for the fact that, because of this rigidity, the gap in public spending feeds into an equivalent gap in GDP and employment, exaggerating the negative effect of the reform.

The same remark applies to sectoral changes (table 6.3). Gaps are limited in the flexible wage specification, with the first iteration underestimating systematically final changes in the complete model. In the fixed wage specification, differences are bigger in size and in the direction of the effect. Discrepancies can be seen between the first iteration and the complete model that come essentially from the overestimation of the drop in real public spending in the former model. This bias generates negative biases in all sectors that provide inputs to the public sector (such as utilities, finance, and services).

Poverty figures show the same pattern. Aggregate results are comparable with the flexible wage specification, and they tend to overestimate the drop in poverty with the flexible wage specification. Poverty effects in the flexible wage case essentially are due to price changes that have been seen to be rather satisfactorily approximated by the first iteration. Results are more surprising in the rigid wage case. Because it tends to overestimate the drop in GDP and employment, one would have expected the initial negative impact on poverty to be smaller than at equilibrium. The explanation of that correction is to be related to sectoral biases for the pure TD rigid wage specification. This result is fully confirmed by the comparison of the growth incidence curves of the MSS and complete IMH rigid specifications (figure 6.3). The first iteration simply misses the increase in poverty because of job losses at the very bottom of the distribution. This does not mean that no job loss occurs in the first iteration, but rather that these losses do not take place in the same part of the distribution because they are not located in the same sectors.

It is thus at the sectoral level that the MSS approach results differ the most from the results of the IMH approach. This is counterintuitive, and larger deviations for the aggregate variables were expected given the incomplete feedback effects of the MSS approach. Results would have been quite different if the initial resolution of the CGE had been undertaken with a single household whose behavior had little to do with the aggregation of individual household behavior in the micro database. At the same time, this relative imprecision of the first-round micro effects points to the interest of resolving the whole model, or at least to iterate between the macro and the micro parts of the full micro-macro model.

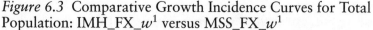

Figure 6.3 Comparative Growth Incidence Curves for Total Population: IMH_FX_w^1 versus MSS_FX_w^1

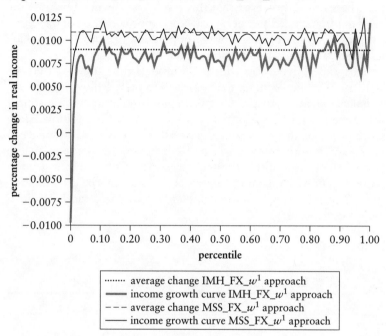

Source: Authors' calculations.

Conclusion

This chapter tries to take into account the microeconomic consequences of a macro policy through the integration of a micro database of households within a conventional CGE framework. This
was done in two ways: (1) through a conventional TD approach
with an aggregate CGE model feeding a micro simulation module
(the MSS model) without any kind of feedback at the macro level;
and (2) through iterations between those two modules to obtain the
solution of an IMH model.

In the simulation of trade liberalization policies undertaken in this
chapter, differences between the two approaches were found to be
important in the presence of rigidities in the labor market, which led
to some rationing situations. In that case, the MSS approach tended
to overestimate the negative impact of the reform on GDP and
employment and, consequently, to underestimate its effect on reducing poverty. In comparison, differences between the two approaches
appeared to be minor in the presence of flexible wages, as most micro

effects were essentially channeled through price-induced changes in real income, rather than quantity adjustment at the micro level. It must be stressed, however, that this result was obtained because the CGE model included a rather satisfactory approximation of the aggregate consumption behavior of the population of households, which itself required several simulations at the micro level.

This experimentation with IMH models thus suggests that the standard TD micro simulation approach to the distributional impact of policies is satisfactory as long as no purely quantitative adjustment is assumed to take place at the micro level. This fits intuition. More work is needed to experiment and measure whether the difference in results is relatively robust to change in behavioral hypotheses, macro closure rules, or to different policy scenarios. Conversely, it is interesting to know that simple iterative techniques can be used to solve integrated models with more complete micro-based market adjustment mechanisms.

Annex 6A

Table 6A.1 Labor Supply Model Estimation Results

Regressor	Coefficient	Standard error	t-statistic	Prob > |t|
Probit				
Constant	1.61683	0.46963	3.44281	0.00029
Education	0.14937	0.00932	16.02265	0
Age	−0.10990	0.02984	−3.68280	0.00012
Age^2	0.00121	0.00030	3.99504	0.00003
Experience	0.02414	0.00976	2.47298	0.00671
Sex of head	−0.02718	0.05456	−0.49819	0.30918
Family size	0.06281	0.00779	8.06703	0
Two-stage Heckman selection model estimations—formal market				
Constant	4.15523	0.55819	7.44413	0
Education	0.22921	0.03320	6.90336	0
Age	0.06746	0.02143	3.14754	0.00084
Age^2	−0.00064	0.00025	−2.59636	0.00476
Experience	−0.01057	0.01798	−0.58781	0.27837
Sex of head	−0.26829	0.08243	−3.25484	0.00058
Family size	0.00591	0.04418	0.13380	0.44679
λ_1	−0.90843	0.25598	−3.54883	0.00020
Two-stage Heckman selection model estimations—informal market				
Constant	3.25639	0.48463	6.71934	0
Education	0.12500	0.03129	3.99533	0.00003
Age	0.05280	0.01901	2.77727	0.00275
Age^2	−0.00055	−0.00055	−2.52059	0.00588
Experience	−0.01826	0.01756	−1.03933	0.14935
Sex of head	0.11637	0.09675	1.20278	0.11456
Family size	0.04344	0.03247	1.33789	0.10650
λ_2	−1.65604	0.25121	−6.59213	0

Annex 6B

Table 6B.1 Education Code Definition

Education code	Level of education
1	Elementary undergraduate
2	Elementary graduate
3	One to three years of high school
4	High school graduate
5	College undergraduate
6	At least college graduate
0	Not reported or no grade

Annex 6C

Table 6C.1 Notations

Variable	Description
p_i	Market price in sector i
w_k	Wage rate by type of labor k
k_i	Capital of sector i
P_i	Profit of sector i
π_{hi}	Specific productivity endowment by household h
Y_i	Supply of sector i
y_h	Income of household h
C_{hi}	Consumption of good j by household h
L_i^d	Labor demand by sector i
$L_{h,k}$	Supply of labor k by household h
ε_h	Household h specific characteristics
α_{hi}	Household h endowment of capital of sector i

Notes

The authors thank D. Boccanfuso, J. Davies, and R. Medhora for very helpful advice and comments, as well as participants at the World Institute for Development Economics Research of the United Nations University (UNU-WIDER) conference in Helsinki, March 2003, for their valuable comments.

1. It is known from the literature on aggregation that properties for aggregating labor supply are more demanding than those for aggregating consumption functions—see Deaton and Muellbauer (1980) and Muellbauer (1981). Note that introducing nonlinearity in labor supply through participation conditions is enough to make aggregation impossible.

2. The FP algorithm could be written in the space of goods and labor rather than in the space of prices.

3. This is the methodology proposed by Rutherford, Tarr, and Shepotylo (2005), but at every step of the algorithm rather than only at the first step.

4. The National Wage and Productivity Commission of the Department of Labour and Employment of the Philippines establishes a grid for minimum wages in formal sector activities. The wage grid is extremely complex because it is region specific, and each region has a multidimensional table specifying the size of the firms, sector of activity, and location characteristics, among other factors. Complete tables can be found on the commission's Web page at http://www.nwpc.dole.gov.ph/.

5. Details of the procedure and a discussion of results can be found in Savard (2006, chapter 3). The simplification with respect to Magnac (1991) consisted of running a univariate probit on participation at the first step, with the identifying assumption that participation depended on the difference between an average of formal and informal earnings and the reservation wage. Then ordinary least squares were run on the earnings within the two segments of the labor market with the standard Heckman correction for selectivity. Finally, arbitrary assumptions were made about the standard deviation of the cost of entry and the unobserved term in the reservation wage.

6. See note 5.

7. These conditions seem to make possible the perfect aggregation of individual demands. Yet full aggregation does not hold because of specific individual savings and tax rates. The authors could have chosen to use Frisch parameters and LES parameters differentiated across households could have been chosen. This choice was raising some calibration difficulties, however. Moreover, it seemed desirable for households to have the same nondiscretionary spending, so that poverty analysis could be based on that minimum basket of goods. The LES parameters in this application are drawn from Pollak and Wales (1969) after establishing some correspondence rule for the definition of goods.

8. In fact, the saving rate is based on disposable income minus the nondiscretionary income—that is, the cost of the minimum basket of consumption goods—assuming that the heterogeneous savings and tax rates are enough to rule out perfect aggregation of household consumption behavior.

9. The information on the type of work performed by the worker is detailed with decomposition into 200 types of work categories. Given the rich set of information, it was not too difficult to classify the workers as formal and informal workers.

10. The complete equation listing can be provided upon a request to the authors.

11. This approach is similar to what is proposed by Agénor, Izquierdo, and Fofack (2003) and Boccanfuso, Cabral, and Savard (2005).

12. For a discussion about the advantages and inconveniences of the two approaches, see Ravallion (1998).

13. It may be easily proven that $\varepsilon = \dfrac{z(\partial FGT_\alpha/\partial z)}{FGT_\alpha} =$ $\alpha\left[\dfrac{FGT_{\alpha-1}}{FGT_\alpha} - 1\right]$, where z is the poverty line and $\alpha > 0$. The initial poverty indexes suggest that ε is approximately the same for $\alpha = 1$ and $\alpha = 2$.

References

Agénor, Pierre-Richard, and Karim El Aynaoui. 2005. "Politiques du marché du travail et chômage au Maroc: une analyse quantitative." *Revue d'économie du développement* 19 (1): 5–51.

Agénor, Pierre-Richard, Alejandro Izquierdo, and Hippolythe Fofack. 2003. "IMMPA: A Quantitative Macroeconomic Framework for the Analysis of Poverty Reduction Strategies." World Bank, Washington, DC.

Armington, Paul. 1969. "A Theory of Demand for Products Distinguished by Place of Production." IMF Staff Paper No. 16, 159–76, International Monetary Fund, Washington, DC.

Boccanfuso, Dorothee, Francois Joseph Cabral, and Luc Savard. 2005. "Une Analyse d'Impacts de la Libéralisation de la Filière Arachide au Sénégal : une Application EGC Multi-ménages." [An Impact Analysis of the Groundnut Sector Liberalization in Senegal. An Application of a Multi-Household CGE Model]/*Perspective Afrique* 1 (1): 32–58.

Bourguignon, François, Anne-Sophie Robilliard, and Sherman Robinson. 2005. "Representative versus Real Households in the Macroeconomic Modelling of Inequality." In *Frontiers in Applied General Equilibrium Modelling*, eds. T. J. Kehoe, T. N. Srinivasan, and J. Whalley. Cambridge: Cambridge University Press.

Bourguignon, François, and Amedeo Spadaro. 2006. "Microsimulation as a Tool for Evaluating Redistribution Policies." *Journal of Economic Inequality* 4 (1): 77–106.

Chen, Shaohua, and Martin Ravallion. 2004. "Welfare Impacts of China's Accession to the World Trade Organization." *The World Bank Economic Review* 18 (1): 29–57.

Coady, David, and Rebecca Harris. 2001. "A Regional General Equilibrium Analysis of the Welfare Impact of Cash Transfers: An Analysis of Progresa in Mexico." TMD Discussion Paper No. 76, International Food Policy Research Institute, Washington, DC.

Cockburn, John. 2006. "Trade Liberalisation and Poverty in Nepal: Computable General Equilibrium Micro Simulation Analysis." In *Globalization and Poverty. Channels and Policy Responses,* eds. M. Bussolo and J. Round. London and New York: Routledge.

Cogneau, Denis, and Anne-Sophie Robilliard. 2001. "Growth, Distribution, and Poverty in Madagascar: Learning from a Microsimulation Model in a General Equilibrium Framework." DIAL Working Paper 2001/19, and IFPRI-TMD Discussion Paper 61, Développement Institutions et Analyses de Long terme, Paris; and International Food and Research Policy Institute, Washington, DC.

Deaton, Angus, and John Muellbauer. 1980. *Economic and Consumer Behaviour*. Cambridge: Cambridge University Press.

Decaluwé, Bernard, Jean-Christophe Dumont, and Luc Savard. 1999. "How to Measure Poverty and Inequality in General Equilibrium Framework." Cahier de recherche, Centre de Recherche en Économie et Finance Appliquées (CREFA), Université Laval, no. 99-20, Québec.

Decaluwé, Bernard, André Martens, and Luc Savard. 2001. *La politique économique du développement*. Montréal: Presse de l'Université de Montréal.

Dervis, Kemal, Jaime de Melo, and Sherman Robinson. 1982. *General Equilibrium Models for Development Policy*. London: Cambridge University Press.

Devarajan, Shantayanan, Hafex Ghanem, and Karen Thierfelder. 1999. "Labor Market Regulations, Trade Liberalization and the Distribution of Income in Bangladesh." *Journal of Policy Reform* 3 (1): 1–28.

Fortin, Bernard, Nicolas Marceau, and Luc Savard. 1997. "Taxation, Wage Controls and the Informal Sector." *Journal of Public Economics* 66 (2): 293–312.

Foster, James, Joel Greer, and Erik Thorbecke. 1984. "A Class of Decomposable Poverty Measures." *Econometrica* 52 (3): 761–66.

Grandmont, Jean-Michel. 1987. "Distributions of Preferences and the Law of Demand." *Econometrica* 55: 155–61.

Heckman, James, and Gilherme Sedlacek. 1985. "Heterogeneity, Aggregation and Market Wage Functions: An Empirical Model of Self-selection in the Labor Market." *Journal of Political Economy* 93: 1077–125.

Hertel, Thomas, and Jeffrey Reimer. 2004. "Predicting the Poverty Impacts of Trade Reform." Policy Research Working Paper No. 3444. World Bank, Washington, DC.

King, Damien, and Sudhanshu Handa. 2003. "The Welfare Effects of Balance of Payments Reforms: A Macro-Micro Simulation of the Cost of Rent-Seeking." *The Journal of Development Studies* 39 (3): 101–28.

Magnac, Thierry. 1991. "Segmented or Competitive Labor Markets?" *Econometrica* 59 (1): 165–87.

Muellbauer, John. 1981. "Linear Aggregation in Neoclassical Labour Supply." *Review of Economic Studies* XLVIII: 21–36.

Pollak, Robert A., and Terrence J. Wales. 1969. "Estimation of the Linear Expenditure System." *Econometrica* 37 (4): 611–28.

Ravallion, Martin. 1998. "Poverty Line in Theory and in Practice." Living Standards Measurement Study Research Paper No. 133. World Bank, Washington, DC.

Riveros, Luis A. 1993. "Equity Impact and the Effectiveness of Adjustment Policies with a Segmented Labor Market: The Case of the Philippines." *Journal of Economic Development* 18 (2): 81–105.

Roy, A. D. 1951. "Some Thoughts on the Distribution of Earnings." *Oxford Economic Papers* 3 (2): 135–46.

Rutherford, Thomas, David Tarr, and Oleksandr Shepotylo. 2005. "Poverty Effects of Russia's WTO Accession: Modeling 'Real' Household and Endogenous Productivity Effects." World Bank Policy Research Working Paper No. 3473. World Bank, Washington, DC.

Savard, Luc. 2006. "Analyse de pauvreté et distribution des revenus dans la cadre de la modélisation en équilibre général calculable." PhD thesis Paris School of Economics—École des Hautes Études en Sciences Sociales.

Savard, Luc, and Epiphane Adjovi. 1998. "Externalités de la santé et de l'éducation et bien-être: Un MEGC appliqué au Bénin." *L'Actualité Économique/Revue d'Analyse Économique* 74 (3): 523–60.

Thomas, Mark, and Luc Vallée. 1996. "Labor Market Segmentation in Cameroonian Manufacturing." *Journal of Development Studies* 32 (6): 876–98.

Vos, Rob, and Niek De Jong. 2003. "Trade Liberalization and Poverty in Ecuador: A CGE Macro-Microsimulation Analysis." *Economic System Analysis* 15 (2): 211–32.

7

Simulating Targeted Policies
with Macro Impacts:
Poverty Alleviation Policies
in Madagascar

Denis Cogneau and
Anne-Sophie Robilliard

The modeling technique presented in this chapter integrates a static micro simulation module of labor supply or income and consumption demand, which is based on cross-sectional survey data with a static (computable general equilibrium [CGE]–type) macro module. This simulation model is designed to study the short- to medium-term impact of policies that select individuals within groups and have economywide implications. The model is applied to the case of large targeted poverty alleviation policies in Madagascar. The model builds on a structural microeconometric model of occupational choices and labor income that is estimated on a standard cross-sectional microeconomic data set derived from a "multitopic household survey" (see Scott 2003). The motivation for building and using this kind of tool is discussed in the first section. This discussion is followed by the micro simulation module and its econometric estimation and presentation of the integration of the macro and micro modules. The chapter concludes with simulations and results.

A Structural Microeconometric Model of Income Generation

This model is a member of the family of applied macro-micro tools that attempt to account for within-group heterogeneity when simulating the counterfactual distributive effect of a given policy or economic shock. In contrast with other approaches of the same family, this tool places greater weight on the microeconometric side of the model; as a consequence, its macroeconomic and multimarket framework is less sophisticated.

The tool employs a structural microeconometric modeling of occupational choices and labor income formation. Advances in microeconometrics allow the consideration of complex production, labor supply, and consumption behaviors of heterogeneous households and individuals confronted with transaction costs, information asymmetries, and employment rationing—that is, various kinds of "market imperfections." Cogneau and Robilliard (2007) consider the nonrecursive behavior of Malagasy agricultural households in the absence of a market for agricultural labor, which prevents the equalization of the productivity of agricultural labor between households. Structural microeconometric estimation may also explicitly consider the market structure that constrains the decisions of various agents. For example, Cogneau (1999, 2001) estimates a labor income and occupational choice model for Madagascar's capital city of Antananarivo under various assumptions on the segmentation (dualism) of the urban labor market. A synthesis of that earlier work follows.

A Simplified Macro Module Augmentation

The structural nature of the microeconomic module paves the way for a consistent connection to a macro module: agents react to prices and other signals that are determined at the macro level. Because even simple microeconomic models do not lead to perfect aggregation, outcomes from micro decisions must be summed up and measured against each other and against other macro aggregates. To achieve a consistent macro-micro equilibrium, some macro variables (such as prices) vary—until all aggregates arising from the micro components (such as the supply of categories of labor, the consumption demand, or total wage earnings) are equal to the corresponding macro aggregates (such as the demand for categories of labor, the domestic supply of consumption goods, and the wage bill). The macro module includes the determination of these latter macro aggregates and the specification of macro closures for each macro-accounting identity. The module built here is a simple three-market CGE model.

Study of Targeted Policies with Macro Impacts

Because of identification and algorithm limitations, structural microeconometric modeling usually precludes a high level of disaggregation of market segments or sectors. As a result, this approach is less suited for either the study of subtle intersectoral reallocations of supply and demand or fine modifications of the price and earnings schedule.[1]

Simulating short-term targeted policies with macro impacts might be the true comparative advantage of this type of model. This notion is explored in this chapter. In this context, "targeted policies" refers to policies that aim to reach specific categories of the population, most often among the poor, through various targeting devices. These devices include not only labor market interventions like wage policies and workfare programs or job creation linked to foreign direct investment, but also land reforms and product market interventions like marketing boards.

The first problem is to evaluate the efficiency of the targeting device. When the targeting is imperfect and depends on self-selection of individuals, a structural microeconometric model may be most useful. For instance, this model can be used to determine how many people will choose the new wage offer from a workfare program or from an export processing zone. Another problem is to assess the overall distributional impact of such policies within and outside the target population, particularly when its magnitude is big enough to have a macroeconomic impact. Under such circumstances, it may be helpful to apply a general equilibrium model with a clearly defined macro closure.

For instance, the integrated macro-micro modeling framework described in this chapter can be used to answer the following questions:

• How many people will benefit from an increase in the minimum wage, and how will this increase be transmitted to other segments in the labor market through a raise in the informal labor earnings?

• What are the respective impacts of a job-creation policy and of a wage policy in a developing country urban labor market?[2]

• How much will a food price subsidy that is operated through a marketing board benefit small farmers, and how much will it benefit the urban poor through a relative food price reduction?

• How much of the workforce will a workfare program attract, and what will be the consequences on the production and prices of other sectors and, hence, on the overall income distribution?

The Microeconometric Model of Income Generation

This section first presents a canonical version of the model and then discusses the basic identification and micro calibration issues. These are followed by some extensions.

The Labor Income Model

The labor income model presented here follows Roy's model (1951), as formalized by Heckman and Sedlacek (1985), and is characterized by Neal and Rosen (1998) as the most convincing model to explain labor income distribution.

In this model, each "individual" pertains to a given family or household whose composition and location are exogenously determined. Working-age individuals (those 15 years and older) have three types of work opportunities: family work, self-employed work, and wage work. Family work includes all kinds of activities supervised by the household head or the spouse, such as family help in agricultural activities, as well as domestic work, nonmarket labor, and various forms of declared "inactivity." Self-employed work corresponds to informal independent market activities. Wage work includes all other kinds of work performed by (mainly) civil servants and large-firm workers.

To self-employed work ($J = 1$) and wage work ($J = 2$), first assign two potential earnings functions. Individual potential earnings, w_{ji}, are the product of a task price, $\pi_j(J = 1, 2)$, and of a fixed idiosyncratic amount of efficient labor that depends on observable characteristics, X_i (education, labor market experience, and geographic dummies), as well as unobservable skills, t_{ji}:

$$(7.1) \qquad \ln w_{1i} = \ln \pi_1 + X_i\beta_1 + t_{1i}$$

$$(7.2) \qquad \ln w_{2i} = \ln \pi_2 + X_i\beta_2 + t_{2i}.$$

Returns to characteristics β_j are differentiated by sector and by gender.

To family work, associate an unobserved individual value that depends on both individual and household characteristics:

$$(7.3) \qquad \ln \tilde{w}_{0i} = (X_{0i}, Z_{0h})\beta_0 + t_{0i},$$

where $\tilde{w}_0$ may be seen as a reservation wage. Vector X_{0i} contains the same variables as X_i (education, labor market experience, and geographic dummies) plus a variable indicating the father's occupation. Vector Z_{0i}, includes the demographic structure of the household and the household's nonlabor income.

Given these elements, the choice of an occupation J can be expressed as follows:

$$(7.4) \quad J = k \quad \text{iff } w_{ki} = \max(\tilde{w}_{0i}, w_{1i}, w_{2i}) \quad \text{for } k = 0, 1, 2 \,.$$

This simple form of the Roy occupational model assumes that the labor market is not imperfect or segmented; in other words, there is no job rationing.[3] In the presence of segmentation, the selection condition in equation (7.4) does not hold in many cases. Some individuals would prefer to work in a given segment but cannot find an available job. Without any loss of generality,[4] one may introduce one segmentation variable defined as the relative cost of entry between wage work and self-employment:

$$(7.5) \qquad \ln \tilde{w}_{2i} = \ln \tilde{\pi}_2 + X_{2i}\tilde{\beta}_2 + \tilde{t}_{2i} \,.$$

Finally, comparing the respective values attributed to the three labor opportunities, workers allocate their labor according to their individual comparative advantage. The selection condition in equation (7.4) is replaced by the following:

$$i \text{ is observed in family work iff } \tilde{w}_{0i} > w_{1i} \text{ and } \tilde{w}_{0i} > \frac{w_{2i}}{\tilde{w}_{2i}}$$

$$(7.6) \quad i \text{ is observed in self-employment iff } w_{1i} > \tilde{w}_{0i} \text{ and } w_{1i} > \frac{w_{2i}}{\tilde{w}_{2i}}$$

$$i \text{ is observed in wage work iff } \frac{w_{2i}}{\tilde{w}_{2i}} > \tilde{w}_{0i} \text{ and } \frac{w_{2i}}{\tilde{w}_{2i}} > w_{1i} \,.$$

Econometric Identification and Micro Calibration

The segmented model contains the simpler "competitive" Roy model as a particular constrained case (Magnac 1991).

For econometric identification, one must assume independence of the residuals $(t_0, t_1, t_2, \tilde{t}_2)$ between individuals—as well as joint normality for the $(t_0, t_1, t_2, \tilde{t}_2)$ vector:

$$(7.7) \qquad (t_0, t_1, t_2, \tilde{t}_2) \rightarrow N(0, \Sigma) \,.$$

Under these assumptions, the occupational choice and labor income model represented by the expressions in equations $(7.1)-(7.3)$ and the series of selection conditions in equation (7.6) may then be estimated by maximum likelihood; one obtains a bivariate tobit, as in Magnac (1991). The coefficients of self-employment benefits and wages are exactly identified, but only some parameters of the family work value (or reservation wage) and of the relative cost of entry are identified, as shown later.

Likewise, only some elements of the underlying covariance structure between unobservables can be identified. Moreover, observed earnings are measured with errors or include a transient component $\varepsilon_j(j = 1, 2)$ that must be taken into account. These unobservable components of earnings do not enter into labor supply decisions of (risk-neutral) individuals. One may then assume for estimation:

(7.8) $(t_0, t_1, t_2, \tilde{t}_2, \varepsilon_1, \varepsilon_2) \rightarrow N(0, \Sigma^*).$

Under these assumptions, eight variance or correlation parameters may be identified: $\rho = \text{corr}\ (t_1 - t_0, t_2 - \tilde{t}_2 - t_0)$, $\sigma_j = \sqrt{\text{var}(t_j + \varepsilon_j)}$, $k = \dfrac{\sqrt{\text{var}(t_1 - \tilde{t}_0)}}{\sqrt{\text{var}(t_2 - \tilde{t}_2 - \tilde{t}_0)}}$, $\lambda_1 = \text{corr}\ (t_1 + \varepsilon_1, t_1 - t_0)$, $\lambda_2 = \text{corr}\ (t_2 + \varepsilon_2, t_2 - \tilde{t}_2 - t_0)$, and $\mu_j = \text{corr}\ (t_j + \varepsilon_j, t_2 - \tilde{t}_2 - t_1)$ for $j = 1, 2$. While all the parameters of potential earnings in self-employment and wage work are identified, only the contrasts $\dfrac{\beta_1 - \beta_0}{\sigma(t_1 - t_0)}$ and $\dfrac{\beta_2 - \tilde{\beta}_2 - \beta_0}{\sigma(t_1 - \hat{t}_2 - t_0)}$ are identified.

For purposes of simulation, one needs to recover the parameters β_0 and $\tilde{\beta}_2$ for $\tilde{w}_0$ and $\tilde{w}_2$, respectively, and the whole covariance structure, Σ^*. Therefore, proceed to a micro calibration, assuming that measurement errors and transient components are white noises (uncorrelated with others). One might then "guesstimate" three kinds of parameters: (1) the variance of measurement errors, (2) the correlation (ρ_{12}) between t_1 and t_2, and (3) the standard error of $(t_2 - \tilde{t}_2 - t_1)$. A linear system of equations is then solved, with the econometrically estimated parameters and the guesstimated parameters as givens and remaining structural parameters as unknowns. Check that the resulting matrix Σ^* is semi-definite positive.

Then draw for each individual a whole set of unobservables $(t_0, t_1, t_2, \tilde{t}_2, \varepsilon_1, \varepsilon_2)$ within the multidimensional normal distribution with the covariance structure Σ^* and constrain the draws to respect the occupational selection conditions in equation (7.6). For instance, for an individual who is observed in the informal sector, start from the observed $t_1 + \varepsilon_1$ and draw all other unobservable components conditionally on it, constraining the draws to respect $w_1 > \tilde{w}_0$ and $w_1 > \dfrac{w_2}{\tilde{w}_2}$. One finally obtains the set $(\tilde{w}_0, w_1, w_2, \tilde{w}_2)$ for each individual at base "prices" $(\pi_1, \pi_2, \tilde{\pi}_2) = (1, 1, 1)$.[5]

An Extension for Nonhead Household Members

Here assume a hierarchical decision-making process within the household. The household head makes his or her decision first, without taking into account the choices of other household members; the household head's spouse then makes his or her decision; and finally, the other working-age, secondary members make their decisions. The latter decisions are simultaneous. In making their choices, the other nonhead members do not consider the consequences of the decision on other household members.

Accordingly, in the case of nonhead members, a variable indicating the link to the household head (spouse/child/other) is added to the Z_0 vector. In the case of spouses, Z_0 also includes the head's occupational choices and earnings. In the case of nonspouse secondary household members, it includes both the head's and the spouse's occupational choice and earnings.[6]

Farm Income and Reservation Wage in Farm Households

Many household members are typically involved in farm activities.[7] To farming households, associate a reduced farm profit function derived from a Cobb-Douglas technology with homogeneous labor:

$$(7.9) \qquad \ln \Pi_{0h} = \ln p_0 + \alpha \ln L_h + Z_h \theta + u_{0h}.$$

The variable L_h stands for the number of members working on the farm, while the vector Z_h includes the amount of land and capital, the household head's education and age, a dummy variable in the case of a female head, and geographic dummies.

Assume that the farm head always works on the farm (at least on a part-time basis; see the part-time extension in annex 7A). As a result, only nonhead members may choose whether or not to participate in farm work. Moreover, $\tilde{w}_0$ is assumed to depend on the individual's contribution to farm profits. Estimate this contribution as $\Delta \Pi_{0h}$, holding fixed the decisions of other household members and the farm global factor productivity u_0:

$$(7.10) \qquad \ln \Delta \Pi_{0h} = \ln p_0 + \ln(L_{h+i}^{\alpha} - L_{h-i}^{\alpha}) + Z_h \theta + u_{0h},$$

where $L_{h+1} = L_h$ and $L_{h-1} = L_h - 1$ if i is actually working on the farm in h, and $L_{h+1} = L_h + 1$ and $L_{h-1} = L_h$, alternatively.

Here again, the labor decision model is hierarchical between the head of the household and nonhead members, and simultaneous among nonhead members. Then write the value of family work as follows:

$$(7.11) \qquad \ln \tilde{w}_{0i} = (X_{0i}, Z_{0h})\beta_0 + \gamma \ln \Delta \Pi_{0i} + t_{0i},$$

where γ stands for the (nonunitary) elasticity of the value of family work in agricultural households to the price of agricultural products.

For estimation, assume that u_0, the idiosyncratic total factor productivity of the household, is independent from $(t_0, t_1, t_2, \tilde{t}_2)$ for all household members.[8] This allows one to follow a limited information approach. In a first step, estimate the reduced profit function (7.10) and then derive an estimate for the individual potential contribution to farm production (7.10); in a second step, estimate the reservation wage equation (7.11), including this latter variable and retaining the wage functions estimated for nonagricultural households.[9] Again, make separate estimations for each gender, excluding the farm heads whose occupational choice is not modeled.

Results of Estimation and of Micro Calibration

The microeconometric model is estimated on a household sample provided by the Enquête Permanente auprès des Ménages (EPM) survey for 1993–94, with approximately 4,500 households and 12,800 individuals ages 15 years and older. The part-time extension presented in annex 7A is estimated. Annex 7B gives the results of the micro calibration procedure for all the coefficients of the four basic variables of the structural microeconomic model: $\tilde{w}_{0i}$, w_{1i}, w_{2i}, and $\tilde{w}_{2i}$.[10] Here the authors comment only on the results that are of importance for the subsequent simulations.

In the farm profit function estimates (not shown), the number of family workers comes out with a coefficient that is consistent with usual orders of magnitude: a doubling of the workforce leads to an increase of about 20 percent in agricultural profits. The amounts of arable land and of capital also come out with a decreasing marginal productivity and a similar impact on profits. Age and education of the farm head also come out with a positive and significant coefficient.

The returns to education are rather close in the self-employment and wage sectors. Returns to labor market experience (or to job tenure) are higher in the wage sector. Self-employment benefits are 25 percent lower in the rural areas. Costs of entry in the wage sector vary negatively with education and experience and, not surprisingly, are 20 to 25 percent higher in the rural areas.

The reservation wage in nonfarm households is positively related to education, the effect of which lies in between the returns to education in the informal sector and the "discounted" returns (monetary returns less cost of entry) in the wage sector. This wage is lower in both the rural area and the Antananarivo *faritany* (region), which translates into higher participation rates in those areas. Almost by definition, household heads are less often inactive and nonlabor income increases the propensity to stay inactive. The demographic structure of the household and the hierarchical decisions of other members play only a minor role in the decision to participate in the labor market.

In farm households, educated people prefer to work outside the farm, whether in self-employment or wage jobs (lower family-work value). When the farm head already works part time in nonagricultural activities, other household members have a higher propensity to do the same. Activity is more diversified out of agriculture in the Antananarivo *faritany*. The estimate of the effect of the marginal productivity of labor has a negative effect on the farm-work value. This effect could stem from the fact that resource-endowed agricultural households, with more land or more capital and hence a higher labor productivity, are more prone (or have more opportunities) to diversify their activities. It should, however, be stressed that this diversification of activity is not frequent among agricultural households. Only 13 percent of the total agricultural households' labor force works outside the farm at least part time, the bulk of which (10 percent) work in part-time informal activities. Diversification is higher for household heads (20 percent work outside of the farm) than for other members (only 10 percent work outside). This absence of real opportunities for diversification of activities among agricultural households, especially the poorest, is one of the most important features of the distribution of income in Madagascar, and it strongly constrains the short-run impact of agricultural price and workfare policies that are examined in the remainder of this chapter. This feature also explains why the authors could not obtain an acceptable estimate for the elasticity (γ, see the previous section) of the farm-work value with respect to the agricultural price, p_0. The remainder of this chapter fixes this elasticity to one, as in other sectors (see annex 7B).

Before turning to the features of the macro-micro integration, it is worth pointing out that this structural microeconomic framework has welfare implications that are only partially taken into account in this chapter. As far as occupational choices are concerned, agents are indeed assumed to derive utility not only from monetary income (whether it comes from labor or other sources), but also from job-specific attributes and from leisure. Nonmonetary arguments of utility are ignored in this analysis, which focuses on the distribution of household real income, that is, the sum of Π_0, w_1, w_2, and other nonlabor income deflated by a household-specific cost of living index (see annex 7C). These arguments are indeed reflected in the two variables $\tilde{w}_0$ and $\tilde{w}_2$, where $\tilde{w}_0$ stands for the utility of leisure or family work (including the relative cost of entry in self-employment)—recalling that in the case of farm households, it includes the profit from farm activities—and $\tilde{w}_2$ stands for the relative disutility of working in the wage sector. A "full-income" concept would sum up $\tilde{w}_0$, w_1, and $\dfrac{w_2}{\tilde{w}_2}$ over individuals within each household. In a first step, however, the authors prefer to use the microeconomic model as a tool only for generating counterfactual income distributions, even at the expense of theoretical consistency from the standpoint of welfare. This choice is led by the fact that $\tilde{w}_0$ and $\tilde{w}_2$ are purely unobserved variables that at the end of this micro calibration procedure, also come out with a high variance (see annex 7C). This variance is why the authors felt that the reliability of full-income counterfactuals was still to be explored, and thus left it for further research.

Macro-Micro Integration

Once micro calibration has been achieved, the segmented occupational choice and labor income model is ready for simulation. If the size of the economic shocks or policies under study is small enough, there is no need to consider macro-level interactions. The microeconometric model can be simulated alone, under the assumption that the variation of goods prices and of factor returns is negligible.[11] Conversely, if the size of the shocks or policies under study is large enough, macro-micro links must be considered.

The database for the macro module comes from a social accounting matrix (SAM) built for the year 1995 (Razafindrakoto and Roubaud 1997). To achieve consistency between micro and macro data, household statistical weights of the 1993–94 EPM were recomputed to comply with the income structure of the 1995 SAM. The reweighting procedure relies on a cross-entropy estimation (Robilliard and Robinson 2003).

Figure 7.1 presents the global structure of the macro-micro integration. Equations in the micro module describe the behavior of individuals and households in terms of their labor supply and consumption demand. At the micro level, all income sources, stemming from individual occupational choices and household-level endowments in capital, are added up in a household income generation equation. Household expenditure is computed as the disposable income after taxes and savings have been subtracted. Consumption demands for the different goods are then derived based on household-specific budget shares (see annex 7C). These household-level consumption

Figure 7.1 Fully Integrated Macro-Micro Model Structure

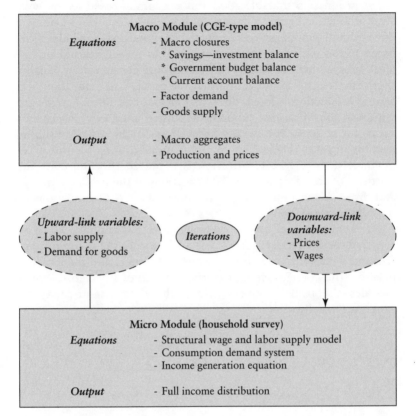

Source: Authors' creation.
Note: CGE = computable general equilibrium.

demands are added up and confronted to goods supply. Relevant prices are adjusted by a *tâtonnement* process so that market equilibrium is achieved. The same applies to labor market equilibrium, with labor supply defined as the sum of the individual occupational choices and wages defined as the adjustment variable. More specifically, the three task prices (π_1, π_2, $\tilde{\pi}_2$) and the agricultural price p_0, introduced above, are the variables that link the micro module to the macro module. The variables p_0 and π_1 are endogenously determined on the goods market equilibrium for agricultural and informal goods, respectively. The variable π_2 is exogenous and may be used to simulate a uniform wage increase in the wage sector, and $\tilde{\pi}_2$ varies endogenously to match labor supply with labor demand in the wage sector.

Only three sectors are considered in this model. The agricultural sector produces a tradable good and is a family-based sector, with total production equal to the sum of household-level productions.[12] The informal sector produces a nontradable good and is an individual-based sector, with total production equal to the sum of individual-level value added augmented by intermediate consumption. Finally, the formal sector produces a tradable good, and total domestic formal production is fixed. Both agricultural and formal goods are imperfect substitutes for exports, the formal good is a *perfect* substitute for imports, and the agricultural good is an *imperfect* substitute for imports. Following common specifications for this class of models, imperfect substitution is captured through constant elasticity of transformation (CET) functions at the production level and through constant elasticity of substitution (CES) functions at the consumption level.[13]

At the macro level, closure rules for three constraints need to be specified for the model to be "closed." They are the (current) government balance, the savings-investment balance, and the external balance (the current account of the balance of payments, which includes the trade balance). These three constraints may be expressed as follows:

$$(7.12) \qquad\qquad GSAV = GINC - pq_f \cdot QG$$

$$(7.13) \quad FSAV = \left(\sum_h mps \cdot Y_h + GSAV - \sum_c pq_c QINV_c \right) / EXR$$

$$(7.14) \qquad \sum_c pwm_c QM_c = \sum_c pwe_c QE_c + FSAV,$$

where $GSAV$ is government savings; $GINC$ is government income; QG is government consumption; $FSAV$ is foreign savings; mps is marginal propensity to save; Y_h is household h net income; $QINV_c$ is investment demand for good c; EXR is the exchange rate; QM_c and QE_c are, respectively, import and export quantities of good c; pq_c is the consumption price of good c; and pwm_c and pwe_c are, respectively, import and export world prices of good c.

Assume that both government and foreign savings are flexible, and that government consumption, the exchange rate, and total investment are fixed.[14] By these closure rules, assume that any large poverty reduction policy, such as those simulated later, will actually be financed by an increase in foreign savings (or, equivalently, by a reduction in current debt service). Whether this assumption is sustainable in the long term remains an open question. This choice of closure was mainly led by the desire to compare the direct and general equilibrium impact of policies without clouding this impact with those stemming from various government revenue-increasing mechanisms, such as flexible direct or indirect tax rates.

Scenarios and Simulations

This chapter explores three simulations with the objective of improving the situation of the poor: a direct subsidy on agricultural prices, a workfare program, and an untargeted transfer program.[15] These policies are compared in terms of both macroeconomic impact and their impact on poverty and income distribution. All experiments are designed so that their ex post costs are equal (in real terms).

Description of the Scenarios

The first simulation looks at the impact of a direct subsidy on agricultural production prices. The subsidy is set at 10 percent and is introduced as a negative tax on producer prices, thus creating a 10 percent gap between producer and consumer prices. Such a policy could be achieved by the intervention of a marketing board on agricultural goods markets, which would buy at high prices (from producers) and sell at 10 percent less (to consumers).

The second experiment simulates the implementation of a workfare scheme. Workfare programs, whereby participants must work to obtain benefits, have been used widely to fight poverty, usually in times of crises caused by macroeconomic or agroclimatic shocks (Ravallion 1999). The workfare scheme studied is assumed to be highly labor intensive. The government buys at a fixed rate the services of labor to build or rehabilitate roads and other infrastructures. Given the occupational choice model described in the previous section, the workfare scheme designed in this experiment can be summarized by two characteristics: the workfare wage level and the corresponding workload. A part-time workfare scheme was designed whereby participating individuals are allowed to continue working (in part) in their original occupation. Whether individuals choose to participate in the workfare program depends on the level of the workfare wage and on their formal, informal, and reservation wages (see the selection rule presented in annex 7A). As discussed, the level of the workfare wage is fixed ex ante so that the ex post cost of the scheme matches the cost of the agricultural price subsidy. The resulting yearly wage is 257,625 Malagasy francs (FMG), which translates into FMG 515,250 in full-time equivalent. Table 7.1 shows official minimum wages in different sectors from 1990 to 1996. This

Table 7.1 Minimum Yearly Wages, 1990–96

(1993 Malagasy francs)

Sector	1990	1991	1992	1993	1994	1995	1996
Agriculture	576,015	614,821	543,323	494,400	554,188	**603,866**	557,053
Nonagriculture	566,458	604,270	533,960	485,880	537,589	**592,923**	547,576
Public	774,965	811,706	716,329	651,828	665,334	**719,102**	653,844

Source: Ministry of Finance and Ministry of Civil Service and Labor, Antananarivo, Madagascar, www.mefb.gov.mg.

database has been scaled to match structural and demographic features of the year 1995. Consequently, the meaningful figures are in the 1995 column (shown in bold in table 7.1). They show that this simulation workfare wage is relatively close to official minimum wages and represents 87 percent of the minimum wage in nonagricultural sectors. Given this workfare wage level, a total of 908,470 workers—corresponding to 12.7 percent of the labor force—choose to participate in the workfare scheme.

The third and last simulation is a uniform, untargeted, per capita transfer program. Again, the amount paid is computed so that the aggregate ex post cost of the program matches the cost of the previous programs. The resulting amount is FMG 17,887 per capita, which will be added to household nonlabor income (and has the corresponding microeconomic effects of an increase in the value of inactivity in nonfarm households).

All three programs share a high budgetary cost equivalent of almost 5 percent of gross domestic product (GDP). They should therefore have large macroeconomic impacts as well as the intended distributional micro impacts.

Targeting Issues

A central issue related to the poverty and income distribution impacts of all three simulations is the targeting properties of each scheme. Obviously, the uniform, untargeted transfer per capita is distributed evenly across quintiles of income, but this is not the case for the agricultural subsidy and workfare simulations. To explore this issue, table 7.2 presents the distribution of individuals in beneficiary households across quintiles of per capita income for these two simulations.

Not surprisingly, the agricultural subsidy appears to have good targeting properties in terms of the distribution of beneficiary households. But this result does not hold when one considers the distribution of the program cost: while 83.9 percent of individuals in the first quintile are in a household that benefits from the agricultural

Table 7.2 Distribution of Beneficiary Households across Quintiles

Quintile	Agricultural subsidy			Workfare scheme		
	Beneficiary households	Row (percent)	Share of program cost (percent)	Beneficiary households	Row (percent)	Share of program cost (percent)
1st	2,184,281	83.9	7.2	821,244	31.5	16.4
2nd	2,073,064	79.5	12.6	842,288	32.3	17.1
3rd	2,073,970	79.4	18.5	919,525	35.2	23.9
4th	1,752,415	67.2	24.0	829,048	31.8	22.0
5th	1,036,771	39.7	37.7	715,063	27.4	20.6
Total or average	9,120,501	69.9	100.0	4,127,168	31.6	100.0

Source: Authors' estimations.
Note: Quintiles are computed using per capita income in the base year. Row percentage figures are shares of beneficiary population by quintile.

subsidy, only 7.2 percent of the total program cost accrues to these households, and the largest share of the cost (37.7 percent) accrues to the last quintile. This result is related to the fact that the price subsidy is proportional to agricultural output and thus, by construction, is regressive in terms of program cost allocation.

When compared with the agricultural subsidy, the workfare scheme appears to be less progressive in terms of the distribution of individuals in beneficiary households, because they are distributed evenly across quintiles. Because the benefits accruing to households are not proportional to their incomes, however, the distribution of the program cost is actually less regressive than in the agricultural subsidy experiment. The targeting performance of the workfare scheme is nevertheless disappointing as it fails to reach a large number of workers in poor households. This is explained by the fact that the reservation value ($\tilde{w}_0$) estimated and calibrated from actual data not only reflects preferences for family work but also includes a cost-of-entry component in outside informal activities. Estimated parameters indicate, for instance, that activity is more diversified out of agriculture in households living in the Antananarivo *faritany* or in urban areas, as well as more diversified in land-rich households. As a result, individuals from poor agricultural households dwelling in remote areas are given large reservation values, which reflect large costs of access to all markets, including the labor market. This cost of access prevents some agricultural workers from seizing the workfare job opportunities. In other words, because the workfare scheme fails to take these costs into account, it is implicitly targeted toward urban areas. As a result, it has a large impact on urban poverty (see the following section, "Simulation Results").

Simulation Results

Table 7.3 shows various price and macro aggregate changes as a result of the three programs. Macro aggregate changes are presented in real terms.

One common point across all three experiments is the increase in the relative price of the agricultural goods. In particular, even the subsidy simulation leads to a 4.7 percent increase in the price of agricultural goods for consumers (relative to the consumer price index). This result stems from large income effects that raise the demand for agricultural products. The workfare program has the strongest impact of all on the agricultural prices (8.2 percent increase against 4.7 and 5.6 percent in the other simulations), because it also leads to a decrease in the labor available for agriculture (see table 7.4).

Results also show that the macroeconomic impact of all three policies is small and positive in terms of GDP.[16] As mentioned earlier, all experiments were designed to equalize their ex post cost. Because

Table 7.3 Macroeconomic Impact of Alternative Policies

Indicator	BASE	Agricultural subsidy	Part-time workfare program	Untargeted uniform per capita transfer
Agricultural price	1.0	4.7	8.2	5.6
Informal price	1.0	1.8	3.5	1.7
Formal price	1.0	−3.0	−5.3	−3.5
Consumption price index	1.0	0	0	0
GDP at market prices	4,713.5	1.0	1.6	1.0
Absorption	4,975.2	4.4	5.0	4.4
Private consumption	4,274.5	5.2	5.9	5.2
Investment	467.2	−0.7	−1.2	−0.7
Government consumption	233.6	0	0	0
Exports	1,144.3	−0.5	1.3	−0.2
Imports	1,406.0	12.0	13.2	12.0
GDP at factor cost	4,424.0	0.3	1.0	0.3
Agricultural value added	1,429.1	0.4	−1.1	0.3
Informal value added	413.6	1.2	1.0	1.7
Formal value added	2,581.2	0.2	2.2	0.1
Cost (FMG, billion)		227.5	228.4	226.8
Cost (percentage of base GDP)		4.8	4.8	4.8

Source: Authors' estimations.

Note: FMG = Malagasy francs; GDP = gross domestic product. Base values are reported in the first column, and percentage changes are reported in the following columns. Cost figures are ex post.

program costs are entirely distributed to the households, all three simulations have the same impact on private consumption.

The employment impact is presented in table 7.4. The top part of the table shows the number of workers by occupational choice, while the lower part presents aggregate values of the sectoral allocation of labor. Results show that the subsidy simulation leads to a mild increase in total employment. In terms of sectoral employment, labor appears to be reallocated from the informal (−5.9 percent) to the agricultural sector (+1.5 percent). As expected, the workfare scheme has a strong impact on urban underemployment, with the number of inactive workers decreasing by almost 18 percent. It also leads to important reallocations of labor out of the agricultural (−3.9 per-cent) and informal sectors (−12.6 percent) into workfare. As a result, the total active population increases by 3.3 percent. Given its design, the workfare program obviously drives transitions out of full-time work and into part-time work. The uniform transfer scheme has a milder impact on the structure of employment.

Table 7.4 Employment Impact of Alternative Policies

Indicator	BASE	Agricultural subsidy	Part-time workfare program	Untargeted uniform per capita transfer
Full-time agricultural workers	4,248.9	2.8	−5.3	1.6
Full-time informal workers	324.6	4.4	−42.2	3.2
Full-time formal workers	527.0	0.4	−2.9	0.4
Part-time workers	874.9	−12.7	67.9	−7.0
Full-time inactive workers	1,144.3	−2.1	−17.7	−1.5
Agricultural labor	4,536.3	1.5	−3.9	0.8
Informal labor	687.0	−5.9	−12.6	−2.9
Formal labor (including workfare)	602.1	0.2	76.1	0.3
Total active workers	5,825.4	0.5	3.3	0.3
Total labor force	7,119.7	0	0	0

Source: Authors' estimations.

Note: Base values are reported in the first column, and percentage changes are reported in the following columns. Part-time workers category includes either part-time formal or informal work with inactivity, part-time formal or informal work with agricultural activity, as well as part-time inactivity, agricultural activity, formal or informal work with workfare in the case of the workfare scheme simulation. Total active workers and sectoral labor are in full-time equivalent, with full-time workers counting for 1.0 and part-time workers counting for 0.5.

Table 7.5 shows results in terms of poverty and income distribution for all households, in both urban and rural areas. Changes in three indicators of inequality are presented: the Gini index and two entropy indexes.

All indicators show that the agricultural price subsidy simulation leads to an improvement in the distribution of income at the national level. A closer look into each area suggests that the decrease in overall inequality is driven both by the convergence in urban and rural per capita incomes and by the decrease in inequality in the urban area. The introduction of a subsidy on agricultural production leaves the inequality within the rural area almost unchanged (the Gini index slightly increases by 0.3 percent), while inequality in the urban area only slightly decreases. As mentioned earlier, the small increase in rural inequality stems from the targeting property of the subsidy, whereby agricultural households with higher incomes benefit more (in absolute terms) than do smaller agricultural households. As a result, changes in poverty indicators are mainly driven by changes in per capita income.

Table 7.5 Social Impact of Alternative Policies, General
Equilibrium Results

All households	BASE	Agricultural subsidy	Part-time workfare program	Untargeted uniform per capita transfer
Per capita income	352.7	4.4	4.6	5.0
General entropy index 0	45.2	−2.5	−7.6	−11.2
General entropy index 1	59.0	−3.0	−6.8	−8.2
Gini index	51.1	−1.3	−3.6	−4.8
Poverty incidence	59.0	−5.0	−6.6	−6.2
Poverty gap	24.9	−8.2	−13.5	−16.3
Poverty severity	13.4	−10.0	−17.4	−24.2
Urban households				
Per capita income	631.1	0.8	3.1	2.7
General entropy index 0	48.1	−1.1	−7.2	−6.2
General entropy index 1	62.8	−0.9	−5.5	−4.5
Gini index	52.7	−0.5	−3.3	−2.6
Poverty incidence	30.5	−1.0	−11.1	−7.0
Poverty gap	10.3	−3.2	−24.0	−19.7
Poverty severity	4.5	−5.1	−29.5	−28.2
Rural households				
Per capita income	260.7	7.3	5.7	6.8
General entropy index 0	33.2	0.8	−8.4	−14.3
General entropy index 1	39.7	0.6	−8.2	−11.3
Gini index	44.0	0.3	−4.1	−6.4
Poverty incidence	68.4	−5.6	−5.9	−6.1
Poverty gap	29.7	−8.8	−12.3	−16.0
Poverty severity	16.4	−10.4	−16.3	−23.8

Source: Authors' estimations.

Note: Base values are reported for the first column, and percentage changes are reported in the following columns.

In terms of poverty reduction, the workfare scheme has a stronger impact than the subsidy program: the poverty headcount is reduced by 6.6 percent, while the subsidy program reduces it by 5 percent. Workfare also has a stronger effect on income distribution, with a 3.6 percent decrease in the Gini index (compared with a 1.3 percent decrease with the subsidy program) and a 17.4 percent decrease in the poverty severity indicator (compared with a 10 percent decrease with the subsidy program). This strong decrease in inequality is explained both by the convergence of average per capita incomes between urban and rural areas and by the decrease of inequality within both areas. The workfare scheme has by far the strongest impact on inequality and poverty in urban areas. Thanks to the workfare scheme, poverty incidence in urban areas decreases by more than 11 percent, whereas it decreases only slightly in the case of the agricultural subsidy and is reduced by 7 percent with the uniform transfer. Although the GDP impact of the untargeted transfer program is mild, both the poverty and income distribution impacts are significant: the program reduces the poverty headcount by 6.2 percent and the Gini index by 4.8 percent, and its impact on poverty severity is the highest among the three experiments. These results again show that the workfare scheme does not achieve much better targeting than the untargeted transfer program and does not satisfactorily reach the poorest of the poor.

In sum, the two targeted programs that have been examined here indeed have large impacts on monetary poverty alleviation, even once general equilibrium effects are taken into account. Given the large budgetary amounts that are transferred to households, this does not come as a surprise. Apart from scaling and financing issues, however, the simulations reveal that there is room to improve the quality of targeting. Indeed, a general subsidy to agricultural producers does not appear to be an adequate scheme for reaching the poorest farmers, because it fails to do better than a uniform per capita transfer or even a workfare scheme—even in rural areas. A general workfare program offering part-time job opportunities paid at about the minimum wage reaches somewhat disappointing results, especially in rural areas. Costs of access to the labor market prevent individuals living in remote areas or in poor autarkic agricultural households from seizing the workfare opportunities. The workfare scheme performance is relatively good in urban areas, where it draws a lot of people out of inactivity or out of informal underemployment, but it falls short in rural areas, where it is outperformed by the untargeted transfer.

All three schemes have been designed to have the same ex post budgetary cost in terms of the total amount of transfer received by households. They all, however, have specific implementation costs that should be taken into account when comparing their relative efficiency. For instance, the implementation of an agricultural subsidy would call for the reconstruction of a marketing board, which raises many institutional issues and might imply high administrative costs. Likewise, the implementation of a workfare scheme has more costs than pure wage costs, no matter how labor intensive it is: organizational and administrative costs, advertisement costs, and input costs (see Ravallion 1999). In this case, however, some of these additional costs are internalized by individuals who give up the workfare job offers when these are located too far from their household. Finally, even the untargeted transfer scheme would entail an additional cost of bringing the cash to the households, even in remote areas.

Comparing Micro Accounting Ex Ante and Ex Post Results

This section turns to a more methodological question and compares the simulation results of three specifications of the model. The first version corresponds to the results of a micro accounting exercise in which neither behavior nor general equilibrium effects would be taken into account. The second version still does not account for general equilibrium effects but allows individuals and households to respond to the shock. The final version accounts for both micro behaviors and general equilibrium effects. It corresponds to the version used above for the analysis of poverty reduction policies. Two types of shocks are examined: the 10 percent agricultural price subsidy analyzed previously and a 20 percent total factor productivity shock in the agricultural sector. The results of both simulations are presented in figures 7.2 and 7.3. These figures show the Lorenz curve (built on income per capita) together with the concentration curves of the benefits of the two shocks under the three specifications of the model.

In figure 7.2, the micro accounting and ex ante curves track closely. Both indicate that the incidence of the subsidy program is progressive. The ex post curve does not reverse that conclusion

Figure 7.2 Benefit Incidence of an Agricultural Subsidy under Various Specifications

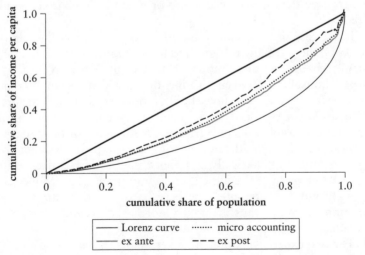

Source: Authors' estimations.

Figure 7.3 Benefit Incidence of a Total Factor Productivity
Shock in the Agricultural Sector

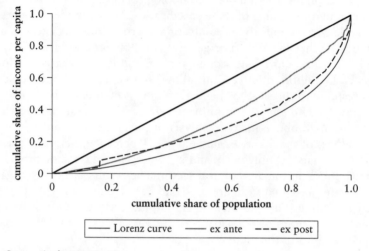

Source: Authors' estimations.

but appears closer to the 45-degree line, indicating that the
program is more progressive than ex ante simulations would
predict. This is reversed in the second simulation (figure 7.3),
where results indicate that taking into account general equilibrium actually leads to the conclusion that the shock is less
progressive than micro accounting or ex ante simulations would
predict.[17]

In the case of Madagascar and of shocks that affect the relative
price of the agricultural good, general equilibrium effects will
mainly change the distribution of the benefits between rural and
urban households. Given the big difference in mean incomes
between urban and rural households, it does not come as a surprise
than any shock that leads to an increase in the relative price of the
agricultural good will "redistribute" the benefits of the program
toward rural households, thus making it more progressive ex post
than ex ante. Symmetrically, any shock that leads to a decrease in
the relative price of the agricultural good (such as a productivity
shock), will "redistribute" the benefits of the program toward
urban households, thus making it more progressive ex post than
ex ante.

The two experiments presented here show that it is not possible
to reach a conclusion on a systematic bias in terms of poverty or
inequality changes when ignoring general equilibrium effects.

Conclusion

This chapter has presented the basic motivations for the construction of an integrated static macro-micro model for a low-income economy. It has outlined the main features of such a model in terms of microeconometric specifications and macro closures. Finally, it has explored the use of this kind of model for the simulation of targeted transfer schemes dedicated to poverty alleviation. These types of transfer schemes might be implemented either following a macroeconomic shock or as permanent safety nets. For purposes of illustration, three large-scale transfer schemes have been simulated and compared: (1) a price subsidy to agricultural producers, (2) a general workfare program proposing part-time job opportunities paid at about the minimum wage, and (3) a uniform unconditional and untargeted transfer provided to each individual regardless of their age and job situation. The macro-micro model yields interesting results on the counterfactual impacts of each program on the overall distribution of income, by taking into account both microeconomic targeting issues and macroeconomic general equilibrium effects. Considerations about the financing of the programs and about their technical implementation costs could supplement the simulations to build realistic, efficient, and sustainable poverty alleviation schemes.

To conclude, it may be useful to review briefly the comparative advantages and disadvantages of the integrated macro-micro approach. The authors first argued that the approach is well suited to incorporating current advances in the microeconometrics of household behaviors and market structures in developing countries. The illustrations presented show the usefulness of a thorough modeling of labor supply behavior in the context of highly segmented markets. However, much remains to be done to improve the modeling of behavior in agricultural households where collective production in family farms does not fit this "individualistic" framework as well. (For an alternative, see Cogneau and Robilliard 2007.) Moreover, it should be emphasized that structural estimation based on cross-sectional data may either overstate or understate the true reaction of poor households with respect to labor incentives. This type of estimation would benefit from the availability of dynamic panel data or from experimental knowledge on the response of poor households to various programs (Duflo 2004).

Second, the authors argued that integrated tools might be desired for the sake of macro-micro consistency, as far as "aggregation issues" and "interlinked welfare issues" are concerned. It should, however, be stressed that such consistency in the modeling of household welfare (labor supply, earnings, consumption) is obtained at the expense of sectoral disaggregation and dynamic considerations. Depending on the policy problem at stake, trade-offs must be solved inside a triangle made of "household heterogeneity," "sectoral detail," and "intertemporal issues." The authors therefore argued that the static integrated tool might be better suited for analyzing the distributional aspects of general development strategies, on the one hand, and for evaluating the impact of short- to medium-term targeted programs with macro impacts, on the other.

Through the applications implemented in this chapter, the authors hope to have shown that integrated macro-micro modeling could be useful in the design of these latter programs. The design of other structural policies, such as minimum-wage increases or foreign-investment-led jobs creation, could also benefit from this type of approach.

Annex 7A: A Part-Time Extension

To account for individuals who wish to pursue outside part-time activities when they also work for the family, one must introduce a "part-time" variable in the wages and benefits equations that accounts for the variability of hours worked:

$$\ln w_{1i} = \ln \pi_1 + X_{1i}\beta_1 + \delta_1 T_{1i} + t_{1i}$$
$$\ln w_{2i} = \ln \pi_2 + X_{2i}\beta_2 + \delta_2 T_{2i} + t_{2i} \, ,$$

with $\delta_1 < 0$, and $\delta_2 < 0$ and where T_{1i} (and T_{2i}) is a dummy variable indicating whether the individual works part-time.[18] One may then redefine full-time incomes as follows:

(A7.1) $\ln \widehat{w}_{1i} = \ln w_{1i} - \delta_1 T_{1i}$

(A7.2) $\ln \widehat{w}_{2i} = \ln w_{2i} - \delta_2 T_{2i} \, .$

Finally, assume that when reservation value is close enough to either full-time wage or self-employment benefits, individuals choose to work (simultaneously or successively) inside and outside the family. The listing of selection rules then becomes

i chooses full-time family work iff

$$\tilde{w}_{0i} > (1 + a)\widehat{w}_{1i} \quad \text{and} \quad \tilde{w}_{0i} > (1 + a)\frac{\widehat{w}_{2i}}{\tilde{w}_{2i}}$$

i chooses family work and self-employment iff

$$(1 + a)\widehat{w}_{1i} > \tilde{w}_{0i} > (1 - a)\widehat{w}_{1i} \quad \text{and} \quad \widehat{w}_{1i} > \frac{\widehat{w}_{2i}}{\tilde{w}_{2i}}$$

i chooses family work and wage work iff

$$(1 + a)\frac{\widehat{w}_{2i}}{\tilde{w}_{2i}} > \tilde{w}_{0i} > (1 - a)\frac{\widehat{w}_{2i}}{\tilde{w}_{2i}} \quad \text{and} \quad \frac{\widehat{w}_{2i}}{\tilde{w}_{2i}} > \widehat{w}_{1i}$$

i chooses full-time self-employment iff

$$(1 - a)\widehat{w}_{1i} > \tilde{w}_{0i} \quad \text{and} \quad \widehat{w}_{1i} > \frac{\widehat{w}_{2i}}{\tilde{w}_{2i}}$$

i chooses full-time wage work iff

$$(1 - a)\frac{\widehat{w}_{2i}}{\tilde{w}_{2i}} > \tilde{w}_{0i} \quad \text{and} \quad \frac{\widehat{w}_{2i}}{\tilde{w}_{2i}} > \widehat{w}_{1i} .$$

For econometric estimation, the likelihood of the model is rewritten according to this new selection rule.

The workfare program that is subsequently simulated introduces a new kind of part-time job offer that is paid at a rate w_3. In this case, once the former selection rule has been run, add the following rules:

if i had chosen full-time family work, i takes the workfare offer iff

$$2w_3(1 - a) > \tilde{w}_{0i}$$

if i had chosen self-employment, i takes the workfare offer iff

$$w_3 > \widehat{w}_{1i}[1 - \exp(\delta_1)]$$

if i had chosen wage work, i takes the job offer iff

$$w_3 > \widehat{w}_{2i}[1 - \exp(\delta_2)] .$$

The two last conditions apply whether i chooses a full-time or part-time option. In the case of a part-time choice, and if the relevant condition holds, this worker relinquishes part-time family work in favor of workfare. In any case, this worker ends up working part-time in self-employment or wage work, and the balance of time in the workfare program. If the first condition holds, the work is then part time in the family, with the remaining time spent in the work-fare program.

Annex 7B: Estimation and Micro Calibration

Table 7B.1 Results from Estimation and Micro Calibration

Variable	β_1	β_2	$\tilde{\beta}_2$	β_0
Men				
Nonfarm households				
Number of years of education (/10)	0.9841	0.8995	−1.3384	0.9429
Number of years of experience (/10)	0.3232	0.5100	−0.7785	0.1533
Number of years of experience squared (/1,000)	−0.3879	−0.6276	1.1335	0.0315
Region of Antananarivo (=1)	−0.0561	−0.0689	0.1520	−0.2380
Rural area (=1)	−0.2504	−0.0891	0.4053	−0.0039
Father in the informal sector (=1)	0	0	0.1901	−0.1696
Father in the formal sector (=1)	0	0	−0.0695	0.0485
Household head in the informal sector (=1)	0	0	0.4913	−0.0505
Household head in the formal sector (=1)	0	0	−0.4124	0.2920
Spouse in the informal sector (=1)	0	0	−0.2107	0.1436
Spouse in the formal sector (=1)	0	0	0.7386	−0.0473
Number of children ages 0 to 9 years old	0	0	0	−0.0641
Number of males ages 10 to 14 years old	0	0	0	−0.0160
Number of males ages 15 to 69 years old	0	0	0	0.0261
Number of females ages 10 to 14 years old	0	0	0	0.0150
Number of females ages 15 to 69 years old	0	0	0	−0.0134
Number of adults ages 70 years and older	0	0	0	0.1188
Household head (=1)	0	0	0	−0.7030
Spouse of the head (=1)	0	0	0	−0.5665
Child of the head (=1)	0	0	0	0.1395
Nonlabor income	0	0	0	0.6465
Household head wage income	0	0	0	0.7335
Spouse wage income	0	0	0	0.2203
Part-time correction	−0.80	−0.43	0	0
Constant	3.8386	3.3470	1.6192	4.8406
Part-time threshold[a]	0.28			

Standard errors (diagonal) and correlation of unobservables

	t_1	t_2	$\tilde{t}_2$	t_0
t_1	0.9740	0.5000*	−0.5020	0.8580
t_2		0.5940	0.0180	0.5110
$\tilde{t}_2$			1.8330	−0.6220
t_0				1.4780

Variable	β_1	β_2	$\tilde{\beta}_2$	β_0
Men				
Farm households				
Number of years of education (/10)	0.9841	0.8995	−1.8892	0.8106
Number of years of experience (/10)	0.3232	0.5100	−1.4856	−0.1862
Number of years of experience squared (/1,000)	−0.3879	−0.6276	3.8351	0.6089
Region of Antananarivo (=1)	−0.0561	−0.0689	−0.5764	−0.8237
Rural area (=1)	−0.2504	−0.0891	0.8868	0.3592
Household head in the informal sector (=1)	0	0	6.6620	−0.6282
Household head in the formal sector (=1)	0	0	−1.5937	0.0513
Number of children ages 0 to 9 years old	0	0	0	−0.0611
Number of males ages 10 to 14 years old	0	0	0	0.0738
Number of males ages 15 to 69 years old	0	0	0	0.0598
Number of females ages 10 to 14 years old	0	0	0	0.0824
Number of females ages 15 to 69 years old	0	0	0	0.0252
Number of adults ages 70 years and older	0	0	0	0.1822
Spouse of the head (=1)	0	0	0	−0.1442
Child of the head (=1)	0	0	0	0.1180
Nonlabor income	0	0	0	−0.3589
Marginal productivity of agricultural labor	0	0	0	1*
Part-time correction	−0.81	−0.44	0	0
Constant	3.8386	3.3470	4.1720	6.1760
Part-time threshold[a]	0.45			

Standard errors (diagonal) and correlation of unobservables

	t_1	t_2	$\tilde{t}_2$	t_0
t_1	0.9740	0.3000*	0.0280	0.8930
t_2		0.5940	0.1040	0.5940
$\tilde{t}_2$			2.0450	−0.4120
t_0				1.7070

(*Continued on next page*)

Table 7B.1 (Continued)

Variable	β_1	β_2	$\tilde{\beta}_2$	β_0
Women				
Nonfarm households				
Number of years of education (/10)	1.0697	1.3439	−1.6047	0.8535
Number of years of experience (/10)	0.2387	0.5243	−0.4425	−0.1333
Number of years of experience squared (/1,000)	−0.2571	−0.6476	0.7708	0.3569
Region of Antananarivo (=1)	−0.2530	0.0541	0.2790	−0.3937
Rural area (=1)	−0.2494	−0.0135	0.3500	−0.1241
Father in the informal sector (=1)	0	0	−0.2720	0.1344
Father in the formal sector (=1)	0	0	−0.2139	0.2915
Household head in the informal sector (=1)	0	0	0.3239	0.1247
Household head in the formal sector (=1)	0	0	−0.1145	0.2320
Spouse in the informal sector (=1)	0	0	−0.3565	0.2135
Spouse in the formal sector (=1)	0	0	−0.4257	0.1466
Number of children ages 0 to 9 years old	0	0	0	0.0038
Number of males ages 10 to 14 years old	0	0	0	−0.0675
Number of males ages 15 to 69 years old	0	0	0	0.0046
Number of females ages 10 to 14 years old	0	0	0	−0.0187
Number of females ages 15 to 69 years old	0	0	0	−0.0124
Number of adults ages 70 years and older	0	0	0	0.1094
Household head (=1)	0	0	0	−0.3917
Spouse of the head (=1)	0	0	0	0.0583
Child of the head (=1)	0	0	0	0.2056
Nonlabor income	0	0	0	1.1474
Household head wage income	0	0	0	0.0574
Spouse wage income	0	0	0	−0.7528
Part-time correction	−0.83	−0.20	0	0
Constant	3.5774	2.4824	2.0197	4.7003
Part-time threshold[a]	0.29			

Standard errors (diagonal) and correlation of unobservables

	t_1	t_2	$\tilde{t}_2$	t_0
t_1	0.9750	0.5000*	−0.4960	0.8760
t_2		0.5590	0.0890	0.3300
$\tilde{t}_2$			1.8810	−0.6530
t_0				1.4520

Variable	β_1	β_2	$\tilde{\beta}_2$	β_0
Women				
Farm households				
Number of years of education (/10)	1.0697	1.3439	−2.3181	0.7551
Number of years of experience (/10)	0.2387	0.5243	−0.5943	−0.2368
Number of years of experience squared (/1,000)	−0.2571	−0.6476	0.4778	0.5286
Region of Antananarivo (=1)	−0.2530	0.0541	−0.1836	−0.5821
Rural area (=1)	−0.2494	−0.0135	0.5646	0.3172
Household head in the informal sector (=1)	0	0	0.1660	−0.6827
Household head in the formal sector (=1)	0	0	−0.8654	−0.1080
Number of children ages 0 to 9 years old	0	0	0	0.0074
Number of males ages 10 to 14 years old	0	0	0	0.1417
Number of males ages 15 to 69 years old	0	0	0	−0.0070
Number of females ages 10 to 14 years old	0	0	0	0.0670
Number of females ages 15 to 69 years old	0	0	0	−0.0311
Number of adults ages 70 years and older	0	0	0	−0.1026
Spouse of the head (=1)	0	0	0	0.0994
Child of the head (=1)	0	0	0	−0.1417
Nonlabor income	0	0	0	0.2221
Marginal productivity of agricultural labor	0	0	0	1*
Part-time correction	−0.84	−0.21	0	0
Constant	3.5774	2.4824	3.9111	6.3980
Part-time threshold[a]	0.55			

Standard errors (diagonal) and correlation of unobservables

	t_1	t_2	$\tilde{t}_2$	t_0
t_1	0.9750	0.3000*	0.0900	0.8340
t_2		0.5590	0.5100	0.0950
$\tilde{t}_2$			1.9590	−0.4470
t_0				1.7470

Sources: Enquête Permanente auprès des Ménages 1993 survey and authors' calculations.

Note: Coefficients in roman type (first two columns) are econometrically estimated. In contrast, the three coefficients with an asterisk (*) are pure guesses. Other guessed coefficients not shown in the table include the two measurement errors variances (which are assumed null) and the $(t_2 - \tilde{t}_2 - t_1)$ standard error (at 2 and 1.5 in nonfarm and farm households, respectively). Coefficients in italics (last two columns) result from a "micro calibration" using both econometric estimates and guessed coefficients. See section titled "Econometric Identification and Micro Calibration" for more details.

a. For the definition of part-time corrections and threshold, see annex 7A.

Annex 7C: A Simple Expenditure System with Heterogeneous Preferences

The macro-micro model tries to make use of the wealth of data available—not only for labor supply and income generation but also for consumption. However, data limitations prevent going too far in that direction. To avoid microeconometric complications, savings and consumption choices are first assumed as separable from labor supply decisions. Second, saving rates derived from the data come out as unreliable; therefore, a fixed saving rate common to all households (and equal to 0.052 in the application) is assumed:

$$(C7.1) \qquad\qquad C_h = (1 - s)Y_h .$$

Household disposable income Y_h is equal to the sum of agricultural benefits (including autoconsumption of goods produced by the household), self-employment benefits and wage earnings, nonlabor income stemming from capital income, and transfers. C_h stands for household h total consumption expenditures.

Third, total consumption is then split between the three composite goods of the model (agricultural, informal, and formal) through idiosyncratic budget shares $\omega_{j,h}$ derived from the data:

$$(C7.2) \qquad C_{j,h} = \omega_{j,h}C_h \quad \text{with } j = 0, 1, 2 \quad \text{and} \sum_{j=0,1,2} \omega_{j,h} = 1 .$$

This specification corresponds to the simplest Cobb-Douglas homothetic utility function for consumption.

Notes

The authors thank the National Institute of Statistics of Madagascar for providing the data presented in this chapter. Special thanks also go to Mireille Razafindrakoto, Francois Roubaud, and members of the MADIO project in Antananarivo for helpful discussions about their research and the Malagasy economy. The authors are grateful to Francois Bourguignon, Jesko Hentschel, Phillippe Leite, Dominique van der Mensbrugghe, Luiz Pereira da Silva, and Abdelkhalek Touhami for discussions about earlier versions of this work.

1. When supplemented with a dynamic demographic module, this approach can be relatively well suited to exploring demo-economic issues like the distributive impact of the HIV/AIDS epidemics (Cogneau and Grimm forthcoming) or general poverty reduction strategies like the long-term impact of education policies (Grimm 2004, 2005).

2. Cogneau (1999, 2001) shows that a macro-micro model of the distribution of income can simulate the historical decrease in poverty observed in the city of Antananarivo during the 1995–99 period, thanks to job creation and minimum-wage increases in the formal sector.

3. Moreover, this simple form assumes that individuals compare self-employment and wage-work opportunities only in terms of earnings; in other words, they do not bring differential nonpecuniary benefits. See Cogneau (2001).

4. The reservation value $\tilde{w}_0$ includes the cost of entry into the informal activities.

5. In econometric estimation, the X vectors include a constant.

6. For estimation, the authors still assume independence for $(t_1, t_2, \tilde{t}_2, t_0)$ between individuals, even among members of the same household.

7. It also might be the case for some nonagricultural occupations. In light of the Malagasy case and data, however, the authors choose to treat nonagricultural self-employment as a purely individual occupation. These data suggest that the great majority of self-employed workers in nonagricultural sectors are running very small, most often individual, businesses.

8. This latter assumption should allow for a direct identification of the $\Delta\Pi_0$ effect in $\tilde{w}_0$, through the effect of u_{0h}. However, as $\Delta\Pi_0$ is presumably affected by large measurement errors, the authors exclude "available land" from the variables in $\widehat{w}_0$, taking it as an instrument for the identification of the effect of $\Delta\Pi_0$.

9. This latter option is rather innocuous for potential earnings outside the farm, as only a small number of individuals declare out-of-farm earnings in agricultural households.

10. More detailed econometric results are available from the authors upon request.

11. Even with small policies, this assumption of no price variation may be violated if there is a strong spatial segmentation of markets. In this latter case, local price variations may matter.

12. Production functions parameters are estimated (see section "Econometric Identification and Micro Calibration") and technical coefficients are taken from the survey. Although all technical coefficients are scaled up so that the sum of intermediate consumption equals national accounts aggregate, they remain household specific for the agricultural production.

13. For the calibration of the agricultural CET function, the share of exports on total production is idiosyncratic and taken from survey data.

14. By Walras's law, one of the system constraints is redundant. System constraints include markets as well as macro balances. In this model, the redundant equation is the external balance equation (7.13).

15. Previously, the authors showed that neither a devaluation of 20 percent nor a fourfold increase in agricultural tariffs could achieve a significant reduction in poverty and inequality indicators (Cogneau, Grimm, and Robilliard 2003).

16. The GDP aggregate does not include the value of goods, services, or infrastructure produced by the workfare program.

17. Under the current version of this algorithm, the authors are not able to distinguish micro accounting from ex ante results in the case of the productivity shock because the shock amounts to changing a technical parameter that does not affect household behaviors in the first round.

18. The authors thank François Bourguignon for a fruitful discussion about this extension.

References

Cogneau, Denis. 1999. "La formation du revenu des ménages à Antananarivo: une microsimulation en équilibre général pour la fin du siècle." *Economie de Madagascar* 4: 131–55.

———. 2001. "Formation du revenu, segmentation, et discrimination sur le marché du travail d'une ville en développement: Antananarivo fin de siècle." DIAL Working Paper 2001/18, Développement Institutions et Analyses de Long terme, Paris.

Cogneau, Denis, and Michael Grimm. Forthcoming. "The Impact of AIDS Mortality on the Income Distribution in Côte d'Ivoire." *Journal of African Economies.*

Cogneau Denis, Michael Grimm, and Anne-Sophie Robilliard. 2003. "Evaluating Poverty Reduction Policies: The Contribution of Microsimulation Techniques." In *The New International Strategies for Poverty Reduction,* eds. J.-P. Cling, M. Razafindrakoto, and F. Roubaud. London: Routledge.

Cogneau, Denis, and Anne-Sophie Robilliard. 2007. "Growth, Distribution, and Poverty in Madagascar: Learning from a Microsimulation Model in a General Equilibrium Framework." In *Microsimulation as a Tool for the Evaluation of Public Policies: Methods and Applications,* ed. A. Spadero. Madrid: Fundacion BBVA.

Duflo, Esther. 2004. "Scaling up and Evaluation." *Annual World Bank Conference on Development Economics 2004: Accelerating Development,* Vol. 1, Report No. 30228. Washington, DC: World Bank.

Grimm, Michael. 2004. "A Decomposition of Inequality and Poverty Changes in the Context of Macroeconomic Adjustment: A Microsimulation Study for Côte d'Ivoire." In *Growth, Inequality, and Poverty: Prospects for Pro-Poor Economic Development,* eds. A. F. Shorrocks and R. van der Hoeven. Oxford: Oxford University Press.

———. 2005. "Educational Policies and Poverty Reduction in Côte d'Ivoire." *Journal of Policy Modeling* 27 (2): 231–47.

Heckman, James, and Guilherme Sedlacek. 1985. "Heterogeneity, Aggregation, and Market Wages Functions: An Empirical Model of Self-Selection in the Labor Market." *Journal of Political Economy* 93 (6): 1077–125.

Magnac, Thierry. 1991. "Segmented or Competitive Labor Markets?" *Econometrica* 59 (1): 165–87.

Neal, Derek, and Sherman Rosen. 1998. "Theories of the Distribution of Labor Earnings." In *Handbook of Income Distribution,* eds. A. B. Atkinson and F. Bourguignon. Amsterdam: North-Holland.

Ravallion, Martin. 1999. "Appraising Workfare." *The World Bank Research Observer* 14 (1): 31–48.

Razafindrakoto, Mireille, and Francois Roubaud. 1997. "Une matrice de Comptabilité Sociale pour Madagascar." *Projet Madio.* INSTAT-DIAL-IRD, Study 9744/E, Antananarivo, Madagascar.

Robilliard, Anne-Sophie, and Sherman Robinson. 2003. "Reconciling Household Surveys and National Accounts Data Using Cross-Entropy Estimation." *Review of Income and Wealth* 49 (3): 395–406.

Roy, A. 1951. "Some Thoughts on the Distribution of Earnings." *Oxford Economic Papers* 3 (June): 135–46.

Scott, Kinnon. 2003. "Generating Relevant Household-Level Data: Multi-topic Household Surveys." In *The Impact of Economic Policies on Poverty and Income Distribution: Evaluation Techniques and Tools,* eds. F. Bourguignon and L. A. Pereira da Silva. Washington, DC: World Bank and Oxford University Press.

8

Wealth-Constrained Occupational Choice and the Impact of Financial Reforms on the Distribution of Income and Macro Growth

Xavier Giné and Robert M. Townsend

How should the financial system of a country be evaluated? How should policy makers determine the appropriate policy response to observed inequality or lack of economic growth? The answers to these questions—put forth by finance ministers, financial sector specialists, academics, and other practitioners and policy experts—generally follow one of two approaches. The first takes the view that the world economy is optimal and that nothing needs to be done because government intervention could lead to a less optimal situation. The second approach is proactive and supports the notion that governments should promote the regulation or liberalization of markets.

The appropriate economic policy advice depends, of course, on the context; but this chapter suggests that policy questions like these are best analyzed with the help of an algorithm that combines theory and data. This chapter provides an example of how an algorithm of this type works, based on earlier published work in Giné and Townsend (2004). In this example, economic theory is used to refine the logic that can be applied to a few key observed facts, and microeconomic data are then used again—to validate the model. In practice, then, one iterates from theory to data and back again.

Model-based advice can be viewed as just another opinion to consider in conjunction with other policy advice; however, model-based opinions emanate from a specified set of assumptions and rules that must be consistent with certain scientific norms within the economics profession. That is, a model requires reduced-form or behavioral equations that often are based on rational or quasi-rational economic behavior. But a model also requires these equations to be consistent with one another, as in explicit definitions of constrained optimality or concepts of equilibrium. More to the point, a model has implications for cross-sectional relationships or the evolution of economic variables over time, and so it can be validated or refuted when confronted with data.

Thus, this chapter proposes that policy recommendations be generated based on somewhat realistic, estimated versions of the reality of a given economy. The logic of the model is made explicit, so this model has the advantage of guiding policy choices because researchers can trace a particular policy recommendation to a given set of assumptions or rules.

The question addressed in chapter 8, along with the proposed algorithm, is that of the potential costs and benefits of financial sector reforms. A major policy concern related to general structural reforms is the idea that benefits will not trickle down. There is concern that the poor will be neglected and that inequality will increase. Similarly, globalization and capital inflows are often claimed to be associated with growth—although the effect of economic growth on poverty is still a much-debated topic.[1]

Not all possible forms of liberalization are (or could be) considered in this chapter. The focus is rather on reforms that (1) increase outreach on the extensive domestic margin (less restricted licensing requirements for foreign and domestic financial institutions, for example), (2) reduce excess capitalization requirements, and (3) enhance the ability to open new branches. These types of reforms are captured in the model, although crudely, by characterizing them as domestic reforms that allow deposit mobilization and access to credit at market-clearing interest rates for a segment of the population that otherwise would not have formal sector savings or credit.

The theory used here to address the costs and benefits of policy reform is a relatively simple general equilibrium model with credit constraints. Specifically, the authors chose from the literature and in this chapter, extend the Lloyd-Ellis and Bernhardt (2000) model (the

LEB model), which features wealth-constrained entry into business and wealth-constrained investment for entrepreneurs. This model has several advantages for purposes of this chapter. It allows for ex ante variation in ability. It has a general (approximated) production technology that allows labor share to vary, and the household occupational choice has a closed-form solution. Finally, the model features a dual economy that captures several widely observed aspects of the development process. These include industrialization with persistent income differentials, a slow decline in the subsistence sector, and an eventual increase in wages—all of which contribute to growth with changing inequality.

The authors extend this occupational choice model that does not include intermediation to an intermediated sector that allows borrowing and lending at a market-clearing interest rate. The intermediated sector is expanded exogenously at the observed rate in the data, given initial participation and the initial observed distribution of wealth. Even though endogenous financial deepening may be preferred (see Greenwood and Jovanovic 1990; Townsend and Ueda 2006), exogenous financial deepening has a peculiar, distinct advantage in this model because it can be varied (either to mimic the data and its upturns and downturns or to keep it flat) and provides a counterfactual experiment. One can thus gauge the consequences of these various experiments and compare them. In short, general equilibrium policy analysis can be applied following the seminal work of Heckman, Lochner, and Taber (1998), despite endogenous prices and an evolving endogenous distribution of wealth in a model where preferences do not aggregate.

In this chapter, the explicit structure of the model is used as given in the occupational choices and investment decisions of households to estimate certain parameters of the model using a variety of distinct microeconomic data sets. But not all parameters of the model can be estimated via maximum likelihood. The rest are calibrated to match the growth rate and observed changes in inequality, labor share, savings, and the number of entrepreneurs reported in the data.

This model can be applied to any economy that has experienced a financial liberalization for which the relevant data are available. The prime example in this chapter is Thailand, from 1976 to 1996.[2] This is a good country to study for a number of reasons. First, Thailand is often portrayed as an example of an emerging market with high income growth and increasing inequality. The gross domestic product (GDP) growth from 1981 to 1995 was 8 percent per year, and the Gini measure of inequality increased from 0.42 in 1976 to 0.50 in 1996. Second, there is evidence that Thailand had a relatively restrictive credit system but also liberalized it during this period (for details, see Klinhowhan 1999; Okuda and Mieno 1999). Third, Jeong (1999) shows that the increase in the number of households with access to formal intermediation did contribute to growth in per capita income during this period. Finally, Thailand experienced a relatively large increase in capital inflows from the late 1980s to the mid-1990s.

This structural, estimated version of an actual economy can then be compared to what would have happened if there had been no expansion in the size of the intermediated sector. Without financial liberalization at estimated parameter values from both data sets, the model predicts a dramatically lower growth rate, a higher residual subsistence sector, nonincreasing wages, and lower and decreasing inequality. Thus, financial liberalization appears to be the engine of growth it is sometimes claimed to be, at least in the context of Thailand.

However, growth and liberalization do have uneven consequences, as the critics insist. The distribution of welfare gains and losses in these experiments is not uniform, because there are various effects that depend on wealth and talent. With financial liberalization, savings earn interest, although the wealthy tend to benefit most. But credit is available to facilitate occupation shifts and to finance setup costs and investment, and quantitatively, there is a striking conclusion. The primary winners from financial liberalization are either talented but low-wealth, would-be entrepreneurs who without credit cannot go into business at all or entrepreneurs with little capital. Modal gains range from 17 percent to 34 percent of the observed overall average of Thai household income.

But there are losers as well. Liberalization induces an increase in wages in later years, and even though this benefits workers, other things being equal, it hurts entrepreneurs because they face a higher wage bill. The estimated welfare loss in both data sets is roughly the same order of magnitude as the observed average income of firm owners overall. This fact suggests a plausible political economy rationale for (observed) financial sector repressions.

Finally, the estimated structure of the model is used to conduct a policy experiment. The economy is "opened up" to the observed foreign capital inflows. These contribute to increased growth, inequality, and the number of entrepreneurs, but they do so only slightly. Otherwise, the macroeconomic and distributional consequences are quite similar to those of the closed economy with liberalization. Indeed, if the expansion is changed to grow linearly (rather than as observed in the data), the model cannot replicate the high growth rates observed in Thailand during the late 1980s and early 1990s, despite large capital inflows at that time.

The steps of the algorithm detailed in the following sections may be applied in a variety of countries. The theory is first presented in detail, followed by a description of the core theory as given in an occupational choice map (for an autarky sector and for a credit sector). The maximum likelihood estimation of most major parameters of the model is then presented, followed by calibration of the remaining parameters, which matches the macro, aggregate data. Simulations are then presented at the estimated and calibrated values for each of two data sets, followed by two extension applications to village economies and other aspects of income distribution. The chapter closes with various measures of the welfare gains and losses associated with the financial liberalization, a discussion of international capital inflows, and conclusions.

Specify the Environment: The General Equilibrium Model

The LEB model begins with a standard production function, mapping a capital input k and a labor input l at the beginning of the period into output q at the end of the period. In the original LEB model,[3] and in the numerical simulations presented in this section, this function is taken to be quadratic. In particular, it takes the following form:

$$(8.1) \qquad q = f(k, l) = \alpha k - \frac{1}{2} \beta k^2 + \sigma kl + \xi l - \frac{1}{2} \rho l^2.$$

The quadratic function in equation (8.1) can be viewed as an approximation for virtually any production function and has been used in applied work (see Griffin, Montgomery, and Rister 1987, and the references cited in that work). This function also facilitates the derivation of closed-form solutions and allows labor share to vary over time.

Each firm has a beginning-of-period setup or fixed cost x, and this setup cost is drawn at random from a known cumulative distribution $H(x, m)$ with $0 \leq x \leq 1$.

$$(8.2) \qquad H(x, m) = mx^2 + (1 - m)x, \quad m \in [-1, 1].$$

This distribution, shown in equation (8.2), is parameterized by the number m. If $m = 0$, the distribution is uniform; if $m > 0$, the distribution is skewed toward high setup cost x, and the converse arises when $m < 0$. This setup cost is supposed to vary inversely with talent—that is, it takes both talent and an initial investment to start a business—but the higher the level of talent, the lower the setup cost. More generally, the cumulative distribution $H(x, m)$ is a crude way to capture and allow estimation of the distribution of talent in the population and is not an unusual specification in the industrial organization literature (for example, Das, Roberts, and Tybout 1998; Veracierto 1998). Unobserved talent is, of course, a key to education choice and other discrete choice models.[4] Cost x is expressed in the same units as wealth and thus has the same units as a utility differential. Every agent is born with an inheritance or initial wealth b. Alternatively, the agent starts the period with wealth saved from the previous period. The distribution of inheritances in the population at date t is given by $G_t(b) : B_t \to [0, 1]$, where $B_t \subset R_+$ is the changing support of the distribution at date t. The time argument t makes explicit the evolution of B_t and G_t over time. The beginning-of-period wealth b and the cost x are the only sources of heterogeneity among the population. These variables are modeled as independent of one another in the specification used in this example and allow the existence of a *unique* steady state.[5]

All units of labor can be hired at a common wage, w, to be determined in equilibrium. (There is no variation in skills for wage work, although this can be added.) There is a storage technology that carries goods from the beginning to the end of the period one-to-one, so the effective interest rate is zero. This assumption puts a lower bound on the gross interest rate in the corresponding economy with credit and limits the input that k firms wish to use in the production of output q, even in the economy without credit. Firms operate in cities, and the associated entrepreneurs and workers incur a common cost of living measured by the parameter v. Alternatively, v captures a fixed cost of leaving agriculture and assumes that firms can operate in rural areas. Under this alternative, setup costs v and x may vary explicitly with distance to a district center or city.

The choice problem of the entrepreneur is as follows:

$$\text{(8.3)} \qquad \begin{aligned} \pi(b, x, w) = \max_{k,l} \quad & f(k, l) - wl - k \\ \text{s. t.} \quad & k \in [0, b - x], \quad l \geq 0, \end{aligned}$$

where $\pi(b, x, w)$ denotes the profits of the firm with initial wealth b, without subtracting the setup cost x, given wage w. Because credit markets have not yet been introduced, capital input k cannot exceed the initial wealth b less the setup cost x—as in expression (8.3). This is the key finance constraint of the model and may or may not be binding, depending on x, b, and w. More generally, some firms may operate, but if wealth b is low relative to cost x, they may be constrained in capital input use k—that is, for constrained firms, wealth b limits input k. Otherwise unconstrained firms are all alike and have identical incomes before netting out the cost x. One can distinguish firms by sector, but the added heterogeneity, though more realistic, complicates the calculation. The capital input k can be zero but not negative.

Even though all agents are born with an inherited nonnegative initial wealth b, not everyone need be a firm. There is also a subsistence sector in which agents earn γ. In the original LEB model, everyone is placed in this subsistence sector initially, at a degenerate steady state distribution of wealth. For various subsequent periods, labor can be hired from this subsistence sector, at subsistence plus cost of living, thus $w = \gamma + v$. After everyone has left this sector (as a laborer or as an entrepreneur), the equilibrium wage will rise. The simulations impose an initial distribution of wealth as estimated in the data and allow the parameter γ to increase at an exogenous imposed rate of γ_{gr}, which also increases the wage, but γ_{gr} could be estimated to be zero.

For a household with a given initial wealth-cost pair (b, x) and wage w, the choice of occupation reduces to an essentially static problem of maximizing end-of-period wealth $W(b, x, w)$ given in equation (8.4):

$$(8.4) \qquad W(b, x, w) = \begin{cases} \gamma + b & \text{if a subsistence worker,} \\ w - v + b & \text{if a wage earner,} \\ \pi(b, x, w) - x - v + b & \text{if a firm.} \end{cases}$$

At the end of the period, all agents take this wealth as a given and decide how much to consume, C, and how much to bequeath, B, to their heirs; that is—

$$(8.5) \qquad \begin{aligned} \max_{C,B} \quad & U(C, B) \\ \text{s. t.} \quad & C + B = W. \end{aligned}$$

In the original LEB model and in the simulations presented in this chapter, the utility function is Cobb-Douglas; that is—

$$(8.6) \qquad U(C, B) = C^{1-\omega} B^{\omega}.$$

This functional form yields consumption and bequest decision rules given by constant fractions $1 - \omega$ and ω of the end-of-period wealth, respectively. Again, indirect utility would be linear in wealth. Parameter ω denotes the bequest motive.[6]

The key to both static and dynamic features of the model is a partition of the equilibrium occupational choice in (b, x) space into three regions: unconstrained firms, constrained firms, and either workers or subsistence workers. These regions are determined by the equilibrium wage w. One can represent these regions as (b, x) combinations yielding the occupational choices of agents of the model, using the exogenous distribution of costs $H(x, m)$ at each period along with the endogenous and evolving distribution $G_t(b)$ of wealth b. The population of the economy is normalized so that the fractions of constrained firms, unconstrained firms, workers, and subsistence workers add to unity.

An equilibrium at any date t given the beginning-of-period wealth distribution $G_t(b)$ is a wage w_t, such that given w_t, every agent with wealth-cost pair (b, x) chooses occupation and savings to maximize equations (8.4) and (8.5), respectively. The wage w_t clears the labor market in the sense that the number of workers, subsistence workers, and firms adds to unity. As is made clear in the following section, existence and uniqueness are ensured. Because of the myopic nature of the bequest motive, the explicit reference to date t often can be dropped.

Characterizing Household Choice: The Occupation Partition

Although the model is essentially dynamic to explain growth and inequality in transition to a steady state, the occupational choice that every household faces on every date is static. In the noninter-mediated sector, this choice depends on the individual beginning-of-period wealth b, cost x, and the economywide wage w. In the inter-mediated sector, it depends only on the cost x and economywide prices w and R. The occupational choice in both sectors is now described in greater detail.

Choices in the Nonintermediated Sector

For an individual with beginning-of-period wealth b facing an equilibrium wage w, there are two critical skill levels: $x^e(b, w)$ and $x^u(b, w)$, as shown in figure 8.1. An individual whose cost level x is higher than $x^e(b, w)$ becomes a worker; if the level is lower, the individual becomes an entrepreneur. Finally, if x is lower than $x^u(b, w)$, the individual becomes an unconstrained entrepreneur whose cost of capital is calculated using the implicit zero interest rate of the storage technology (see figure 8.1). The exact specification can be used to derive these curves and cutoffs. For a complete set of equations, see Giné and Townsend (2004).

To define x as the maximum fixed cost, such that for any $x > x^*$, the agent will *never* be an entrepreneur. More formally, and suppressing the dependence of profits on the wage w, x^* is such that

(8.7) $x^* = \pi^u - w$, where $\pi^u = \max_k \pi(k, w)$,

Figure 8.1 Occupational Choice Map

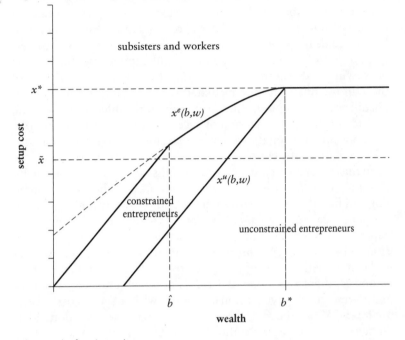

Source: Authors' creation.

if $x > x^*$, the maximum income as an entrepreneur will always be less than w; therefore, the agent is always better off becoming a worker. Denote by b^* the wealth level of an entrepreneur with cost x^* so that this individual is just unconstrained. That is, $b^* = x^* + k^u$, where $k^u = \arg\max_k \pi(k, w)$. Finally, note that for b less than $\hat{b}$, the potentially binding constraint is financing the setup costs x, even with $k = 0$.

Choices in the Intermediated Sector

A major feature of the baseline model is the credit constraint in equation (8.3) that is associated with the absence of a capital market. For example, a talented person (low fixed cost) may be unable to become an entrepreneur because that person cannot raise the necessary funds to buy capital. Likewise, some firms cannot capitalize at the level they would choose if they could borrow at the implicit interest rate of the storage technology. The most obvious variation to the baseline model is to introduce credit to a market and allow the fraction of the population in this market to increase over time. This is what is meant by a financial liberalization in the context of this chapter.[7]

The authors consider an economy with two sectors of a given size at date t, with one sector open to borrowing and lending. Agents born in this sector can deposit their beginning-of-period wealth in the financial intermediary and earn gross interest R on this amount. If they decide to become entrepreneurs, they can borrow at the interest rate R to finance their fixed cost and capital investment. The borrowing and lending rate is assumed to be the same for all of those in the financial, intermediated sector. Again, in this context, liberalization does not mean a reduction in the interest rate spread; it instead means an expansion of access on the extensive margin.

Labor (unlike capital) is assumed to be mobile, so there is a unique wage rate w for the entire economy, common to both sectors.

In the intermediated sector, gross profits do not depend on wealth or setup costs. Because all entrepreneurs operate the same technology and face the same factor prices w and R, they will all operate at the same scale and demand the same (unconstrained) amount of capital and labor, regardless of their setup cost or wealth. The decision to become an entrepreneur, a worker, or a subsistence worker is dictated by the value of the fixed cost. Indeed, given factor prices w and R, there is a value of $\tilde{x}(w, R)$ at which an agent would be indifferent to the two options. Anyone with a setup cost greater than $\tilde{x}(w, R)$ will be a worker, and vice versa. The thick dotted line in figure 8.1 represents the threshold fixed cost $\tilde{x}(w, R)$.

Figure 8.1 thus shows the overlap of the relevant occupational map in each sector. Thick solid curves represent the nonintermediated sector, and a thick dotted line represents the intermediated sector, thereby partitioning the (b, x) space into different regions that (as explained later) will experience a differentiated welfare impact from a financial liberalization.

As in a standard two-sector neoclassical model, the factor prices R and w can be found, solving the credit and labor market-clearing conditions.[8]

Estimating Some Key Parameters from Cross-Section Data

This section explores the idea that the occupational choice is static, to estimate some of the parameters of the model. If the initial wealth b and the wage w are observable, while x is not, then the likelihood that an individual will be an entrepreneur in the nonintermediated sector can be determined entirely as in the occupation partition diagram, from the curve $x^e(b, w)$ and the exogenous distribution of talent $H(x, m)$. That is, the probability that an individual household with initial wealth b will be an entrepreneur is given by $H(x^e(b, w), m)$, with the likelihood that cost x is less than or equal to $x^e(b, w)$. The residual probability $1 - H(x^e(b, w), m)$ corresponds to the likelihood that the individual household will be a wage earner.

The fixed cost x enters additively into the entrepreneur's problem defined at wealth b. Thus, setup costs can be large or small relative to wealth (depending on how the 1997 Thai baht is converted into LEB model units).[9] The authors therefore searched over various scaling factors s to map wealth data into the model units. In a related move, they pinned down the subsistence level γ in the model by using the estimated scale s to convert to LEB model units the baht earnings of those in Thai subsistence agriculture.

Now let θ denote the vector of parameters of the model related to the production function and scaling factor, that is, $\theta = (\beta, \alpha, \rho, \sigma, \xi, s)$. Suppose that there is a sample of n households with y_i as a zero-one indicator variable for the observed entrepreneurship choice of household i. Then with the notation $x^e(b_i | \theta, w)$ for the point on the $x^e(b, w)$ curve for household i with wealth b_i, at parameter vector θ with wage w, the explicit log likelihood of the entrepreneurship choice for the n households can be written as follows:

$$(8.8) \qquad L_n(\theta, m) = \frac{1}{n} \sum_{i=1}^{n} y_i \ln H[x^e(b_i | \theta, w), m]$$
$$+ (1 - y_i) \ln\{1 - H[x^e(b_i | \theta, w), m]\} .$$

In equation (8.8), the parameters to be searched are again the production parameters $(\beta, \alpha, \rho, \sigma, \xi)$, the scaling factor s, and the skewness m of $H(\cdot, m)$.

Intuitively, however, the production parameters in vector θ cannot be identified from a pure cross-section of data at a given point in time. Essentially, only three parameters, not five, are determined. The regions represented in figure 8.1 are determined by $\hat{b}, b^*$, x^*. However, one can fully identify the production parameters by exploiting the variation in the wages over time observed in the data, as two of these cutoffs move with wage.[10]

The derivatives of the likelihood in equation (8.8) can be determined analytically, and then with the given observations of a database, standard maximization routines can be used to search numerically for the maximum.[11] The standard errors of the estimated parameters can be computed by bootstrap methods. And comparable estimates can be made for other countries. Dynamic simulations are sensitive to the scale parameter s. High values increase the likelihood function but give the initial economy so much wealth that initially there is high consumption, low saving, and negligible growth. In practice then, the scale parameter can be calibrated as part of the algorithm that follows. Likewise, numerical maximization routines are improved in accuracy if there is a priori information about x^*, and so x^* may be included in the following calibration exercise. (Likelihood estimation routines are available from the authors.)

The primary database featured in these calculations is the widely used and highly regarded Socio-Economic Survey[12] (SES) conducted by the National Statistical Office in Bangkok, Thailand. The sample is nationally representative and includes eight repeated cross-sections collected between 1976 and 1996. As in the complementary work of Jeong and Townsend (2003), the calculations in this chapter are restricted to relatively young households (with members ages 20–29), whose current assets might be regarded as somewhat exogenous to their recent choice of occupation. This sample is also restricted to households with no recorded transaction with a financial institution in the month before the interview (a crude measure for lack of financial access), as assumed in the LEB model. However, the SES does not record direct measures of wealth. From the ownership of various household assets, the value of the house, and other rental assets, Jeong (1999) estimates a measure of wealth based on principal components analysis that essentially estimates a latent variable that can best explain the overall variation in home ownership and other household assets (for details, see Jeong 1999; Jeong and Townsend 2003).

Observations for the first available years are used (1976 and 1981) to obtain full identification because the household wages varied over these two periods (see figure 8.2). The sample consists of a

Figure 8.2 Occupational Choice Maps, Socio-Economic Survey Data and Townsend-Thai Data

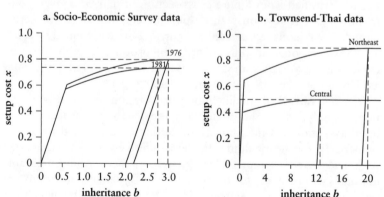

Source: National Statistical Office of Thailand, Bangkok (http://www.nso.go.th/); authors' data.

total of 24,433 observations—with 9,028 observations from 1976 and 15,405 from 1981.

The second data set is a specialized but substantial cross-sectional survey of 2,880 households conducted during May 1997 (Townsend-Thai data).[13] Because the LEB model is designed to explain the behavior of those agents without access to credit, the sample presented here is restricted to households that reported having no relationship with any credit institution (formal or informal), which is another strength of the survey.[14] A disadvantage of the second data set is that, as a single cross-section, there is no temporal variation in wages. Thus, the production parameters are identified by dividing the observations into two subsamples of households in the northeast and central regions, which exploits regional variation in the wages.[15] The final sample consists of a total of 1,272 households, with 707 households from the northeast region and 565 households from the central region.

Table 8.1 reports the estimated parameters and the standard errors. The parameter γ for both data sets was found by multiplying an estimate of the subsistence level from the data by the scaling factor estimated. For the SES data, the authors used the mean income of farmers in 1976, which amounted to 19,274 Thai baht.

Table 8.1 Maximum Likelihood Estimation Results

	Socio-Economic Survey data		Townsend-Thai data	
Indicator	Coefficient	Standard error	Coefficient	Standard error
Scaling factor				
s^a	1.4236	0.00881	1.4338	0.03978
Subsistence level				
γ	0.02744	0.00119	0.01538	0.00408
Fixed-cost distribution				
m	−0.5933	0.05801	0.00559	0.17056
Technology				
α	0.54561	0.06711	0.97545	0.00191
β	0.39064	0.09028	0.0033	0.00013
ρ	0.03384	0.00364	0.00966	0.00692
σ	0.1021	0.02484	0.00432	0.00157
ξ	0.2582	0.03523	0.12905	0.04146
Number of observations	24,433		1,272	
Log-likelihood	−8,233.92		−616.92	

Source: Authors' computations.

Note: Socio-Economic Surveys were conducted by the National Statistical Office in Bangkok, Thailand.

a. The parameter value and standard error reported are multiplied by a factor of 10^6.

Analogously, they used the average income of workers in the northeast region without access to credit (as reported in the Townsend-Thai data), or 10,727 baht. The wages for the two time periods in the model units at the estimated scaling factor s were $w_{76} = 0.048$ and $w_{81} = 0.053$ for the SES data set, and $w_{NE} = 0.016$ and $w_C = 0.037$ for the two regions in the Townsend-Thai data set. The maximized value of the likelihood function obtained using the SES data was $-8,233.92$, whereas the Townsend-Thai data set yielded a value of -616.92.

Calibration of Primary Parameters against Dynamic Paths

The cost of living v and the "dynamic" parameters, namely, the savings rate ω and the subsistence income growth rate γ_{gr} must still be determined (as well as other parameters if it is not clear that these have been reliably estimated in the maximum likelihood estimation routines). One way to determine these parameters is calibration: look for the best v, ω, and γ_{gr} (and other combinations) according to some metric relating the dynamic data to be matched with the simulated data.

The Data

The Thai data used here are the growth of GDP, the Thai national savings rate, labor share, the fraction of entrepreneurs, and the Gini coefficient. (Giné and Townsend 2004 describe the data in more detail.)

The data show an initially high net growth rate of roughly 8 percent in the first three years, which then fell to a more modest 4 percent up through 1986. The period 1986–94 displayed a relatively high and sustained average growth rate of 8.43 percent, and within that period, from 1987 to 1989, the net growth rate was 8.83 percent. During this same period, the Thai economy GDP growth rate was the highest in the world (at 10.3 percent). These high growth periods have attracted much attention. Labor share was relatively stable at 0.40 and rising (after 1990) to 0.45 by 1995. A trend from the 1990–95 data was used to extrapolate labor share for 1996. Savings as a percentage of national income were roughly 22 percent from the initial period to 1985. Savings then increased to 33 percent after 1986, in the higher growth period. Although typical of Asia, these numbers are relatively high. The fraction of entrepreneurs was remarkably steady, but slightly increasing, from 14 percent to 18 percent. The Gini coefficient stood at 0.42 in the 1976 SES and increased more or less steadily to 0.53 in 1992. Inequality decreased slightly in both the 1994 and 1996 rounds, to 0.50. This downward trend mirrors the rise in the labor share during the same period, and both may be explained by the increase in the wage rate. This level of inequality is relatively high, especially for Asia, and rivals many countries in Latin America. Other measures of inequality (Lorenz curve, for example) display similar orders of magnitude within Thailand over time and relative to other countries. (For a more detailed explanation, see Jeong 1999.)

The fraction of population with access to credit was estimated at 6 percent in 1976 and increased to 26 percent by 1996. The data also reveal that as a measure of financial deepening, access to credit grew slowly in the beginning and more sharply later (from 1986 onward). The authors recognize that this measure of intermediation is at best limited and not what they would like to have, and it seems likely that these levels are inaccurate.

Issues in the Calibration Method

FINANCIAL LIBERALIZATION

Begin with the standard benchmark occupational choice model, shutting down credit altogether. Then consider an alternative intermediated economy, with two sectors, one open to credit and saving and the other remaining nonintermediated. Only labor is mobile, hence a unique wage rate, whereas capital cannot move to the other sector. In other words, a worker residing in the nonintermediated sector may find a job in the credit sector but will not be able to deposit wealth in the financial intermediary. The relative size[16] of each sector is assumed to be exogenous and changing over time (given by the fraction of people with access to credit as shown in figure 8.3). This is the key measure of liberalization.

INITIAL WEALTH DISTRIBUTION

The initial 1976 economywide distribution of wealth is relevant for dynamic simulations.[17] As mentioned earlier, Jeong (1999) constructs a measure of wealth from the SES data using observations on both household assets and the value of owner-occupied housing units.

Figure 8.3 Foreign Capital Inflows and Financial
Liberalization

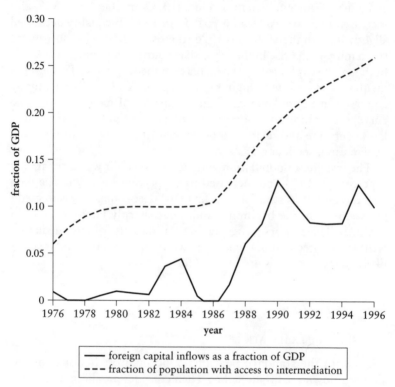

Source: Authors' creation.

The Metric

Any calibration exercise requires a metric to assess how well the
model matches the data. The authors used the normalized sum of
the period-by-period squared deviations of the predictions of the
model from the actual Thai data.[18] The deviations are normalized in
the five variables by dividing them by their corresponding mean
from the Thai data. More formally,

$$(8.9) \qquad C = \sum_{s=1}^{5} \sum_{t=1976}^{1996} w_{st} \left[\frac{z_{st}^{\text{sim}} - z_{st}^{\text{ec}}}{\mu_{z_s}} \right]^2,$$

where z_s denotes the variable s, t denotes time, and w_{st} is the weight
given to the variable s in year t.[19] Finally, sim and ec denote "simulated" and "Thai economy," respectively, and μ_{z_s} denotes the variable z_s mean from the Thai data.

The search covers the cost of living v, subsistence-level growth rate γ_{gr}, and the bequest motive parameter ω using a grid of 20^3 points or combinations of parameters.[20]

All of the statistics except for the savings rate have natural counterparts in the model. "Savings" is considered to be the fraction of end-of-period wealth bequeathed to the next generation. The savings rate is then computed by dividing this measure of savings by net income.

The simulation routines are available from the authors. But roughly speaking, given the parameters and initial distribution of wealth—a guessed wage and interest rate—the routines determine household occupational choices and intermediated sector borrowing and lending choices. Then, if the labor market and credit market do not clear, the interest and wages are adjusted using a bisection algorithm. Having found the market-clearing prices, equilibrium wealth at the end of period is determined—as is wealth at the beginning of the subsequent period. The process begins again.

Simulated and Actual Economies

This section illustrates the simulation results using the calibrated and estimated parameters.

Simulations with Parameters from the Townsend-Thai Data

The simulation featured here is generated from the economy with *no access at all to intermediation* at the Townsend-Thai parameters and displays similar characteristics to the simulation that uses the SES data parameters (figures 8.4 and 8.5). Essentially, the Thai economy fails to grow except toward the end of the 1976–96 period, and then only at the rate of exogenous technological change, γ_{gr}. Now consider the intermediated economy at these parameter values. If all variables are equally weighted each year, the calibrated parameters[21] are $v = 0.004$, $\omega = 0.267$, and $\gamma_{gr} = 0.006$. The corresponding graphs are presented in figure 8.4.

The model does well here at explaining the levels and changes in all variables. Particularly striking is the growth rate of income, which although somewhat low in levels, tracks the Thai growth experience. The model also does remarkably well in matching labor share and the Gini measure of inequality. It underpredicts the fraction of entrepreneurs, however, although it is able to replicate a positive trend. As usual, the model features a flatter savings rate—although it does well at matching the last subperiod (1988 to 1996). Economywide growth is driven primarily by growth in the intermediated sector, where the bulk of the economy's entrepreneurs lie in

Figure 8.4 Intermediated Model, Townsend-Thai Data, 1976–96

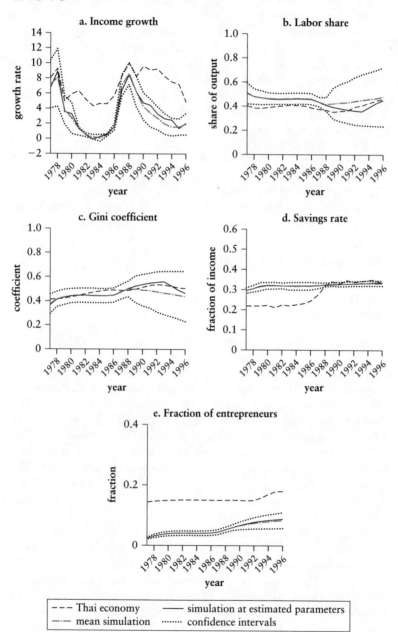

Source: Authors' creation.

Figure 8.5 Intermediated Model, Socio-Economic Survey
Data, 1976–96

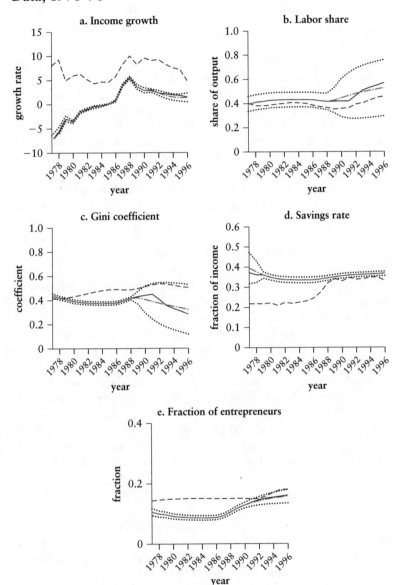

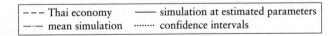

Source: Authors' creation.

addition to a relatively high number of workers from both the inter-mediated and nonintermediated sectors.[22]

Village Economies

The same algorithm can be applied to more aggregated data. Felkner and Townsend (2004) have village-level data from a census administered by Thailand's Community Development Department (a ministry of the interior agency) to male village leaders biannu-ally from 1986 to 1996. Using a principal components analysis of the fraction of households in a village owning tractors, motorcy-cles, pickup trucks, and toilets, the authors estimated the initial distribution of cross-village wealth. Also, according to the village leaders, the history of credit access from formal providers is known (with regard to the Bank for Agriculture and Agricultural Cooper-atives and commercial banks). So the increasing weight of the inter-mediated sector is known for the 1986–96 period, and the model is thus simulated (at trial parameter values) to predict wages and interest rates, among others. Then, knowing the history of credit intervention in a village, predictions are made for the fraction of households in each village that should be represented as firms (those engaged exclusively in trade and handicrafts, for example). Finally, using mean square error criteria (as in the calibration sec-tion), most of the key parameters (except for the end-of-sample year 1996) are reestimated in an effort to match the observed entre-preneurial rate to the rate predicted by the data. In particular, if the parameter m of the cost distribution is allowed to vary in the obvi-ous way with distance (so that villages far from main roads are more likely to have high costs), then the predictions of the model are reasonably good, and correlations of prediction errors with observables and with clusters of urbanization are small.

Inequality Decompositions and the Dynamics of Change

It is interesting to explore more fully how well the LEB occupational choice model can track growth and the change in inequality. Jeong and Townsend (2003) reconfirm that the model does reasonably well with growth, by tracking movements in GDP (even though the model has no aggregate shocks), particularly the expansion of incomes in the late 1980s. The model also does quite well with a Theil measure of income inequality, and though that measure is lower than in the data, the model picks up the decrease in inequality observed during the 1990s in Thailand, when wages began to increase. But the model underestimates the actual number of entrepreneurs, overpredicts the income differential over wage earners, exaggerates the impact of occupation shifts on increases in inequality, and underestimates the inequality within occupations. Making access to the financial sector endogenous helps to remedy some of these anomalies.

Micro Impact: The Distribution of Gains

A goal of this analysis is to identify a measure of the welfare impact of the observed financial sector liberalization. And because there can be general equilibrium effects in the model from this liberalization, the appropriate welfare comparison must be made clear. The analysis that follows compares the economy with the exogenously expanding intermediated sector to the corresponding economy without an intermediated sector, at the same parameter values. The criterion will be end-of-period wealth—or what households in the model seek to maximize. For a given period, then, a household will be characterized by its wealth b and beginning-of-period cost x; and it will be asked how much end-of-period wealth would increase (or decrease) if that household were in the intermediated sector in the liberalized economy, as compared with the same household in the economy without intermediation, a restricted economy.[23]

If, in fact, the wage is the same in the liberalized and restricted economies, then this is also the obvious, traditional partial equilibrium experiment that entails a simple comparison of matched pairs, each person with the same wealth-cost (b, x) combination but residing in two different sectors of a given economy, one with intermediated sector treatment and one without. The wage is the same with and without intermediation in both SES and Townsend-Thai simulations before 1990, when the subsistence sector is not depleted.

If the wage is different across the two economies, this cross-sector comparison does not measure the net welfare impact of the financial sector liberalization. Instead, it measures end-of-period welfare differences across sectors of a given economy that has experienced price changes due to liberalization. To be more specific, those in the nonintermediated sector of the liberalized economy will experience the impact of the liberalization through wage changes. Workers in the nonintermediated sector may benefit from wage increases, but entrepreneurs in the nonintermediated sector suffer losses, because they face a higher wage. There is, of course, a similar price impact for those in the intermediated sector, but there is a credit effect there as well. And such wage effects are present using the parameters estimated from both data sets after 1990.

More to the point, differences in estimates for a given economy provide an inaccurate assessment of welfare changes if liberalization influences the wage. In this case, differences in the estimator of income of laborers would identify only changes in income from savings, because both sectors face a common wage. Analogously, losses due to wage changes would not be captured in a comparison of entrepreneurial profits across both sectors.[24]

Implicit in this discussion is another problem that has no obvious remedy, given the model presented in this chapter. Although households in the model maximize end-of-period wealth, they pass on a fraction of that wealth to their heirs. Thus, the end-of-period wealth effects of the liberalization are passed on to subsequent generations. The problem is that there is no obvious summary device; households do not maximize discounted expected utility, as in Greenwood and Jovanovic (1990) and Townsend and Ueda (2006), for example. So the authors do not attempt to circumvent the problem in this chapter but rather present the more static welfare analysis for various separate periods.

They first look at the liberalized economy in 1979, three years after the initial policy start-up (in 1976), using the overall best fit: the Townsend-Thai data economy with financial sector liberalization. As noted earlier, the wage has not yet increased as a result of the liberalization. Its value is 0.0198 in the liberalized and restricted benchmark economies. And the interest rate in the intermediated sector of the liberalized economy is very high, at 93 percent. This reflects the high marginal product of capital in an economy with a relatively low distribution of wealth.

Figure 8.6a displays the corresponding end-of-period wealth percentage changes in the same (b, x) space. Because the wage is the same in both sectors, agents will only benefit from being in the credit sector, not only because they can freely borrow at the prevailing rate if they decide to become entrepreneurs but also because they can deposit their wealth and earn interest on it. The wealth gain resulting from interest rate earnings can best be seen by fixing x and moving along the b axis, noting the rise.

If, however, one looks at the highest wealth, $b = 0.5$ edge, the wealth changes that correspond to changing setup costs x can be tracked. Moving forward from the rear of the diagram in figure 8.6a, at high x the wealth increment is shown to be constant; however, these households had workers in both economies, so setup costs x were never incurred. So the wealth increment drops for households with entrepreneurs in the no-credit economy that invested some of their wealth in the setup costs x. Those with high x gain the most,

Figure 8.6 Welfare Comparison, Townsend-Thai Data, 1979

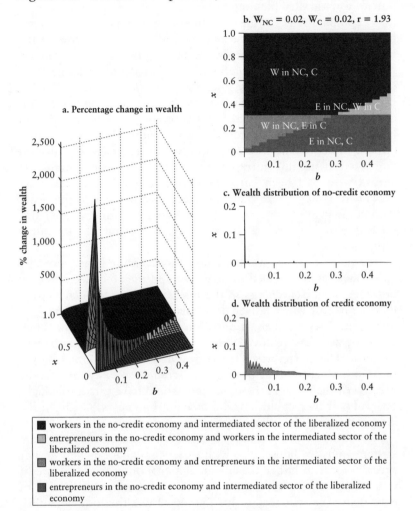

Source: Authors' creation.

by quitting that investment and becoming workers in the inter-mediated sector. Thus, the percentage of wealth increment drops as *x* decreases. A trough is reached, however, when the household head decides to remain an entrepreneur. Lower setup costs benefit entrepreneurs in the intermediated sector more than in the corre-sponding no-credit economy, however, because the residual funds can be invested at interest. Hence, the back edge rises as *x* decreases further.

Figure 8.6b displays the corresponding occupation partition, but now with variables representing given beginning-of-period (b, x) combinations for the corresponding occupation of a household in both the no-credit economy and the credit sector of the intermediated economy. The darker shading in figure 8.6b denotes households with (b, x) combinations that do not change their occupation as a result of the liberalization—that is, they are entrepreneurs (E) in the no-credit (NC) economy and in the intermediated sector of the liberalized (C) economy, or workers (W) in both instances. The lighter shading denotes households that switch: these include low-wealth, low-cost agents who had been workers but became entrepreneurs; and high-wealth, high-cost agents who had been entrepreneurs but became workers. As explained earlier, figure 8.6b represents the overlap of the occupational maps in both sectors. For the credit sector, the key parameter is $\tilde{x}(\hat{w}, R)$, whereas for the no-credit sector, it is the curve $x^e(b, w)$.

The most dramatic welfare gains, however, are experienced by agents who are compelled to be workers in the no-credit economy but become entrepreneurs in the intermediated sector. Although their setup cost was relatively low, their wealth was not enough to finance it. They were constrained on the extensive margin. When credit barriers are removed, however, these entrepreneurs benefit the most. The sharp vertical rise corresponds to those on the margin of becoming entrepreneurs in the no-credit economy. Intuitively, because of their low x, these workers would have earned the highest profits if they could have become entrepreneurs. Credit in the intermediated sector allows that option.

A problem with this analysis, however, is that it may compute welfare gains for households with (b, x) combinations that do not actually exist in either the liberalized economy or the no-credit economy. In other words, those households have zero probability to exist under the endogenous distribution of wealth. To remedy this, figure 8.6c and 8.6d display the wealth distribution of the no-credit economy and the wealth distribution of the credit economy (over both sectors), respectively, in 1979.

The upper part of table 8.2 displays the welfare gains from liberalization in 1979 for both weighting distributions. The mean gains correspond to roughly 1.5 times and twice the average household yearly 1979 income[25] using the intermediated economy wealth distribution and the nonintermediated economy wealth distribution, respectively, as weighting functions. The modal gains are significantly lower, at roughly 17 or 19 percent of the 1979 average household yearly income.

Table 8.2 Welfare Gains and Losses, Intermediated and Nonintermediated Economic Wealth Distribution

Indicator	Intermediated economic wealth distribution			Nonintermediated economic wealth distribution		
	1997 Thai baht	*U.S. dollars*	*Percentage of income*	*1997 Thai baht*	*U.S. dollars*	*Percentage of income*
From Townsend-Thai data (1979)						
Welfare gains						
Mean	82,376	3,295	200.93	61,582	2,463	150.21
Median	22,839	914	55.71	3,676	147	8.97
Mode	7,779	311	18.97	6,961	278	16.98
Percentage of population		100			100	
From Socio-Economic Survey data (1996)						
Welfare gains						
Mean	76,840	3,074	100.54	83,444	3,338	109.18
Median	25,408	1,016	33.24	20,645	826	27.01
Mode	25,655	1,026	33.57	18,591	744	24.32
Percentage of population		86			95	
Welfare losses						
Mean	117,051	4,682	107.59	115,861	4,634	106.50
Median	113,705	4,548	104.51	112,097	4,484	103.04
Mode	117,486	4,699	107.99	118,119	4,725	108.57
Percentage of population		14			5	

Source: Authors' calculations.

Note: SES = Socio-Economic Surveys conducted by the National Statistical Office in Bangkok, Thailand.

A contrast is offered by the welfare comparison from the simulation using the "best fit" estimated maximum likelihood estimation parameters from the SES data in 1996. The wage is 0.05 in the nonintermediated economy and runs to 0.08 in the intermediated one. Thus, agents who remain workers in the credit sector are better off in no small part because they earn a higher wage, and those who remain entrepreneurs in both economies end up losing somewhat because they face higher labor costs (although they may gain because of the savings rate). The interest rate in the intermediated sector has fallen to 9 percent.

These welfare gains and losses are reported in the lower part of table 8.2. Using the intermediated economy wealth distribution as weighting function, the model predicts that 86 percent of the population benefits from the financial sector liberalization, and even more benefit (95 percent) if the nonintermediated wealth distribution is used. The modal welfare gains of those who gain correspond to roughly 34 percent (when the intermediated wealth distribution is used as weighting function) and 24 percent (nonintermediated wealth distribution) of the 1996 average household yearly income. The mean losses, for those who are worse off, amount to 1.08 times or 1.06 times the average household yearly income for the sample of entrepreneurs for intermediated and nonintermediated wealth distribution, respectively. Thus, it seems that

Figure 8.7 Welfare Comparison, Socio-Economic Survey Data, 1996

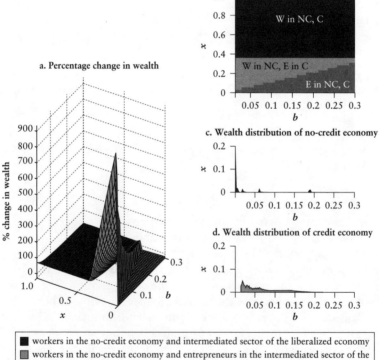

Source: Authors' creation.

a fraction of the population loses a great deal from the liberalization policy (see also figure 8.7).

Macro Impact and Policy Evaluation

Figure 8.3 (see page 256) displays in a solid line capital inflows as a fraction of GDP. The data are from the Bank of Thailand as reported in Alba, Hernandez, and Klingebiel (1999). From 1976 to 1986, private capital inflows to Thailand remained relatively low at an average of 1.05 percent of GDP. From 1986 to 1988, however, they increased rapidly to 10 percent of GDP and remained at that average level until 1996.

This enhanced capital availability was funneled through the financial sector and thus is modeled here as additional capital for households with access to the financial market (those residing in the credit sector). The authors ran this extended (open-economy) version of the model at the estimated and calibrated parameters and compared it with the previous closed-credit economy model at the same estimated and calibrated parameter values from the two data sets.[26] Although not shown, capital inflows contributed to a larger number of entrepreneurs and larger firm size, especially in the late 1980s and early 1990s. Since the marginal product of labor increases with capital utilization, more labor is demanded, and thus the fraction of subsistence workers is depleted earlier. Labor share rises and inequality decreases, both relative to the actual path and relative to the earlier simulation. The interest rate tends to be lower with capital inflows. Nevertheless, the welfare changes are small—indeed, almost negligible.

Because the surge in capital inflows coincides with the phase of high growth of per capita GDP, it has often been portrayed as an important factor in that high growth. To disentangle the extent to which the phase of high growth was due to increased participation in the credit market versus additional capital availability from capital account liberalization, the authors simulated the economy at the estimated and calibrated parameter values, allowing for international capital inflows but using a linearized credit participation from 6 percent to 26 percent (that is, a 1 percent increase per year for each of the 20 years). As shown in figure 8.8, this version of the model fails to match the upturn in GDP growth as compared with the benchmark credit economy. Thus, it seems from the model that capital inflows per se were not the cause of the high growth that Thailand experienced in the late 1980s.

Figure 8.8 Access to Capital and Foreign Capital Inflows, Socio-Economic Survey Data and Townsend-Thai Data

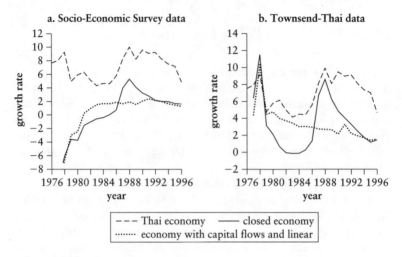

Source: Authors' creation.

Conclusion

This chapter describes how an algorithm that combines theory and data can be used to provide useful information about the relative impacts of financial liberalization.

Although the magnitude of the welfare gains and losses depends on the assumptions of the model, and the plausibility of these depends on the context, the advantage of this approach is that it can be used by researchers to trace the effects of particular recommendations to given sets of assumptions or rules. Thus, because the logic of the model is made explicit, it becomes easier to improve the model to better characterize the economy.

For example, in related work, Paulson and Townsend (2001) use the Townsend-Thai data to estimate (using maximum likelihood methods) not only the LEB model featured in this chapter, but also the collateral-based lending model of Evans and Jovanovic (1989) (the EJ model), and also the incentive-based lending of Aghion and Bolton (1997) and Lehnert (1998) (the ABL model). Observed relationships of entrepreneurship, investment, and access to credit as functions of wealth and talent suggest that the ABL model best fits the data, but the EJ model fits well for those with relatively low levels of wealth and those in the northeast region of Thailand, and the

LEB model discussed in this chapter is a close contender. This finding suggests that a calculation of the welfare gains and losses to
financial intermediation based on these other models would be
worthwhile, even though the average and modal estimates presented
in this chapter should not be rejected out of hand. It seems plausible, however, that the dramatic gains found near the loci when
wealth can only cover the setup costs x (or the 45-degree line) would
be vulnerable to alternative specifications.

The growth and inequality literature that relies on these under-
pinning models presupposes (as in the LEB model discussed in this
analysis) an overlapping generations model with a bequest motive
or a simplistic, myopic solution to the household savings problem.
More work is needed to make the models dynamic and to couple
households with firms and model the intertemporal decision problems confronted by firms. But given the preliminary results presented in this chapter, that work appears to be warranted.

Notes

1. See, for example, Gallup, Radelet, and Warner (1998) and Dollar
and Kraay (2002) for evidence that growth helps reduce poverty. For concerns about these approaches, see Ravallion (2001, 2002).

2. The focus here is on this 20-year transitional period, not on the financial crisis of 1997. The authors' own view is that one needs to understand
the growth that preceded the crisis before analyzing the crisis itself.

3. The authors used the functional forms contained in the 1998 working
paper, although the published 2000 version contains slight modifications.

4. In extended models, this would be the analog to the distribution of
human capital, although the education investment decision obviously is not
modeled in this chapter. Related extensions allow wealth and talent to be
correlated.

5. The authors also estimate the Lloyd-Ellis and Bernhard (LEB) model
for various stratifications of wealth (above and below the median, for example) to see how parameter m varies with wealth. This way, wealth and talent are allowed to be correlated. Even though the point estimates of m vary
significantly, simulations with the different estimates of m are roughly similar. If correlation between wealth and ability were allowed, there could be
poverty traps, as in Banerjee and Newman (1993). The authors do recognize
that in practice, wealth and ability may be correlated. In related work,
Paulson and Townsend (2001) estimate (with the same data used here in
chapter 8) a version of the Evans and Jovanovic (1989) model that allows
the mean of unobserved ability to be a linear function of wealth and education. Evans and Jovanovic find the magnitude of both coefficients to be

small. Karaivanov (2003) allows a correlation between parameter m and wealth for a series of exogenously specified incomplete market models. Buera (2003) develops a dynamic model that endogenizes the relationship between wealth and talent.

6. More general monotonic transformations of the utility function $U(C, B)$ are feasible, allowing utility to be monotonically increasing but concave in wealth. In any event, the overall utility maximization problem is converted into a simple end-of-period wealth maximization problem. More realistically, the model can be interpreted as having an exogenously imposed myopic savings rate ω, which is later calibrated against the data. Attention can then be focused on the nontrivial endogenous evolution of the wealth distribution.

7. The model is, at best, a first step in distinguishing between agents with and without access to credit. In this context, it is assumed that intermediation is perfect for a fraction of the population and nonexistent for the rest. Allocation of a household into the intermediated sector is an exogenous treatment.

8. Note that, in particular, *net* aggregate deposits in the financial intermediary can be expressed as total wealth deposited in the intermediated sector minus credit demanded for capital and fixed costs. For low levels of aggregate wealth, the deposits will constrain credit and the net will be zero. However, note that net aggregate deposits can be strictly positive if there is enough capital accumulation, in which case the savings and the storage technology are equally productive, and both yield a gross return of $R = 1$.

9. The relative magnitude of the fixed costs will drop over time (as wealth evolves).

10. The appendix in Giné and Townsend (2004) details how the coefficients are estimated and how the production parameters are recovered.

11. In particular, the "fmincon" routine of the MATLAB Optimization Toolbox software was used, starting from a variety of predetermined guesses.

12. See Jeong (1999) for details about the Socio-Economic Survey (SES); for an application of the SES data, see Schultz (1997) or Deaton and Paxson (2000).

13. Robert M. Townsend is the principal investigator for this survey. See Townsend and others (1997) and Paulson and Townsend (2001) for details.

14. These households could have borrowed from friends and relatives, although the bulk of the borrowing through this source consists of consumption loans rather than business investments.

15. Unfortunately, estimating a model that features a unique wage by exploiting the geographic variation in the wage observed in the data is a contradiction. Costly migration could be introduced, but that explicit approach is not taken in these calculations. Some confidence might,

however, be drawn from the fact that these are secondary data—and that its estimates are compared to those from the SES data set, with its temporal variation in wages consistent with the estimated model.

16. The intermediated sector, with its distribution of wealth, is assumed to be scaled up period-by-period according to the exogenous credit expansion. Alternatively, a sample from the no-credit sector distribution of wealth could have been selected (with the corresponding fraction to the exogenous expansion), but the increase is small and would have made little difference in the numerical computations.

17. This estimated measure of wealth is likely to differ (in scale and units) from the wealth reported in the Townsend-Thai data; these calculations allow for a different scaling factor to convert SES wealth into the model units. In other words, the authors employ *two* scaling factors to calibrate the model, using the parameters estimated with the Townsend-Thai data. One is estimated with maximum likelihood techniques and converts wealth and incomes reported in the data, whereas the other is calibrated and converts the SES wealth measure used to generate the economywide initial distribution.

18. In computing the growth rate, one observation is lost, so the time index in the formula given in equation (8.9) is from 1977 to 1996 for the growth rate statistic.

19. All variables are weighted equally to focus on a particular period; more weight may be given to those years. Analogously, all the weights may be set to one variable to assess how well the model is able to replicate that variable alone. All weights are renormalized so that they add up to unity.

20. As mentioned earlier, when the Townsend-Thai data are used, a grid of 20 scaling factors is searched for the initial distribution of wealth.

21. The scaling factor chosen for the initial distribution is 15 percent of the one used to convert wealth when using the maximum likelihood estimation.

22. It is important to conduct a robustness check to see whether the results are sensitive to estimated calibrated parameters. In these calculations, robustness is checked in two ways. First, parameters are changed one at a time and checked to see whether the new simulation differs significantly from the benchmark simulation. Alternatively, one could see how sensitive the model is to changes in *all* of the estimated parameters in one simulation. For details on this approach, see Jeong and Townsend (2003) and Giné and Townsend (2004).

23. If the comparison had been conducted using an intermediated economy (in which the intermediated sector is fixed at 6 percent), then when agents living in the credit sectors of both economies were compared, the welfare gains and losses that arose (because of interest rate levels) were larger in the economy that did not experience liberalization. Therefore, wealthier but less talented workers in the benchmark economy may be

better off without liberalization, because they already earn a higher interest rate income.

24. A cross-country comparison would be more accurate if one could control for the underlying environment, but countrywide aggregates would conceal the underlying gains and losses in the population.

25. The 1979 average household yearly income is estimated from the SES data. Actual SES data are not available for 1979, so it is interpolated using the average annual growth rate of SES data between 1976 and 1981.

26. In addition, the cost-of-living v, subsistence-level growth rate γ_{gr}, and the bequest motive parameter ω for this open-economy version were recalibrated and found to have even fewer differences compared with the closed-economy model. In particular, the calibrated bequest motive parameter ω is lower for both data sets in the open-economy version, so that the depletion of subsistence workers occurs at a slower rate.

References

Aghion, Philippe, and P. Bolton. 1997. "A Theory of Trickle-Down Growth and Development." *Review of Economic Studies* 64 (2): 151–72.

Alba, P., L. Hernandez, and D. Klingebiel. 1999. "Financial Liberalization and the Capital Account: Thailand 1988–1997." World Bank, Washington, DC.

Banerjee, A., and A. Newman. 1993."Occupational Choice and the Process of Development." *Journal of Political Economy* 101 (2): 274–98.

Buera, F. J. 2003. "A Dynamic Model of Entrepreneurship with Borrowing Constraints." University of Chicago. http://economics.uchicago.edu/download/buera_applications2003.pdf.

Das, M., M. Roberts, and J. Tybout. 1998. "Experience, Expectations and Export Dynamics." http://citeseer.ist.psu.edu/642470.html.

Deaton, Angus, and C. Paxson. 2000. "Growth and Saving among Individuals and Households." *Review of Economics and Statistics* 82 (2): 212–25.

Dollar, David, and Art Kraay. 2002. "Growth Is Good for the Poor." *Journal of Economic Growth* 7 (3): 195–225.

Evans, D., and B. Jovanovic. 1989. "An Estimated Model of Entrepreneurial Choice under Liquidity Constraints." *Journal of Political Economy* 97: 808–27.

Felkner, J., and Robert M. Townsend. 2004. "The Wealth of Villages: An Application of GIS and Spatial Statistics to Two Structural Economic Models." Paper presented at the Center for Humanities, Arts, and Social Sciences EPIC workshop, "Spatial Thinking in the Social Sciences and Humanities," on December 18 and 19, 2006. http://www.chass.uiuc.edu/events_gis_conference_dec_2006.html.

Gallup, J. L., S. Radelet, and A. Warner. 1998. "Economic Growth and the Income of the Poor." Harvard Institute for International Development.

Giné, Xavier, and Robert M. Townsend. 2004. "Evaluation of Financial Liberalization: A General Equilibrium Model with Constrained Occupation Choice." *Journal of Development Economics* 74: 269–307.

Greenwood, J., and B. Jovanovic. 1990. "Financial Development, Growth, and the Distribution of Income." *Journal of Development Economy* 98: 1076–107.

Griffin, R., J. Montgomery, and M. Rister. 1987. "Selecting Functional Form in Production Function Analysis." *Western Journal of Agricultural Economics* 12 (2): 216–27.

Heckman, James, L. Lochner, and C. Taber. 1998. "Explaining Rising Wage Inequality: Explorations with a Dynamic General Equilibrium Model of Labor Earnings with Heterogeneous Agents." *Review of Economic Dynamics* 1: 1–58.

Jeong, H. 1999. "Education and Credit: Sources of Growth with Increasing Inequality in Thailand." PhD thesis, University of Chicago, Population Research Center 98-12. http://ideas.repec.org/p/fth/chiprc/98-12.html.

Jeong, Hyeok, and Robert M. Townsend. 2003. "Growth and Inequality: Model Evaluation Based on an Estimation-Calibration Strategy." USC Institute of Economic Policy Research Paper No. 05.10. Available at SSRN: http://ssrn.com/abstract=661283.

Karaivanov, A. 2003. "Financial Contracts and Occupational Choice." PhD thesis, Department of Economics, University of Chicago.

Klinhowhan, U. 1999. "Monetary Transmission Mechanism in Thailand." Master's thesis, Thammasat University, Bangkok, Thailand.

Lehnert, A. 1998. "Asset Pooling, Credit Rationing, and Growth." Working Paper 1998–52, Finance and Economics Discussion Series, Federal Reserve Board, Washington, DC.

Lewis, A. 1954. "Economic Development with Unlimited Supplies of Labor." *Manchester School of Economic Studies* 28: 139–91.

Lloyd-Ellis, H., and D. Bernhardt. 2000. "Enterprise, Inequality, and Economic Development." *Review of Economic Studies* 67 (1): 147–68.

Okuda, H., and F. Mieno. 1999. "What Happened to Thai Commercial Banks in Pre-Asian Crisis Period: Microeconomic Analysis of Thai Banking Industry." *Hitotsubashi Journal of Economics* 40 (2): 97–121.

Paulson, Anna, and Robert M. Townsend. 2001. "The Nature of Financial Constraints: Distinguishing the Micro Underpinnings of Macro Models." http://cier.uchicago.edu/papers/Paulson/PaulsonTownsend1.pdf.

———. 2004. "Entrepreneurship and Financial Constraints in Thailand." *Journal of Corporate Finance* 10: 229–62.

Ravallion, Martin. 2001. "Growth, Inequality, and Poverty: Looking Beyond Averages." *World Development* 29 (11): 1803–15.

————. 2002. "The Debate on Globalization, Poverty, and Inequality: Why Measurement Matters." Policy Research Working Paper No. 3038, World Bank, Washington, DC.

Schultz, T. P. 1997. "Diminishing Returns to Scale in Family Planning Expenditures: Thailand 1976–81." Yale University, New Haven, CT. http://www.econ.yale.edu/~pschultz/thai.pdf.

Townsend, Robert M., with Anna Paulson, Sombat Sakuntasathien, Tae Jeong Lee, and Michael Binford. 1997. Questionnaire Design and Data Collection for National Institute of Child Health and Human Development grant, "Risk, Insurance and the Family," and National Science Foundation grants.

Townsend, Robert M., and Kenichi Ueda. 2006. "Financial Deepening, Inequality, and Growth: A Model-Based Quantitative Evaluation." *Review of Economic Studies* 73 (1): 251–93.

Veracierto, M. 1998. "Plant Level Irreversible Investment and Equilibrium Business Cycles." Working Paper Series WP-98-1, Federal Reserve Bank of Chicago. (Revised) http://ideas.repec.org/p/fip/fedhwp/wp-98-1.html.

PART IV

Macro Approach with Disaggregated Public Spending

9

Aid, Service Delivery, and the Millennium Development Goals in an Economywide Framework

François Bourguignon, Carolina Díaz-Bonilla, and Hans Lofgren

The United Nations (UN) Millennium Summit in 2000 witnessed the historic adoption of the Millennium Development Goals (MDGs) by the global community. These goals committed the international community to achieving by 2015 an ambitious vision of development that encompasses not only higher incomes, but also broader human development (HD) goals related to health, education, and access to water and sanitation. Two years later, in Monterrey, the international community met again to address the challenge of *financing* the MDGs, where it was recognized that a substantial increase in official development assistance (ODA) would be required to reach the MDGs. But it was also recognized that donors and recipients had parallel responsibilities. Aid alone would not be enough—donor commitment to provide more resources needed to be matched by recipient policies and programs that would ensure that incremental assistance was well used.

Over the last few years, some encouraging signs have demonstrated progress toward these goals. Many developing countries have accelerated growth and reduced poverty by reforming domestic institutions and integrating their economies into global markets. But this progress has been uneven. Many countries, particularly in Sub-Saharan Africa, lag behind in growth and remain off track in terms of achieving the goal of halving poverty by 2015. Regarding the nonpoverty MDGs, the picture is also mixed. Although some countries have made impressive advances toward health and education objectives, others—even some with a strong growth performance—lag behind.

This mixed performance raises important questions. First, faster growth is a facilitating factor for MDG achievements on the HD goals. Thus, slow growers might find it difficult to make progress on the nonpoverty MDG fronts. It is also the case, however, that improved health and education standards can increase productivity and accelerate growth at a later stage. These improvements can bring positive synergies when service access improves simultaneously in different areas (health, education, water, and sanitation), which ultimately may increase the efficiency of service delivery or reduce its cost. To the extent that growth and higher incomes can generate increased funding for services and raise service demand, investing more today in nonpoverty MDGs could trigger a virtuous circle of growth and human development.

Second, growth and HD service delivery may conflict. The need to finance HD investments may crowd out investments and growth in other parts of the economy, making the allocation of government resources between human development and public infrastructure (including roads, power, and irrigation) a critical policy issue. Another potential source of conflict is that relative costs of government services will rise if productivity growth within the government is slower than in the private economy. These tensions work in the other direction as well. Increased employment of teachers, health personnel, and other skilled workers may drive up wages and reduce the number of skilled workers available for private sector employment, at least in the short and medium terms.

Various approaches have been used to plan and monitor progress toward achieving the MDGs and to evaluate the additional (or total) public resources, including foreign aid, needed to meet them. Clemens, Kenny, and Moss (2004) and Reddy and Heuty (2004) surveyed a large number of studies that forecast and cost MDGs. As emphasized by Vandemoortele and Roy (2004), however, data availability and simplifying analytical assumption severely affected the quality of quantitative estimates of all these studies.

Four major sets of limitations affect studies on MDGs' achievement. First, many sectoral studies have focused on individual MDGs, but even those studies that consider multiple goals often fail to properly account for the interdependencies that exist among different MDGs and among policies designed to reach them. Second, MDG-related policies interact with the rest of the economy (namely, the private sector) by altering prices of specific factors (such as skilled labor) and their overall supply. Third, intertemporal equilibrium consistency is seldom checked. Financing needs, debt accumulation, and the intertemporal sustainability of fiscal policies need to be integrated in a complete study on strategies to achieve the MDGs. Fourth, as stressed by Devarajan, Miller, and Swanson (2002), the policy and institutional environment is as important a component of success in achieving the MDGs as the availability of public resources or financial assistance. Keeping these potential limitations in mind, the authors briefly report on some recent studies and approaches in use at the United Nations and the World Bank.

The United Nations Development Programme (UNDP) *Human Development Report* (2005) addresses most of the MDGs, projecting trends for individual countries, aggregated to regions and globally. Policies and links between MDGs are not considered. The authors point out that it is problematic to make projections on a goal-by-goal basis, given strong links between different MDGs. Nevertheless, their approach may be adequate for their purpose—that is, to highlight the fact that if current trends continue, most countries will fail to achieve most MDGs. The report, however, is not designed for analysis of MDG strategies. With the more ambitious objective of helping countries design Poverty Reduction Strategy Papers (PRSPs), Christiaensen, Scott, and Wodon (2002) developed SimSIP (Simulations for Social Indicators and Poverty), a set of tools that address different aspects of strategy analysis (also applicable to MDGs), including target setting and assessments of costs and fiscal sustainability.

The Excel-based tools are user-friendly and analytically simple.[1] The objective of the target-setting module is to assess the realism of targets related to poverty, health, education, and basic access to water and sanitation. The module provides alternative specifications for forecasting these indicators on the basis of econometrically estimated equations that include gross domestic product (GDP), urbanization, and time as arguments. The cost analysis, which covers the same set of indicators (except for poverty), is based on fairly detailed modules that consider input needs and assessments about future wage changes. The module for analysis of fiscal sustainability compares the estimated costs of achieving targets to available public funding (based on assumptions about GDP growth, tax collection, and the level of sustainable deficits). The target-setting module is a useful tool for assessing target realism; however, the fiscal sustainability component is relatively weak. This weakness reflects the fact that a set of independent tools cannot capture interdependencies between GDP growth, MDG targets, program costs (including wage changes), and alternative financing approaches.

The different publications of the UN Millennium Project report represent a more detailed sectoral approach (see, for example, UN Millennium Project 2005). Its main feature is to estimate and add up the costs of specific interventions in areas such as education, health, and public infrastructure. As implemented, this is essentially a fixed-coefficient–fixed-price planning exercise. This approach—rich in detail—has typically ignored or simplified the synergies across the MDGs and, more important, the interactions with the broader economy.

Agénor and others (2005) apply a novel approach to MDG analysis to Niger.[2] Recognizing the need for an economywide perspective, they combine a macro model with an MDG module. Government spending has different repercussions depending on whether it is identified as being used for education, health, or infrastructure. The MDG module is used for postcalculations of MDGs and other social indicators, including poverty, malnutrition, literacy rate, infant mortality, life expectancy, and access to safe water. The determinants of most of these indicators are estimated using cross-section, cross-country data for a sample of developing countries (when feasible, limited to Sub-Saharan Africa), allowing for links between MDGs. A key strength of this approach is that it requires relatively little data and draws on econometrically estimated parameters. The macro model is highly aggregated, however, presenting two limitations: (1) it has only one production sector (meaning that one dollar of additional government demand for investment in infrastructure has the same direct effect on production and imports as one dollar of additional government demand for education), and (2) it does not include intermediate inputs, factor markets, or factor wages (rents). These limitations restrict the model's ability to analyze key aspects of MDG strategies, such as the labor market repercussions of scaled-up government services and Dutch disease effects (characterized by an appreciating real exchange rate, a shift of resources toward nontradable goods, and lower export growth). Its high level of government and labor market aggregation (only "educated labor" is used in production) makes it more difficult to draw on for Public Expenditure Reviews (PERs) and in other contexts for fiscal analysis. Nevertheless, the model can provide useful macro insights for strategy analysis and may be developed further to address some of these limitations.

The links between growth, service delivery, and MDG achievements outlined above demonstrate that a more sophisticated framework is needed. The analysis must consider macroeconomic factors and trade-offs between objectives. For example, the prospect of significant increases in foreign aid (for most countries in Sub-Saharan Africa, external assistance required to meet the MDGs in 2015 may require more than a doubling of aid flows) leads to concerns over the possibility of Dutch disease. A related critical issue is the pace at which large, aid-financed programs should be scaled up. Rapid initial expansion may drive up costs more quickly and could be more expensive in real present-value terms. Conversely, given time lags, especially in education, expanding investment too slowly may make it impossible to achieve the MDGs by 2015. A coherent analytical framework is needed to capture macro-micro links, Dutch disease effects, and timing issues.

The need to evaluate and provide policy advice on such trade-offs—across sectors and over time—has led to innovative research efforts. This chapter presents Maquette for MDG Simulations (MAMS), which was produced within a research program on the MDGs conducted at the World Bank. MAMS is an economywide framework designed to analyze the interactions between the delivery of HD services (health, education, water, and sanitation), the MDGs, growth, and foreign aid. The framework is equally applicable to the analysis of the same set of policy issues in the context of Poverty Reduction Strategies (PRSs). MAMS belongs to the class of dynamic general equilibrium models, but it has been substantially augmented to capture key processes that generate MDG outcomes as well as feedbacks to the rest of the economy.

MAMS does not replace detailed sectoral studies, but instead complements and draws on the research that underpins sector strategies for achieving the MDGs. Without sector studies to provide a strong empirical basis, the analysis of MDG strategies in an economywide framework loses much of its power. By fully embedding such strategies in a comprehensive economywide framework, MAMS fills a gap in the toolkit that is available to policy analysts. Especially for low-income countries, the policy challenges related to the MDGs cannot be well understood unless sector issues are viewed in the context of constraints in the macro environment and in labor markets.

This chapter is divided into two sections. The next section presents the model structure, emphasizing the features that distinguish MAMS from other computable general equilibrium (CGE) models, particularly the feedbacks from and links between different MDG goals and the rest of the economy. This discussion is followed by a set of simulations that illustrates how MAMS captures some of the

MDG issues discussed in this introduction. The conclusion outlines a possible future research agenda.

Model Structure and Key Mechanisms

A key premise of the model is that government spending and MDG outcomes are linked in a dynamic way, with several outside influences. But that relationship is not a simple, invariable one for three essential reasons:

• The returns to scale of government spending vary with the level of service delivery. At low levels, increasing returns may prevail as network effects, learning effects, and synergies are predominant. At high levels of service delivery, government spending may suffer from decreasing returns to scale. Water supply, health care, and education can be provided relatively easily in densely populated areas, but doing so becomes increasingly expensive as coverage expands to remote areas. When mortality rates are already low, it becomes increasingly difficult to reduce these rates further. Similarly, if completion rates in education are already high, it is difficult to ensure that the last percentages of children complete the program.

• Effectiveness of government spending depends on many variables. For example, spending on education becomes more effective if health conditions improve (reducing absenteeism at schools), public infrastructure improves (facilitating access to schools), income levels rise (and parents are less inclined to keep children at home), or skill premiums increase (triggering a greater incentive to finish formal education). In general terms this means that spending on services becomes more effective if demand conditions for those services are more favorable.

• Costs of service delivery change with macroeconomic conditions. The services are often skill intensive and in many cases also capital intensive. The more intense the MDG effort, the stronger the impact on costs as skilled labor becomes scarcer and financial conditions become tighter. From a general budgetary perspective, the impacts on costs are even larger because changes in macroeconomic conditions affect not only MDG spending, but also other, non-MDG government spending (as well as the competitiveness of the private sector).

The first two aspects (changing returns to scale and impact of demand variables) are captured in the "MDG production functions" introduced in MAMS. The last aspect (macroeconomic interactions) is captured as the MDG production functions are incorporated in a dynamic CGE framework that also includes detailed fiscal accounts.

The dynamic framework not only reflects the key macroeconomic interactions, but also allows planning to target the MDGs in 2015 and to incorporate autonomous baseline forecasts.

The Production of the MDGs

MAMS focuses on the subset of MDGs that is most costly and has the greatest interaction with the rest of the economy: universal primary school completion (MDG 2, measured by the net primary completion rate), reduced under-five and maternal mortality rates (MDGs 4 and 5), halting and reducing the incidence of HIV/AIDS and other major diseases (part of MDG 6), and increased access to improved water sources and sanitation (part of MDG 7). Achievements in terms of poverty reduction (MDG 1) are also monitored.[3] Because of their impact on overall growth and, through that, on poverty, investments in public infrastructure are explicitly taken into account. This consideration also allows the modeling of the positive influence of infrastructure on the effectiveness of spending on social sectors.

The modeling of the production of a typical MDG (except for MDG 2—primary school completion for all—which is discussed later in the context of the education sector) consists of two blocks of equations: the first models the production of MDG-related services; the second defines MDG outcomes as a function of service delivery and other determinants.[4] In the first block, the production of MDG-related services, substitution possibilities among the three broad categories of inputs (labor, capital goods, and intermediate products) are assumed to be negligible. Assuming fixed input-output coefficients, the inputs required for a level Q of service delivery are as follows:

$$L = \alpha_L Q$$

(9.1)
$$K = \alpha_k Q$$

$$INT = \alpha_{INT} Q \, ,$$

where L is the labor requirement (for example, teachers or nurses), K is the capital requirement (for example, classrooms or hospital beds), and INT represents intermediate inputs (for example, textbooks or medicine).

Aggregate labor L results from the combination of three different kinds of labor: those with less than completed secondary education (N), those with completed secondary education (S), and those with completed tertiary education (T). The elasticity of substitution between the different forms of labor is assumed to be constant, and the government is assumed to use the most cost-effective combination of different labor types. The demand for specific education categories thus depends on education premiums. Under the assumption of constant substitution elasticity, ω, the demand is given by the following:

$$N = \alpha_N \left(\frac{W}{W_N} \right)^{\omega} L$$

(9.2)
$$S = \alpha_S \left(\frac{W}{W_S} \right)^{\omega} L$$

$$T = \alpha_T \left(\frac{W}{W_T} \right)^{\omega} L \, ,$$

where W_N, W_S, and W_T are the respective wages for workers with less than secondary, completed secondary, and completed tertiary schooling, and W is the average wage across all workers—and the unit cost of aggregate labor, L. The positive coefficients, α, describe the structure of the labor demand by education category for given unit costs of the various categories.

The capital stock is built up over time through investments and deteriorates at a constant depreciation rate (δ).

(9.3) $I_t = K_{t+1} - (1 - \delta)K_t \, .$

The investment in the current period (t) is chosen such that the required capital stock in the next period, as given by the capital demand equation (9.1), is achieved. Government capital spending on MDGs will be large when service delivery is expanding and will reduce to replacement investment when the level of service delivery is constant.

Intermediate purchases include domestically produced products and imported products, with the two linked through a constant elasticity of substitution demand function. As for labor, cost reduction by the government implies that the demand for domestic (INT_d) and imported (INT_m) intermediate inputs takes the following form:

$$INT_d = \alpha_d \left(\frac{P}{P_d} \right)^{\sigma} INT$$
(9.4)
$$INT_m = \alpha_m \left(\frac{P}{P_m} \right)^{\sigma} INT \, ,$$

where P is the unit price of the aggregate intermediate input (INT); P_d and P_m are the price of the domestic and imported goods, respectively; and $\sigma(\geq 0)$ is the elasticity of substitution. As before, α is a positive coefficient.

The second block of equations defines MDG achievements, relating service delivery and other determinants to MDG indicators (for MDGs 4, 5, 7a, and 7b). The changing returns to scale are represented by a logistic curve, showing increasing returns to scale at low levels of development indicators and decreasing returns to scale at high levels of development indicators.

$$(9.5) \qquad MDG_k = ext_k + \frac{\eta_k}{1 + e^{\gamma_k + \beta_k Z_k}} \, ,$$

where MDG_k is the indicator used to monitor MDG k; Z_k is an intermediate variable that summarizes the influence of the determinants of MDG performance; ext_k is the extreme (maximum or minimum) level of the indicator (for example, 1 or 100 percent for completion rate); β_k shows the responsiveness of the indicator to changes in Z_k; γ_k determines whether increasing or decreasing returns prevail at the starting point; and η_k is used to replicate the initial MDG value and the slope of the function, which is positive if declines in the MDG indicator denote an improvement (mortality rate) and negative in the reverse situation (for example, rates of access to safe water). The intermediate variable, Z_k, is defined by the following Cobb-Douglas relationship:

$$(9.6) \qquad Z_k = Q_k^{\phi_k} \cdot \prod_{i=1}^{n} D_{ik}^{\phi_{ik}} \, .$$

Table 9.1 lists the arguments (for example, service levels, Q_k, and other determinants, D_{ik}) that defined Z_k in the Ethiopia application. Simulation results are discussed at the end of this chapter. These

Table 9.1 Determinants of MDG Achievements

		Other determinants		
MDG	Per capita real service delivery	Per capita household consumption	Public infrastructure	Other MDGs
4	X	X	X	7a, 7b
5	X	X	X	7a, 7b
7a	X	X	X	
7b	X	X	X	

Source: MAMS version for Ethiopia was developed by the authors.

Note: MDG = Millennium Development Goal. The MDGs referred to in this table are defined as follows: MDG 4: reduce by two-thirds the mortality rate among children under five; MDG 5: reduce by three-quarters the maternal mortality ratio; MDG 7a: halve the proportion of people without sustainable access to safe drinking water; and MDG 7b: halve the proportion of people without sustainable access to sanitation services. The target year is 2015 and the reference year is 1990. The services related to these MDGs are health (disaggregated by technology) and water-sanitation services. Other determinants should be added if they are important in the context of a particular country study; if any of the determinants listed in the table are unimportant, then they can be omitted (or given an elasticity of zero). MDG 2 is covered in the following discussion of education.

variables are identified by sectoral studies underpinned by econometric analysis. They include other MDGs—better access to water and sanitation may improve health outcomes (MDGs 4 and 5)—as well as infrastructure or consumption per capita. For example, a higher level of consumption per capita may influence health achievements positively. Pregnant women who are better fed face reduced health risks for themselves and for their babies. Among the "other determinants," per capita household consumption and other MDGs represent demand-side factors, whereas public infrastructure facilitates both demand and supply.

To implement the first block of MDG equations, data are required on government spending by function (one or more health sectors, water and sanitation, other public infrastructure, and other government) and type of outlay (current versus capital). Current outlays must be disaggregated into payments to different types of labor (wages) and intermediate inputs.[5] This information, complemented by elasticities of factor substitution, is similar to what is required for other (nongovernment) sectors in a standard CGE model and can easily be built into the model's social accounting matrix (SAM). In parallel with data on payments to labor, information is also needed on the number of people employed. The information needed for this block typically can be found in sectoral studies and databases of governments, international organizations, and other research institutions.

For the second block of MDG equations, which translates government services into MDG indicators, information is needed on (1) base-year values and 2015 targets for MDG indicators; (2) extreme values for MDG indicators; (3) a set of elasticities of MDG indicators with respect to the relevant determinants (with one version provided in table 9.1);[6] (4) the position of the initial situation (in terms of MDG_k or Z_k) relative to the inflection point (at which the function switches from increasing to decreasing returns to scale); and (5) a scenario indicating one set of 2015 values for the arguments of equation (9.6) under which the MDG in question is achieved. It is relatively straightforward to collect the base-year values and 2015 targets. With respect to the extreme values for MDG indicators, function (ext_k) can be determined by pure logic (for example, the maximum share of the population with access to a service is 1) or international experience (the minimum observed maternal mortality rate across countries). For a set of elasticities of MDG indicators, it is possible to draw on a growing body of econometric research, in particular in the areas of health and education. Although sometimes contradictory, the findings of these studies provide broad support for inclusion of the determinants referred to in table 9.1.[7] Econometric estimates of basic MDG elasticities are hampered by the fact that it is difficult or impossible to observe the full functional form—at least among countries for which it can be asserted that MDG outcomes are generated by the same processes. These outcomes are difficult to achieve because they are concentrated within a limited range that is far from MDG targets and extreme outcome values. Given this fact, econometric analysis must be complemented with other approaches to be able to fully parameterize the MDG production functions. Sectoral studies of MDG strategies and discussions with experts make it possible to determine the position of the initial situation and a scenario indicating one set of 2015 values. Using this information, one can infer from the logistic function the rate at which marginal returns decline and ensure that MAMS is consistent with sectoral studies. In sum, if data are available for these five scenarios, it is possible to calibrate the η_k, γ_k, β_k, and φ_k parameters.[8]

The treatment of education is more complex than that of health and other MDGs. The model gives a complete account of the sector, dividing it into different cycles (or levels): primary, secondary, and tertiary. The primary cycle is needed because it is linked to MDG 2. The higher cycles are needed to link education to the labor market, provide a complete picture of the dynamic fiscal consequences of achieving MDG 2, and expand the education system. In each grade in each cycle, a student may pass, drop out, or repeat the grade next year. Students who pass may proceed to a higher grade within the cycle or graduate from the cycle. In the latter case, they may continue to the next cycle or exit from the school system. The two-block structure and the functional forms, described above for the other MDGs, also apply to education. However, the second block—equations (9.5) and (9.6)—is applied to two types of behavioral outcomes in all cycles: entry rates (to the first grade of any cycle, out of the qualified population[9]) and passing rates (from each grade within a cycle). More specifically, in the logistic functions, equation (9.5), the left-hand-side variables are the shares of students that pass their current grade (one variable per cycle) and the shares, out of the relevant population, that start the first year (also one variable per cycle). The extreme value for all of these variables is one. Other behavioral rates are computed on the basis of the share variables that are defined by the logistic. Rates of repetition and dropout are scaled up or down on the basis of changes in passing rates. The students who pass are split into graduates from the cycle and passers within the cycle, which assumes that as entry and passing rates improve, the students who pass eventually become evenly distributed across the grades within the cycle.

Each logistic equation (9.5) is associated with a Cobb-Douglas equation—compare equation (9.6)—where the relevant Z variable is defined. The arguments determining Zs in education may be similar to those appearing in table 9.1. In the Ethiopia application, the arguments determining the educational Zs include education services per student enrolled, per capita household consumption, public infrastructure, and health performance (proxied by the value for MDG 4). As noted, apart from the service argument, these variables all influence the demand side; public infrastructure may also facilitate service supply. The education equations include an additional demand-side argument, wage incentives (measured by the relative wage gain students would enjoy if, instead of entering the labor market with their current education achievement, they would study enough to climb one notch in the labor market).

As the indicator for MDG 2—universal primary school completion (every child should complete a primary cycle of education)—the authors use the net (on-time) completion rate, that is, the share of the population in the relevant age cohort that graduates from the primary cycle in the right year. It is computed on the basis of relevant entry and graduation rates. For example, for a four-year primary cycle, the value for MDG 2 in year t is the product of the entry rate in $t-3$ and the graduation rates in $t-3$, $t-2$, $t-1$, and t. Rising completion rates in the primary cycle tend to increase the number of students in subsequent cycles, raising demands on services if quality is to be maintained. With a time lag, education expansion increases the supply of skilled labor in the economy.

The data requirements for education and its MDG are more extensive than for the noneducation MDGs. In addition to the information that is needed to cover the production of services (which is identical), it is necessary to know base-year rates and elasticities for a wider range of outcomes and enrollment numbers in each cycle.

General Equilibrium and the Dynamics of MDG Attainment

The MDG production functions are integrated in a standard, open-economy CGE model in the tradition that goes back to Derviş, de Melo, and Robinson (1982). The simultaneous determination of MDG achievement, supply and demand of private goods and services, and factor market equilibrium is a key feature of MAMS. Because MAMS is a general equilibrium model, it accounts for numerous important interactions between the pursuit of the MDGs and economic evolution.

Two important such interactions are the economywide impact of additional public spending caused by the MDGs and the impact of

MDGs on growth. Additional government services needed to reach the MDGs require additional resources—for example, labor, intermediate inputs, and investment funding—that compete with other demands in competitive labor, goods and services, and, possibly, loanable funds markets. This may generate substantial wage hikes for skilled labor given the combination of a small supply (especially in low-income countries) and rapid demand expansion. Conversely, as (the bulk of) school graduates enter the labor force as skilled labor, MAMS captures the positive impact of education on the growth potential of the economy.

In the loanable funds market of the model, investments in capital for MDG services compete with other investments for available savings. The outcome depends on the mechanisms through which the economy achieves balance between savings and investment. If MDG-related additional public spending is partly financed by foreign resources (grants or loans), the impact on domestic private consumption and investment may be limited or even positive. However, larger inflows of foreign aid tend to generate Dutch disease effects. In the medium to long run, the most important determinant of the size of such effects is the import share of the additional spending that these inflows finance—if it is low, Dutch disease effects tend to be strong.[10] In the model, the appreciation of the real exchange rate caused by the inflow of foreign currency provides the incentives required for suppliers to export a smaller share of their output and for demanders to switch from domestic outputs to imports. The resulting increase in the trade deficit is covered by the inflow of foreign currency brought about by aid. As a complement to foreign resources, MDG strategies are, at least in part, financed with domestic resources, either taxes or borrowing. In the model, selected tax rates may be adjusted endogenously to meet targets for government savings or foreign aid. Alternatively, tax rates may adjust in response to changes in fiscal solvency indicators (like the ratio between government debt and GDP), ensuring that these indicators remain unchanged. Of course, the cost of higher taxes is reduced private savings and consumption spending, with a negative impact on growth and on efforts to reduce poverty.

The fact that MAMS is a dynamic model makes it possible to take into account that many of the links between MDGs, factor markets, and growth operate with significant time lags. The expansion of MDG services may follow different time paths, approaching target levels at constant growth rates or doing so with different degrees of front- or backloading. These lags are particularly important in modeling progress in education and its impact on the economy. Indeed, the model accounts for the growth and change in the age structure of the population, the multiyear duration of the various education cycles, and the time lags between expansion in the number of students and graduates at low levels of education and changes in the skill structure of the labor force. For example, improved primary school completion rates affect the skill structure of the labor force with considerable delays.

The dynamic structure of the model is mostly recursive. The bulk of endogenous decisions of economic agents depends on the past and the present, not the future. However, some features may be nonrecursive. For instance, the government's current investment decisions are driven by future decisions on service provision (in health, education, and other areas). In this context, a multiyear simultaneous model solution is preferable to the usual recursive algorithm. Quite important, this approach makes it possible to simulate highly relevant scenarios under which the government endogenously selects growth patterns for government services that are subject to the constraint that certain MDGs be achieved by 2015, while also considering the roles of other determinants of MDG performance. In this case, the government is assumed to have perfect foresight: its decisions in early periods depend on future decisions and the future evolution of the economy.

The model structure has been designed to address four broad groups of issues, each of them crucial to the interaction between growth, aid, and MDGs:

• The model describes the mechanisms through which service delivery and other determinants of MDG achievements interact, capturing the roles of the demand and supply sides of MDG services.

• The model analyzes competition for scarce resources (labor, investment funding, and other goods and services) between MDG services and other sectors, as well as the role of MDG services in adding to the resources of the economy via the labor market and by promoting long-run growth in incomes and investments.

• The model captures the impact of alternative foreign aid scenarios on the production of tradable goods (Dutch disease phenomena) and its role in adding to the pool of savings, thereby mitigating resource competition between MDG services and other sectors.

• The model may be solved simultaneously for the full planning horizon, permitting it to produce future scenarios and analyze the impact of the sequencing of large programs.

MDG Strategy Simulations for Ethiopia

The preceding discussion shows how MAMS is designed to address key aspects of MDG strategies. This section illustrates some of the features of MAMS through a set of simulations of the evolution of the Ethiopian economy. Among other things, these simulations address the following questions: What effects do selected MDG strategies have on MDG indicators, economic growth, exports, the labor market, and the roles of the government and the private sector in the economy? How much does it cost to achieve the MDGs? What roles may synergies among MDGs or between MDGs and the economy have in reducing these costs? How are the effects of MDG strategies influenced by the availability of more or less foreign aid? What kinds of trade-offs may Ethiopian policy makers have to face given limited foreign aid and domestic resource constraints?[11]

To answer these questions and illustrate key model features, the authors designed a set of simulations with MAMS applied to an Ethiopian database. The first simulation (Base) corresponds to a simple extrapolation of current trends and is used as a benchmark for comparison with other scenarios. In this first simulation, MDGs are not reached by 2015. Conversely, the second scenario is designed to reach the MDGs, with foreign aid filling any financing gap. This simulation, entitled MDG-Base, provides a first indication of the effects of pursuing an MDG strategy, including its costs and the need for foreign resources. Two variants on this scenario explore the impact of less foreign aid combined with heavier reliance on domestic financing through direct taxes (MDG-Mix) and improved government productivity (MDG-Gprd). Finally, to explore trade-offs, the authors analyzed the impact of scenarios with less foreign aid and less government spending either on human development or on infrastructure (with MDG-HDcut and MDG-Infcut, referred to in the tables, as two examples). In case resources to reach all the MDGs were not available, this permits calculating what is the cost of reaching a specific MDG in terms of the others. Selected results from these simulations are presented in tables 9.2–9.7 and figures 9.1–9.4.

Under MDG-Base, the authors imposed full achievement of the education, health, and water-sanitation MDG targets. The evolution of MDG 1 is monitored using a simple constant-elasticity relationship between the headcount poverty rate and real GDP per capita.[12] Foreign aid in grant form is assumed to fill any financing gap.[13] This scenario constitutes a strong and extended economic shock. Tables 9.4 and 9.5 show that achievement of these targets requires rapid expansion in the provision of the MDG-related government services and therefore rapid expansion of current and capital public spending. In water and sanitation, current public expenditures increase at an average annual growth rate of 21 percent, whereas capital spending increases at a rate of 40 percent. Both in primary education and infrastructure, the current and capital growth rates are, respectively, 15 percent and 24 percent. Of course,

Table 9.2 Impacts on MDG Indicators

MDG indicator[a]	2005	Base	MDG-Base	MDG-Mix	MDG-Gprd	MDG-Infcut	MDG-HDcut	Target
					Rate in 2015			
1. Headcount poverty rate (percent)	33.8	27.8	18.7	22.6	18.6	21.3	18.6	19.2
2. First cycle primary net completion rate (percent)	29.1	48.1	99.9	99.9	99.9	99.9	93.8	100.0
4. Under-five mortality rate (per 1,000 live births)	156.2	110.5	68.0	68.0	68.0	67.9	79.0	68.0
5. Maternal mortality rate (per 100,000 live births)	580.0	387.2	217.5	217.5	217.5	217.2	260.1	217.5
7a. Access to safe drinking water (percent)	24.4	26.4	62.5	62.5	62.5	62.5	59.5	62.5
7b. Access to improved sanitation (percent)	12.0	14.1	54.0	54.0	54.0	54.0	50.6	54.0

Source: World Bank staff simulations with the MAMS model.
Note: MDG = Millennium Development Goal; Base = business-as-usual scenario; MDG-Base = core MDG scenario; MDG-Mix = MDG scenario with a smaller increase in foreign aid; MDG-Gprd = MDG scenario with increased government productivity; MDG-Infcut = MDG scenario with reduced spending on infrastructure (human development focus); MDG-HDcut = MDG scenario with reduced spending on human development (growth focus).
a. The 1990 values are as follows: 38.4 (MDG 1); 24.0 (MDG 2); 204.0 (MDG 4); 870 (MDG 5); 25.0 (MDG 7a); 8.0 (MDG 7b). The targeted changes relative to the 1990 value are as follows: 50 percent reduction (MDG 1); reach 100 percent in 2015 (MDG 2); two-thirds reduction (MDG 4); three-fourths reduction (MDG 5); 50 percent reduction in share without (MDG 7a); and 50 percent reduction in share without (MDG 7b).

Table 9.3 Impacts on Macroeconomic Indicators
(levels in 2005, average annual percent compound growth rate, 2006–15)

Indicator	2005 (US$ millions)	Base	MDG-Base	MDG-Mix	MDG-Gprd	MDG-Infcut	MDG-HDcut
			Real annual growth 2006–15 (percent)				
Absorption[a]	10,153	3.5	8.5	6.5	7.8	7.6	7.9
GDP at market prices	8,528	3.5	5.7	4.8	5.9	5.2	5.7
Private consumption	6,734	3.1	5.4	1.8	5.0	4.7	5.5
Government consumption	1,458	4.0	8.4	8.6	8.4	8.7	6.8
Private investment	942	4.4	8.5	3.0	7.6	7.2	8.3
Government investment	1,019	4.0	20.0	20.3	18.2	17.9	18.4
Exports	1,283	3.7	−1.0	1.1	1.0	−0.7	0.6
Imports	2,908	3.4	12.8	9.1	10.7	11.2	11.4
GDP at factor cost (total)	7,704	3.6	5.5	4.7	5.5	5.0	5.5
GDP at factor cost (private sector)	7,101	3.5	5.2	4.3	5.3	4.6	5.4
GDP at factor cost (government)	603	4.0	8.7	8.8	8.6	8.9	7.3
Real exchange rate (index)	1.0	0.2	−3.4	−0.9	−1.8	−2.9	−2.5
	2005 (percent)		*Percentage of GDP in 2015*				
Absorption[a]	119.1	118.6	141.7	137.4	137.6	138.7	138.5
Private consumption	79.0	76.0	72.1	58.6	72.9	71.2	74.3
Government consumption	17.1	17.9	22.1	24.4	19.0	23.9	19.0
Private investment	11.0	12.1	12.0	8.9	12.1	11.5	12.5
Government investment	12.0	12.6	35.5	45.5	33.6	32.0	32.7
Exports	15.0	15.6	5.7	9.7	8.1	6.4	7.3
Imports	−34.1	−34.2	−47.4	−47.1	−45.7	−45.1	−45.9

Source: World Bank staff simulations with the MAMS model.

Note: MDG-Base = core MDG scenario; MDG-Mix = MDG scenario with a smaller increase in foreign aid; MDG-Gprd = MDG scenario with increased government productivity; MDG-Infcut = MDG scenario with reduced spending on infrastructure (human development focus); MDG-HDcut = MDG scenario with reduced spending on human development (growth focus).

a. Absorption is the sum of private and public consumption and investment.

these rates of growth are also those of inputs in those services, for example, numbers of teachers and classrooms in primary education. As a result of this acceleration in public spending for the MDGs, the GDP share of the government (measured by the sum of government consumption and investment) is almost doubled, increasing from 29.1 percent in 2005 to 57.6 percent in 2015—see table 9.3.

Table 9.4 Impacts on Government Current Expenditures

Expenditure	2005 (US$ millions)	Base	MDG-Base	MDG-Mix	MDG-Gprd	MDG-Infcut	MDG-HDcut
			Real annual growth 2006–15 (percent)				
1st cycle primary education	95.1	4.0	15.6	15.9	15.7	16.4	9.3
2nd cycle primary education	68.0	4.0	12.9	12.9	12.9	12.9	12.9
Secondary education	55.9	4.0	11.2	11.2	11.2	11.2	11.2
Tertiary education	51.3	4.0	13.1	13.1	13.1	13.1	13.1
Low-tech health	22.0	4.0	14.7	15.5	14.7	16.0	8.3
Medium-tech health	31.0	4.0	11.9	12.6	11.9	13.0	6.8
High-tech health	110.7	4.0	15.5	16.4	15.5	16.9	8.8
Water and sanitation	16.3	4.0	21.4	21.9	21.5	21.9	20.4
Public infrastructure	17.0	4.0	15.4	15.4	15.4	12.3	15.4
Other government	990.8	4.0	4.0	4.0	4.0	4.0	4.0

	2005 (percent)			*Percentage of GDP in 2015*			
1st cycle primary education	1.1	1.1	2.7	2.8	2.2	3.0	1.5
2nd cycle primary education	0.8	0.8	1.5	1.6	1.2	1.6	1.5
Secondary education	0.7	0.8	1.2	1.2	0.9	1.2	1.1
Tertiary education	0.6	0.7	1.2	1.3	1.0	1.3	1.2
Low-tech health	0.3	0.3	0.6	0.7	0.5	0.7	0.3
Medium-tech health	0.4	0.4	0.6	0.7	0.5	0.7	0.4
High-tech health	1.3	1.4	3.0	3.7	2.7	3.6	1.7
Water and sanitation	0.2	0.2	0.8	0.9	0.7	0.9	0.7
Public infrastructure	0.2	0.2	0.5	0.5	0.4	0.4	0.5
Other government	11.6	12.2	10.0	10.9	8.8	10.6	10.1
Domestic interest payments	0.2	0.7	0.5	0.6	0.5	0.5	0.5
Foreign interest payments	0.8	1.1	0.6	0.9	0.7	0.7	0.7
Total recurrent public spending	18.2	19.6	23.2	25.9	20.3	25.2	20.2

Source: World Bank staff simulations with the MAMS model.

Note: MDG-Base = core MDG scenario; MDG-Mix = MDG scenario with a smaller increase in foreign aid; MDG-Gprd = MDG scenario with increased government productivity; MDG-Infcut = MDG scenario with reduced spending on infrastructure (human development focus); MDG-HDcut = MDG scenario with reduced spending on human development (growth focus).

Compared with the Base scenario, annual real GDP growth under MDG-Base accelerates strongly for government activities (from 4 percent to 8.7 percent) and more moderately but yet substantially for the private sector (from 3.5 percent to 5.2 percent; see table 9.3). In comparison with the Base simulation, the present value (PV) of total

Table 9.5 Impacts on Government Investment Expenditures

Expenditure	2005 (US$ millions)	Base	MDG-Base	MDG-Mix	MDG-Gprd	MDG-Infcut	MDG-HDcut
		Real annual growth 2006–15 (percent)					
1st cycle primary education	18.6	4.0	24.1	24.7	24.3	25.6	12.4
2nd cycle primary education	13.6	4.0	24.4	24.4	24.4	24.4	24.4
Secondary education	26.6	4.0	21.1	21.1	21.1	21.1	21.1
Tertiary education	36.7	4.0	24.9	24.9	24.9	24.9	24.9
Low-tech health	16.3	4.0	28.0	29.5	28.0	30.4	14.9
Medium-tech health	23.9	4.0	22.6	23.8	22.6	24.6	11.3
High-tech health	45.3	4.0	29.6	31.1	29.5	32.1	15.9
Water and sanitation	15.4	4.0	40.4	41.1	40.5	41.1	38.6
Public infrastructure	378.4	4.0	24.6	24.6	24.6	18.9	24.6
Other government	444.3	4.0	4.0	4.0	4.0	4.0	4.0

	2005 (percent)						
		Percentage of GDP in 2015					
1st cycle primary education	0.2	0.2	0.9	1.2	0.9	1.1	0.4
2nd cycle primary education	0.2	0.2	0.7	0.9	0.6	0.7	0.7
Secondary education	0.3	0.3	1.0	1.3	1.0	1.1	1.1
Tertiary education	0.4	0.5	1.9	2.4	1.8	2.1	2.0
Low-tech health	0.2	0.2	1.1	1.5	1.0	1.4	0.4
Medium-tech health	0.3	0.3	1.0	1.4	1.0	1.3	0.4
High-tech health	0.5	0.6	3.4	4.8	3.2	4.4	1.2
Water and sanitation	0.2	0.2	2.6	3.4	2.5	2.9	2.4
Public infrastructure	4.4	4.7	19.2	24.0	18.2	13.0	20.3
Other government	5.2	5.5	3.7	4.6	3.5	4.0	3.9
Total public capital spending	12.0	12.6	35.5	45.5	33.6	32.0	32.7

Source: World Bank staff simulations with the MAMS model.

Note: MDG-Base = core MDG scenario; MDG Mix = MDG scenario with a smaller increase in foreign aid; MDG-Gprd = MDG scenario with increased government productivity; MDG-Infcut = MDG scenario with reduced spending on infrastructure (human development focus); MDG-HDcut = MDG scenario with reduced spending on human development (growth focus).

foreign aid over the 2006–15 period is more than quadrupled, reaching US$31 billion. In the final year, 2015, foreign aid is US$81 per capita or 37 percent of GDP (table 9.6). This huge inflow of foreign aid causes the onset of Dutch disease, which manifests itself in an appreciation of the real exchange rate, depressed exports, and larger

Table 9.6 Impacts on Government Revenues
(as share of GDP)

Revenue	2005 (percent)	Base	MDG-Base	MDG-Mix	MDG-Gprd	MDG-Infcut	MDG-HDcut
				Percentage of GDP in 2015			
Direct taxes	6.3	6.0	5.8	24.8	5.8	7.9	3.6
Import taxes	6.4	6.2	7.0	6.3	6.8	6.9	6.9
Other indirect taxes	3.3	6.2	5.9	6.0	6.1	5.9	6.0
Central bank borrowing	1.2	1.4	1.1	1.2	1.1	1.1	1.1
Other domestic borrowing	2.0	2.5	1.9	2.2	2.0	2.0	2.0
Foreign borrowing	5.8	4.2	2.4	3.4	2.8	2.7	2.7
Foreign grants	5.1	5.7	34.6	27.4	29.2	30.7	30.7
Net other capital inflows and errors	0	0	0	0	0	0	0
Total	30.1	32.2	58.7	71.4	53.8	57.2	53.0
Memorandum items							
Total public expenditures	30.1	32.2	58.7	71.4	53.8	57.2	53.0
Foreign aid per capita (US$)[a]	16.2	18.5	80.8	51.4	61.9	67.5	67.5
Present value (PV) of foreign aid (2005 US$ billions)		6.9	31.4	20.2	26.5	26.7	26.7

Source: World Bank staff simulations with the MAMS model.

Note: MDG-Base = core MDG scenario; MDG-Mix = MDG scenario with a smaller increase in foreign aid; MDG-Gprd = MDG scenario with increased government productivity; MDG-Infcut = MDG scenario with reduced spending on infrastructure (human development focus); MDG-HDcut = MDG scenario with reduced spending on human development (growth focus).

a. Foreign aid per capita includes an allowance for aid outside the government budget. In per capita terms, aid in the government budget was around US$11 in 2005.

imports, thus allowing the economy to fully use the foreign currency inflow that comes with foreign aid.

Figure 9.1 shows the expansion of foreign aid per capita in the various scenarios. It can be seen that it increases monotonically, except for a decline in 2011. The decline reflects two factors. First, the period of big investments—in schools and teacher training—to support rapid expansion in primary education comes to an end, reducing government spending needs. Second, the model captures an Ethiopia-specific threshold effect based on expert assessments. Private sector productivity is boosted because the public infrastructure capital stock exceeds a threshold above which productivity-enhancing network effects are triggered in the private sector.

Figure 9.1 Foreign Aid per Capita

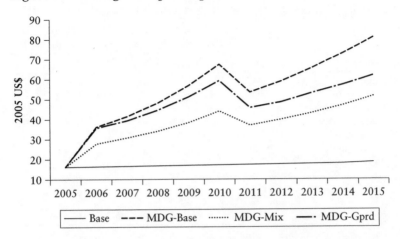

Source: World Bank staff simulations with the MAMS model.
Note: MDG-Base = core MDG scenario; MDG-Mix = MDG scenario with a smaller increase in foreign aid; MDG-Gprd = MDG scenario with increased government productivity.

Part of the huge increase in public spending in pursuit of MDGs is due to changes in unit costs caused by the increase in the demand of several types of goods and services. Of particular importance are wage developments, which depend on what happens in the education system (influencing supply) and government services (driving demand changes). Labor supply growth by workers with little or no education (the bulk of the labor force) declines, given that an increasing share of the children—by 2012, close to all—pass primary school, with many continuing beyond this level (see table 9.7). As a result, GDP growth is affected negatively in this first stage. For the more educated (but much smaller) segments of the labor force, supply growth accelerates gradually as more students graduate from higher cycles. Demand for more educated labor in government services grows quickly throughout most of the simulation period, especially up to 2012 (the year in which everyone in the primary-school cohort has to start the cycle and, after this, manage to successfully proceed through the different grades, graduating in 2015). Conversely, demand growth for this type of labor in the private sector is relatively steady. The combined impact of these demand- and supply-side changes is relatively rapid wage growth for the least educated throughout the period (albeit starting and remaining at a low level). For the two more educated groups, wages grow rapidly until around 2012 and, after this, start to decline as

Table 9.7 Impacts on Labor and Capital

(levels in 2005, average annual percent compound growth rate, 2006–15)

Wages and return to capital	*2005 birr per year (thousands)*	Base	MDG- Base	MDG- Mix	MDG- Gprd	MDG- Infcut	MDG- HDcut
		Nominal annual growth 2006–15 (percent)					
Labor (<secondary education)	0.8	−0.4	3.9	2.4	3.4	3.2	3.4
Labor (secondary education)	2.1	−0.7	1.6	0.2	0.6	1.1	1.1
Labor (tertiary education)	9.6	2.2	3.4	2.2	1.8	3.3	2.7
Private capital	2.7	−0.4	0.4	1.1	0.4	0.1	0.6

Factor quantities	*2005 birr per year (millions)*						
		Real annual growth 2006–15 (percent)					
Labor (<secondary education)	29.8	3.5	1.9	1.9	1.9	1.9	2.2
Labor (secondary education)	2.3	3.9	5.0	4.9	5.0	4.9	4.8
Labor (tertiary education)	0.2	1.9	4.4	4.2	4.3	4.2	4.4
Private capital[a]	76.7	3.5	4.9	2.9	4.7	4.6	4.8
ICOR		3.7	6.8	7.6	6.7	6.5	6.2

Source: World Bank staff simulations with the MAMS model.

Note: ICOR = incremental capital-output ratio; MDG-Base = core MDG scenario; MDG-Mix = MDG scenario with a smaller increase in foreign aid; MDG-Gprd = MDG scenario with increased government productivity; MDG-Infcut = MDG scenario with reduced spending on infrastructure (human development focus); MDG-HDcut = MDG scenario with reduced spending on human development (growth focus).

a. Private capital units = billions of constant 2002 birr.

the supply of skilled workers starts to accelerate. Comparing MDG-Base to Base, private sector employment expansion for more educated labor is minor (given competition from the government), whereas its employment contraction for the least educated labor type is similar to that of the government. Private sector GDP growth under MDG-Base is boosted by more rapid productivity growth. Figure 9.2 shows the evolution of wages for the segment that has completed secondary but not tertiary education, for MDG-Base and other simulations.

In this analysis, the costs of achieving the MDGs are influenced by the fact that MDG achievements do not depend only on the supply of relevant services, but also on progress in terms of a set of other determinants: other MDGs, availability of public infrastructure, household consumption per capita, and wage premia (influencing education decisions). To assess the role that such "synergies"

Figure 9.2 Real Wages of Labor with Secondary Education

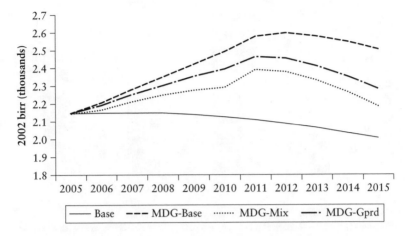

Source: World Bank staff simulations with the MAMS model.

Note: MDG-Base = core MDG scenario; MDG-Mix = MDG scenario with a smaller increase in foreign aid; MDG-Gprd = MDG scenario with increased government productivity.

can play in influencing costs, the authors compared the costs for MDG-Base with the costs of primary education, health, and water sanitation in three separate scenarios (where MDGs were achieved in each of these areas separately).[14] The results—not reported here—indicate that the present value of total costs in these three areas is 22 percent higher when the MDGs are pursued separately compared with the costs for MDG-Base, where they are pursued simultaneously. The differences are primarily due to savings in health. This result suggests that bottom-up costing exercises that do not consider the economywide context of MDG strategies may be misleading, often overestimating the costs.

The scenario MDG-Base looks unfeasible. It is unlikely that donors will be willing to provide foreign aid in the required amounts. Moreover, such a huge expansion of foreign aid and the government GDP share most likely would generate severe governance problems.[15] Given this, alternatives need to be considered. The next scenario, MDG-Mix, considers one alternative. It has been constructed to address the following question: in a setting with less foreign aid, what would be the consequences of pursuing the same MDG targets (in health, education, and water sanitation) and maintaining the same real growth in other areas of government spending (including infrastructure)? MDG-Mix is identical to MDG-Base

Figure 9.3 Present Value of Foreign Aid

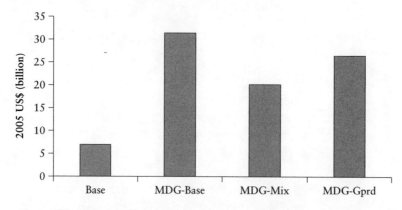

Source: World Bank staff simulations with the MAMS model.

Note: MDG-Base = core MDG scenario; MDG-Mix = MDG scenario with a smaller increase in foreign aid; MDG-Gprd = MDG scenario with increased government productivity.

except for the fact that the increase in foreign grant aid relative to the base scenario is only half as large; in per capita terms, foreign aid reaches US$51 in 2015 (see table 9.6). The PV of total foreign aid in 2006–15 falls from US$31.4 billion to US$20.2 billion (see figure 9.3 and table 9.6). As a result of reduced foreign aid, the appreciation of the real exchange rate is less pronounced, whereas export growth increases and import growth slows down. Direct tax collection adjusts to ensure that government receipts are sufficient to cover government spending. The direct tax increase is huge, going from a share of GDP of 6.3 percent in 2005 to close to 25 percent in 2015. Such an increase has a strong dampening impact on growth in household factor incomes, consumption, savings, and investments, resulting in slower growth in the private capital stock and private GDP, the latter falling from 5.2 percent under MDG-Base to 4.3 percent under MDG-Mix. Government demand (the sum of government consumption and investment) reaches almost 70 percent of GDP, exceeding the highest share in the world.[16] As a result of slower GDP growth, the MDG target for poverty reduction is not met. Compared with MDG-Base, more rapid growth is needed in government spending in education, health, and water-sanitation services to achieve the MDG targets. This spending is required because of slower growth in per capita household consumption, that is, a source of weaker synergy effects, influencing the demand side for different government services.

Although the scenario MDG-Mix has a more realistic outcome for foreign aid, it has the drawbacks of reducing private and overall GDP growth, achieving only a subset of the MDGs (MDG 1 is far from being reached) and generating an even larger government share in GDP.

To explore the potential for government productivity in facilitating progress toward the MDGs, the authors constructed a second alternative scenario (MDG-Gprd) that has more rapid government productivity growth but otherwise is identical to MDG-Base. Under MDG-Gprd, the productivity of government labor and intermediate input use improves by an additional 1.5 percent per year, and government investment efficiency grows at the same annual rate.[17] Compared with MDG-Base, the results include noteworthy declines in foreign aid needs (to US$26.5 billion; US$61.9 per capita in 2015) and declines in the GDP share for the government (to 52.6 percent). The deterioration in terms of poverty reduction, private consumption growth, and GDP growth is minor. In an additional simulation, not reported elsewhere in this chapter, the authors let the productivity improvement of the government be doubled, to 3 percent per year. The result is a further strengthening of these outcomes: the PV of aid declines to US$22.7 billion and the government GDP share in 2015 falls to 45.7 percent, without any significant impact on poverty reduction. Although these scenarios highlight the importance of improving government efficiency, such efficiency gains may be particularly difficult to bring about in the context of rapid government expansion.

These simulations exemplify the type of questions that MAMS can address under scenarios that achieve MDG targets. They suggest that in the face of constraints (on foreign aid, domestic resources, and the scope for productivity improvement), the government may have to confront difficult trade-offs, adjusting downward the MDG targets it strives to achieve by 2015. If these targets are not adjusted, taxes and government spending may become excessive or unreasonable relative to the total size of the economy, with a negative impact on private sector development and household consumption.

The remaining scenarios analyze trade-offs between spending on infrastructure and human development in a setting with reductions in foreign aid relative to MDG-Base. Under the scenario MDG-HDcut, the government receives 85 percent of the aid under MDG-Base. It maintains its spending on infrastructure and cuts spending on HD MDGs (here defined to include primary education, health, and water sanitation).[18] Compared with MDG-Base, GDP growth is virtually unchanged. The required reduction in domestic final demand (driven by the fact that with less foreign aid, the country has to live with a smaller trade deficit) is spread quite evenly across private and government consumption and investment. The key result is that, for the HD MDGs, the country achieves 91.6 percent of the increase required to meet the MDGs; for the poverty objective, however, 102.6 percent of the required drop is achieved (that is, a slight overachievement). Conversely, if the country maintains a 100 percent achievement rate for its HD MDGs while cutting spending on infrastructure (the scenario MDG-Infcut), 89.3 percent of the required fall-in-poverty MDG is achieved. The driving force behind this outcome is that, during the simulation period, spending on infrastructure has a considerably stronger impact on GDP growth than spending in the HD area—annual GDP growth for MDG-HDcut is close to MDG-Base. For MDG-Infcut, a significant slowdown occurs (by 0.5 percent in annual growth), partly because of the lag in the effect of human development on growth. Figure 9.4 provides a broader perspective on trade-offs between human development and poverty reduction in the face of foreign aid constraints. It summarizes trade-offs for a larger set of simulations with alternative cuts in foreign aid—the simulations along each curve have identical levels of foreign aid in the final year and, in PV terms, for the period 2006–15.

Figure 9.4 Trade-Offs between Human Development and Poverty Reduction

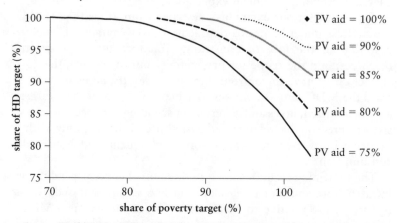

Source: World Bank staff simulations with the MAMS model.

Note: HD = human development; PV = present value. Along a given curve, the present value of aid is kept constant. The point at the upper right corner of the graph (PV aid =100%) corresponds to the core MDG simulation (MDG-Base). The results for MDG-Base are as follows: the HD target is achieved to 100 percent; the poverty target is achieved to 102.8 percent; and the PV of aid 2006–15 = US$31.4 billion.

Conclusion

This chapter has described the design and application of the MAMS model, intended to focus on strategies and trade-offs related to efforts to achieve the MDGs over the next decade. The scenarios presented exemplify the use of MAMS. Other examples of issues that MAMS can address include the effects of front- or backloaded increases in government MDG services, reallocation of government spending from unproductive areas, foreign debt forgiveness, and alternative allocations of resources between government and the private sector in the context of a fixed foreign aid envelope. In settings less focused on full achievement of the MDGs (for example, growth analysis), MAMS provides results for MDG indicators along with more standard economic indicators, making it possible to maintain a focus on poverty and human development. This tool can simulate the effects of the level and, more important, the structure of public spending, using a level of disaggregation rarely found in economywide modeling—see tables 9.4–9.6.

One virtue of the MAMS framework is that it provides a comprehensive perspective on the MDG challenge through its representation of the entire economy. The analysis highlights the fact that changes in wages and exchange rates influence domestic relative prices and the domestic purchasing power of foreign aid, thereby invalidating simplistic costing and aid-forecasting exercises. Unlike such exercises and strict sectoral approaches, MAMS facilitates an examination of how the different goals complement one another, while at times competing for resources. Moreover, by focusing explicitly on the goals themselves, rather than simply on more resources, MAMS supports efforts to move away from traditional reliance on measuring "inputs" (such as teachers hired or foreign aid received) to measuring "outcomes" (the goals themselves). This, in turn, encourages greater attention to the consideration of the appropriate sequencing of resources, priorities, and policies to reach the MDG targets.

Currently, the MAMS framework is being applied to 6 countries in Africa and 18 countries in Latin America (in a project managed by the UNDP). This broad application suggests that it is a valuable tool for strategy analysis in a wide range of countries, not only in low-income countries, for which it was initially designed and for which the economywide interactions between development, external aid, and the MDGs are the strongest.

The MAMS framework has particular operational appeal for the World Bank. The government of Ethiopia has drawn on results from MAMS in its MDG strategy document (FDRE 2005a, 2005b). The World Bank is drawing on MAMS simulations in its country-level dialogue on Ethiopia's PRS as well as in ongoing studies on aid, labor, and population. Similarly, the International Monetary Fund (IMF) uses results from MAMS in the formulation of its MDG scenarios for Ethiopia (IMF 2006). MAMS has also provided inputs to several recent World Bank and IMF documents on MDGs, aid, fiscal policy, and growth (World Bank and IMF 2004, 2006; Patillo, Gupta, and Carey 2005; World Bank 2005b). In dialogues with the government of Ethiopia and other partners inside and outside the World Bank, the authors have found that issues related to labor and education, synergies, long-run macro issues (including growth and financing), and trade-offs between human development and infrastructure are of particular interest. They have also learned that it is important to view model-based analysis and the development of a multipurpose database as part of an ongoing process based on multiple tools—in this case substituting a simpler macro framework for MAMS when the micro foundations of scenarios were not available to the degree of detail required for MAMS.

As more countries move ahead with ambitious PRSs that are built around accelerating progress toward achieving the MDGs, availability of an operational tool to integrate detailed sector analysis within an economywide framework to capture the interactions between and trade-offs among MDG-related and other expenditures is invaluable. Properly used, MAMS can enrich the dialogue among the different partners in the development community to establish coherent long-term strategies for achievement of the MDGs.

Notes

The authors acknowledge the initial inspiration of Luiz Pereira da Silva and significant contributions from Maurizio Bussolo, Ahmed Kamaly, Jeff Lewis, Hans Timmer, and Dominique van der Mensbrugghe, as well as the assistance provided by Denis Medvedev and Shuo Tan. Comments and suggestions have been provided by Ishac Diwan, Enrique Ganuza (United Nations), Pablo Gottret, Wafik Grais, Jee Peng, Sherman Robinson (University of Sussex), Agnès Soucat, and Rob Vos (United Nations). The views and findings in this paper are those of the authors and not necessarily those of the World Bank, its executive board, or member country governments.

1. The SimSIP tools and related documentation can be downloaded from www.worldbank.org.

2. Agénor, Bayraktar, and El Aynaoui (2005) include more detail on the macro model.

3. MAMS is compatible with any standard treatment of economywide modeling of poverty, including representative household approaches,

micro simulation, and more simple relationships based on a constant elasticity of the poverty rate with respect to GDP or household consumption per capita.

4. This presentation is simplified, highlighting key mechanisms. For a detailed technical documentation of MAMS, see Lofgren and Díaz-Bonilla (2006).

5. The national accounts rarely ascribe value added to government capital—by accounting conventions, only labor creates value added in the government sector—making it impossible to derive coefficients of the MDG production functions from value-added shares as is standard practice in the calibration of private sector production functions. The assumption of Leontief production functions made earlier is justified by that difficulty, as well as by the lack of information about the substitutability between capital and labor in these service sectors.

6. For each argument, these "full" elasticities are the product of two elasticities: the elasticity of the MDG indicator with respect to Z_k—equation (9.5)—and the elasticity of Z_k with respect to the argument in the constant-elasticity function (φ_k and φ_{ik})—equation (9.6).

7. For examples of the literature on health that support the statements in this paragraph, see Glewwe and Jacoby (1995), Lavy and others (1996), Anand and Bärnighausen (2004), and Baldacci and others (2004). Similarly, the authors' statements on education draw on Anand and Ravallion (1993), Deolalikar (1998), Case and Deaton (1998), Mingat and Tan (1998), Baldacci and others (2004), and World Bank (2005a). For more details, see Kamaly (2006).

8. A simultaneous-equation model can be solved to generate the values of η_k, β_k, and γ_k that permit the logistic function to (1) replicate base-year MDG_k; (2) have an inflection point at a specified distance relative to the initial Z_k; and (3) exactly achieve the MDG for the value of Z_k, which is defined by the specified MDG scenario. The preceding scenario assumes that the user relies on exogenous values φ_k and φ_{ik} (elasticities of Z_k with respect to Q_k and D_{ik}). Alternatively, if the user wants to impose the "full" base-year elasticities of MDG_k with respect to Q_k and D_{ik}, then the model has to be extended in two ways: (1) in one set of new equations, these elasticities are imposed and, at the same time, the parameters φ_k and φ_{ik} are endogenized; and (2) in a second set of equations, Z_k is defined as a constant-elasticity function of Q_k, D_{ik}, φ_k, and φ_{ik}. It is then no longer possible to impose a value a priori for Z_k because its value depends on φ_k and φ_{ik}, which now are endogenous. The prespecified scenario is only one out of an infinite number of scenarios that generate the same MDG_k value in 2015. For example, in simulations targeting the MDGs, the actual need for services, Q_k, will vary depending on the evolution of the other arguments, D_{ik}, in equation (9.6).

9. For the first grade of primary school, the qualified population includes everyone in the relevant age cohort (often those who are six years

old, but this may vary across countries). For the first grades of secondary and tertiary education, those qualified include those who graduated from the preceding cycle in the previous year. In addition, any cycle can have additional entrants (most important, slightly older students who start primary school but also potentially other entrants from outside the school system, such as migrants from abroad).

10. For an analysis of Dutch disease effects of foreign aid, see Heller (2005).

11. Different aspects of Ethiopia's MDG strategy are explored in Lofgren and Díaz-Bonilla (2005) and in Sundberg and Lofgren (2006).

12. GDP per capita was preferred to household consumption per capita given that GDP is much less influenced by the level of foreign aid in a given year, providing a better indicator of the long-run capacity of the economy to sustain a flow of household consumption.

13. For the sake of clarity, note that for the BASE scenario (and, unless otherwise noted, all other scenarios), the following variables clear the three macro balances: (1) the government balance—foreign grants; (2) the balance of payments—the real exchange rate; and (3) the saving-investment balance—private investment. The domestic consumer price index is the model *numéraire*. (The limited changes in these rules for other scenarios are indicated below.)

14. In other words, the cost of primary education was defined as the cost of government spending in this area when only MDG 2 was targeted, the cost of health on the basis of government health spending in a simulation in which only MDGs 4 and 5 were targeted, and the cost of water and sanitation on the basis of government costs in this area when MDGs 7a and 7b were targeted.

15. Given the large trade deficit, which permits absorption (total domestic final demand) to reach 142 percent of GDP, there is a big difference between the government share in absorption (around 41 percent) and its share in GDP (around 58 percent). The same observation applies to the other MDG scenarios.

16. In 2002, the most recent year with a comprehensive data set, the largest GDP share for the sum of government consumption and investment in any developing country was 65.5 percent (for Eritrea). Few countries exceeded 40 percent. Note, moreover, that this percentage does not include major redistribution schemes (like pay-as-you-go pension systems or health insurance) as in the countries with the highest share of public spending over GDP.

17. For MDG-Base, the rates of total factor productivity growth are 1.1 percent for the government (only for labor) and private health services and 1.9 percent for the rest of the private sector.

18. In terms of macro closure rules, for the scenarios analyzing spending trade-offs, the government budget is cleared by adjustments in a selected spending area, not by adjustments in foreign grants.

References

Agénor, Pierre-Richard, Nihal Bayraktar, and Karim El Aynaoui. 2005. "Roads out of Poverty? Assessing the Links between Aid, Public Investment, Growth, and Poverty Reduction." Policy Research Working Paper No. 3490, World Bank, Washington, DC.

Agénor, Pierre-Richard, Nihal Bayraktar, Emmanuel Pinto Moreira, and Karim El Aynaoui. 2005. "Achieving the Millennium Development Goals in Sub-Saharan Africa: A Macroeconomic Monitoring Framework." Policy Research Working Paper No. 3750, World Bank, Washington, DC.

Anand, Sudhir, and Till Bärnighausen. 2004. "Human Resources and Health Outcomes: Cross-country Econometric Study." *The Lancet* 364: 1603–609.

Anand, Sudhir, and Martin Ravallion. 1993. "Human Development in Poor Countries: On the Role of Public Services." *Journal of Economic Perspectives* 7 (1): 135–50.

Baldacci, Emanuele, Benedict Clements, Sanjeev Gupta, and Qiang Cui. 2004. "Social Spending, Human Capital, and Growth in Developing Countries: Implications for Achieving the MDGs." IMF Working Paper No. 04/217, International Monetary Fund, Washington, DC.

Case, Anne C., and Angus Deaton. 1998. "School Quality and Educational Outcomes in South Africa." Paper 184, Princeton, Woodrow Wilson School, Development Studies, New Jersey.

Christiaensen, Luc, Chris Scott, and Quentin Wodon. 2002. "Development Targets and Costs." In *A Sourcebook for Poverty Reduction Strategies,* ed. Jeni Klugman. Vol. 1. Washington, DC: World Bank.

Clemens, Michael A., Charles J. Kenny, and Todd J. Moss. 2004. "The Trouble with the MDGs: Confronting Expectations of Aid and Development Success." Working Paper No. 40, Center for Global Development, Washington, DC.

Deolalikar, Anil B. 1998. "Increasing School Quantity vs. Quality in Kenya: Impact on Children from Low- and High-Income Households." *Journal of Policy Reform* 2 (3): 223–46.

Derviş, Kemal, Jaime de Melo, and Sherman Robinson. 1982. *General Equilibrium Models for Development Policy.* New York: Cambridge University Press.

Devarajan, Shantayanan, Margaret J. Miller, and Eric V. Swanson. 2002. "Goals for Development: History, Prospects, and Costs." Policy Research Working Paper No. 2819, World Bank, Washington, DC.

FDRE (Federal Democratic Republic of Ethiopia). 2005a. *Ethiopia: Building on Progress: A Plan for Accelerated and Sustained Development to End Poverty (PASDEP) (2005/06–2009/10).* Addis Ababa: Ministry of Finance and Economic Development.

————. 2005b. *Ethiopia: The Millennium Development Goals (MDGs) Needs Assessment Synthesis Report*. Addis Ababa: Ministry of Finance and Economic Development.

Glewwe, Paul, and Hanan Jacoby. 1995. "An Economic Analysis of Delayed Primary School Enrollment and Childhood Malnutrition in a Low Income Country." *Review of Economics and Statistics* 77 (1): 156–69.

Heller, Peter S. 2005. "'Pity the Finance Minister': Issues in Managing a Substantial Scaling Up of Aid Flows." Working Paper No. 05/180, International Monetary Fund, Washington, DC.

IMF (International Monetary Fund). 2006. "The Federal Democratic Republic of Ethiopia: Selected Issues and Statistical Appendix." IMF Country Report No. 06/122, International Monetary Fund, Washington, DC.

Kamaly, Ahmed. 2006. *An Econometric Analysis of the Determinants of Health and Education Outcomes in Sub-Saharan Africa*. Washington, DC: World Bank.

Lavy, Victor, John Strauss, Duncan Thomas, and Philippe de Vreyer. 1996. "Quality of Health Care, Survival and Health Outcomes in Ghana." *Journal of Health Economics* 15 (3): 333–57.

Lofgren, Hans, and Carolina Díaz-Bonilla. 2005. "An Ethiopian Strategy for Achieving the Millennium Development Goals: Simulations with the MAMS Model." Draft paper, Development Prospects Group, World Bank, Washington, DC.

————. 2006. "MAMS: An Economywide Model for Analysis of MDG Country Strategies." Technical documentation, Development Prospects Group, World Bank, Washington, DC.

Mingat, Alain, and Jee-Peng Tan. 1998. "The Mechanics of Progress in Education." Policy Research Working Paper No. 2015, World Bank, Washington, DC.

Patillo, Catherine, Sanjeev Gupta, and Kevin Carey. 2005. "Sustaining Growth Accelerations and Pro-Poor Growth in Africa." IMF Working Paper No. WP/05/195, International Monetary Fund, Washington, DC.

Reddy, Sanjay, and Antoine Heuty. 2004. "Achieving the MDGs: A Critique and a Strategy." *Harvard Center for Population and Development Studies Working Paper Series* 14 (3).

Sundberg, Mark, and Hans Lofgren. 2006. "Absorptive Capacity and Achieving the MDGs: The Case of Ethiopia." Chapter 6 in *The Macroeconomic Management of Foreign Aid: Opportunities and Pitfalls*, eds. Peter Isard, Leslie Lipschitz, Alexandros Mourmouras, and Boriana Yontcheva. Washington, DC: International Monetary Fund.

United Nations Development Programme. 2005. *Human Development Report 2005: International Cooperation at a Crossroads: Aid, Trade and Security in an Unequal World*. New York: Oxford University Press.

United Nations Millennium Project. 2005. *Investing in Development: A Practical Plan to Achieve the Millennium Development Goals.* New York: United Nations Development Program, Earthscan.

Vandemoortele, Jan, and Rathin Roy. 2004. "Making Sense of MDG Costing." Poverty Group, United Nations Development Programme, New York. http://www.undp.org/poverty/docs/prm/MakingsenseofMDGcosting-August.pdf.

World Bank. 2005a. "Education in Ethiopia: Strengthening the Foundation for Sustainable Progress." Human Development Department (AFTH3), February 28, World Bank, Washington, DC.

————. 2005b. *Global Monitoring Report: Millennium Development Goals: From Consensus to Momentum.* Washington, DC: World Bank.

World Bank and the International Monetary Fund. 2004. "Aid Effectiveness and Financing Modalities." Background Paper for the October 2 Development Committee Meeting, Washington, DC.

————. 2006. "Fiscal Policy for Growth and Development: An Interim Report." Background Paper for the April 23 Development Committee Meeting, Washington, DC.

10

Conclusion: Remaining Important Issues in Macro-Micro Modeling

François Bourguignon, Maurizio Bussolo,
and Luiz A. Pereira da Silva

The benefits of a stable macroeconomic environment are undisputed and, for many developing countries, the main challenges for macro policies have shifted from a stabilization phase—where key objectives included balanced budgets, moderate to low inflation, and sustainable positions for the current account and government debt—to a poststabilization phase. In this new phase, governments are engaged in an effort to improve the efficiency and quality of public spending, taxation, and economic management. Policy makers are still concerned with macro stability, but they also need to consider, for example, the fiscal implications of scaling up pro-poor interventions such as conditional cash transfers; or reconcile the tension between the need of additional external resources (through foreign aid, international remittances, or commodities exports) and the ensuing pressure on the real exchange rate; or regulate imperfect markets while avoiding excessive red tape and governance issues. Accelerating growth and, at the same time, fighting poverty and unequal access to opportunities are the main goals of this new phase. Evaluating the policies of this new phase in terms of their contribution toward the attainment of these goals is a difficult exercise, but demand for these evaluations from policy makers, practitioners, and researchers is rapidly increasing. This volume is a response to this growing demand.

The studies in this volume provide clear illustrations of the important advantages that come from adopting a macro-micro integrated approach to evaluate the impact of macroeconomic policies on poverty and income distribution and the macro effects of micro policies directed toward reducing poverty and inequality. In fact, this integrated approach is the only one that can overcome such crucial difficulties as creating macro counterfactuals or accounting for the macro effects of scaling up micro interventions. It is also the only one that permits determining with some precision who are the winners and losers in a reform at the macroeconomic level and what are the macro and second round effects of micro policies directed toward specific agents or sectors. In a broad perspective, this macro-micro approach also represents the "natural" methodological approach to assess the contributions of growth and distribution to the development process.

The preceding chapters warned that linking a macro model with a household-level micro model, irrespective of the degree of integration between the macro and micro parts, could be challenging. The authors of the studies in this book demonstrated various ways to overcome this challenge, but major difficulties as well as under-researched areas remain. These concluding remarks highlight some of these challenges.

The first difficulty any empirical method faces is data quality. In the context of a macro-micro modeling framework, this issue is compounded by data reconciliation. Most developing countries now have the technical capacity to gather and document national accounts statistics, and these statistics—along with ancillary data from central banks, customs authorities, and other agencies—usually provide a fair, if not always accurate and timely, macro picture for the economy. Many topics, such as better measurement of employment by skill level or capital stocks, still require attention. Alongside these developments in macro data availability and quality, collection of micro data, mainly in the format of household surveys, has become more and more common for many countries. Efforts by national agencies and international organizations have improved the quality and thematic coverage of these surveys. An outstanding issue is that of generating more panel data sets—that is, linking consecutive surveys so that households and individuals can be followed through time. Panel data would be especially useful in estimating intertemporal behavior and thus would help with building more detailed dynamic models. Panel data could also facilitate the validation of many of the macro-micro techniques described in this volume,[1] even though most of these techniques do not aim at mimicking panel data (in the sense that these techniques do not focus on tracing the history of specific households).

Notwithstanding these positive developments, a systematic attempt to reconcile micro and macro data is missing in most if not all countries. Obvious differences in definition aside, measurements for the same aggregate from two sources should be reconciled. As mentioned in the introduction, the availability of macro and micro data that are in synch not only is a requirement for the construction of a consistent quantitative model, but also can directly benefit policy making. The well-known case of private consumption in India (also cited in the introduction) is exemplary in this sense: consumption growth and poverty reduction rates calculated from the surveys appear to be much slower than the same rates estimated from national accounts. And so supporters of additional market-friendly reforms of the Indian economy appeal to the positive results from the national accounts, whereas opponents of the reforms use the sluggish poverty reduction shown in the surveys as a proof against the recent or further liberalizations.

The second major challenge is better modeling of growth or, more generally, the dynamics of economic systems. Dynamic macro-micro modeling largely remains comparisons of two cross-sections of households in different states of the economy at two points in time, under the implicit assumption that macro dynamics are somehow independent from distribution or heterogeneity parameters at the micro level. A proper treatment of growth is required to better understand the links between micro and macro phenomena.

A brief digression on the "aggregation problem" is useful here. An aggregation problem exists whenever the aggregate agents' behavior, such as aggregate private demand, cannot be "treated as if it were the outcome of the decision of a *single* maximizing consumer" (Deaton and Muellbauer 1980: 148). When aggregation conditions do not hold, macro models or models with representative agents do not necessarily tell the whole story and, in particular, miss out on some important interactions between distribution and growth. It turns out that aggregation conditions tend to be quite stringent and, as Deaton and Muellbauer (1980: 149) observe, this has "tempted many economists to sweep the whole problem under the carpet or to dismiss it as of no importance." The intuitively appealing way of writing off the aggregation issue often consists of assuming that the heterogeneity in circumstances of individual agents cancels out. But again, adopting this view severely limits not only the possibility of assessing poverty/distribution impacts of macro policies or appraising macro consequences of micro interventions, but it also hinders the proper modeling of growth. Macro literature on endogenous growth has repeatedly emphasized the key role of nonlinearity and market imperfections. Notably, these same two features are sufficient to break the aggregation conditions.[2] In these *aggregation problematic* situations, a macro-micro modeling approach can be helpful. And its usefulness in terms of improving an understanding of the growth process is definitely an underresearched area.

The recent literature on the inequality of opportunities (see Roemer 1998; Roemer et al. 2003; Bourguignon, Ferreira, and Menendez 2007) has shown that unequal initial distribution or unequal access to education, health, and other human development factors leads to *inequality traps* in which investment opportunities are missed and institutional arrangements tend to be biased to maintain a status quo that favors those with more influence. These, in turn, result in lower growth. These direct links between greater equity and higher efficiency allow conceiving "efficient redistributions" and, more generally, to overcome the old idea of a dichotomy between distribution and efficiency and therefore growth. Empirical models where these ideas could be tested have to overcome relevant obstacles; in particular they have to deal with the (very) long run, namely, with the large time lags between the achievements of a more equal distribution of opportunities and its effects on growth. Chapter 8 in this volume, as well as Heckman, Lochner, and Taber (1998), is a good example of this promising research on growth and distribution complementarities. More has to be done and care must be taken to stay close to the data.

A second area of microeconomic research that promises interesting results in terms of linking growth and distribution is that of modeling firms' behavior. The importance of modeling heterogeneity of households has been clearly shown by the studies in this volume, but the importance of modeling heterogeneity of production and investment decisions by firms is perhaps as essential, especially when the focus of the analysis is on the determinants of productivity and growth. A simple example can clarify the issues. Many studies (for example, Tybout and Westbrook 1995; Nickell 1996; Pavcnik 2002; Lopez-Cordova 2003; De Hoyos and Iacovone 2006; Fernandes 2007) have identified a positive relationship of competition, mainly in the form of increased penetration of foreign suppliers in cases of trade liberalization and economic performance. This effect may be different across heterogeneous firms, however, with *good* firms (that is, those closer to the technological frontier) benefiting disproportionately and *bad* firms being affected negatively. The heterogeneity across firms is enormous and so is their behavior. Solely owned firms with no employees (that is, the self-employed) are quite different from large corporations, and within the large group of small and medium enterprises (SMEs), significant variation exists. Besides, the same enterprise may change its behavior because of its age, sectoral shocks, macroeconomic pressures, and other factors. A single micro simulation model cannot capture this complexity. The proper modeling of entry, growth, survival, or exit of firms; the effects of macro policies thereon; and the aggregate macro results of firms' behavior, as well as a combination of approaches, are needed. This combination may include some variation of the macro-micro integrated framework presented in this volume, clearly adapted to deal with firms, but it may also include other methods. Realistically, however, even if it would be nice to have such a firm-focused macro-micro simulation tool, developing it will take years. As in the case of households, the issue is one of "aggregation" and its related features of nonlinearity and market failures. Perhaps an intermediate step, before getting to the final complete model, may be possible and should be attempted. This intermediate model could, for example, include the following characteristics. If empirical observation shows that SMEs behave differently from large firms, then an intermediate model could include two representative firms, with possibly some market power for the large firm. Continuing with the example, the faster churning through entry and exit observed for SMEs could be modeled by larger adjustment parameters in the familiar cost-of-investment model. The real issue is whether enough is known about the evolution of the structure of individual firms to summarize it through a few representative aggregate firms. And it is true that having a dynamic micro simulation model based on a sample of firms would be the first best; but again, at this stage this looks unrealistic, and an intermediate step seems an acceptable second best.

Counterparts to these two frontiers of microeconomic research—modeling inequality of opportunity and heterogeneous firms—exist at the macro level. The amount and the nature of public spending—for example, spending more on education may be an obvious mechanism to remedy inequality in the distribution of opportunities—have macro effects on growth. These effects have been taken into account by the endogenous growth models developed in the macro literature of the 1990s, but the reliability and policy relevance of these types of studies have been questioned. Apart from the generally scarce robustness of the empirical results (Gemmell 2007), most of the models are in reduced form (and partial equilibrium), so tracing the direct effects of policy interventions on agents' behavior is not possible. An example of a structural model in which the growth and the general equilibrium effects of public expenditure programs are accounted for is given by the MAMS model described in chapter 9 of this volume (Bourguignon, Diaz-Bonilla, and Lofgren), but more needs to be done.

Another area of fruitful macro-micro research includes the development of structural models that identify clear channels through which the quality of governance and, more generally, policies aimed at improving the investment climate can affect actual investment levels, productivity gains, and ultimately growth. There is a strong link with what was mentioned above on the literature on firms' behavior. Research developments may allow assessments of how heterogeneous firms react to macro policies and shocks, and perhaps even how firms are affected by policies that change the institutional environment. Large and small firms in the same sector may react differently and, for instance, take opposite decisions in terms of investment plans. Appropriately aggregating these micro results and linking them back to a macro model where other general equilibrium effects can be accounted for may be a useful step forward.

Advancing research in macro-micro modeling can be highly relevant for policy. Development theories increasingly insist on the importance of institutional arrangements, but it is known that institutions are endogenous to the development process and that their quality often depends on which coalitions control economic and political power. Reforms that may be necessary to improve the institutions and thus accelerate growth may negatively affect these coalitions and may thus be opposed. A better understanding of the political economy of institutional change seems thus quite important to single out and successfully implement politically feasible reforms. Analytical tools such as those presented in this volume may be very helpful in this political economy analysis. After all, central results of a macro-micro framework consist of identifying winners and losers of a reform and assessing what compensation must be given for a reform to be undertaken.

Therefore, in a broad sense, macro-micro modeling can not only disentangle the complex mutual interactions between distribution and growth, but it can also be viewed as a relevant tool in the political economy analysis of macro and micro policies and perhaps even of institutional change.

Notes

1. Validation exercises are also possible with a sequence of cross-section data sets, as shown in chapter 5.

2. A simple example of nonlinearity is given by the labor participation decision. Not all individuals participate in the labor market, but participation is expected to increase as wages rise. At the micro level this can be

obtained in two ways: either an individual increases his or her working hours, or someone who was not working enters the labor market. Modeling both of these effects becomes impossible if aggregate labor supply is treated as coming from a representative worker. Similar discontinuities can be observed when workers move from informal to formal employment. Examples of imperfect markets also abound. These range from the cases of monopolistic power to situations of asymmetric information affecting markets of all types: goods, factors, credit, education, and the like.

References

Barro, R. 1990. "Government Spending in a Simple Model of Endogenous Growth." *Journal of Political Economy* 98: 103–17.

Bourguignon, F., F. H. G. Ferreira, and M. Menendez. 2007. "Inequality of Opportunity in Brazil." *Review of Income and Wealth* 53 (4): 585–618.

De Hoyos, R., and L. Iacovone. 2006. "Impact of NAFTA on Economic Performance: A Firm-Level Analysis of the Trade and Productivity Channels." Working paper, Inter-American Development Bank, Washington, DC.

Deaton, Angus, and John Muellbauer. 1980. *Economic and Consumer Behaviour.* Cambridge, U.K.: Cambridge University Press.

Fernandes, A. M. 2007. "Trade Policy, Trade Volumes and Plant-Level Productivity in Colombian Manufacturing Industries." *Journal of the European Economic Association* 71 (1): 52–71.

Gemmell, N. 2007. "The Composition of Public Expenditure and Economic Growth: A Report to the World Bank." Unpublished manuscript, World Bank, Washington, DC.

Heckman, J., L. Lochner, and C. Taber. 1998. "Explaining Rising Wage Inequality: Explorations with a Dynamic General Equilibrium Model of Labor Earnings with Heterogeneous Agents." *Review of Economics Dynamics* 1: 1–58.

Lopez-Cordova, E. 2003. "NAFTA and Manufacturing Productivity in Mexico." *Economia: Journal of the Latin American and Caribbean Economic Association* 4 (1): 55–88.

Nickell, S. J. 1996. "Competition and Corporate Performance." *Journal of Political Economy* 104 (4): 724–46.

Pavcnik, N. 2002. "Trade Liberalization, Exit and Productivity Improvements: Evidence from Chilean Plants." *Review of Economic Studies* 69 (1): 245–76.

Roemer, John E. 1998. *Equality of Opportunity.* Cambridge, MA: Harvard University Press.

Roemer, J. E., R. Aaberge, U. Colombino, J. Fritzell, S. P. Jenkins, I. Marx, M. Page, E. Pommer J. Ruiz-Castillo, M. J. S. Segundo, T. Traanes,

G. Wagner, and I. Zubiri. 2003. "To What Extent Do Fiscal Regimes Equalize Opportunities for Income Acquisition among Citizens?" *Journal of Public Economics* 87: 539–65.

Tybout, J. R., and M. D. Westbrook. 1995. "Trade Liberalization and the Dimensions of Efficiency Change in Mexican Manufacturing Industries." *Journal of International Economics* 39 (1–2): 53–78.

World Bank. 2005. *World Development Report 2006: Equity and Development*. Washington, DC, and New York: World Bank and Oxford University Press.

Index

Figures and tables are indicated by f and t, respectively.